PRINCIPLES OF MANAGEMENT:
A Programmed-Instructional Approach

D0806996

Principles of Management

A Programmed-Instructional Approach

THIRD EDITION

Leonard J. Kazmier
Arizona State University

McGraw-Hill Book Company
New York St. Louis San Francisco Düsseldorf Johannesburg
Kuala Lumpur London Mexico Montreal New Delhi Panama
Paris São Paulo Singapore Sydney Toronto

PRINCIPLES OF MANAGEMENT:
A Programmed-Instructional Approach

1234567890KPKP7987654

This book was set in Baskerville by Textbook Services, Inc. The editors were Thomas H. Kothman, Harriet B. Malkin, and Claudia A. Hepburn; the designer was Pencils Portfolio, Inc.; and the production supervisor was Bill Greenwood.
Kingsport Press, Inc., was printer and binder.

Library of Congress Cataloging in Publication Data

Kazmier, Leonard J
  Principles of management.

  Includes bibliographies.
  1. Management—Programmed instruction. I. Title.
HD31.K36 1974   658.4'007'7   73-12765
ISBN 0-07-033450-1
ISBN 0-07-033451-X (pbk.)

To Lorraine

CONTENTS

II PLANNING

III ORGANIZING

PREFACE

This book has been designed as an effective aid to the development of an understanding of the major functions of management and the skills that lead to managerial success, be it in business firms or other kinds of organizations in which the planning, organizing, directing, and controlling of activities are required. The study of the process of management is based on the assumption that there are common activities and skills that lead to managerial success in a wide variety of fields and in various kinds of organizations. These universal principles of management serve as the focal point for the topics covered in this book.

Several distinct approaches have been developed for studying and describing the practice of management. Although the organization of this book follows the management process approach in that it is based on an analysis of the principal management functions of planning, organizing, directing, and controlling, an introduction to the quantitative and behavior approaches to studying managerial activity is included in the description of the functions. For example, both the basic findings in the area of human motivation and the application of these findings are discussed in some detail in Part 4 on the management function of directing. Similarly, the quantitative decision-making techniques are described in Part 2 on planning, and the systems-oriented Program Evaluation and Review Technique (PERT) is included in Part 5 on controlling. Whereas the behavioral, quantitative, and systems-oriented approaches to management have resulted in productive research during recent years, it is the author's viewpoint that the one approach best suited to communicating management concepts at an introductory level and with an applications orientation is the functional approach to management.

As compared with the second edition of this book, the third edition has been updated to reflect recent developments and has again been expanded in the number of discussion questions and case studies. One new chapter, concerned with staffing the organization, has been added to the book. Other significant additions include material on the cultural framework of management in Chapter 1, statistical decision analysis in Chapter 5, barriers to communication in Chapter 10, managerial power and disciplining in Chapter 13, and budgetary control in Chapter 15. Every chapter in this third edition has at least two case studies or case problems, as compared with the one case study typically included with each chapter in the second edition.

The Use of This Book

For academic application, this programmed-instructional book has been developed for use in undergraduate courses in the principles of management, organization and management, or organization behavior, or for early graduate school exposure for those students who do not have an undergraduate background in management or administration. It can be used in conjunction with a book of readings, case studies, or business simulations, or can be used as a supplement to other textbooks in management. In covering the basic facts, concepts, and theory in an effective self-instructional manner, the book prepares the student for more meaningful discussion and class participation aimed at the application of management principles. Thus, more class time can be spent on such activities as the analysis of case studies, discussions of readings, and participation in business games. Essentially, the format of this book makes it possible for the instructor to reduce the amount of time devoted to lecturing about management principles and to increase the amount of time that can be spent in class activities concerned with applications. When used in conjunction with more comprehensive textbooks in management and administration, the completion of equivalent chapters in this book provides the student with a conceptual framework in which the more comprehensive material can be studied.

Because of the applications orientation of this book, the previous editions have been widely used in management development programs. Since the chapters have been developed to be as independent of one another as possible, they can be covered in any desired order, with the omission of earlier chapters not affecting the coverage of later chapters in most cases. For the purposes of historical and conceptual overview, however, it is desirable that the first two chapters be the first area covered. Because of the specific topic content of each chapter, one instructional possibility is to have participants in management development programs develop additional short case descriptions for group discussion, thereby increasing their understanding of the concepts which are presented as well as developing case problems oriented toward the specific concerns of the participants.

Case Books, Books of Readings, and Business Games

Barton, Richard F.: *The IMAGINIT Management Game,* Allyn and Bacon, Inc., Boston, 1973.

Carlson, John G. H., and Michael J. Misshauk: *Introduction to Gaming: Management Decision Simulations,* John Wiley & Sons, Inc., New York, 1972.

Carroll, Stephen J., Jr., Frank T. Paine, and John B. Miner: *The Management Process: Readings and Cases,* New York: The Macmillan Company, 1973.

Champion, John M., and Francis J. Bridges: *Critical Incidents in Management,* 2d ed., Richard D. Irwin, Inc., Homewood, Ill., 1969.

Donnelly, James H., Jr., James L. Gibson, and John M. Ivancevich: *Fundamentals of Management: Selected Readings,* Business Publications, Inc., Austin, Tex., 1971.

Farmer, Richard N., Barry M. Richman, and William G. Ryan: *Incidents for Studying Management and Organization,* Wadsworth Publishing Company, Inc., Belmont, Calif., 1970.

Henshaw, Richard C., and James R. Jackson: *The Executive Game,* 2d ed., Richard D. Irwin, Inc., Homewood, Ill., 1972.

Hicks, Herbert G.: *Management, Organizations, and Human Resources: Selected Readings,* McGraw-Hill Book Company, New York, 1972.

Koontz, Harold, and Cyril O'Donnell: *Management: A Book of Readings,* 3d ed., McGraw-Hill Book Company, New York, 1972.

McFarlan, F. Warren, James L. McKenney, and John A. Seiler: *The Management Game: Simulated Decision Making,* The Macmillan Company, New York, 1970.

Terry, George R.: *Management: Selected Readings,* Richard D. Irwin, Inc., Homewood, Ill., 1973.

Cross-Reference Table to Other Textbooks

The table following provides a cross reference between the major parts of this book and the equivalent chapters in a number of textbooks in the area of organization and management. This table will be helpful when the book is used in conjunction with one of these texts, or for general reference purposes.

Acknowledgment

As with the previous editions of this book, I owe a debt of gratitude to the students at Arizona State

University and at the University of Notre Dame who participated in the field testing of preliminary versions of this programmed-instructional material. Similarly, I express gratitude to the companies who made available the information which serves as the basis for the case studies included in the book. Of course, the names used in the case descriptions are fictitious. I owe special thanks to the several reviewers, whose identities are unknown to me, who gave so generously of their time and effort in recommending changes to the previous edition and then again in evaluating the changes that were included in the manuscript for this edition. Finally, without the enthusiastic assistance of Sharon Brommer, Lori Miller, and Janet Thrasher, timely completion of the manuscript copy would not have been possible.

Leonard J. Kazmier

Cross-Reference Table to Selected Textbooks

The numbers for each book refer to the chapters associated with each part of this book.

TEXTBOOKS	PART I INTRODUCTION	PART II PLANNING	PART III ORGANIZING	PART IV DIRECTING	PART V CONTROLLING	PART VI SYSTEMS CONCEPT
Albers, Henry H.: *Principles of Management: A Modern Approach*, 3d ed., John Wiley & Sons, Inc., New York, 1969.	1–3	14–17	5–13, 25–26	18–19, 22–24	20	4, 21
Cleland, David J., and William R. King: *Management: A Systems Approach*, McGraw-Hill Book Company, New York, 1972.	1	8–12	3–5, 13	15	16	2, 7, 1 17
Dale, Ernest: *Management: Theory and Practice*, 3d ed., McGraw-Hill Book Company, New York, 1973.	1–7	13, 18–20, 26	8–12, 14	15–16	17	24–25
Donnelly, James H., James L. Gibson, and John M. Ivancevich. *Fundamentals of Management: Functions, Behavior, Models*, Business Publications, Inc., Austin, Tex., 1971.	1–3	4, 13–17	5, 9, 11	7–8, 10, 12	6, 18	
Filley, Alan C., and Robert J. House: *Managerial Process and Organizational Behavior*, Scott, Foresman and Company, Glenview, Ill., 1969.	1–4	5–8	9–14, 17	15–16	8	
Flippo, Edwin B.: *Management: A Behavioral Approach*, 2d ed., Allyn and Bacon, Inc., Boston, 1970.	1	2–5	8–13, 16	6–7, 14–15, 17–19, 23	20–22	
Haimann, Theo, and William G. Scott: *Management in the Modern Organization*, Houghton Mifflin Company, Boston, 1970.	1–2	4–9	10–24	25–28	29–32	3, 33
Haynes, W. Warren, and Joseph L. Massie: *Management: Analysis, Concepts, and Cases*, Prentice-Hall, Inc., Englewood Cliffs, N.J., 1969.	1–4	11–12, 15–20	5–8	9–10, 29	13–14	21–26

TEXTBOOKS	PART I INTRODUCTION	PART II PLANNING	PART III ORGANIZING	PART IV DIRECTING	PART V CONTROLLING	PART VI SYSTEMS CONCEPTS
Hicks, Herbert G.: *The Management of Organizations: A Systems and Human Resources Approach*, 2d ed., McGraw-Hill Book Company, New York, 1972.	12, 24	3–4, 13–16, 29	1–2, 5–6, 17, 25	7–11 18–22	23	30
Hodge, Billy J., and Herbert J. Johnson: *Management and Organizational Behavior: A Multidimensional Approach*, John Wiley & Sons, Inc., New York, 1970	1–3	13–15	10–11, 18	9, 12, 19–20	16–17	4–8
Kast, Fremont E., and James E. Rosenzweig: *Organization and Management: A Systems Approach*, McGraw-Hill Book Company, New York, 1970	1–4	13–15	6–7, 9	8, 10–11	16	5, 12
Koontz, Harold, and Cyril O'Donnell: *Principles of Management: An Analysis of Managerial Functions*, 5th ed., McGraw-Hill Book Company, New York, 1972	1–5	6–11	12–24	25–28	29–32	
Longenecker, Justin G.: *Principles of Management and Organizational Behavior*, 3d ed., Charles E. Merrill Publishing Company, Columbus, Ohio, 1973.	1–3	4–8	9–12, 15–19	10, 20–23, 24	24–26	2
McFarland, Dalton E.: *Management: Principles and Practices*, 3d ed., The Macmillan Company, New York 1970.	1-3,23	4-9	14-19	12,20-22	10–11	13
Miner, John B.: *The Management Process: Theory Research and Practice*, The Macmillan Company, New York, 1973.	1-3,16	4-6	7-9,15	10-12	13–14	

Cross-Reference Table to Selected Textbooks *(Cont.)*

TEXTBOOKS	PART I INTRODUCTION	PART II PLANNING	PART III ORGANIZING	PART IV DIRECTING	PART V CONTROLLING	PART VI SYSTEMS CONCEP'
Newman, William H., Charles E. Summer, and E. Kirby Warren: *The Process of Management: Concepts, Behavior, and Practice*, 3d ed., Prentice-Hall, Inc., Englewood Cliffs, N.J., 1972	1	11–19	2–7, 10	8–9, 20–23	24–27	
Richards, Max D., and Paul S. Greenlaw: *Management Decision Making*, 2d ed., Richard D. Irwin, Inc., Homewood, Ill., 1972	1	2–3, 12, 14–19	8–11	5–7	13	4
Scanlan, Burt K.: *Principles of Management and Organizational Behavior*, John Wiley & Sons, Inc., New York 1973.	1-2	3-7	8-12 15-16	13-14 17-21	22–24	
Sisk, Henry L.: *Management and Organization*, 2d ed., South-Western Publishing Company, Cincinnati, 1973.	1-3	4-8	9-14	15-19	20–22	23
Starr, Martin K.: *Management: A Modern Approach*, Harcourt Brace Jovanovich, Inc., New York, 1971	1	4–10	13	14–15	11–12	2–3
Terry, George R.: *Principles of Management*, 6th ed., Richard D. Irwin, Inc., Homewood, Ill., 1972	1–5	6–8, 10–13	14–18, 22	9, 19–21	23–26	

TO THE STUDENT

The format of this book is different from that of a typical textbook in that each section of the chapter is made up of a series of short paragraphs, called *frames*, which not only present you with some information but also require you to answer key questions about the material. The answers to these questions are provided along the left margin of each page. Please cover these answers until you have tried to answer each question on your own, and then compare your answer with the one given in the margin. By following this recommended procedure you will gain two advantages that will increase your learning effectiveness: having independent practice, and being able to check on whether you understand the concepts and remember important facts as you do your reading.

The questions in the introductory chapters will probably seem easy to you. However, the development of the material in this book is relatively fast-moving and comprehensive, with little repetition, and so you will find that close attention on your part is necessary. If you do not understand why the answer given in the margin differs from yours, place a question mark in the margin as a reminder to ask for clarification of the concept during class discussion. A review section is included at the end of each chapter. You can use this as an overall self-test after completing the chapter, as well as for later review. Each frame in the review section refers to the frame numbers with which it is related in that chapter. If you have any difficulty answering the questions in the review, consult the referenced frames immediately, while the problem is still fresh.

Best success in your study of the principles of management, and in your application of the concepts included in this book!

PRINCIPLES OF MANAGEMENT:
A Programmed-Instructional Approach

INTRODUCTION

In Chapter 1 we consider four important influences on the development of management concepts: Taylor's scientific management movement, Fayol's general principles of management, the application of the behavioral sciences, and the systems and quantitative approach to management. We conclude this chapter by considering the cultural framework within which management principles are applied. This chapter serves as a general introduction to the materials covered in the rest of the book.

Chapter 2 is concerned with a description of the so-called "functional approach" to the study of management concepts. This approach is also often referred to as the management process approach, and involves an orientation on the functions performed by managers in any type of organization. The functions which are identified and described in Chapter 2 are those of planning, organizing, directing, and controlling. The functional approach to management serves as the principal basis for organizing the contents of this book.

Chapter **one**

THE DEVELOPMENT OF MANAGEMENT CONCEPTS

Any attempt to formulate general management concepts is based on the assumption that there is a common set of principles underlying successful managerial performance in a diversity of fields. The purpose of this chapter is to review briefly some of the influences on the development of management concepts during this century. From the standpoint of the history of human managerial activity, these are, of course, relatively recent influences. Thus, we shall discuss Taylor's scientific management, Fayol's general principles of management, the influence of the behavioral sciences, and the systems approach to management. We conclude the chapter by considering some of the cultural factors which have influenced managerial decisions during the past decade.

A TAYLOR'S SCIENTIFIC MANAGEMENT

Frederick W. Taylor is generally acknowledged to be the founder of the scientific management movement. His overall goal was higher industrial efficiency, in the form of either higher productivity or lower unit cost. What distinguishes scientific management from other approaches is not so much its goal, but the basic assumptions, specific objectives, and techniques by which industrial efficiency is to be achieved. The techniques of scientific management reflect Taylor's belief that the *planning* of tasks needs to be separated from the *doing*. His book, *The Principles of Scientific Management*, was first published in 1911.

1 One of the assumptions underlying scientific management is that the application of the *methods of science* to problems of management will lead to high industrial efficiency. It was in this sense that

Taylor   Frederick _____ believed management should be "scientific."

2 Observation, measurement, and experimental comparison are among the principal methods of

science   _____ that can be applied to problems
management   of _____ .

3 A second basic assumption is that the incentive of high wages will promote the mutuality of interest between workers and managers that will result

efficiency (or
productivity, etc.)   in high industrial _____ .

4 Thus two basic assumptions underlying the techniques of scientific management are that industrial efficiency can be improved through the

science   application of the methods of _____
high   and the payment of [high / low] wages.

5 Several specific objectives are included in the scientific management approach to improving industrial efficiency. One is the *standardization of working conditions*. Determining the best temperature and humidity for achieving productivity has to do with the standardization of _____ _____ .

working
conditions

6 The provision for work breaks of optimum duration and frequency is another example of standardization of _____ to achieve higher industrial _____ .

working conditions

efficiency

7 Closely related to the objective of standardizing working conditions is the *standardization of work methods*. Determining the best procedure for doing a job is an example related to standardization of _____ _____ .

work methods

8 *Motion study* is the observation of all the motions that compose a particular job and the determination of the best set of motions that leads to the greatest efficiency. Therefore, _____ _____ is a technique used to attain the specific objective of standardizing work methods.

motion study

9 Taylor concentrated on observing and measuring the performance of high producers in order to discover and develop standardized _____ methods for particular jobs.

work

10 The use of motion-picture cameras to record worker movements and work methods is included in the technique of _____ _____ .

motion study

11 In addition to the standardization of _____ _____ and the standardization of _____ _____ , Taylor believed that the planning of a *large daily task* promotes industrial efficiency.

working conditions

work methods

12 Just as motion study is a technique related to

work methods
daily task

the standardization of _____ _____ , *time study* is related to the planning of a large _____ _____ for each worker.

13 The use of a stopwatch is related to the technique of _____ _____ .

time study

14 Determining the appropriate production standard for a particular job can be accomplished by using the technique of _____ _____ .

time study

15 On the other hand, observing the detailed job performance of a number of workers in order to discover the best way to do a job is related to the technique of _____ _____ .

motion study

16 Another specific objective of scientific management is that encouragement to stay in a job should be given to [high / low] producers, whereas encouragement to transfer to a different job should be given to [high / low] producers.

high

low

17 Accordingly, for those producing above standard the per-unit pay under the Taylor Differential Piecework Plan is [higher / lower] than it is for those producing below standard.

higher (Note that not only overall pay but also per-unit pay is higher.)

18 As a result, job transfers for employees producing above standard are [encouraged / discouraged] by the use of the Taylor Differential Piecework Plan, whereas job transfers for those producing below standard are [encouraged / discouraged].

discouraged

encouraged

19 Thus two basic assumptions of scientific management are that industrial efficiency can be attained through the application of the methods of _____ and the payment of _____ _____ .

science
high wages

20 Of the techniques of scientific management, studies of rest breaks, lighting, and the like are related to the objective of defining standardized

working
conditions

_____ _____ .

21 Motion study is related to the objective of defining standardized _____ _____ .

work methods

22 The use of the Taylor Differential Piecework Plan is related to the objective of encouraging high producers to _____ while encouraging low producers to _____

stay in the job (etc.)
transfer to another
job (etc.)

_____ .

23 The production standard to be used in a wage incentive system can be determined by using the technique of _____ _____ .

time study

24 Although the historical connection is not direct, recent work in operations research, which emphasizes the application of the methods of science to managerial decision making, is a further development of one of the operating assumptions of Taylor's scientific _____ .

management

B FAYOL'S GENERAL PRINCIPLES OF MANAGEMENT

In contrast to Taylor's emphasis on management techniques applicable at the working, or operative, level, Henri Fayol's approach to developing management concepts is oriented toward the higher levels of the organization. The so-called "functional approach" to the study of management is a direct outgrowth of Fayol's work. Because all of Chapter 2 is devoted to describing the functional approach to management, our coverage of Fayol's work in this chapter is restricted to providing a brief exposure to the overall framework that Fayol followed in his development of management concepts.

Henri Fayol was a French industrialist who published his observations about general management principles in 1916 in French, under the title *Administration Industrielle et Générale*. However, this monograph was not translated into English until 1929 and was not published in the United States until 1949.

25   Fayol identified six activities which he believed had to be accomplished in all organizations. Referring to Figure 1.1, we see that organizational activity concerned with the optimum use of capital is the

financial   _____ activity.

1. Technical
2. Commercial
3. Financial
4. Security
5. Accounting
6. Managerial

Figure 1.1   Fayol's identification of the activities to be accomplished in all organizations.

26   Continue referring to Figure 1.1 for the following frames. The buying, selling, and exchange functions in an organization are related to the

commercial   _____ activity.

27   Production   would   be   classified   as   a

technical   _____ activity in Fayol's analysis.

28   The determination of present financial position is included in the _____ activity.

accounting

29   Protection of property would be included in

security   the _____ activity.

30   Finally, Fayol identified the functions of planning, organizing, commanding, coordinating, and

managerial   controlling as being included in _____ activity.

31   Most of Fayol's analysis of organizational activities was devoted to the area listed in the preced-

managerial

ing frame, i.e., the analysis of _____ activity.

32   Fayol held that the importance of managerial ability increases as one goes up the chain of command. Consequently, one would expect that managerial skill is the most important component of job

top

performance in [first-level / top] management positions.

33   Fayol also identified a number of principles of management, listed in Figure 1.2, which apply in varying degrees in all managerial situations. We shall discuss some of these principles briefly in the frames that follow, in order to illustrate his approach to managerial problems. These fourteen concepts, then, are considered to be the most im-

management

portant principles of _____ .

1. Division of work
2. Authority and responsibility
3. Discipline
4. Unity of command
5. Unity of direction
6. Subordination of individual interest to general interest
7. Remuneration of personnel
8. Centralization
9. Scalar chain
10. Order
11. Equity
12. Stability of tenure of personnel
13. Initiative
14. Esprit de corps

Figure 1.2   Fayol's general principles of management.

34   *Remuneration of personnel* concerns the importance of the remuneration system being fair and affording maximum satisfaction to employee and employer. This principle is similar to one of the basic assumptions underlying the field of

scientific
management

_____   _____ , which we discussed in the preceding section of this chapter.

35   The *scalar chain* refers to the chain of superiors from the highest to the lowest rank, which should be short-circuited only when scrupulous following of it would be detrimental. This principle suggests, for example, that an employee **should not** [should / should not] feel free to contact his immediate superior's superior.

36 The *unity of command* principle suggests that an employee should receive orders from [**only one** / several] superior(s).

37 *Initiative* is conceived of as the thinking out and execution of a plan. Fayol suggests that since it is one of the "keenest satisfactions for an intelligent man to experience," managers should "sacrifice personal vanity" in order to permit subordinates to exercise it. Fayol thus appears to suggest that managers should share some of their decision-making authority with their **subordinates** _____ .

38 The principle of *division of work* suggests that specialization within an enterprise leads to a higher level of **efficiency (or productivity, etc.)** _____ .

39 "A place for everything (everyone) and everything (everyone) in its (his) place" concerns the principle of *order*. The use of a formal organization chart in a company would be [**consistent** / inconsistent] with the objective of this principle.

40 *Stability of tenure of personnel* suggests that high employee turnover is [advantageous / **detrimental**] to an organization.

41 In concluding his discussion of management principles, Fayol stated that he had tried to present only those that he had the most occasion to use in his career as a manager. Thus the principles [were / **were not**] regarded as being exhaustive.

42 In addition to his description of organizational activities and principles of management,

functions

Fayol considered the specific *functions*, or elements, of management. These universal elements, or _____ , constitute the essence of the managerial job.

43 Although we are making only brief reference to this aspect of Fayol's work for the present, it constitutes a major part of his writing. Planning, organizing, commanding, coordinating, and controlling were identified by Fayol as being the _____ of management.

functions (or elements)

44 Throughout Fayol's writings there is an emphasis on the universality of management functions and principles. Therefore, he believed that political, religious, philanthropic, and other organizations [would / would not] all be able to apply his principles.

would

45 Because their interests were directed toward different aspects of managerial work in organizations, the methods and principles developed by Taylor and Fayol are typically considered to be [conflicting / complementary].

complementary (the principles and techniques used are not contradictory)

C   INFLUENCES OF BEHAVIORAL SCIENCE ON MANAGEMENT CONCEPTS

The behavioral science approach to management concerns the application of the methods and findings of psychology, social psychology, and sociology for the purpose of understanding organizational behavior. Historically, the first significant use of the behavioral science approach to management problems occurred in the famous series of studies in the Hawthorne Plant of the Western Electric Company during the late 1920s and early 1930s; the studies are usually referred to as the *Hawthorne studies*. The researchers began these studies with the intention of investigating the relationship between physical conditions of work and employee productivity. However, they found that the social variables were more important than the physical variables as factors affecting productivity. As a result, their research had an unexpected outcome.

46 The development of the field of *human relations*, which is the study of human behavior at work for the purpose of developing higher levels of productivity and personal satisfaction, was a direct

Hawthorne

result of the _____ studies.

47 Several people made significant contributions to the studies in the Hawthorne Plant. However, Elton Mayo, a principal consultant in the Hawthorne studies, is generally considered to be the

human

founder of the field called _____ relations.

48 To Taylor, human relations problems stood in the way of production and should be removed. To

(Elton) Mayo

_____ [name], human relations became a broad new area of study in order to improve morale and productivity, and was not considered simply as a "problem."

49 For example, in the Hawthorne Plant, Mayo found that the piecework systems in use led to extensive conflicts between workers and time-and-motion-study experts. Thus employee reactions to

were not

piecework systems [were / were not] those desired by Taylor.

50 The Hawthorne studies provided evidence that, in addition to being a formal arrangement of functions, an organization is a social system whose success depends on the appropriate application of

behavioral
(or social)

_____ science principles.

51 Early human relations research tended to focus on employee satisfaction and morale, the im-

plicit assumption being that high morale leads to
[high / low] productivity.

high

52 Later research has indicated that the initial assumption about the relationship between morale and productivity was oversimplified. Furthermore, because the scope of organizational application has increased, many writers prefer the term "behavioral science approach to management" in place of
the term "human _____ ."

relations

53 The area of *employee motivation* continues to be of prime interest in the _____ _____ approach to management.

behavioral
science

54 A determination of the factors that lead to high productivity as well as to high morale in an organization is included in the study of employee
_____ .

motivation

55 Another area of behavioral science research is the study of the organization as a *social system*. Studies of role, status, and status symbols are included in viewing the organization as a _____ system.

social

56 Studying the functions of informal groups and their effect on organizational success is also consistent with viewing the organization as a
_____ _____ .

social system

57 Increasingly, the area of *leadership* and its relationship to organizational success have been included in _____ science research.

behavioral

58 The problem of distinguishing between successful and unsuccessful managerial behavior is included in the study of leadership. Since the study of leadership includes consideration of environmental factors that affect a leader's success, it [includes / does not include] more than the study of the leader himself.

includes

motivation
social
leadership

59 In addition to studying employee _____ , viewing the organization as a _____ system, and studying the process of _____ , the behavioral science approach to management directs attention to *communication* and its relationship to organizational success.

communication

60 The study of the factors related to achieving understanding in two-person situations is included in the behavioral interest in _____ .

communication

61 Furthermore, consideration of the best structuring and use of the channels of contact in an organization is included in the study of _____ .

motivation
social system
leadership
communication

62 The four areas of application of the behavioral science approach to management discussed so far have been employee _____ , considering the organization as a _____ _____ , _____ , and _____ .

behavioral science

63 Finally, an interest in *employee development* is included in the _____ _____ approach to management theory.

development

64 Studying and applying the principles leading to efficiency in learning are included in the area of employee _____ .

employee
development

65 A study of the factors leading to appropriate application of what has been learned to a new situation is also included in the interest in _____ _____ .

communication

66 Reviewing this section briefly, the area of behavioral science application that emphasizes the importance of common understanding and its assessment is _____ .

67 The area of behavioral science research that focuses on the personal factors underlying high productivity, as well as high morale, is the area of employee _____ .

motivation

68 Charting the informal pattern of relationships in an organization is included in the research perspective which views the organization as a _____ _____ .

social system

69 The area having to do with identifying personal characteristics and situational factors leading to managerial success is that of _____ .

leadership

70 The area concerned with the continued upgrading of employee skills, including managerial skills, is that of employee _____ .

development

71 The five areas of managerial application of behavioral science methods and findings which have been introduced in this chapter are employee _____ , viewing the organization as a _____ _____ , _____ , _____ , and employee _____ .

motivation
social system
leadership
communication
development

72 As we have indicated, the Hawthorne studies mark the beginning of the human relations field and the subsequent interest in applying behavioral science methods and principles in the study of managerial problems. In the book that serves as a comprehensive report of these studies, Roethlisberger and Dickson summarize one of the studies by reporting:

The study of the bank wiremen showed that their behavior at work could not be understood without considering the informal organization of the group and the relation of the informal organization to the total social organization of the company.[1]

[1]F. J. Roethlisberger and William J. Dickson, *Management and the Worker*, Cambridge, Mass.: Harvard University Press, 1939, p. 551.

Of the five areas of behavioral science application we have discussed, the one that is represented in this excerpt is that of viewing the organization as a

social system   _____ _____ .

D THE SYSTEMS AND QUANTITATIVE APPROACH TO MANAGEMENT CONCEPTS

Historically, the systems approach is the most recent contributor to management theory and techniques. As is also true for the other contributions which we have discussed, certain ingredients included in this approach can be traced to early historical antecedents, but they have undergone recent significant development resulting in a distinct approach to organization and management. In this case, the significant historical event is represented by the development of operations research (OR) in the British military services during World War II. In this section we introduce the general characteristics of the systems approach that was stimulated by the development of OR, consider the associated use of mathematical models and quantitative methods, and discuss the role of communication and decision processes in the systems orientation.

73 In general, a *systems approach* indicates a primary interest in studying whole situations and relationships, rather than organizational segments. In this sense, if product design, manufacture, and marketing were largely accomplished independently of one another by specialized managers, the

inconsistent   procedure used would be [consistent / inconsistent] with the systems approach.

74 The general characteristics of the systems viewpoint are described in some detail in Chapter 17, where that viewpoint is used as the basis for summarizing some of the major concepts in this book. As indicated by our example, even though specialized knowledge is still considered to be important, the application of the systems approach results in the need to develop people who are [technical specialists / generalists].

generalists

75 In the case of a business organization the term "system" could mean "social system" and thus have a behavioral orientation, or it could apply to functional relationships and decision processes and thus have a relatively impersonal orientation. The systems approach associated with operations research concerns the identification of appropriate mathematical models as the basis for determining best decisions, and therefore it is relatively [behavioral / impersonal] in its orientation.

impersonal

76 Thus, whereas the continued development of the behavioral science applications since the Hawthorne studies has mainly led to developments in such areas as [employee motivation / decision-making techniques], the continued development of the systems approach stemming from operations research has led to developments in [employee motivation / decision-making techniques].

employee
motivation

decision-making
techniques

77 We shall discuss the techniques associated with operations research in Chapter 5. For now we can observe that, as an overall approach, the most important characteristic of OR is its orientation toward [whole systems / particular problems].

whole systems

78 Even though the systems orientation of OR is its most important contribution to management theory, the quantitative techniques have come to be widely used in many specialized problem areas, such as production and distribution. Therefore, many people think of the collection of such techniques as linear programming, Monte Carlo methods, and game theory as constituting the definition of _____ research.

operations

79 As it has continued to develop in recent years,

the systems approach not only includes an interest in mathematical models and the quantitative techniques associated with operations research, but it has also resulted in viewing the organization as a communication and decision-making system. In the context of the systems approach "communication" refers to [channels provided for information flow / factors influencing changes in behavior].

channels provided
for information
flow

80 From this standpoint, whereas many of Fayol's general principles of management were concerned with [division of formal authority / communication structure], the systems approach to management tends to view any organization as representing a ————————— ————————— .

division of formal
authority

communication
structure

81 The Program Evaluation and Review Technique (PERT) is a planning and controlling method which represents the systems approach in its orientation and is extensively used in the aerospace and defense industries. Described in detail in Chapter 16, this technique [cuts across / closely conforms to] the established specialized departments in a firm.

cuts across (and
thus has a
wholistic
orientation)

82 The systems approach to management shares a number of characteristics with Taylor's earlier work in that both are relatively impersonal in orientation, emphasize the use of the methods of science, and have resulted in contributions to the planning process. As if to highlight this similarity, the quantitative systems approach has frequently been called "management science," as contrasted to Taylor's ————————— ————————— .

scientific
management

83 However, the scope and techniques associated with these two contributors to the practice of management are quite different. The approach oriented toward study of entire situations with identification of best organizationwide decisions is

management
science (or
systems
approach);
scientific
management

————————— ————————— , whereas
the approach oriented toward identifying best
methods of work within an established system is
————————— ————————— .

84 Another development that has added fuel to
growing interest in the systems approach is the use
of electronic data processing in commercial applications beginning in the early 1950s. The applications particularly relevant to the systems approach
are those that are concerned with [rapid sequences
of computations, such as in payroll / processing of
information for general management use].

processing of
information for
general
management use

85 The full potential of the computer is represented when it is used to develop information for
more effective decision making, rather than when
it is simply used as a rapid calculator. To the extent
that current procedures associated with "instructing" the computer through computer programs
can be simplified, the use of such equipment in
conjunction with the systems approach to management will be [curtailed / enhanced].

enhanced (since
the need to write
individual
programs now
limits computer
use when the
problem is
nonrepetitive)

E THE CULTURAL FRAMEWORK OF MANAGEMENT

The coverage in the preceding sections of this
chapter has been concerned with management as
an internal process, and this is also the main orientation of the entire book. By "internal" we mean
that the focus is on the things that managers
should do within the organization to achieve organizational objectives. However, in addition to the
internal process the cultural framework within

which the organization exists represents the external process which may (and should) influence the specific decisions made by managers. Of course, the cultural factors which exist in different countries are likely to differ. But the point particularly developed in this concluding section of the chapter is that a manager needs to be aware of changing cultural influences in our own society in order to be effective in applying the principles of management developed in this text.

86 The general manager of a steel mill in Sweden can analyze his organizational objectives and apply principles of management in a manner similar to his American counterpart. However, because the mill is located in a different (socialistic) political system, the _____ influences are likely to be quite different.

cultural (or external)

87 Even within the context of a particular country, cultural changes take place which influence the appropriateness of particular managerial actions. Managerial alertness to cultural changes is therefore a prerequisite to the successful application of the principles of _____ presented in this book.

management

88 In the remainder of this section we discuss four external, or cultural, factors that have been particularly important in the United States during the past decade: the internationalization of business, the increase in minority group participation, the concern for the ecology, and the rise in individual self-expression. Given the nature of these cultural influences, has it been possible for a business firm or other type of organization to ignore these developments? [Yes / No] Why or why not?

No
These developments have resulted in governmental legislation (etc.).

_____

_____

_____

_____

89 Of course, the four areas of development which we consider do not cover all of the changes taking place in our society, but indicate the kinds of developments that should be given attention by managerial personnel. The first development, the *internationalization of business*, identifies the fact that the United States as well as foreign firms have been increasingly active [within their own countries only / on a global scale].

on a global scale

90 Not only has trade among countries increased, but business firms have increasingly established subsidiaries in other countries. Thus, this worldwide orientation is what we have in mind when we speak of the _____ of business.

internationalization

91 Of course the multinational scope of business activities has also opened the door to a number of problems, including the existence of different political systems, changing monetary exchange rates, and different ways of "doing business" in different countries. But given the mutual opportunities to develop new markets, such difficulties [have / have not] prevented the internationalization of business during the past decade.

have not

92 A second important external factor influencing organizations in this country during the past decade is the movement toward greater *minority participation* in our society. These concerns have resulted in specific government regulations to increase employment opportunities for such groups as blacks, Mexican-Americans, women, and those over forty years of age. As a result, the use of such established personnel selection methods as employment tests [has / has not] been affected.

has (since some of these tests have been judged to include a cultural bias)

93 Thus, two external factors which have had a profound affect on the organizational perspective of managers during the past decade are the _____ of business and the increase in _____ group participation.

internationalization

minority

94 A third cultural influence has been the increasing *concern about the ecology* of our country. Some years ago it was considered entirely acceptable for a steel mill to dispose of wastes in the local environment, both in the air and in adjoining streams and rivers. Such a managerial attitude is now [unlikely / impossible].

impossible (since
federal and state
legislation now
exists in respect to
such activities)

95 Outside the area of waste disposal as such, managers today are likely to be very much aware of the visual and cultural impact of company facilities and the necessity of replenishing natural resources where possible. All such concerns are reflective of the manager's awareness of the national interest in our _____ .

ecology

96 Finally, a fourth area of development in our culture during the past few years, and one that is more difficult to "pin down," concerns the increased interest in individual *self-expression*. In an era in which there is less conformity to specific modes of dress and hairstyle, the assembly-line approach to organizing jobs by which each individual does a repetitive task hundreds or thousands of times per day is likely to be viewed as providing [sufficient / insufficient] opportunity for self-expression.

insufficient

97 Thus, the motivational and disciplinary problems in automobile assembly plants which have been reported during the past few years are at least in part related to the increasing desire for _____ by people in our society.

self-expression

98 If the management of a company or an industry chooses to ignore certain cultural developments, the effects nevertheless eventually occur in one way or another. For example, minority group participation was formalized through governmental legislation. However, if business and other organizations are to provide a leadership role in our society, then they [should / should not] wait for such external actions as governmental legislation to take place.

should not

99 Aside from the legislative aspects of cultural change, historically it can be observed that organizations which recognized the implications of technological developments achieved greater success. Similarly, organizations which recognize the implications of such cultural developments as the increasing desire for individual self-expression are [more / less] likely thereby to achieve organizational success.

more

Review

100 The approach founded by Frederick Taylor that has the major objective of attaining higher industrial efficiency by separating the planning from the doing of tasks is called _____ _____ . (Introduction to Section A)

scientific
management

101 Two assumptions underlying the specific objectives and techniques of scientific management are that industrial efficiency can be attained through the application of the methods of _____ and the payment of _____ _____ . (Frames 1 to 4)

science
high wages

102 Studies of the relationship between employee productivity and such physical factors as lighting, temperature, humidity, and rest pauses concern the objective of defining standardized _____ _____ . (Frames 5, 6, and 20)

working
conditions

103 Standardized work methods can be determined by applying the technique of

motion

_____ study, whereas setting the production level to be used as the standard for a wage incentive system can be accomplished by the

time

application of the technique of _____ study. (Frames 7 to 24)

104 In contrast to Taylor's work in studying first-level management, Henri Fayol centered his atten-

higher-level (etc.)

tion on _____ management. (Introduction to Section B)

105 The organizational activity with which most of Fayol's writings are concerned is the

managerial

_____ activity. (Frames 25 to 31)

106 In Fayol's analysis, planning, organizing, commanding, coordinating, and controlling are

functions (or
elements)

considered to be the _____ of management. (Frames 30 to 32, 42 to 45)

107 Fayol also listed and described fourteen general principles of management, ranging from "division of work" to "esprit de corps." He believed that these principles, based on his own experiences

incomplete

as a manager, represented a(n) [complete / incomplete] listing. (Frames 33 to 41)

108 The third important influence on management concepts is the application of the methods

behavioral science

and results of the _____ _____ approach. (Introduction to Section C)

109 The famous studies that led to widespread application of behavioral science principles to problems of management have been called the

Hawthorne

_____ studies. (Frames 46 to 52)

110 The area of behavioral science application that is concerned with determining employee goals

motivation

is employee _____ , whereas studying

the influence of informal groups on individual performance is related to viewing the organization

social system   as   a   _____   _____.
(Frames 53 to 56, 72)

111 Attempting to discover the basis for the success or failure of individual managers involves the

leadership   area of research in _____ . (Frames 57 and 58)

112 Determining the factors related to conveying

communication   understanding has to do with _____ whereas improving the performance of organiza-

development   tional members involves employee _____ . (Frames 59 to 71)

113 The systems approach to management traces its recent growth to the development of

operations   _____ research during World War II. (Introduction to Section D)

114 As applied in business organizations, the systems approach to management has resulted in particular interest being given to [behavioral fac-

information and   tors / formal authority / information and decision
decision processes   processes]. (Frames 73 to 85)

115 The appropriateness of particular managerial actions is influenced by certain external, or

cultural   _____ influences, as well as by managerial principles as such. (Frames 86 to 88)

116 The multinational scope of activities of firms in all countries in the past few years is a cultural development which has been referred to as the

internationalization   _____ of business, while a cultural development in our own country has been the increas-

minority   ing participation of _____ groups in organizations. (Frames 89 to 93)

117 Increasing national concern about polution and about the quality of our environment is

ecology   included in the concern about the _____ , while
organizing jobs so that an individual is required to
do a repetitive task in an automated fashion may
run counter to the increased desire for individual

self-expression _____ in our society.
(Frames 94 to 99)

Discussion Questions

1. Do you think that there are universal principles of management that affect the success of, for
example, sales managers as well as productions
managers?

2. Describe the kind of work done for the purpose of improving industrial efficiency that would
be an application or development of Taylor's scientific management.

3. In what respect have Fayol's general principles
of management resulted in contributions to management methods that are different from the techniques of Taylor's scientific management?

4. What are some major areas of behavioral
science research that have had an impact on management theory?

5. How is the term "system" generally defined in
the systems approach to management? Discuss the
similarities and differences between this approach
and each of the others discussed in this chapter.

6. Since a manager's job is concerned with achieving organizational objectives as efficiently as possible, why should factors outside the organization,
such as the concern for minority rights, influence a
manager's decisions?

7. The use of Taylor's scientific management
during the 1920s was frequently accompanied by

managerial abuses of the approach, in that the techniques of the system were often used without the overall philosophy of gaining worker cooperation and sharing the gains associated with the system. Consider the possible relationship between such abuses and events in United States industry during the 1930s.

8. Fayol's conclusion that management principles are universal, and apply to any area of managerial endeavor, was considered to be a controversial position at the time he made his observations at the turn of the century. Today there is little question about the universality of management concepts. Why the difference? Is it because a science of management has been developed based on managerial principles that have been tested and proved?

9. Some writers in the area of management principles have suggested that the systems and the behavioral science approaches to studying management are likely to be the most influential in terms of generating new concepts and techniques during the next decade. Consider some reasons why this belief might be true.

10. In conjunction with the preceding question, it has also been suggested that no matter what approaches to developing new management principles prove to be productive during the next decade, the functional approach to management will continue to be the most popular method by which to summarize and communicate these principles. Consider some reasons why this might be true.

Case Study: Consultants' Reports

The Corby Manufacturing Company is a manufacturer of industrial power tools located in the Midwest. During the last five years, since the appointment of Phillip Sherman to the presidency, the company has been particularly successful in

broadening its product lines and achieving technological improvements in existing products. Although a controller and a personnel manager are
included in the top management group, the large
majority of the company's middle and top management have a background in professional engineering, reflecting the nature of the company's products and customers.

Although the company is considered to be one of
the most successful in its field, Sherman has taken
special notice of the fact that profits did not keep
pace with advances in sales during the past year,
even with outside-of-company factors considered.
As Sherman perceives the situation, the very success that the company has enjoyed has also created
operating difficulties at the management level. He
finds, for example, that he can no longer keep tabs
on all the areas of managerial activity in the firm.
Where five years ago there were twenty managers
at the departmental level and above, there are now
thirty-five managers, resulting in greater difficulties in coordinating sales, manufacture, and shipment of the various products. Sherman does not
consider the situation to be serious now, but he is
concerned about the possibility that, as the firm
continues to grow, this symptom of a developing
organization problem will become more serious.

In order to obtain an objective diagnosis of the
company's situation as a basis for developing a plan
of action, Sherman retained two consultants, representing two different management consulting
firms, to carry out a diagnostic survey of company
operations at the managerial level. Very briefly,
the first consultant reports that there is a basic
need to develop a greater awareness of the managerial skills among company executives. Among
his specific recommendations he proposes a series
of conferences, to include all levels of management, aimed at defining organization objectives
and leadership and decision-making skills. He

suggests that the company needs to determine what factors really motivate managers and employees, and to make use of this knowledge in organizing work groups as well as in evaluating the financial compensation system itself.

The second consultant reports that areas of authority and responsibility are not clearly designated and that the formal organization structure does not reflect present organizational needs. Accordingly, he proposes that a major company reorganization at this point in company growth is desirable. The objective of this reorganization will be to define the principal functions being carried out in the company and to group operating activities according to these functions at all organizational levels. Of course, this reorganization will have to be accomplished with complete top management participation, and the resulting organization structure should not only better serve present needs, but should also provide the framework for further organizational growth.

Mr. Sherman had planned to take immediate remedial actions in areas where both consultants agreed and to further study their other observations and recommendations. Upon reading their reports, however, he finds it difficult to find any area of agreement between the two analyses.

1. Given that both consultants studied the same firm, why are their results so different?
2. In what respects are the consultants in implicit agreement?
3. Which report do you believe provides the better basis for further action? Why?

Case Study: The Old-Line Foreman

John Norris has worked for United Electric Company since 1946, upon his release from military service after World War II. Following several

years' experience as a production worker he was
promoted to foreman of a manufacturing section
in 1953. By 1960 he was promoted to general
foreman of an entire department. The performance of his department was so exceptional that in
1965 he was considered for promotion to assistant
plant manager. However, the fact that his formal
education did not include any work at the college
level led to some question about whether his
preparation for such a position was adequate, particularly since as a matter of policy the company
wants assistant plant managers to be qualified for
promotion to plant manager. Further, John Norris
himself indicated that he preferred to remain in
the type of managerial position in which the
human relations factors are the primary ones affecting job performance. From this standpoint, he
enjoyed working close to the operative level at
which the "work was really being done" in the company.

During the past few years the department headed
up by John Norris has continued to do well, but
George Malcolm, the plant manager, has taken
note of the fact that the department does not have
the exceptional quality and cost performance it
once exhibited. He recognizes that an individual,
or a department, cannot be at a "peak" all of the
time, but his review of the performance statistics of
the past several years now indicates a downtrend
that, if continued, will soon lead to performance at
an unacceptable level. During the annual appraisal
interview, therefore, Mr. Malcolm decided that it
would be well to discuss this apparently deterio-
rating situation in some detail with John Norris.

As usual, George Malcolm first reviewed the areas
of departmental strength and the areas of possible
improvement with John during the appraisal conference. Then, in a broader vein he indicated
overall satisfaction with John's work, but expressed
his concern about the deterioration in performance in recent years. He asked John what his

thoughts were about why his department no longer displayed the exceptional levels of performance that were once typical of those areas working under his supervision. John's immediate reaction to this question made it obvious that he was indeed very much aware of the decline, and that it had distressed him.

"You're right, George," he replied. "The people in my department are performing adequately, but nothing like the way they were a few years ago. And it's all because of the kind of people that we've been hiring lately. I'm as much for equal rights as the next man, but I also know that if I'm going to be responsible for the work in my department then I should have the authority to choose the kind of people who I think will work well for me when they're sent to me by the personnel department. Over the years I've found that young fellows whose fathers have skilled trades jobs in manufacturing plants work out best for me, because they've usually got a good background in mechanical things and also understand about discipline in a production situation. But, as I say, during the past few years the personnel department has said that because of equal opportunity reasons, I can't follow my own standards anymore. These minority group people just don't seem to follow directions the same way. What's worse, even the other young fellows they've been sending me don't seem any better. Instead of following through and doing the job as instructed, they start asking 'why' and talk about 'doing their own thing.' I'll tell you, until we get another depression to remind these fellows what it's all about, we can forget about getting much out of them except minimum performance. You know what I'm talking about, don't you George?"

1. In what respects is John Norris correct in his diagnosis of the developing problem in his department?
2. In what respects is John's diagnosis incorrect?

3. What should George Malcolm do to achieve some corrective and remedial results?
4. What should George Malcolm do in the broader context of his responsibilities as plant manager?

Suggested Readings*

Andrews, K. R.: "Toward Professionalism in Business Management," *Harvard Business Review*, vol. 47, no. 2, March-April 1969.

Ansoff, H. E., and R. G. Brandenburg: "The General Manager of the Future," *California Management Review*, vol. 12, no. 3, Spring 1969.

Davis, K., and R. L. Blomstrom: *Business, Society, and Environment: Social Power and Social Response*, 2d ed., McGraw-Hill Book Company, New York, 1971.

England, G. W., and R. Lee: "Organizational Goals and Expected Behavior among American, Japanese, and Korean Managers: A Comparative Study," *Academy of Management Journal*, vol. 14, no. 4, December 1971.

Fayol, H.: *General and Industrial Management*, Pitman Publishing Corporation, New York, 1949.

Johnson, R. A., F. E. Kast, and J. E. Rosenzweig: *The Theory and Management of Systems*, 3d ed., McGraw-Hill Book Company, New York, 1973.

Koontz, H.: "The Management Theory Jungle," *Academy of Management Journal*, vol. 4, no. 3, December 1961.

——— **(ed.):** *Toward a Unified Theory of Management*, McGraw-Hill Book Company, New York, 1964.

Mayo, E.: *The Human Relations of an Industrial Civilization*, Harvard University Press, Cambridge, Mass., 1933.

Mockler, R. J.: "The Systems Approach to Business Organizations and Decision Making," *California Management Review*, vol. 11, no. 2, Winter 1968.

Narver, J. C.: "Rational Management Responses to External Effects," *Academy of Management Journal*, vol. 14, no. 1, March 1971.

Peterson, R. B.: "A Cross-Cultural Perspective of Supervisory Values," *Academy of Management Journal*, vol. 15, no. 1, March 1972.

Roethlisberger, F. J., and W. J. Dickson: *Management and the Worker*, Harvard University Press, Cambridge, Mass., 1933.

*Also see the cross-reference table in the Preface.

Taylor, F. W.: *The Principles of Scientific Management*, Harper and Brothers, New York, 1911.

Chapter two

THE
FUNCTIONS
OF
THE
MANAGER

Stemming from the work of Henri Fayol, the functional approach to management focuses upon the managerial *activities* that have to be carried out in order to achieve organizational objectives. In this chapter we consider the characteristics of the major management functions of *planning, organizing, directing*, and *controlling*. There is no universal agreement regarding which activities constitute the major management functions, but these four are listed by the large majority of writers in the field. Along these lines, some have added the function of "staffing" to this list. Fayol himself identified a fifth function he called "coordinating," and in the last section of this unit we discuss why coordinating is better considered an objective of management rather than a function of management. The four major functions described in this chapter serve as the principal basis for organizing the topics in the remainder of this book, and therefore the ideas introduced in this chapter are more fully developed in later chapters.

A THE FUNCTIONAL APPROACH TO MANAGEMENT

In addition to focusing upon what managers do, the functional approach to the study of management emphasizes the universal applicability of the functions. Thus, whether in a small business firm, a governmental agency, or a large corporation, whether on the general management level or in a specialized area of work, all managers are involved in carrying out the functions of planning, organizing, directing, and controlling.

1 Universal applicability and the focusing upon what managers do is descriptive of the _____ approach to studying the process of management.

functional

2 *Management* functions should not be confused with *organizational* functions. Thus finance, production, and sales are examples of _____ functions, whereas planning, organizing, directing, and controlling are _____ functions.

organizational

management

3 Is a manager whose area of activity is restricted to one organizational function, such as production, nevertheless concerned with the several management functions? [Yes / No]

Yes

4 Figure 2.1 illustrates the relationship between some representative organizational functions and the management functions. The figure indicates, for example, that a manager who has a primary assignment in the organizational function of production can effectively carry out this assignment by appropriate use of the management functions of

planning
organizing
directing
controlling

_____ , _____ , _____ , and _____ .

5 Viewed from the other standpoint, Figure 2.1 indicates that effective planning for a firm as a whole requires planning for each of the

organizational

_____ functions represented in that firm.

Representative organizational functions

Management functions	Production ↓	Sales ↓	Finance ↓	Personnel ↓
Planning →				
Organizing →				
Directing →				
Controlling →				

Figure 2.1 The relationship between organizational functions and management functions.

6 Therefore, the relationship between organizational and management functions is such that a manager must typically [choose to do one or the other / give attention to both].

give attention to
both

7 In addition to the difference between organizational and management functions, another distinction that needs to be made is between _managerial_ and _technical_ activities. To the extent that an executive is carrying out the functions of planning, organizing, directing, and controlling, he is involved in _____ activities.

managerial

8 On the other hand, to the extent that a manager does not delegate nonmanagerial tasks but carries them out himself, he is involved in _____ activities.

technical

9 When a senior accountant directs the efforts of a group of junior accountants, he is performing _____ work. When he himself audits certain records or reports, he is doing _____ work.

managerial
technical

10 Therefore, is all of a manager's time necessarily spent carrying out management functions? [Yes / No]

No

11 Since these managers are closest to the technical work being done, the time spent on technical activities is usually greatest at the [top / middle / first-level] managerial level.

first-level

12 In effect, we are suggesting that a manager is *not* a manager when he is doing technical work. Similarly, an employee who does not have a managerial title is in fact working as a manager when he has responsibility for any of the _____ functions.

management

13 Therefore, the absolute distinction between managers and nonmanagers that is implied by position titles is generally [accurate / misleading].

misleading

14 Just as the time spent on managerial and technical activities varies with managerial level, the proportion of time spent on planning and organizing, as contrasted to directing and controlling, also varies with the _____ level.

managerial

15 Top managers, who need to be concerned

about the future position of the organization, are likely to spend relatively more time on the functions of [planning and organizing / directing and controlling].

planning and
organizing

16 On the other hand, first-level managers, whose prime responsibility is to see that work already scheduled is accomplished, are likely to spend more time on the functions of [planning and organizing / directing and controlling].

directing and
controlling

17 Though he included coordinating in his analysis, Fayol had difficulty in distinguishing coordinating from the other management _____ .
In this chapter we regard coordinating not as a function, but as an objective related to all of the functions.

functions

18 In the following sections of this chapter, we briefly consider the descriptions of the four management functions of _____,
_____, _____, and
_____ . More complete development for each of these functions takes place in later chapters.

planning
organizing
directing
controlling

B PLANNING

From the standpoint of logical progression, the function of planning precedes activities in organizing, directing, and controlling. And within planning, the first logical and necessary step is the identification of the organization's objectives. Following the identification of objectives, necessary policies, procedures, and methods can then be determined.

19 In discussing organizational objectives, we cannot ignore the fact that the groups of people associated with an organization have their own personal objectives that affect the organization's success. The owner and employee groups, for example, are considered to be [within / outside]

within

outside

the firm, whereas suppliers and customers are [within / outside] the firm.

20 From this standpoint, equitable distribution of economic gains to the various groups associated with an enterprise [enhances / diminishes] the likelihood of long-run success.

outside

enhances

21 However, an organization can also be viewed as an entity with its own objectives. In their search for a universal organizational objective, management theorists have considered three general objectives: profit, growth and survival, and the product or service objective. Of these, the objective most frequently associated with privately owned firms is _____ .

profit

22 For a number of reasons, to be discussed in Chapter 3, most writers in management prefer to identify the production of an economic value in the form of a product or service as being the universal objective of all organizations. This objective assigns particular importance to the influence of [owners / employees / customers] on organization success.

customers

23 As part of the process of defining specific operating objectives, such factors as expected demand, technological changes, and governmental fiscal policy have to be considered. Such factors have been called *planning premises* because they [are / are not] subject to the firm's direct control.

are not

24 The determination of *policies*, which are general statements that guide decision making in the organization, typically follows the identification of the organization's specific operating _____.

objectives

25 In contrast to the needs of top management personnel, a first-level manager needs relatively [specific / broad] policy statements to guide his decision making.

specific

26 Accordingly, policies are often classified according to the _____ level affected.

managerial (or
organizational)

27 Furthermore, it is also useful to classify policies according to the way they were formed and according to the organizational function involved. An example of the latter would be the company's _____ policies.

finance (or
production, sales,
etc.)

28 Whereas a "general guide for decision making" defines a _____ , a _procedure_ specifies the sequence of steps to be taken to attain an objective.

policy

29 On the other hand, a _method_ specifies how some one step of a procedure should be performed, and is thus more detailed than either a _____ or a _____ .

policy procedure

30 Overall, the identification of the organization's objectives and the formulation of policies, procedures, and _____ are all components of the planning process.

methods

31 Though the skill of _decision making_ is involved in all management functions, it is especially important in determining the manager's effectiveness in carrying out the function of _____ .

planning

32 In addition to research interest in creativity, there has been extensive application of quantitative methods to improve managerial skill in _____ making.

decision

33 Some of the techniques of operations research (OR) are presented and discussed in Chapter 5. The development of OR has resulted in expanded application of _____ methods in managerial decision making.

quantitative

C ORGANIZING

The organization chart, which is a kind of model representing the formal organization, indicates the grouping of activities, authority relationships, and certain communication channels. As such, the organization chart represents the result of the management function of organizing. The function itself consists of determining the activities to be performed in an organization, grouping these activities, and assigning managerial authority and responsibility to people employed in the organization.

34 As indicated in the introduction above, the results of the process of organizing are typically represented by means of an organization

chart   _____ .

35 *Departmentation*, which is the grouping of

activities (etc.)   _____ , in a business enterprise can be done on the basis of several different factors.

36 For example, grouping of activities according to such factors as sales, finance, production, and the like is departmentation based on organiza-

functions   tional _____ .

37 Grouping of activities according to the number of people, the product, the territory, the customer, and the process involved are other bases

departmentation   for _____ .

38 As an organization expands, growth may take place in either a vertical or a horizontal direction. The addition of more levels of management repre-

vertical   sents _____ growth, whereas the addition of more organizational functions, with the number of levels held constant, represents

horizontal   _____ growth.

39 Determining the ideal *span of management*, i.e.,

the number of employees whose work can be effectively supervised by one manager, has been a long-standing problem related to the management function of _____ .

organizing (Of course, this also becomes a directing problem.)

40 Whereas classical writers tended to search for an ideal span of _____ for all situations, contemporary writers emphasize the importance of such factors as the organization level involved, the type of activity, the type of personnel, and the type of organization.

management

41 Overall organizational structure is greatly affected by whether the enterprise tends toward a philosophy of managerial *centralization* or *decentralization*. Concentration of authority at top management levels is reflective of managerial _____ .

centralization

42 On the other hand, wide dissemination of authority in the organization is reflective of a managerial philosophy of [centralization / decentralization].

decentralization

43 Identification of *line* and *staff* activities, and definition of the authority relationships between the two, constitutes another dimension of the management function of _____ .

organizing

44 Activities that are directly concerned with attaining company objectives are classified as line activities, whereas those that have an indirect relationship are classified as [line / staff] activities.

staff

45 There are various ways in which the staff gives assistance in attaining the organization's objectives, sometimes involving even staff control of _____ activities.

line

46 Further, the manager needs to be aware that in every enterprise an *informal social organization*

in addition to   exists [instead of / in addition to] the formal one
defined and constructed by the manager.

47   The informal organization serves as an additional communication medium, making possible

faster   [faster / slower] flow of information within an enterprise, though the information may or may not be accurate.

48   From what you know about the tendency of people to communicate and get together outside formal organization channels, would you expect it to be possible to eliminate the informal organiza-

No   tion in an enterprise? [Yes / No]

49   Finally, an organization has to be staffed, which includes the determination of personnel needs and the selection, appraisal, and training of the people who are required. Therefore, such personnel functions can also be considered an inherent part of the management function of

organizing   ——————————— .

D   DIRECTING

The function of directing involves guiding and supervising the efforts of subordinates toward the attainment of the firm's goals. Through research in human motivation, leadership, communication, and employee development, the behavioral sciences have contributed substantially to our understanding of this function in recent years.

50   In contrast to the classical economic-man assumption, which suggested that amount of pay is the only factor determining worker productivity, recent findings emphasize the diverse motives un-

more   derlying behavior, thus resulting in [more / less] complex motivational models which are

more   [more / less] realistic.

51   The facts that a multiplicity of motives exists and that these motives are not necessarily compati-

motive ble with one another suggest that a person must often make a choice about which _____ he will attempt to satisfy.

52 The supervisor has the choice of using *positive* or *negative* motivational methods. Motivating people by threatening to reduce their current levels of

negative satisfaction involves _____ motivation.

53 On the other hand, the promise of increased

positive satisfaction involves _____ motivation.

54 Since a supervisor's *communication skill* is related to his effectiveness in guiding people's behavior, it is also directly related to his effectiveness in

directing the management function of _____ .

55 The passing of information and understanding from one person to another defines the process

communication of _____ .

56 In a communication situation involving two people the channel is relatively simple. On the other hand, a formal organization can be viewed as being made up of a number of decision centers in-

channels terconnected by communication _____ .

57 In addition to the areas of motivation and communication, studies by behavioral scientists in the area of *leadership* have increased our understanding of the management function of

directing _____ .

58 Classical studies of leadership success tended to be focused exclusively on the characteristics of the principal person in the situation, that is, the

leader _____ himself.

59 However, contemporary studies of leadership have included consideration of the situational factors that affect the appropriateness of specific lead-

increasing

ership methods, thus [increasing / reducing] the number of factors that have to be included in studies of leadership.

directing

60 Finally, one of the practical difficulties faced by supervisors is employee *resistance to change.* Therefore, the methods by which such resistance can be overcome are also relevant to carrying out the management function of _____ .

E CONTROLLING

The fourth management function, that of controlling, is concerned with evaluating performance in an organization and applying necessary corrections. The control process includes the steps of establishing standards, comparing actual results with the standards, and taking corrective action.

late

61 To define standards only for the culmination of a process, rather than for points along the way, results in errors or discrepancies being detected relatively [early / late] in the process. For this reason, *strategic control points* which are used as focal points for control action *within* a process, are typically identified.

strategic control

62 Rather than inspect every unit of work in process, it is typical to select only a portion of inspection at a _____ _____ point.

standards

63 The standards with which results are compared may be of several types. Quantity, cost, time use, and quality measurements are four types of _____ which we shall discuss in Chapter 15 on the control process.

control

64 On the other hand, budgets, statistical control reports, and break-even-point analysis are among the *control devices* used to achieve effective management _____ .

cost

65 Of the classical control devices, the budget is by far the most frequently used, and it is particularly associated with control in respect to [cost / time].

time

66 On the other hand, PERT, which is described in detail in Chapter 16, is particularly associated with control in respect to [cost / time].

No

67 Managers who rely on the use of formal control systems frequently assume that people will automatically correct their behavior when informed of a discrepancy from defined standards. Is this necessarily true? [Yes / No]

resist

68 The tendency to want to avoid unpleasant facts, failure to accept the organization's goals, and objections to "outside" staff groups are among the reasons why individuals might [cooperate with / resist] a formal control system.

Yes

69 In American industry there has been a general movement toward emphasizing the advantages of self-control in contrast to centralized control of individuals and organizational units. Is it possible that this approach might *not* be successful in another country at this time? [Yes / No]

F COORDINATING

Contemporary writers in the field of management regard coordinating as an objective of management, rather than as a function in itself. Thus, successful coordination of activities results from effectively carrying out the functions of planning, organizing, directing, and controlling.

70 One reason for a lack of coordination between two departments might be that their respective objectives, policies, procedures, or methods are not consistent across departmental lines. In this case, the lack of coordination can be traced to a failure to carry out the management function of

planning   _____ .

71 On the other hand, a failure to define authority relationships so that they are similarly understood by the various organizational units and personnel involved would signify a failure in the

organizing   _____ function.

72 The failure of a unit or of specific personnel to carry out assigned functions according to schedules previously agreed upon reflects a lack of coordination probably related to management

directing   weakness in the function of _____ .

73 Finally, in the case in which one segment of an organization considers an output to be acceptable whereas another does not, the discrepancy in defining the standard involves difficulty in the

controlling   management process of _____ .

74 Thus, a successfully coordinated enterprise results from effectively carrying out the management

planning   functions of _____ ,
organizing   _____ , _____ , and
directing
controlling   _____ .

75 When a lack of coordination is detected, the appropriate action is to identify the management

function   _____ requiring improvement.

76 Throughout this chapter we have always listed the management functions in the same order so as to highlight their sequential relationship. As shown in Figure 2.2 on page 48, the first function

planning   requiring managerial attention is _____ , while the last one in the sequence, which culminates in the attainment of organization objectives,

controlling   is _____ .

77 Of course, managers are typically involved in all of the management functions on a continuing

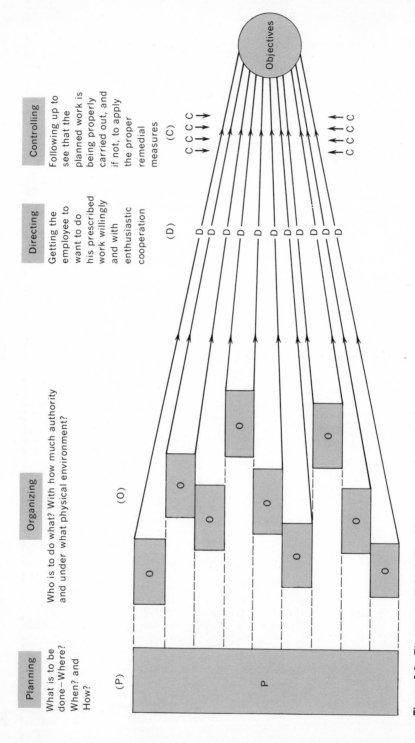

Figure 2.2 The sequential relationship among the functions of management. (Adapted from George R. Terry, *Principles of Management*, 6th ed., Richard D. Irwin, Inc., Homewood, Ill., 1972, p. 85. Reproduced with permission.)

basis as a result of overlaps in company projects. Because of this, the sequential relationship among the functions that is described in Figure 2.2 tends

masked   to be [masked / highlighted].

Review

functional

78 The approach to developing management concepts that focus on universal management activities is the _____ approach. (Introduction to the chapter, Introduction to Section A)

organizational

management

79 Production is an example of an _____ function, whereas controlling is an example of a _____ function. (Frames 1 to 6)

No

80 Is it true that, by definition, all the things that a manager does are considered managerial activities? [Yes / No] (Frames 7 to 10)

technical

81 As compared with those at other managerial levels, top managers spend the largest portion of their working time carrying out managerial activities, rather than carrying out nondelegated, or _____ , activities. (Frames 11 to 13)

Top
First-Level

82 Which level of management would be most involved in the function of planning? [Top / First-level] In the function of directing? [Top / First-level] (Frames 14 to 18)

planning

83 The identification of organizational objectives and the formulation of policies, procedures, and methods make up the _____ process. (Frames 19 to 33)

organizing

84 The determination and grouping of activities and the definition of authority relationships in the organization are involved in the management function of _____ . (Frames 34 to 49)

85 Guiding and supervising the efforts of subordinates toward the attainment of the organization's
directing   goals describes the function of _____ .
(Frames 50 to 60)

86 Establishing standards, comparing actual results with standards, and taking corrective action
are the steps included in the process of
controlling   _____ . (Frames 61 to 69)

87 A coordination problem within an enterprise
signifies that there has been a failure in performing at least one of the management _____
functions   _____ . (Frames 70 to 75)

88 In terms of their sequential relationship, the
four functions of management are appropriately
identified in the following order:
planning   _____ , _____ ,
organizing
directing   _____ , and _____ .
controlling   (Frames 76 and 77)

Discussion Questions

1. What are management functions, as contrasted to management "skills," for example?

2. What is the relationship between the management functions and the organizational functions in
a firm?

3. When is a manager a manager? When is he a
technical specialist?

4. We have always listed the management functions in a particular order in this chapter. Why?

5. Why is coordinating properly considered a
management objective rather than a management
function?

6. The use of many managerial techniques is associated with more than one of the functions. For

example, budgeting is considered to be a planning tool as well as a controlling device. Does this indicate that the functional approach to management is not really descriptive of the actual practice of management?

7. Should employees who are nonmanagers be concerned about principles of management? Why?

8. As indicated in the introduction to this chapter, there is no universal agreement about which functions represent *the* functions of management. For example, an alternative listing to the one used in this book is: planning, organizing, staffing, directing, and controlling. Another is: planning, organizing, activating, and controlling. A third is: planning, organizing, motivating, communicating, and controlling. Do these differences suggest that the "functional approach to management" is too diverse from the standpoint of being considered a common approach?

Case Study: The New Manager

After two years in the research and development department of the Altec Company, a manufacturer of electrical components in the aerospace industry, Bill Jeffries gained a reputation as an innovator and idea man who worked well with the other members of the fifteen-man department. In addition to his generally superior performance, two of his projects resulted in patents of significant competitive value. With the retirement of Joe Stephenson, the former department manager, several of the senior department members were considered likely candidates for the job. However, because of Bill's record of achievement and in order to boost the level of overall departmental performance, the president of Altec asked Bill Jeffries to assume the duties of department manager. Bill accepted the appointment and felt highly complimented at the level of confidence in him that the promotion implied.

After six months as manager of the research and development department, however, Bill Jeffries has begun to question the wisdom of his decision to accept the appointment. Worse, he now wonders whether the president also questions the wisdom of the decision to offer him the position. Although no official comment has been made thus far, he is well aware that no significant product improvement has come out of the R&D department in the last six months. Although he has publicly taken the position that it is too early to assess the results of the work during this period, he doesn't in fact see any significant improvements resulting from the work now under way.

There appears to be no motivational or morale problem in the department, for the other members accepted Bill's appointment almost immediately, unexpected though it was, and have been enthusiastic about the research freedom that they have had under his leadership. As one of the department members commented, "I've finally had a chance to look into some technical problems that I haven't been able to get to during the past couple of years." Generally, the department members believe that Bill is too impatient for results, considering the nature of their work. And because of his obligations concerning departmental correspondence, executive meetings, and various personnel functions relating to the department, Bill has not found the time to extend his earlier research in the directions he believes would result in further patents of competitive advantage to the firm.

1. Why was the position of the department manager offered to Bill Jeffries? What is your evaluation of the president's approach to this executive assignment decision?
2. In what ways might the company president's approach to executive selection and development be improved?

3. If the present condition of nonproductivity continues, should Bill Jeffries be relieved of the responsibility for managing the department?

4. In his position as department manager, what can Bill do to "find time" and make progress in the research areas he judges to be promising?

Case Study: Selection of a Senior Buyer

As manager of purchasing in a large manufacturing company, Bill Perkins faced the necessity of replacing his senior buyer, George Carlson, who was leaving the company. The logical choice was Mr. T. J. Smith, because he had the greatest number of years of experience in the department. Further, because of his excellent record as a buyer and his many good merit reviews he was the highest paid of the fifteen buyers in the department.

After determining that Mr. Smith was in fact interested in the position, Mr. Perkins began holding individual conferences with each of the buyers in the department to keep them informed about the likely appointment and to determine if there might be any adverse reaction to such appointment. Three of the first six men with whom he talked expressed their regrets with his choice for senior buyer based on doubts they had about Mr. Smith's managerial ability. Further, each of the three buyers thought that he was better qualified than Smith for the position, and they went so far as to hint that they would look for other positions if Mr. Smith was promoted to the supervisory post.

In order to maintain maximum harmony in the purchasing department, Perkins began looking outside the department for a man to appoint as senior buyer. He finally found a man, Mr. Ralph Peterson, who was in a supervisory position in the purchasing department of the state government and who was very interested in the position. He appointed Peterson to the position and introduced him to the other buyers as a man who had successfully supervised such operations in his previous job.

Although Ralph Peterson took charge immediately and began studying all of the various aspects of the product lines with which the buyers were involved, his attempts to supervise the buying activities were largely ineffective. Invariably, the buyers in the department gave him industry-related reasons why his suggested procedures could not be followed. Instead of following the directives of their new senior buyer they kept doing things the old way or devised new procedures of their own to take care of new types of buying problems. After about four months it was obvious that Ralph Peterson was being systematically bypassed, and the buyers were doing things increasingly on their own. Consequently, there was an absence of any actual leadership in the buying department, and at this late date Bill Perkins again began looking for another person to head up the buyers.

1. From the information given in the case description, why do you think Ralph Peterson failed in his appointment as senior buyer?
2. Should Bill Perkins have consulted with his men in respect to his original intention of appointing Mr. Smith to the supervisory position? Should he have stuck with that decision?
3. Was the decision to appoint someone from outside the company as the senior buyer appropriate, or should it have been the most qualified person from within the company?
4. What should Mr. Perkins do now?

Suggested Readings*

Barnard, C. I.: *The Functions of the Executive,* Harvard University Press, Cambridge, Mass., 1938.

*Also see the cross-reference table in the Preface.

Davis, R. C.: *The Fundamentals of Top Management,* Harper & Brothers, New York, 1951.

Fayol, H.: *General and Industrial Management* Pitman Publishing Corporation, New York, 1949.

Koontz, H.: "A Model for Analyzing the Universality and Transferability of Management," *Academy of Management Journal,* vol. 12, no. 4, December 1969.

Urwick, L. F.: *The Elements of Administration,* Harper & Brothers, New York, 1944.

———: "Papers in the Science of Administration," *Academy of Management Journal,* vol. 13, no. 4, December 1970.

PLANNING

Viewed as a managerial function, the process of planning includes the identification of organization objectives and the selection of policies, procedures, and methods designed to lead to the attainment of these objectives. In terms of the skill involved, effective decision making plays a major part in contributing to the success of the planning function.

Chapter 3 is concerned with the types of objectives associated with organizational activity, with special attention given to the concept of management by objectives. The discussion on the environment of planning includes consideration of the external premises that affect the planning function, while sales forecasting is viewed from the standpoint of being an internal premise.

In Chapter 4 we consider the formulation of the policies, procedures, and methods which are directed toward the achievement of organization objectives. Within this context, the general steps included in the process of decision making are also described.

Chapter 5 begins with a general description of operations research as a systems-oriented method of analysis based on the use of a mathematical model. After a general description of a number of quantitative decision-making techniques, the chapter includes illustrative examples of the application of linear programming and statistical decision analysis.

Chapter **three**

ORGANIZATIONAL OBJECTIVES AND PLANNING PREMISES

The first step in the planning process is that of designating organizational objectives and identifying the environmental factors, or premises, that define the framework of opportunities and limitations affecting planning. In this chapter we begin by considering the types of group and organizational objectives that affect operations in a firm. We then extend this orientation on objectives by describing *management by objectives* as an approach affecting planning at all levels within the organization. In the third section of this chapter we describe the environment of planning and some of the external premises that affect the planning function. In the last section we discuss sales forecasting as an internal premise affecting the planning function.

A TYPES OF OBJECTIVES

Organization objectives have been discussed by economists and management theorists both in terms of the firm as a whole and in terms of the groups of people who have an interest in the performance of the firm. In this section we first consider the particular objectives of the several groups of people within and outside the firm. The listing of the groups is not intended to be exhaustive, but it should illustrate the extent to which the management of a company needs to consider different group objectives which affect overall organizational effectiveness. Following this, we discuss the organization as an entity and evaluate several approaches that have been used in the attempt to identify the universal organizational objective, i.e., the objective held in common by all firms and organizations. In this context we discuss the profit objective, the survival and growth objective, and the product or service objective.

1 People associate themselves with an organization in order to satisfy their own objectives. Therefore, before considering the objectives of a firm as such, we find it useful to identify some of the groups of people associated with a firm and to consider their objectives. For our purposes we shall discuss *owners* (or investors), *managers*, and *employees* as examples of groups that are located
within [within / outside] the firm. On the other hand, we shall discuss vendors, customers, and government
outside as groups that are [within / outside] the firm.

2 Considering only the economic-objectives for the groups within the firm, we can describe the owners as being oriented toward earning a profit

_____, whereas the managers and the employees are described as being oriented toward

salary (or wage, etc.)

earning a _____.

3 For the groups outside the company, vendors look to the firm as a customer and thus as a source of sales revenue; governmental units at the local, state, and federal levels look to the firm as a source of tax revenue (as well as having broader considerations); and customers look to the firm as a suppli-

products (or services)

er of _____ .

4 In exchange for the economic benefits or values obtained from the firm, each of the groups we have discussed contributes to the firm's effectiveness. Thus, vendors provide the firm with raw material, employees devote their services to the firm, and owners (investors) provide the firm with

capital

_____ .

5 Although each group is in an interchange with the firm, each may view itself as competing with one or more of the other groups for the economic gains generated by the firm's activity. Thus, employees may take the attitude that the amount of money available to wages and salaries is reduced by

owners (or investors)

profits paid to _____ .

6 Figure 3.1, on page 62, shows the relationships we have been discussing. It indicates that each group contributes to the firm's effectiveness, represents a demand upon the firm's resources, and may in this particular case consider itself in compe-

five

tition with as many as _____ [number] other groups for those resources.

7 Without the contribution of each group represented in Figure 3.1, the existence or effectiveness of the firm would be threatened. Therefore, one of the primary tasks of company management is to allocate available resources so that a balance is achieved among the competing interests of the several groups represented. For example, what would be the likely effect of reducing the salaries of professional employees in the company?

_____

_____

_____

_____

Many competent employees would be likely to leave the company, thus impairing its effectiveness.

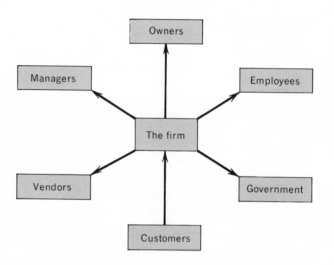

Figure 3.1 Some of the groups associated with a firm's activities.

8 Thus, from the standpoint of our discussion thus far, organizational objectives might be studied by considering the objectives of the several competing _____ that have interchange with the organization.

groups

9 In addition to the objectives of the specific groups, an overall organization objective would seem to be desirable to provide a direction for the firm's activities. Within the framework of the free enterprise system, for example, it might be said that the one objective all business firms share is the desire to earn a _____ .

profit

10 Although all the groups associated with a firm are jeopardized in the absence of profitable operations, the group most directly and immediately affected is the _____ group.

owner (or investor)

11 Therefore, one possible disadvantage of identifying *profit* as the principal goal of all organizations is that we may be confusing the objectives of a specific group, namely, the owners, with the principal objective of the _____ .

organization (or firm)

12 Another disadvantage of identifying profit as a universal organizational objective is that any management theory based on this premise could not be readily applied to nonprofit organizations. Yet an underlying assumption that has stimulated the development of management concepts and principles is that such principles are applicable [only in profit-oriented enterprises / in all types of organizations].

in all types of organizations

13 In considering organization objectives some writers in the field have concluded that the objective of *organizational survival and growth* characterizes all formal organizations. This viewpoint also assumes that the groups that make up the organization and the organization as such [can / cannot] be considered distinct and separate entities.

can

14 The viewpoint that all organizations have the common objective of survival and growth is particularly applicable to business firms whose form of ownership is the [sole proprietorship / partnership / corporation].

corporation

15 When the ownership of an enterprise is other than corporate, the firm legally ceases to exist with the death of an owner or co-owner. Thus, the general objective of survival and growth does not appear to apply very well to a firm that is legally organized as a _____ _____ or a _____ .

sole proprietorship partnership

16 Important as each may be in its own right, neither the profit objective nor the objective of survival and growth fully qualifies as a universal objective for all organizations, whether publicly or privately owned and regardless of legal form or ownership. Therefore, some writers in this field have suggested that the ultimate objective of any formal organization can be identified as a *product* or *service*. In our discussion of the groups of people associated with company activities, we particularly identified an interest in the product or service with the

customer ———————— group.

17 Thus, just as profit was criticized as a general objective because it was too closely associated with a particular group of people, so also might an orientation toward a product or service be criticized. However, unlike profit, the product or service objective can be used to study the operations of [privately owned firms only / either private or public organizations].

either private or
public
organizations

18 Another advantage of focusing on a product or service as the "reason for existence" of any organization is graphically illustrated in Figure 3.2. The ultimate source of funds used to finance the activities of an organization is associated with the

customer ———————— .

19 Whether the output is in the form of a product or a service, every firm or organization exists to create something of economic value. From this standpoint, the principal objective of the Chevrolet Division of General Motors is to manufacture

automobiles ———————— . The principal objective of

merchandise for
sale (etc.)

Sears Roebuck is to provide ————————
———————— .

20 Since profit is what is "left over" after the demands of every group except those of the owners have presumably been satisfied, it is a convenient basis for measuring the firm's effectiveness

product in providing a _____ or a
service _____ desired by consumers.

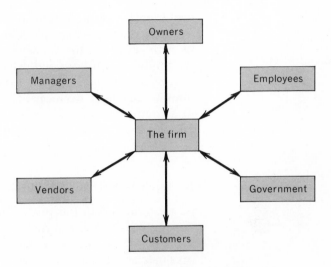

Figure 3.2 A schematic diagram representing the flow of funds in the operation of an established firm.

21 Thus, although profit may be an indicator of a firm's success or failure, it does not specifically identify the *basis* for that success or failure. In a free enterprise system, the economic value of a firm's products or services is ultimately decided by
customer the _____ group.

22 In the case of public organizations and monopolies, profit as such may be nonexistent or inapplicable as a way of evaluating organizational performance. Nevertheless, the size of the agency or firm and its continued existence are still decided by consumers (though indirectly) in their activities as citizens and voters. For example, charitable organizations depend directly on public contributions and support. Government programs depend on ultimate support by the electorate. Thus, all organizations, whether private or public, share the

product; service

common primary objective of providing a
_____ or a _____ of eco-
nomic value.

23 Identifying the product or service objective as
the universal objective of all organizations provides
us with the basis for evaluating the activities of
both public institutions and privately owned firms.
Furthermore, since a firm's profitability is dependent on customer decisions, careful identification
of a company's product or service goals makes it
more   [more / less] likely that the firm will earn a profit
as the result of its operations.

B   MANAGEMENT BY OBJECTIVES

As we indicated in the preceding section, the ultimate objective of an organization as an entity is
the creation of economic values in the form of
products or services. The individual divisions and
departments in a firm may not be producing
completed products or services, but all of them
should be contributing to the creation of these economic values. In a sense, the concept of *management by objectives* is an extension of the product or
service objective to the operating units within the
firm. This concept suggests the need for a hierarchy of compatible objectives within the organization and suggests further that these objectives
identify the economic contribution of each segment of the organization in measurable terms.

24 The management-by-objectives approach focuses on the economic contribution of each of the
operating units in the firm. In order to achieve the
firm's product or service objective effectively, the
specific objectives of the operating units that make
compatible   up the firm need to be [identical / compatible].

25 Since each unit has a designated type of work,
specific objectives will not be identical, but they do
need to be compatible. One way of achieving this
compatibility throughout the organization is to as-

certain that in each of the several functional areas of work the objectives at each organizational level contribute to those at the next higher organizational level. The outcome, then, is referred to as a

objectives

hierarchy of _____ .

26 Figure 3.3, on page 68, illustrates the hierarchy of objectives for a selected segment of an organization. The overall objective of this company is

a product

identified as being [profit / a product / a service].

27 In Figure 3.3 we have identified a hierarchy of objectives within the personnel and industrial relations division. In addition to the division objective, objectives are also identified at the levels of the

department
section

_____ and _____ .

28 Further, note that at each of the organizational levels the objectives are defined in terms of

measurable goals

[detailed procedures / measurable goals].

29 Thus, the philosophy of *management by objectives* requires that for the several organizational

hierarchy

levels a _____ of objectives be identified and that these objectives be specified in the

goals

form of measurable _____ .

30 The approach that focuses on defining *measurable goals* and ascertaining that these goals *contribute to the overall product or service objective* of the organization (rather than focusing on the particular methods and procedures to be followed in the

management
by objectives

organization) is called _____

_____ .

31 The identification of objectives constitutes the first essential step in the managerial process of planning. Since management by objectives has a direct influence on methods of organizing, directing, and controlling, as well as on planning, it has become a basis for describing and improving

managerial activity
as a whole

[planning / managerial activity as a whole].

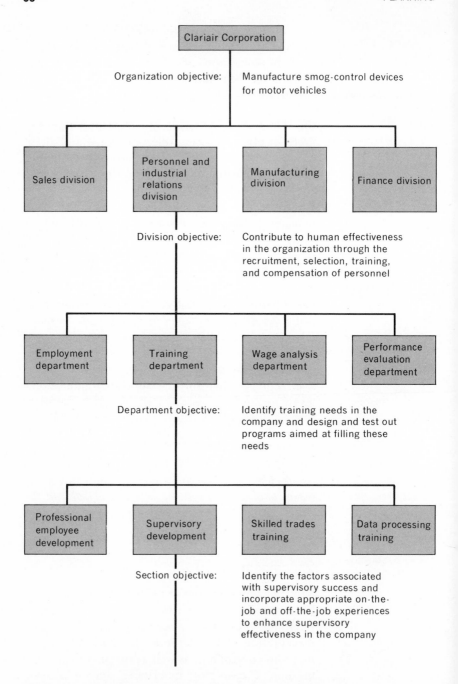

Figure 3.3   A hierarchy of objectives for a selected segment of a company.

32 Because personal commitment to the goals of an operating unit makes it more likely that those goals will be accomplished, individual participation in defining these goals is typically [encouraged / discouraged].

encouraged

33 The management-by-objectives approach also provides the basis for evaluating the performance of operating units and individuals in the organization by comparing the goals specified for a particular time period with the goals actually _____ during that period.

achieved (etc.)

34 Finally, since performance evaluation within the management-by-objectives approach is oriented toward objective work goals rather than employee characteristics and personal traits, needed changes in employee and managerial performance are [more / less] easily achieved by this approach.

more

C THE ENVIRONMENT OF PLANNING

As we have indicated in the preceding section, the process of planning begins by designating organizational and unit objectives. In addition, we must consider the various possible strategies or courses of action that will lead to the achievement of these objectives. Since the organization does not exist in a vacuum, managers have the responsibility of assessing the various external factors that either limit the company's action possibilities or provide the opportunity for action aimed at accomplishing objectives. In this section we shall identify some of the major environmental factors and discuss their effect on the planning process. Because these factors represent external constraints on planning, some writers in the field of management have referred to these factors as *external planning premises*.

35 Although the order in which we shall discuss the environmental factors does not imply an order of importance, it is certainly true that the level of *political stability* is one of the most important factors affecting the planning process. In the absence of a politically stable environment, business planning tends to be limited to the [long / short] run.

short

36 The factor of political stability has been particularly important for firms engaged in international operations. For example, one of the important factors affecting managerial planning in South American countries is the relatively high level of political [stability / instability].

instability

37 On the other hand, firms engaged in business operations in Western Europe in recent years have been able to carry out the planning function in a climate of political [stability / instability].

stability

38 Although international illustrations provide particularly vivid contrasts in political stability, this is a factor that operates on our domestic scene as well. Other factors being equal, business firms prefer to locate in states and municipalities with an [established / emerging] pattern of political stability.

established

39 Similarly, we would predict that during periods of political uncertainty at the national level, such as at the inauguration of a new President, long-range planning commitments by business firms tend to [increase / decrease].

decrease

40 Closely associated with the factor of political stability is the nature of *government fiscal and monetary policy, regulations*, and *controls*. The fiscal and monetary policy affects the overall economic environment within which planning takes place. For example, if businessmen conclude that federal fiscal policy is aimed more at maintaining a high level of employment and economic growth than at avoiding inflation, their commitment to capital investments is [more / less] likely.

more

41 Specific fiscal and monetary policies may affect some types of firms more than others and may indirectly benefit one industry at the expense of another. For example, if interest rates on home mortgages were to be maintained at a high level while excise taxes were removed from airline fares, airline   the [construction / airline] industry would tend to benefit by such a policy.

42 *Governmental regulations and controls* also tend to affect firms in some industries more than in others. As compared with toy manufacturers, for example, airlines and railroads operate under a high   relatively [high / low] level of governmental regulation and control.

43 With the growth of our industrial system, the extent of control and regulation by all levels of government has been consistently on the increase   [increase / decline].

44 Thus, no industry has experienced a decline in the importance of governmental regulation and control, although in some industries a general level of stability has existed. In recent years, for example, governmental controls in the area of hous- stable   ing standards have been relatively [stable / expanding], whereas governmental controls in au- expanding   tomobile safety have been [stable / expanding].

45 Another factor in the environment of planning is the overall *trend in employment, productivity, and income.* Unless a company finds itself in a declining industry, as these values tend upward, the overall demand for products and services tends rise   to [rise / fall / stabilize].

46 Incidentally, if a firm is in a declining industry, managerial action in regard to objectives is certainly necessary. For example, with the recent decline in birth rate in the United States a firm that has specialized in the manufacture of baby food

dietetic foods

might well consider expanding its product offerings to include [infant wear / dietetic foods].

47 In a country in which the prospects for continued increases in employment, productivity, or income become bleak, long-range commitments by business firms are likely to [increase / decrease].

decrease (thereby adding to the poor prospects)

48 The factor of *changing price levels* is another influence on the planning process. The situation which leads to the greatest difficulty in planning is the one in which prices in an industry are [slowly increasing / slowly declining / subject to change in unanticipated ways].

subject to change in unanticipated ways

49 Of course, the general movement of prices in the economy is associated with the nature of governmental fiscal policy. At least since World War II, federal fiscal policy has resulted in a general and continuing price [rise / decline].

rise

50 Price movements in particular industries do not necessarily follow general price movements in the economy. During the past fifteen years, for example, television receivers have generally declined in price from year to year. Thus if a manager concludes that a general price increase of 3 percent for consumer goods is likely during a planning interval, the assumption that the selling price of his firm's products will increase by about 3 percent is [warranted / unwarranted].

unwarranted

51 All of the environmental factors that we have discussed thus far seem to presume unchanging engineering concepts. But the fact that *technological changes* are likely is itself a factor that affects planning. Again, this factor may be more important in some industries than in others. For example, of the following two industries the factor of technological change is especially important as a planning factor in the [automobile / aerospace] industry.

aerospace

52 But the very example we have just cited indicates the increasing importance of technological change in all industries, since even the relatively stable automobile industry has experienced major technological improvements in manufacturing techniques and may be even more drastically affected by the possible development of [more safety features / different power systems].

different power systems

53 By hindsight, the impact of the technological changes that have already occurred appears obvious, and business history is abundant with examples of firms that failed to recognize the planning implications of such technological developments as the jet engine in aircraft propulsion. At the point of planning, however, these implications are, of course, uncertain. For example, during the early 1960s the Chrysler Corporation invested substantially in the development of a turbine-powered car. On the basis of later developments, this investment appears to have been [warranted / unwarranted].

unwarranted (This is the author's opinion, based on the absence of any subsequent developments in turbine-powered cars. But work on trucks has continued.)

54 Thus far we have considered political stability; governmental fiscal policy; trends in employment, productivity, and income; price levels; and technological change as environmental factors that constitute important planning premises. An additional external factor that would be given first consideration by many managers is the *expected demand* for the kind of product or service provided by the company. Studies and reports published by various governmental agencies and trade associations are most useful for forecasting the level of expected sales for a particular [company / industry].

industry

55 We shall consider sales forecasting as a technique for predicting a particular company's sales in the following section of this unit. At this point, however, we might observe that as a firm grows, the likelihood that the sales forecast is based on detailed studies conducted by the firm itself [increases / decreases].

increases

56 Finally, a group of external planning premises that has to do with the acquisition of goods and services by the firm has been referred to as the "factor market." This includes consideration of the availability of *land, labor, raw materials and parts, and capital* in a given geographic area. These factors are particularly relevant for planning activities directed toward [level of production / location of facilities].

location of
facilities

57 The availability of land is one of the factors affecting plant or company location. In this context, "land" refers to [available acreage as such / acreage with necessary transportation facilities and utilities].

acreage with
necessary
transportation
facilities and
utilities

58 In terms of the *labor* factor, firms often locate their facilities in an area where people with the needed skills already live. From this standpoint, an industrial machinery manufacturer is most likely to find people with needed skills in the [Midwest / West], whereas people with aerospace experience are most likely to be located in the [Midwest / West].

Midwest

West

59 To the extent that a manufacturer is dependent on certain *raw materials or parts*, he will tend to locate his facilities close to the source of supply. For example, the early development of the steel industry in and around Pittsburgh was influenced by the availability of _____ in that area.

coal

60 As is true for the other environmental factors affecting planning, the source of raw materials or parts may be of relatively less importance in some industries because of their transportability. Thus, of the following two types of companies, the one that is less affected by the location of raw materials and parts is the [lumber company / electronic equipment manufacturer].

electronic
equipment
manufacturer

61 Finally, and in some cases most importantly, a firm's planning alternatives are affected by *capital availability*. Along these lines, studies indicate that the two principal causes for the bankruptcy of small business establishments are lack of management skill and shortage of capital. However, even a large firm's ability to obtain financing for new ventures is limited, especially if it has experienced recent product [successes / failures].

failures

D SALES FORECASTING AND PLANNING

Since the anticipated revenues associated with a sales forecast determine the economic limitations with which plans have to conform, the forecast represents an important influence on the function of planning. The sales forecast differs from the external planning premises in that it is not an environmental factor as such, but rather is developed by the firm itself. Because of this, some writers in the field of management have referred to the sales forecast as an *internal planning premise,* to distinguish it from the external, or environmental, factors. Since it is developed by the firm itself, the sales forecast can also be considered a planning technique in its own right. In this section we consider the general nature of sales forecasting and then discuss the principal methods that have been used for arriving at such forecasts: the jury of executive opinion method, the sales force composite method, the users' expectation method, and the statistical methods.

62 The sales forecast can be considered a planning premise in that it defines certain limits for all other _____ activities in the firm.

planning

63 As contrasted to the environmental factors
internal   that affect planning, the sales forecast is an [inter-
nal / external] planning premise.

64 The sales forecast can also be regarded as a
planning technique. As such, it is particularly
useful when the market demand for a firm's prod-
unstable   ucts or services has been historically [stable / un-
stable].

65 The sales forecast provides a company with
the basis for determining anticipated revenues and
for planning associated investments and other expenditures. Because of these significant uses, the
final decision regarding forecasted sales is the
responsibility of [technical specialists in this field /
the top   the top management of a company].
management of a
company

66 Our discussion of the specific methods of sales
forecasting will generally proceed from the technically simplest to the more sophisticated methods,
but the use of any of the techniques in a company
indicates an active concern about the level of
sales (and   _____ in a future period.
revenues)

67 The *jury of executive opinion* is the oldest and
simplest of the sales forecasting methods. By this
method the opinions of all members of top management are pooled in order to arrive at an overall
sales estimate. One advantage of this method is
that it may force all key executives to obtain infor-
increasing   mation relevant to the forecast, thus [increas-
ing / decreasing] their awareness of market fac-
tors that affect company success.

68 Furthermore, since the sales forecast has a
direct effect on the planned budgets for the
various operating divisions of an enterprise, the
participation of key executives in sales forecasting
makes general acceptance of the budgets
more   [more / less] likely.

69 However, the jury of executive opinion method may result in combining poorly founded hunches and opinions, thus resulting in an overall forecast with [high / low] reliability.

low

70 Further, since no one individual or department has the primary responsibility for collecting and analyzing the data necessary for the forecast in the jury of executive opinion method, improvement of forecasting techniques from one period to the next is [likely / unlikely].

unlikely

71 The first method of sales forecasting we have discussed, which represents an attempt to pool the best judgments of the company's key executives, is the _____ method.

jury of executive
opinion

72 The *sales force composite method* also represents a combination of the opinions of a number of people but in a way quite different from the jury of executive opinion. In the jury of executive opinion method each manager submits a forecast for [a particular segment of the market / the entire market].

the entire market

73 On the other hand, in the sales force composite method each participating individual submits his forecast for only a particular segment of the market. Typically, salesmen are asked to forecast sales for their districts, and then these are reviewed by regional sales managers and higher-level executives. This method of sales forecasting has the advantage of being based on the judgment of those people in the company who are [closest to the consumer market / experts in sales forecasting].

closest to the
consumer market

74 Furthermore, participation in sales forecasting by those who have to "make good" on the forecasts may provide a sales incentive during the period of forecast. However, this factor is also a major source of weakness of the sales force composite method. When forecasts are used to set sales quotas, the original forecasts by sales personnel tend to be [optimistic / pessimistic].

pessimistic

75 A further difficulty of the sales force composite method is that the individual salesman tends to give undue weight to present market conditions and cannot, after all, include consideration of company or competitor product developments unknown to him. From this standpoint his sales forecast tends to be [too high / too low / either high or low].

either high or low

76 Thus, the sales forecasting method that has the advantage of being based on close contact with the consumer and the weakness of not including enough consideration of future economic and product developments is the _____ _____ composite method.

sales force

77 Like the jury of executive opinion method and the sales force composite method, the *users' expectation method* is also based on a composite of individual judgments or opinions. As the name implies, however, in this method the opinions are those of the potential _____ .

users (or customers, etc.)

78 The opinions obtained from the customers have to do with their purchasing plans during the planning period under consideration. A company's success in obtaining this information is enhanced if it is made clear that individual customer intentions will be kept confidential and if it is also clear that such information [does / does not] constitute a commitment to buy.

does not

79 The users' expectation method is particularly useful when there are only a few customers. This is most likely to be true for products or services supplied to [consumers in general / industrial customers].

industrial customers

80 If there are a large number of customers, the use of sampling techniques becomes necessary in the _____ expectation method.

users'

81 A weakness of this technique is that a firm may rely too heavily on opinions that are themselves not well founded. Thus, the composite sales forecast obtained can be no more reliable than the sum of the collective customer opinions that are obtained by the _____ method.

users'
expectation

82 Thus far in our discussion of sales forecasting we have considered the jury of executive opinion method, the sales force composite method, and the users' expectation method. Finally, the _statistical methods_ represent the last group of methods we shall consider. As the name implies, this includes application of [a particular technique / a number of possible alternative techniques].

a number of
possible
alternative
techniques

83 Among the most popular of the statistical techniques is _trend analysis_, by which the historical trend in the sales of a company's products is projected for the purpose of predicting sales during the planning period. Thus, the use of trend analysis is based on the assumption that the factors that have influenced changes in sales volume in the past [will / will not] continue to operate.

will

84 Some of the more sophisticated statistical methods, such as _correlation analysis_, are directed at identifying the underlying causes affecting previous changes in sales volume. However, both trend analysis and correlation analysis are dependent on the availability of [current / historical] data.

historical

85 The use of a _mathematical model_ represents still another step in sophistication, since in this case the analyst attempts to incorporate all known causative variables in one mathematical formulation. The model might, for example, require use of consumer income figures, consumer debt, and present

sales

sales level in a _____ forecast for the planning period.

86 Through careful analysis of historical data, influences on the company's sales volume that are not otherwise obvious might be detected by one of

statistical

the _____ methods.

87 On the other hand, by the use of the statistical methods the effect of new products or marketing

cannot

developments [can / cannot] be readily determined.

88 In total, we have discussed the strengths and weaknesses associated with four approaches to

jury of executive

sales forecasting: the _____

sales force

opinion method, the _____ _____

users'

composite method, the _____ expecta-

statistical

tion method, and the _____ methods.

89 In practice, a company typically uses a combination of these methods (rather than just one of them) in arriving at a final sales forecast. For example, Figure 3.4 portrays a situation in which

three

_____ [number] independent forecasts of sales are forwarded to a management committee for final consideration.

90 As we indicated at the very outset of this section, the implications of the sales forecast are so great that final responsibility for the forecast is

top

typically assigned to the company's _____

management

_____ .

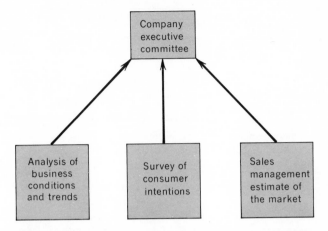

Figure 3.4 Example of the use of several independent sources of information for the sales forecast.

Review

91 Several different groups can be identified as having an interest in the activities of a firm and achieving certain goals by their interaction with it. An example of such a group within the company is the _____, whereas an example of a group outside of the company is the _____ . (Frames 1 to 8)

owners, managers, or employees

vendors, customers, or government

92 In considering the underlying common objectives of all organizations as entities, an objective that may be more of a "measuring stick" of success than the objective as such is _____ . (Frames 9 to 15)

profit (The objective of survival and growth might also be so regarded.)

93 The general organization objective that highlights the "reason for existence" for business firms, as well as for other organizations, and also takes cognizance of the ultimate source of the funds that contribute to profit and make survival and growth

product
service

possible is the objective of _____ or
_____ . (Frames 16 to 23)

94 The approach to planning, as well as to the
management functions in general, which represents a type of extension of the firm's product or
service objective to the operating units of the firm

management by
objectives

is called _____.
(Frames 24 to 28)

95 An important feature of the management-by-
objectives approach is the requirement that within
the organization a hierarchy of objectives be

measurable results

defined in terms of [designated procedures / measurable results]. (Frames 29 to 34)

96 Of the environmental factors affecting planning, the factor of political stability has particularly

international

influenced firms in their [domestic / interna-
tional] operations, whereas concern about government fiscal and monetary policy has been most

domestic

prevalent on the [domestic / international] scene.
(Frames 35 to 44)

97 With good prospects for continued growth in
employment, productivity, and income, business

long

firms are more likely to make [short- / long-] term
commitments. The situation in changing price

changing in
unanticipated
ways (etc.)

levels which leads to the greatest difficulty is the
one in which prices are _____
_____ . (Frames 45 to 50)

98 The factor of technological change as a plan-

virtually all

ning premise affects [only a few / virtually all] industries today. The expected demand for the kind
of products or services provided by the company is

external

still another [internal / external] planning premise. (Frames 51 to 55)

99 The so-called "factor market," which includes

consideration of the availability of land, labor, raw materials or parts, and capital, is the final environmental factor we discussed. As far as labor is concerned, the typical need nowadays is for

skilled

[unskilled / skilled] personnel. Overall, the factor market as an environmental factor is most relevant for planning [volume of production / location of

location of
facilities

facilities]. (Frames 56 to 61)

100   As contrasted to the environmental factors that affect planning, sales forecasting is considered

internal

to be an _____ planning premise. (Frames 62 to 65)

101   The method of sales forecasting which is generally least sophisticated when used alone, and which represents a pooling of top management

jury of executive
opinion

opinion, is the _____ _____ method. (Frames 66 to 71)

102   The method by which the judgments of field representatives and sales personnel are first reviewed and then combined in order to arrive at a

sales force
composite

sales forecast is the _____ _____ method. (Frames 72 to 76)

103   The method of sales forecasting based on combining customer reports regarding their buying intentions during the planning period is the

users' expectation

_____ method. (Frames 77 to 81)

104   Finally, the methods that include such quantitative and analytical techniques as trend analysis, correlation analysis, and the use of mathematical

statistical

models are the _____ methods. (Frames 82 to 88)

105   In practice, the sales forecasts developed by business firms tend to be based on the use of [a

a combination of
methods

particular method in preference to others / a combination of methods]. (Frames 89 and 90)

Discussion Questions

1. Is it useful to consider the objectives of the several groups of people associated with a firm's activities? Why or why not?

2. What do you think is the "real" objective of business firms?

3. In response to a question posed by a financial analyst at a public meeting, a corporate officer in a conglomerate (multiproduct) firm has stated that it is the objective of his company to earn a fair profit in each fiscal period, considering the required investment of resources and business risks involved. Comment on his statement.

4. In what respects are the "product or service" objective and "management by objectives" related?

5. Discuss the impact of management by objectives on the way the functions of planning, organizing, directing, and controlling are carried out.

6. What is the particular factor associated with management by objectives which often represents an advantage over an approach which specifies the *way* that departmental functions are to be carried out?

7. We have identified the sales forecast as an internal planning premise. In what respects might it be considered an external premise? In what respects is it not a premise at all, but rather part of the planning process itself?

8. Is it unrealistic to expect top managers to become involved in the details of sales forecasting?

Case Study: Planning in a Staff Department

As manager of the training department in the Clariair Corporation, Mark Anderson has been assigned responsibility for determining training and development needs within the company and presenting the results of such studies, along with recommended courses of action, to his immediate superior, who is a vice president in charge of personnel and industrial relations. Further, Mark's department has responsibility for implementing the decisions of the company's administration committee by designing and conducting training and development programs that are used as prototypes for programs conducted in the company's geographically decentralized facilities.

The training department contains four sections, each specializing in a particular type of job represented in the company. Thus the department includes sections whose principal work concerns professional employee development, supervisory department, skilled trades training, and data processing training.

During Anderson's regular weekly meeting with his section supervisors the topic of department and section objectives came up for discussion. Specifically, some section supervisors defined their objectives in terms of providing *requested* training services, whereas others included the *discovery* of training needs in the objectives. As a result of the diversity of views expressed in the meeting, Mark Anderson recognized the need to devote further departmental attention to this area, and therefore posed the following question to his section supervisors: "What are the objectives that guide the activities in your section?"

He has requested that the answer to this question be included in a report to be submitted to him by each supervisor within the next two weeks.

1. What immediate positive results are likely to come from Mark Anderson's request?
2. In what respects is his request incomplete?
3. What are the weaknesses, if any, in his overall approach to the task of defining objectives?
4. What would be the most effective way of proceeding after the written reports are submitted by the section supervisors?

Case Study: A Decline in Government Contracts

The Rolamar Electronics Company was established in 1955 and experienced rapid growth during the 1950s and 1960s through its success in bidding on and being awarded government contracts for the development and manufacture of military electronics equipment. As would be expected, the company is heavily oriented toward research and development, and the electronic components developed by the company have always been at the forefront of state-of-the-art developments. By the beginning of the 1970s, however, the growth in government contracts had peaked and thereafter began to decline. Funding for the associated area of space communication systems, particularly in regard to manned space flights, was also reduced by the government. The company has gathered together a top-caliber engineering team, and Elroy McMann, the founder and company president, would like to see the research group kept intact. If government funding of space programs were to be again increased, for example, the company would be in a favorable position to obtain government contracts if the present research and development team were kept together. However, with the expiration of a major contract in eight months the company cannot maintain the present work force without other sources of revenue.

Mr. McMann discussed this situation at some length with his top executives. As the result of this discussion, Mr. Richard Sloan, who is manager of the research and development group, has proposed a specific product area that the company might enter as some of the military electronics work is reduced. He suggests that the engineers who have been involved in developing the electronics components for military applications have the capability of developing amplifier systems, stereo systems, and radio receivers that would be technologically much superior to systems now commercially available. Richard Sloan was particularly aware of this opportunity because many of his engineers have built "sound systems" of various kinds for their own homes and apartments. "All we have to do is to tap this capability," said Sloan, "and within a year we can have a stereo system on the market that is superior to anything now available to the general consumer."

1. If the proposal presented by Mr. Sloan is accepted, what is the implication from the standpoint of the company's objectives?
2. Given the technological capability of the research and development personnel, what are some reasons for caution in respect to the proposal?
3. If the proposal were successfully implemented, what would be the probable effect on the president's desire to maintain the technological team intact?
4. What other types of products or service opportunities might the company consider as government contracts are reduced?

Suggested Readings*

Colm, G.: *Forecasting Sales*, Studies in Business Policy, no. 106, National Industrial Conference Board, New York, 1963.

Drucker, P. F.: *The Practice of Management,* Harper & Brothers, New York, 1954.

*Also see the cross-reference table in the Preface.

Levinson, H.: "Management by Whose Objectives?" *Harvard Business Review*, vol. 48, no. 4, July–August 1970.

Mali, P.: *Managing by Objectives: An Operating Guide to Faster and More Profitable Results*, John Wiley & Sons, Inc., New York, 1972.

Mason, R. H., J. Harris, and J. McLoughlin: "Corporate Strategy: A Point of View," *California Management Review*, vol. 13, no. 3, Spring 1971.

O'Donnell, C.: "Planning Objectives," *California Management Review*, vol. 6, no. 2, Winter 1963.

Reichard, R. S.: *Practical Techniques of Sales Forecasting*, McGraw-Hill Book Company, New York, 1966.

Tosi, H. L., J. R. Rizzo, and J. S. Carroll: "Some Factors Affecting the Success of Management by Objectives," *The Journal of Management Studies*, vol. 7, no. 2, May 1970.

——, ——, and ——: "Setting Goals in Management by Objectives," *California Management Review*, vol. 12, no. 4, Summer 1970.

Wikstrom, W. S.: *Managing by and with Objectives*, Studies in Personnel Policy, no. 212, National Industrial Conference Board, New York, 1968.

Chapter four
POLICIES, PROCEDURES, AND METHODS

After organization objectives have been identified, the function of planning is concerned with the selection and definition of the policies, procedures, and methods necessary to achieve overall organizational objectives. Each of these "levels" of planning activity is considered in turn in this chapter. Whether it be at the level of determining policies, procedures, or methods, the process of decision making is an essential component of the planning function. Therefore, the factors that lead to effective diagnosis, discovery of alternatives, and analysis in decision-making situations are considered in the last part of this chapter.

A POLICIES

Whereas objectives are necessary to give direction to individual and group efforts in the organization, policies are general statements which serve as the guidelines by which these objectives are to be attained. Policies have been classified on the basis of the organizational level which they affect, the way they are formed in the organization, and the area of work to which they apply.

1 A business firm may have the specific objective of attaining greater market penetration in its product field; relying on price competition to achieve this objective would be an example of a business

policy _____ .

2 Policies have been defined as general statements or understandings which guide decision making by subordinates in the various departments of an enterprise. By this definition, do such statements have to be set down in writing in order to be considered policies? [Yes / No]

No

3 Whether or not they have been written down, policies serve as broad, comprehensive guides for

decision making _____ _____ in the organizations.

4 Policies may be classified in several ways. One classification that is useful is based on the organizational level of the managers affected. Thus *basic, general, and departmental policies* identify the organi-

level   zational _____ of policy application.

5 The *basic policy*, which is very broad in scope and affects the organization as a whole, is used

top   mainly by [top / middle / first-level] managers.

6 A policy of marketing a competitive product for each one offered by a major competitor is an

basic   example of a _____ policy.

7 The *general policy*, which is more specific, typically applies to large segments of the organization but usually not to all of it. It is used mainly by [top / middle / first-level] managers.

middle

8 A policy that purchasing agents should work with local contractors whenever possible is an example of a _____ policy.

general

9 The *departmental policy* is most specific in nature and applies to everyday activities at the departmental level. It is used mainly by [top / middle / first-level] managers.

first-level

10 The policy that employees are expected to call when they are going to be absent because of illness is a _____ policy.

departmental

11 In summary, there are three types of policies, based on the scope and managerial level affected. These are _____ , _____ , and _____ policies.

basic; general
departmental

12 The general policies relate primarily to the activities of _____ managers, the departmental policies are of most concern to _____ managers, and basic policies affect _____ managers most directly.

middle

first-level

top

13 Another classification of policies is based on the way they are formed in the organization. *Originated policy, appealed policy,* and *imposed policy* are three types of policy based on the way they are _____ .

formed

14 An *originated policy* is one initiated by the managers of a company for the purpose of guiding themselves and their subordinates. Typically, the relationship between originated policy and organizational objectives [is / is not] fairly close.

is

15 The decision to promote the sale of service

contracts with equipment sales to ensure that customers maintain the equipment properly is an example of _____ policy.

16 An *appealed policy* is also formulated by a company manager. The distinction is that the appealed policy comes into existence from the appeal by a manager to his superior about handling an exceptional case; this is the basis for its being called _____ policy.

17 Since appealed policy is based on the handling of individual cases, which may each involve special circumstances, is there any danger that such policy will be incomplete, uncoordinated, and perhaps inconsistent? [Yes / No]

18 In the absence of a previously specified policy, a manager asks his superior what to do about an overdue account receivable. The superior's decision constitutes the formulation of _____ policy.

19 When managers find themselves continually occupied in formulating appealed policy, it indicates that not enough attention had been given to formulating the type of policy we previously discussed, that is, _____ policy.

20 *Imposed policy* is formed as the result of some external influence on the organization, such as action by a governmental unit, trade association, or labor union. In general, the importance of imposed policy has been [increasing / decreasing] with the development of industrialization.

21 Would you expect that the imposed policy in General Motors would be very similar to the imposed policy in the Ford Motor Company? [Yes / No]

originated

appealed

Yes

appealed

originated

increasing

Yes (since they are subject to the same governmental, trade association, and union pressures)

22 A policy of equipment depreciation that is formulated because of Air Force contract requirements is an example of _____ policy.

imposed

23 Based on the way they are formed in the organization, we have discussed three types of policies:_____, _____,and _____ .

originated
appealed
imposed

24 The type of policy which would be similar for different companies within the same industry is _____ policy.

imposed

25 The policy specifically formulated to establish guidelines needed to achieve organizational objectives before any problems have been encountered is _____ policy.

originated

26 The type of policy whose abundance indicates a lack of appropriate managerial attention to anticipating needed guidelines for decision making is _____ policy.

appealed

27 Finally, another classification of policies is based on the *area of work* to which the policies apply. Although a number of categories could be discussed, we shall consider *sales, production, finance*, and *personnel* as major areas of _____ in business firms.

work

28 *Sales policies* have to do with such decisions as the selection of the product to be manufactured, its pricing, the sales promotion to be carried out, and the selection of distribution channels. Since these are interdependent areas of decision making, close coordination of these efforts [is / is not] essential.

is

29 A decision to restrict the distribution of a certain brand of beer to the Midwest area constitutes a _____ policy.

sales

30 *Production policies* include such decisions as whether or not to make or buy a needed component, the location of production facilities, the purchase of production equipment, and the inventories to be maintained. Can production policies be formulated without regard to the sales policies of

No   the enterprise? [Yes / No]

31 The decision to locate new plants within a certain distance from a major market area constitutes

production   a _____ policy.

32 *Finance policies* are concerned with such matters as capital procurement, depreciation methods, and the use of available funds. As such, they

would   [would / would not] directly affect all other areas of policy formulation.

33 The decision to lease rather than buy all needed warehouse space is an example of a

finance   _____ policy.

34 *Personnel policies* concern personnel selection, development, compensation, morale development, and union relations. Is it important that these policies be consistent throughout the company?

Yes   [Yes / No]

35 The decision that applicants should be placed in an apprentice program on the basis of ability

personnel   tests is an example of a _____ policy.

36 The four types of policies based on area of work that have been discussed above are the

sales; production   _____, _____, _____,

finance; personnel   and _____ policies.

37 Obviously, any given policy can be described in terms of each of the three major classification

managerial (or   systems we have discussed: the _____

organizational)   level involved, the _____ in which the

way (method, etc.)   policy was formed, and the area of _____

work   affected.

38 The employment manager of a company has informed his superior that he is unable to hire certain technical personnel in the local community, and, as a result, the industrial relations director decides that these personnel should be recruited in a distant city. From the standpoint of managerial

general   level, this is a _____ policy, from the standpoint of the way it was formed it is an

appealed   _____ policy, and from the standpoint

personnel   of the area of work it is a _____ policy.

39 The top managers of a company decide that the firm will concentrate its merchandising efforts in the electronic equipment field. This can be

basic; originated   described as a _____, _____,

sales   and _____ policy.

40 Because of the requirements of a union-management contract, foremen are directed to use only certain time-study methods in determining production standards. This can be described as a

departmental   _____, _____, and

imposed   _____ policy.

production

B PROCEDURES AND METHODS

A statement of *procedure* is more specific than a policy statement in that it enumerates the chronological sequence of steps to be taken in order to achieve an objective. A *method*, on the other hand, specifies how some one step of a procedure is to be performed.

41 A description of how each of a series of tasks is to take place, when it will take place, and by whom it is to be accomplished is normally included in a

procedure   statement of a _____ .

42 A set of specific instructions for processing orders, which may include activities in the sales, accounting, and production departments, is an ex-

procedure   ample of a specified _____ .

43   Figure 4.1 shows an example of a procedure.
employment   In this case, an _____ procedure is
described.

1. Preliminary (screening) interview
2. Application form
3. Check of references
4. Aptitude tests
5. Employment interview
6. Approval by the supervisor
7. Physical examination
8. Orientation

Figure 4.1   Outline of a typical employment procedure.

44   As compared with policies, procedures allow
less   [more / less] latitude in managerial decision making.

45   In contrast to a procedure, a description of
how some one step of a procedure is to be per-
method   formed is called a _____ .

46   Is it possible that a method would involve just
one department and just one person in that
Yes   department? [Yes / No]

47   The specified technique to be used in adminis-
method   tering an aptitude test is a _____ ,
whereas the sequence of steps involved in the
employment function shown in Figure 4.1 makes
procedure   up a _____ .

48   *Methods improvement* refers to improvements in
the manner of performing specific tasks. Historically, replacement of manual methods by mechanical means has been a popular approach to
methods   _____ _____ .
improvement

49   From a broader point of view, *work simplification* applies to efforts to make a particular task, or a
whole series of tasks, more efficient and economi-

procedures

cal. Therefore, work simplification can apply to changes in either methods or _____ .

work simplification
(The effect is usually broader in scope than methods improvement.)

50 In recent years, electronic equipment has been importantly involved in achieving _____
_____ .

b

51 Which do you think is more likely? [a / b]

a. a change in a particular method will dictate a change in overall procedure.
b. a change in overall procedure will affect the need for a particular method.

procedures

52 Since a change in procedure may make certain steps, and hence methods, in that procedure unnecessary, it follows that work simplification should begin with a study of the existing [methods / procedures].

methods;
procedures

53 Unless the work simplification is itself planned, however, it is easier to achieve improvement and simplification in _____ than in _____ .

easier

54 For example, as compared with simplification of the overall personnel selection procedure, which may involve several departments, improvements in the method of administering an aptitude test is [easier / more difficult].

policies
procedures
methods

55 In summary, in the first two sections of this chapter we have described three levels of planning that are related to achieving organizational objectives. These are the determination of _____, _____, and _____ .

56 A chronological description of the steps

to be taken in attaining an objective is a

procedure   _____ , whereas the specification of
how a particular step should be carried out is a

method   _____ .

57 Improvements and simplification in either
procedures or methods are referred to as

work simplification   _____ _____ .

C DECISION MAKING

Decision-making skill is the key to successful planning at all levels. This involves more than the selection of a plan of action, for at least three phases—
diagnosis, discovery of alternatives, and *analysis*—have
to be completed before a choice can be made.

58 The sequence of decision-making activities is
of considerable importance. Successful analysis of
alternatives depends on previous discovery of appropriate alternatives, and this phase, in turn,

diagnosis   depends on accurate _____ .

59 The function of the first phase in decision

diagnosis   making, that of _____ , is to identify
and clarify a problem.

60 An accurate diagnosis depends on a *definition
of organizational objectives* with which present results
are compared. This is consistent with our previous
observation that objectives are the focal point for

planning   the managerial function of _____ .

objectives   **61** After organizational _____ are
identified, diagnosis then involves *identifying major
obstacles* to their attainment. Along these lines, it
should be observed that describing a problem

does not   [does / does not] necessarily identify the obstacles.

62 For example, identifying a problem as involving the marketing function is at the level of a
description, whereas locating specific failures in

obstacles

the within-company communication system constitutes an identification of _____ .

objectives

obstacles

Decrease

63 In addition to defining organizational
_____ and identifying major
_____ , the diagnosis phase of deci-
sion making usually involves recognizing the factors in the situation that cannot be changed. Would
the latter action tend to increase or decrease the
number of possible solutions to the problem?
[Increase / Decrease]

unlikely

64 In the diagnosis phase of decision making,
care should be taken to avoid "blocking out" alternatives that are in fact possible. For example, the
marketing executive who accepts the present product distribution system as a fixed factor is
[likely / unlikely] to consider an obvious alternative system.

diagnosis

65 The first phase of the decision-making process, which we have just discussed, is that of
_____ . This phase is followed by the
discovery of *alternative courses of action*.

alternative

66 It is in this second phase of discovering
_____ courses of action that the element of creativity is especially important.

Yes

67 Are there marked individual differences
among people in regard to creative thinking?
[Yes / No]

more

68 Granting the importance of individual differences in creativity, there are several organizational variables that affect the likelihood of creativity. One obvious, but often overlooked, factor is
that rewarding creative behavior makes it
[more / less] likely to occur.

69 Thus the manager who brushes aside novel
suggestions with little consideration does not en-

creativity courage the development of _____ on the part of his subordinates.

70 Another factor affecting creativity is the level of stress in the environment. Although some stress is stimulating, psychological research in this area indicates that high stress leads to either behavioral disruption or behavioral rigidity, neither one of which is conducive to creativity. Accordingly, peo-

less ple in a "high-pressure" organization are [more / less] likely to be creative, although they may be productive in routine tasks.

71 In comparing successful research organizations with successful production organizations, we would therefore expect to find less emphasis on

research day-to-day schedules in the [research / production] organizations.

72 Finally, creative thought and new solutions cannot take place without allowing *time* for acquiring and considering the necessary factual material. This suggests that "thinking time," during which

is no overt progress is obvious, [is / is not] time productively spent.

73 Thus there are at least three factors that affect the creativity climate. Creativity is enhanced when

rewarded it is _____, when the level of
stress (etc.) _____ is appropriate, and when adequate
time _____ is available for considering the problem.

74 Following diagnosis and the discovery of alter-
decision- natives, the final phase of the _____
making _____ process is that of *analysis*, which involves comparing the possible courses of action and choosing one of the alternatives.

75 To the extent that a manager bases his decisions on hunches or inner feelings, the process of choice is based on intuition. In a totally intuitive

analysis

approach, the third phase of decision making, that of _____ , might appear to be virtually absent.

76 That the basis for the choice of an alternative is not clear, even to the decision maker himself, is one weakness or disadvantage of relying on

intuition

_____ in making decisions.

77 As an alternative to the intuitive approach, the method of *factual analysis* requires that the factors or reasons underlying hunches be identified and evaluated, thus increasing the extent to which the

public

analysis process is [personal / public].

78 Identifying, and possibly listing, the advantages and disadvantages related to each of the alternatives is one example of the method of

factual analysis

_____ _____ .

79 Would you expect that it would often be useful to quantify the various factors involved in

Yes

the factual analysis? [Yes / No]

80 A method of analysis that relies on the quantification of all factors, and that has been found useful in decision making, is operations research. This method is sometimes referred to by the first

OR

letters of the two words, that is, _____ .

81 One of the features of the operations research approach to analyzing decision-making situations is the construction of a model for the situation. Consistent with the quantitative orientation of OR,

mathematical

the model used is typically a [physical / mathematical] model.

82 Thus the operations research approach, which is described in detail in the following chapter, places emphasis on the importance of identifying and quantifying all variables involved in a decision-making situation and constructing a mathematical   _____ model to represent the situation.

Review

83 As the first step in planning, organizational

objectives   _____ must be identified. (Introduction, Section A, Frame 1)

84 Following the identification of objectives, the

policies

procedures

methods

planning process includes the selection and definition of _____ , _____ , and _____ . (Introduction to the chapter)

85 Policies, which serve as general guides for decision making by managers, can be classified in several ways. On the basis of the organizational level of the managers directly affected, policies are

basic

general

departmental

described as being _____ , _____ , or _____ . (Frames 2 to 12)

86 For example, the type of policy that applies to large segments of an organization but not to all of it, and which is of greatest concern to middle man-

general

agers, is the _____ policy. (Frames 7 and 8)

87 There are also three types of policies, based on the way they are formed in the organization.

originated

appealed

imposed

These are _____ , _____ , and _____ policies. (Frames 13 to 23)

88 A great deal of which type of policy formulation indicates that top managers have not successfully anticipated the policy needs of the organiza-

Appealed

tion? _____ policy. (Frames 16 to 26)

89 The third classification of policies we discussed is based on the area of work to which they

sales

apply. On this basis, there are _____ ,

production; finance   _____, _____, and
personnel   _____policies. (Frames 27 to 36)

90 The decision to lease rather than purchase retail sales outlets is an example of the formulation
finance   of _____ policy. (Frames 32 and 33)

91 Any policy can be described from the standpoint of all three classification systems we have discussed. The decision that all first-level supervisors in the company are to be held accountable for the development of their subordinates can be classified
departmental   as a _____, _____, and
originated   _____ policy. (Frames 37 to 40)
personnel

92 A description of how each of a series of tasks is to take place, when it will take place, and by whom it is to be accomplished is normally included in a
procedure   statement of _____ . (Frames 41 to 44)

93 By contrast, the detailed specification of how some one step of a procedure is to be performed is
method   a statement of _____ . (Frames 45 to 57)

94 The selection of a plan of action represents the culmination of the decision-making process. The process itself is made up of at least three
diagnosis; discovery   phases: _____, _____
of alternatives   _____, and _____ . (Frames 58
analysis   to 78)

95 It is in the discovery of alternatives phase that creativity is particularly important in decision making. Creative behavior is made more likely
rewarded   when it is _____, when the level of
stress   _____ is appropriate, and when adequate
time   _____ is available for considering a problem.
(Frames 66 to 73)

96 The extension of factual analysis, which is based on mathematical model building and which

operations
research (OR)

has been found to be useful in decision making, is
called _____   _____ .
(Frames 79 to 82)

Discussion Questions

1. The term "strategies" is frequently used to
denote specific courses of action that can be taken
to achieve an organization's goal, usually in the
context of a competitive environment. How does
this definition relate to the definition of "policies"
given near the beginning of this chapter?

2. A manager states that in his organization most
policies are defined as the result of an appeal
rather than being originated, and that this has the
advantage of having policies where they are most
needed and avoiding unnecessary policy statements. Do you agree with him?

3. In what ways does effective planning on the
departmental level in an organization depend on
actions taken "higher up" in the organization?

4. Policies have been classified in various ways.
Why is a single classification system not sufficient?

5. Consider the difference between methods improvement and work simplification. Why is the latter approach to be preferred in most instances?

6. We have suggested that several distinct types
of activities make up the decision-making process.
Discuss these, indicating the probable consequences associated with omitting any of the activities.

7. What is the role of creativity in planning? Do
you think individual creativity can be developed,
or is it inborn?

8. Though some managers believe that "experience is the best teacher," others hold that "experience is a dangerous basis for decision making." Can you reconcile these two views?

Case Study: Krueger Metal Products Corporation

The Krueger Metal Products Corporation specializes in the installation of heating and air conditioning equipment in a metropolitan area of about one million people. Although the company usually installs nationally known equipment, it engages in limited manufacturing of certain components used with the heating and cooling systems, particularly for commercial installations. Since it was established some thirty years ago, the company has earned a reputation for quality work.

Gerald Carter has been with the company as sales representative for two years. During this period he believes that the company has missed a number of opportunities to obtain lucrative contracts because of the conditions under which he is forced to operate. Particularly in the case of commercial installations, he does not have the authority to make any decisions or commitments during preliminary contract negotiations; he has to withhold discussion of price, completion time, and credit arrangements until after each of the technical experts in these areas has reviewed the job and made formal commitments. By this time, a competing firm has frequently already completed negotiations and obtained the contract. Mr. Carter considers this a continuing problem, and feels hamstrung in that he sees himself as "selling the product," but without authority to specify how, when, for how much, and under what conditions.

1. In what respects do you think Mr. Carter is justified in his complaint?
2. In what respects is he perhaps not justified?

3. What can he do to improve his situation?

4. If this is something of an organizational problem, rather than one confined to Gerald Carter, what should be done on a companywide basis to improve the situation?

Case Study: A Wage and Salary Policy Problem

The Conklin Manufacturing Company is a medium-sized firm located in the Midwest and involved in the manufacture of valves and related metal fittings. The company has had the policy of paying above-average wages to its employees and expecting in return an above-average commitment to producing quality products. For several years, one particular group of inspectors has been supervised by Mr. Ed Haley. Ed's philosophy has been to give his people what he considered to be adequate, but not extravagent, increases in salary at the time of each annual salary review. As a result of this philosophy many of the inspectors have now reached the top classification grade and the top salary within that grade.

Recognizing that the cost-of-living adjustments to the salary scales, which are also made annually, do not provide an opportunity for any real improvement in income, Ed Haley has consulted with George Nowak, the wage and salary administrator, about the problem. Nowak has refused to authorize either higher grades for the inspectors or higher top salaries for the existing grades. His position is that the company's wage scale is in line with and in fact exceeds the wage scales of comparable companies in the same area, and he has wage survey data which support his position.

Several of the inspectors have been at top salary for over two years, and the absence of any merit increases is becoming a major morale problem in the department. Because Ed Haley is within two months of retirement, his designated successor, Bill Reilley, has also been approached by several of the inspectors about the problem. Bill has responded by consulting with the plant manager about the situation. The answer he received is that all possible avenues for a solution have been explored and that there is no alternative to consistent application of the company wage and salary policies.

1. From the standpoint of the inspectors, in what respect is their complaint justified and in what respect is it not justified?
2. Should the company policy regarding maximum pay in grade be made more flexible? Why or why not?
3. How might Ed Haley have prevented the present problem from developing?
4. If this problem is in fact occurring throughout the organization, what change should the company consider in its wage and salary policies?

Suggested Readings*

Herold, D. M.: "Long-Range Planning and Organizational Performance: A Cross-Validation Study," *Academy of Management Journal*, vol. 15, no. 1, March 1972.

Holloman, C. R., and Hendrick, H. W.: "Adequacy of Group Decisions as a Function of the Decision-Making Process," *Academy of Management Journal*, vol. 15, no. 2, June 1972.

LeBreton, P. P., and D. A. Henning: *Planning Theory,* Prentice-Hall, Inc., Englewood Cliffs, N.J., 1961.

Mason, R. H., J. Harris, and J. McLoughlin: "Corporate Strategy: A Point of View," *California Management Review*, vol. 13, no. 3, Spring 1971.

Mockler, R. J.: "Theory and Practice of Planning (Keeping Informed)," *Harvard Business Review*, vol. 48, no. 2, March–April 1970.

*Also see the cross-reference table in the Preface.

Steiner, G. A.: *Top Management Planning*, The Macmillan Company, New York, 1969.

Thune, S., and R. House: "Where Long-Range Planning Pays Off," *Business Horizons*, vol. 13, no. 4, August 1970.

Weisselberg, R. C., and J. G. Cowley: *The Executive Strategist*, McGraw-Hill Book Company, New York, 1969.

Chapter **five**
QUANTITATIVE DECISION-MAKING TECHNIQUES

In recent years, there has been an accelerated application of quantitative techniques for the purpose of improving managerial decision making. The use of a systemwide point of view and quantification of all variables in the decision-making situation, closely related to the development of operations research, are given emphasis by this approach. In this chapter, we introduce the steps included in operations research, give an illustration of a mathematical model, briefly discuss the use of some specific quantitative techniques, and provide illustrative applications of linear programming and statistical decision analysis.

A   OPERATIONS RESEARCH

Operations research includes more than the application of mathematical methods to decision-making situations, although the mathematical methods are largely the "language" of the approach. There are several ingredients, or steps, that make up the OR approach. These are:

1. A systemwide, or enterprisewide, orientation
2. Specific identification and measurement of the goals of the system
3. Specific identification and measurement of all variables that affect goal attainment
4. Construction of a mathematical model to represent the situation being studied

1 In its approach to management decision making, operations research emphasizes the use of a [departmental / systemwide] point of view.

systemwide

2 A synonym for "entire system," as it would apply in a business firm, would be _____ .

the entire firm (or the entire organization, etc.)

3 On this basis, would you expect OR studies to be departmental, that is, within particular departments of an enterprise, or interdepartmental? [Departmental / Interdepartmental]

Interdepartmental

4 Of course, even though a systemwide point of view is encouraged, a particular problem may involve just specific functions within the enterprise. Thus, if an inventory problem is being studied, the entire enterprise [is / is not] necessarily involved.

is not

5 Once a problem or activity of interest has been identified, the first thing that an operations researcher would do is to identify the _____ of the process or activity.

goals (or objectives)

6 What might be one goal of a medical supply warehouse?

Not running out of
supplies, minimum
inventory,
minimum spoilage,
etc.

_____

_____

_____

7 Thus an overall objective for a firm might involve several subgoals. However, merely identifying the goals is not enough. We must also be able to

measure (or
quantify)

_____ their attainment.

8 After identifying goals and determining how they should be measured, we then identify the

variables (factors,
etc.)

_____ that affect goal attainment in the process.

9 And after these variables are identified, the way in which they are to be _____ must

measured (or
quantified)

also be determined.

10 After the goals and all variables involved have been identified and quantified, study of the system of relationships then "sets the stage" for constructing or choosing the appropriate _____

mathematical (or
quantitative)

model.

11 A "good" mathematical model is one that accurately represents the pattern of relationships in a system. Therefore, the complexity of the mathe-

does not

matical techniques used [does / does not] necessarily indicate the adequacy of the model.

12 Which of the following is the better state-

a

ment? [a / b]

  _a._ The mathematical model must fit the problem of interest.
  _b._ The problem must fit an available mathematical model.

13 Therefore, consistent use by an analyst of a particular mathematical technique, such as linear programming, to the exclusion of other techniques, suggests that either he is studying just particular organizational activities or that his

mathematical
models

_____ _____ are often inappropriate.

14 Summarizing the steps in OR, we see that the

goals

variables

_____ of the activity are first identified and quantified, then the _____ that affect goal attainment are identified and quantified, and

mathematical
model

finally a _____ _____ is chosen or constructed.

15 In general, the application of operations research is more appropriate in which of the following two situations? [*a* / *b*]

b (since a common
mathematical
model could then
be used in
conjunction with
repeated
decisions)

a. A large number of decisions are to be made involving different problems.

b. A large number of decisions are to be made in the same problem area.

B   ILLUSTRATION OF A MODEL

A mathematical model can involve the use of any of a number of mathematical or statistical tools. In order to make our discussion of mathematical models more meaningful, an algebraic model utilizing the technique of differential calculus in its solution is illustrated in this section. An understanding of calculus is not necessary to appreciate the role this technique serves in the model.

16 As a simplified example, suppose that the rated quality of customer service in a particular type of department store increases with number of employees only up to a point, and then actually decreases. In this example, the quality of customer service (one of the goals of the store) is a function

Number of
employees

of what variable?_____
_____

17 Incidentally, can you think of any reason why the quality of customer service might decrease beyond some point of adding personnel?

Perhaps the
employees get too
involved with one
another instead of
serving the
customers (etc.).

_____
_____
_____
_____

18 Assuming that we have been able to quantify the relationship between the variable and the goal in this particular problem, illustrate the *general form* of this relationship on the following graph.

Quality of customer service

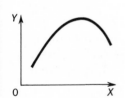 

Number of employees

19 The graph above can be considered a symbolic model for this problem. Suppose that this relationship can be represented by the equation $Y = 14X - \frac{1}{2}X^2$. The equation, then, is the

mathematical

_____ model representing the situation being studied.

20 Referring to the graph shown in Frame 18, what does the X represent in the equation $Y = 14X - \frac{1}{2}X^2$?

Number of
employees

_____

21 Referring to the graph shown in Frame 18,

what does the Y represent in the equation $Y = 14X - \frac{1}{2}X^2$?

Quality of
customer service

_____

22 The optimum, or best, solution for this simplified problem is to find that value of X for which Y is
maximum   a [minimum / maximum] value.

23 One way in which the value of X resulting in the maximum value of Y could be found is by taking different values of X and calculating the effect on the value of Y. Given that $Y = 14X - \frac{1}{2}X^2$, what is the quality of customer service associated with having six employees in the store? Do your calculations below.

$Y = 14(6) - \frac{1}{2}(6)^2$
$Y = 84 - \frac{1}{2}(36)$ _____
$Y = 84 - 18$ _____
$Y = 66$ _____
        _____

24 Refer to Figure 5.1. The table and graph indicate the value of Y associated with each of several values of X. At what value of X is Y maximized?
14        $X = $ _____

25 At fourteen employees, what is the quality of
98   customer service? $Y = $ _____

26 In the figure, note that with either fewer or more than fourteen employees the quality of customer service is [increased / decreased].
decreased

27 The same solution could have been achieved more quickly through the application of differential calculus. On the graph in Figure 5.1, note the value of Y with respect to changes in the value of X first increases and then decreases. The optimum solution in this case is at the point where the *rate of change* for Y is zero, because at this point Y is at its
maximum   [minimum / maximum] value.

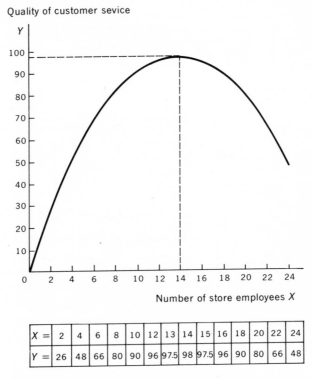

Quality of customer sevice

X =	2	4	6	8	10	12	13	14	15	16	18	20	22	24
Y =	26	48	66	80	90	96	97.5	98	97.5	96	90	80	66	48

Figure 5.1 Graphic and tabular representation of the equation $Y = 14X - \frac{1}{2}X^2$.

28 For illustrative purposes, the solution to this problem using differential calculus is presented below. If you have not studied calculus, you need not be concerned about the specifics of this solution.

$Y = 14X - \frac{1}{2}X^2$	basic mathematical model
$dY/dX = 14 - X$	rate of change of Y with respect to X
$0 = 14 - X$	point of optimization, where rate of change equals zero
$X = 14$	value of X at point of optimization

29 For our illustrative example, the optimum solution was that of attaining a maximum value of Y, the goal. Give an example of a goal for which we would want to attain the minimum value possible.

Amount of waste, waiting time, cost, etc.

_____

_____

30 Thus the optimum solution can be the attainment of either a _____ or a

minimum

maximum

_____ , depending on the goal involved.

C SOME QUANTITATIVE TECHNIQUES

In the section just concluded, we had an illustration of the use of calculus in finding the optimum solution in a decision-making situation. In this section, we briefly discuss some uses of probability analysis, queuing theory, game theory, the simulation method, and linear programming in decision making.

31 Calculus, probability analysis, queuing theory, game theory, the simulation method, and linear programming are among the quantitative techniques used to find _____ solutions in decision-making situations.

optimum

32 The application of _probability analysis_ is appropriate whenever the value of one or more variables in the model cannot be definitely specified, but the likelihood of the value being at various levels is [known / unknown].

known

33 If a manager knows that "there is only a 5 percent chance that consumer demand for January will be less than 10,000 units," has the risk been removed from his decision making? [Yes / No]

No

34 If a manager has determined the specific

minimize

probabilities associated with various events, he can act to [minimize / maximize] the overall risk associated with his decision acts.

35 In many situations, not only the degree of risk but also the expected gain, or expected monetary value, associated with each possible

decision (or
decision act)

_____ can be ascertained.

36 Expected monetary values can be determined for sequential acts as well as individual acts. Because this method of analysis has been given increasing attention in recent years, Section E of this chapter is devoted to illustrating the computation of expected monetary values. In general, when expected monetary values are determined, that decision act is best for which the expected value is

maximized

[minimized / maximized].

37 In contrast to the use of probability analysis, *queuing theory* is applicable to waiting-line situations, such as may be involved when several departments use a centrally located computer. When departments or items must wait for service of some kind, the delay in service represents a cost in the organization. Is there also a cost involved in

Yes

reducing or eliminating waiting lines? [Yes / No]

38 Thus balancing the cost of bottlenecks against the cost of idle capacity is the principal characteristic of the type of problem to which

queuing

_____ theory can be applied.

39 A facility that is too small incurs high costs of waiting by customers, whereas a facility that is too large incurs high idle-time costs. The optimum solution to this type of problem is the one which

minimizes

[minimizes / maximizes] the sum of the two types of cost.

40 In what decision-making area might queuing

theory be applied in a self-service department store?

Determining the number of checkout stands to be provided (etc.)

_____

_____

_____

41 In our endeavor to achieve an optimum solution to organizational problems, we have thus far discussed the use of three quantitative decision-making techniques: _____,

calculus

probability

queuing theory

_____ analysis, and _____

_____ .

42 *Game theory* is another technique used to maximize expected gain or minimize expected loss. As the word is generally used, is a game typically played against an opponent? [Yes / No]

Yes

43 As the name implies, game theory is a method for the study of situations in which two competitors are similarly motivated to maximize gain or minimize loss, and the success of one can be achieved only at the expense of the other. In addition to considering his own strategy, the decision maker must also consider what the strategy of his

opponent (or competitor)

_____ will be.

44 Determining the pricing and marketing strategy of a department store by considering the expected strategy of a prime competitor is a decision-making situation in which the application of

game theory

_____ _____ might be appropriate.

45 The fifth quantitative technique we now describe is *linear programming*. This technique of analysis has been applied extensively, and is useful when there are several variables which affect the attainment of a desired goal and the problem is to choose the best combination of values for these variables. As the name of this technique implies,

linear

the relationship between each one of the variables and the goal must be [linear / nonlinear]. That is, a constant change in a variable results in a constant change in goal attainment.

46 For example, a hat manufacturer who wants to determine the quantity of each of several types of hats to manufacture in order to maximize revenue could attempt a mathematical analysis of the problem using the technique of _____

linear
programming

_____ .

does not (But if the
relationship is
linear for a certain
range of values,
the technique can
be used within that
range.)

47 Suppose that the hat manufacturer finds that the markup for certain hats gets progressively smaller as production of that type of hat is increased. Because of the nonlinear relationship between production volume and revenue, this problem [does / does not] lend itself to the use of linear programming.

linear

48 Despite the restriction that relationships must be approximately _____ , the technique of linear programming has had extensive application in production, transportation, and inventory problems. Because of this, we shall present a relatively detailed example of its application in Section D of this chapter.

calculus
probability
analysis; queuing
theory; game
theory; linear
programming

49 The five quantitative techniques we have discussed so far are _____ , _____ , _____ , _____ , and _____ .

50 Finally, the last technique we discuss is the *simulation method*. This method incorporates features common to both mathematical models and probability analysis. It is particularly useful when there are several variables affecting results, and further, when these variables are themselves uncertain and

subject to probability analysis. Therefore, the simulation method is useful in decision situations that
complex   are relatively [simple / complex].

51 The value of some outcome, such as the inventory level for a particular item at a future point in time, is dependent on such uncertain factors as level of sales, delivery time, and spoilage or inventory loss. Since there are several factors involving a different probability distribution for each factor, the probabilities associated with the several possible inventory levels can be determined by applica-
simulation   tion of the _____ method.

52 When the simulation method was first developed it was called the *Monte Carlo method*, because a modified roulette wheel was used to simulate the outcome of each variable affecting the result. The use of this name also indicated that the outcome it-
probabilistic   self is [deterministic / probabilistic] in nature.

53 Instead of manually operated roulette wheels, computers are now used to generate the results of a large number of "trial runs" when the
simulation   _____ method is used.

54 By way of summary, let us review the appropriate application of the six quantitative decision-making methods we have briefly discussed. The analytic approach that is appropriate when a decision maker attempts to maximize his gain or minimize his loss by considering the strategy of a
game theory   rational competitor is _____ .

55 In a particular company, it has been found that product development per dollar spent on research and development first increases and then decreases; that is, the relationship is curvilinear. The mathematical technique that might be useful to determine the optimum research and develop-
calculus   ment expenditure in this case is _____

56 The problem of determining how many machine repairmen to have on call so as to minimize the combined cost of the repairmen's idle time and the machine idle time lends itself to the use of

queuing theory _____ _____ .

57 Given the situation in which each of a number of transportation routes has a direct relationship to total transportation cost and in which the objective is to find that combination of routes which minimizes the total cost, the applicable mathematical

linear programming technique   would   be   _____ _____ .

58 Making an investment decision on the basis of considering both the possible gain associated with each act and the likelihood of that gain involves the

probability analysis application of _____.

59 Finally, given a situation in which the development time for a new product depends on the time required to complete several major project segments, each of which requires an uncertain amount of time, the probabilities that the total required time will be at various levels can be determined by using the _____ method.

simulation

D AN ILLUSTRATIVE APPLICATION OF LINEAR PROGRAMMING

Because of the extensive application of linear programming to decision-making situations, an example of its use in a production planning problem is given in this section.

60 Suppose that a furniture manufacturer specializes in just two types of products, tables and hutches, which we shall refer to as products A and B, respectively. Referring to Figure 5.2, what is the gross revenue associated with producing each unit

$60; $80 of product A? _____ Of B? _____

Product	Gross revenue per unit	Process 1: cutting and trimming	Process 2: assembling	Process 3: finishing
A (Tables)	$60	1.8 hrs	3.0 hrs	1.5 hrs
B (Hutches)	$80	2.0 hrs	2.0 hrs	4.0 hrs

Figure 5.2 Process times for two products.

61 In Figure 5.2, each table requires 1.8 hours of cutting and trimming, 3.0 hours of assembling, and 1.5 hours of finishing, for a total of 6.3 hours. Similarly, each hutch involves _____ hours of cutting and trimming, _____ hours of assembling, and _____ hours of finishing for a total of _____ hours.

2.0
2.0
4.0
8.0

62 Assuming a market for as many tables and/or hutches as we decide to produce, what are we trying to optimize through the application of linear programming in this particular problem?

_____

gross revenue (See next frame.)

63 In this decision-making situation, the optimum solution is that level of production for A and for B that results in the highest gross revenue. Referring to Figure 5.2, we can state this objective in the form of an equation as

80

Maximize: $60X_A + $ _____ X_B

where X_A and X_B represent the number of units of each product to be produced.

64 In the language of linear programming, *constraints* represent the limitations that affect the values of one or more of the variables. In a product-mix problem, the fact that production capacity is limited by the existing facilities represents a major source of constraints. For each of the three production processes, we shall assume the availability of just 1,800 working hours per month. Thus for process 1, $1.8X_A + 2X_B \leq 1,800$; that is, the hours of process 1 devoted to producing units of product A plus the hours devoted to producing product B must be equal to, or less than, 1,800 hours per month. In view of this restriction, can we plan to produce 500 tables and 500 hutches per month (refer to Figure 5.2)? [Yes / No] Why or why not? _____

_____

_____

_____

_____

No.
The total
number of
required hours for
process 1 would
equal 1,900 hours,
which exceeds the
capacity in that
department.

65　In view of the constraint $1.8X_A + 2X_B \leq 1,800$, can we plan to produce 900 hutches and no tables? [Yes / No] _____

_____

_____

_____

Yes, the constraint
does not demand
that we produce
both products.

66　Similarly, how would you state the restriction, or constraint, of having just 1,800 hours per month available for process 2 (refer to Figure 5.2)?

_____ $X_A + $ _____ $X_B \leq 1,800$

3; 2

67　State the 1,800-hour constraint for process 3 in the form of an equation. _____ . .

$1.5X_A + 4X_B \leq 1,800$

68　For this problem, we have stated the objective as

Maximize: $60X_A + 80X_B$

subject to the constraints:

$1.8X_A + 2X_B \leq 1,800$

$3X_A + 2X_B \leq 1,800$

$1.5X_A + 4X_B \leq 1,800$

Are there any other restrictions imposed in this problem? [Yes / No]

Yes (see next frame)

69 There is an additional category of restrictions that is perhaps so obvious that we hardly think of it in these terms. This restriction is that neither X_A nor X_B can be negative in value (which is, of course, impossible in the practical sense, since we cannot produce a negative quantity of something), so the quantities of products A and B to be produced must be ≥ 0 (equal to or greater than zero). Symbolically, the nonnegativity constraint for A is

$X_B \geq 0$ $X_A \geq 0$, and for B it is _____ .

70 We shall now proceed to solve this linear programming problem by the graphic method. There are algebraic methods of attaining the optimum solution, which we shall briefly consider later. In that the solution can be visually portrayed by the graphic method, this method of solution is

the least   [the least / among the more] complex.

71 The first step in the graphic solution to a linear programming problem is to chart the constraints on the graph. The first restriction, for the available time in process 1, is $1.8X_A + 2X_B \leq 1,800$. If we were to produce only tables and use the full 1,800 hours of process 1, how many tables would be manufactured?

1,000   _____ Similarly, how many hutches would be produced if only hutches were manufactured?

900   _____

72 Refer to Figure 5.3. The line on the graph

$1.8X_A$; $2X_B$ represents the equation _____ + _____

1,800   = _____ . Note that the values of X_A and X_B at which this line intersects each axis are equal to the values we just computed in the previous frame.

73 Since the constraint stated "less than or equal to," the feasible-solution area is the entire shaded area below the line of restriction. Why doesn't the feasible-solution area extend below or to the left of

Number of hutches

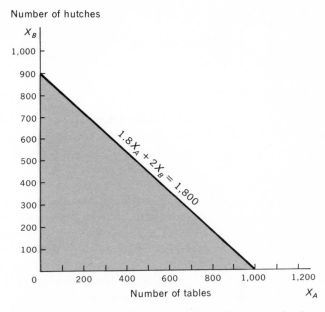

Figure 5.3 The graphic representation of a constraint in linear programming.

the two axes of the graph? _____

Because of the nonnegativity constraints for X_A and X_B (because neither X_A nor X_B can have a negative value).

_____
_____
_____
_____
_____
_____

74 In the graphic solution of a linear programming problem, the area of the graph whose values conform to, or satisfy, the restrictions in the problem is called the _____

feasible-solution   _____ area.

75 Suppose the production restriction for process 1, which is protrayed in Figure 5.3, were the only constraint in this problem, other than the nonnegativity constraints. How many feasible solutions to this problem would there be (not necessarily all op-

A great number are
possible because
all combinations of
values for X_A and
X_B in the shaded
area qualify as
possible solutions.

timum)?

_____

_____

_____

_____

_____

76 As far as the *constraints* in this problem are concerned, is the decision to produce no tables and no
hutches within the feasible-solution area?

Yes
[Yes / No]

77 Many solutions are possible, but there is only
one optimum solution. Looking back at Figure 5.2,
and recalling that our objective is to maximize
$60X_A + 80X_B$, what is the optimum solution with
only the one major restriction involved? Produce

0; 900
_____ [number] tables and _____
[number] hutches.

78 At the production level of 900 hutches and no

$72,000
tables, the gross revenue, which is _____ , has
been maximized; that is, this production plan rep-

optimum
resents the _____ solution to the
problem with only the one major restriction.

79 Of course, the solution we have just discussed
is not the final solution, because only one constraint was considered. Refer to Figure 5.4. We
have now entered the two remaining constraints
on the graph. Is the feasible-solution area now
larger or smaller than before we added the

Smaller
remaining two constraints? [Larger / Smaller]

80 In Figure 5.4, the feasible-solution area is
such that we cannot possibly use the full

1
1,800-hour capacity for process _____ .

81 Since we want to maximize gross revenue, the
optimum solution lies somewhere along the line
YZX in Figure 5.4, and, specifically, it is at point *Y*,
Z, or *X*. No point within the shaded area could

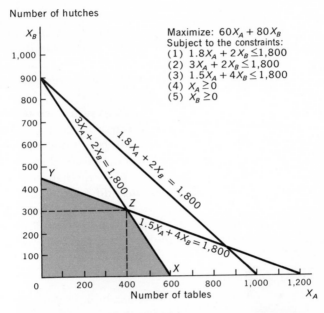

Number of hutches

Maximize: $60X_A + 80X_B$
Subject to the constraints:
(1) $1.8X_A + 2X_B \leq 1,800$
(2) $3X_A + 2X_B \leq 1,800$
(3) $1.5X_A + 4X_B \leq 1,800$
(4) $X_A \geq 0$
(5) $X_B \geq 0$

$3X_A + 2X_B = 1,800$

$1.8X_A + 2X_B = 1,800$

$1.5X_A + 4X_B = 1,800$

Number of tables

Figure 5.4 The graphic solution of a linear programming problem.

maximize gross revenue because all these points involve unnecessary idle capacity in processes

2; 3 _____ and _____ .

82 Using the data from Figure 5.4, complete the following chart:

	TABLES (A)		HUTCHES (B)		
Point on graph	No. of units	Revenue per unit	No. of units	Revenue per unit	Total revenue
Y	0	$60	450	$80	$36,000
Z	___	$60	___	$80	$____
X	___	$60	___	$80	$____

400; 300; 48,000
600; 0; 36,000

83 The optimum solution to this problem, then, is to produce _____ [number] tables and

400

300   _____ [number] hutches. At these productions levels all the restrictions are satisfied, and
gross revenue is maximized; that is, no other product mix within the feasible-solution area would
yield a higher gross-revenue figure.

84   In this example we have had two variables
which affected the goal of maximizing gross revenue, the number of units of products A and B, and
thus a two-dimensional graph was required in the
solution. Since each additional variable, or product, would add another dimension to the graph,
the graphic method of solving a linear program-
two   ming problem is useful when only _____
(Conceivably, a   [number] variables are involved in the problem.
three-dimensional
graph could also
be constructed.)

85   An algebraic technique for solving more
complex linear programming problems is the
simplex method. There are actually several varia-
tions to the technique, but it is particularly applica-
large   ble whenever a [small / large] number of variables
is involved in the problem.

86   The optimum product mix in a plant capable
of producing twelve different products in ten different departments, with different production
times involved, could be determined by applying
simplex   the _____ method of solving a linear
programming problem.

87   A simplified version of the simplex method,
which was developed specifically for problems involving the movement of products from several
sources to several destinations, has been referred
to as the *transportation method*. Would this technique
apply to the kind of linear programming problem
that we used to illustrate the graphic method?
No (since ours was   [Yes / No]
a product-mix
problem)

88 Suppose that we have four factories producing similar merchandise and seven warehouses that are geographically dispersed. Determining how much of the production of each factory should be shipped to each warehouse could be done by using the _____ method of solving the linear programming problem.

transportation
(also by the more
involved simplex
method)

89 Of the three methods that we have discussed for solving linear programming problems, the mathematically most complex is the _____ method, the least complex is the _____ method, whereas intermediate in complexity is the _____ method.

simplex
graphic
transportation

E ILLUSTRATIVE APPLICATIONS OF STATISTICAL DECISION ANALYSIS

Probability analysis plays a role in a number of quantitative methods. The method of analysis by which economic consequences as well as probability values are considered for the purpose of determining the best decision act has been referred to as *statistical decision analysis.* In the context in which a final commitment by the choice of some one act is required, the analysis typically begins by constructing a table of conditional economic consequences, or a *decision table.* When a sequence of decision acts is required, a *decision tree* typically is constructed to aid in the analysis. In this section we illustrate the application of statistical decision analysis in these two types of situations using relatively simple examples.

90 Suppose a manufacturer faces the decision of whether or not to manufacture and market a particular product. The possible decision acts are "manufacture" or "don't manufacture." For the purposes of our simplified example we classify the possible levels of market demand as being "low," "moderate," or "high" at the required price level. Therefore, if the decision table to be constructed is to include a row for each possible decision act and a column for each possible state, then in this case

2   the decision table will have _____ [number]
3   rows and _____ [number] columns.[1]

91 The basic framework for the decision table is presented below. The next step is to enter the values in the cells of the table, which should be the conditional economic consequence (dollar result) for the decision act for that row and the state for that column. For example, if the product is not manufactured then the economic consequence would be zero gain no matter what the state, since there can be no gain (or loss) if the product was not marketed. Therefore, enter the appropriate values in the second row of the table below.

	STATE S_1 (LOW DEMAND)	STATE S_2 (MODERATE DEMAND)	STATE S_3 (HIGH DEMAND)
DECISION ACT			
D_1 (manufacture)			
D_2 (don't manufacture)			

0; 0; 0

92 Now, in order to fill in the first row of the decision table we need to know more about the risk situation. Suppose that the capital investment which is required is such that if demand is low there will be a net loss of $300,000 (gain of −$300,000), if demand is moderate there will be a gain of $50,000, and if demand is high there will be a gain of $250,000 (all in present dollar values).

[1]Some textbooks in decision analysis follow the opposite convention and designate the possible states in the rows of the decision table and the available acts as column headings. Therefore, the reader should be alert to this possible difference when referring to different books.

In row 1: −300,000;
50,000; 250,000

Accordingly, enter these values in the appropriate cells of the table in Frame 91.

93 In constructing the decision table, or payoff table, for a decision situation, we identify every possible decision act and every possible economic consequence depending on the state which occurs. For example, referring to the table in Frame 91 we see that the consequence associated with manufacturing the product and moderate market demand developing is a _____ [gain / loss].

$50,000; gain

94 Since statistical decision analysis includes the use of probability values as well as economic consequences, the next step is to determine the probability of each state (of demand, in this case). On the basis of previous experience with similar products as well as a market study, suppose that the probability values associated with low, moderate, and high market demand are determined to be 0.20, 0.50, and 0.30, respectively. Enter these values in the table below.

0.20; 0.50; 0.30

DECISION ACT	STATE S_1 (LOW DEMAND) ($P =$____)	STATE S_2 (MODERATE DEMAND) ($P =$____)	STATE S_3 (HIGH DEMAND) ($P =$____)
D_1 (manufacture)	− $300,000	$50,000	$250,000
D_2 (don't manufacture)	0	0	0

95 The final step leading to the identification of the best act is to determine the expected monetary value (EMV) for each possible act. Arithmetically, this is simply the sum of the products of each conditional value for an act multiplied by the respective probability. In this case, three products are summed for each of the two acts. Therefore, for the illustrative decision problem the expected monetary values are:

−300,000; 50,000
250,000; 40,000

$$\text{EMV}(D_1) = 0.20 \ (\underline{\hspace{2cm}}) + 0.50 \ (\underline{\hspace{2cm}})$$
$$+ \ 0.30 \ (\underline{\hspace{2cm}}) = \underline{\hspace{2cm}}$$

0; 0
0; 0

$$\text{EMV}(D_2) = 0.20 \ (\underline{\hspace{2cm}}) + 0.50 \ (\underline{\hspace{2cm}})$$
$$+ \ 0.30 \ (\underline{\hspace{2cm}}) = \underline{\hspace{2cm}}$$

D_1

Yes

0.20 (which is the
probability of
experiencing a
loss)

96 Comparing the expected monetary values for the available decision acts, the best decision in this case is $[D_1 \ / \ D_2]$. Is it possible that the "best act" will turn out to be the incorrect one in a particular decision situation? [Yes / No] What is the probability of this occurring in our illustrative problem? $P = \underline{\hspace{2cm}}$.

97 Thus, the choice of the "best act" in statistical decision analysis does not assure the correctness of each decision, but is oriented toward optimizing the average economic result over the long run, when many such decisions are made. As contrasted to the situation above, frequently the decision problem is more complicated in that the first decision to be made leads sequentially to the necessity of making other decisions based on intermediate results. For example, the first decision may be whether or not to develop a product, and then the second decision may be concerned with the level of manufacturing if the product is in fact successfully developed. This type of problem is portrayed in Figure 5.5 As indicated in this figure, the graphic device used to analyze a decision problem involv-

decision tree

ing sequential decisions is the _____ .

98 The decision tree portrays all decision acts and the states that can occur in their sequential order of occurrence. In Figure 5.5, note that the points of required decision are designated by the

☐

symbol _____ , while the points at which chance events occur are designated by the symbol

○

_____ .

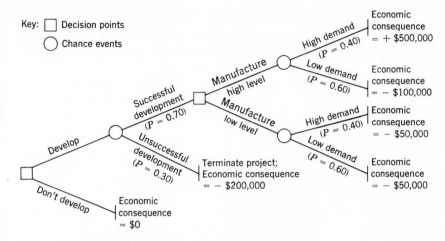

Figure 5.5 Decision tree for the sequential decision problem.

99 In Figure 5.5 two points of decision are identified: first, whether or not to _____ the product, and then if the product is successfully developed, the level of _____ of the product.

develop

manufacturing

100 The value of decision tree analysis is that it permits the decision maker to "look ahead" to the implications of an initial decision. In this case, we would not want to begin development of the product if later market prospects did not look good. For this reason, as we illustrate in the following frames, the computational analysis using a decision tree proceeds from right to left, rather than left to right. In terms of "looking ahead," one observation we can make by referring to Figure 5.5, even without any further calculation at this point, is that the decision to develop the product will prove to be the right one only if (1) the product [can / cannot] be developed and (2) subsequent demand for the product is [high / low].

can

high

101 The determination of the best act at each decision point is similar to decision table analysis,

in that the act with the largest EMV is designated
as the best act. Figure 5.6 repeats the decision tree
with EMV values identified for all acts. To illustrate that these values have been calculated as
before, note that the EMV of $140,000 for "Manu-
facture high level" was determined by summing
two products as follows:

+$500,000 $0.40 (_____) + 0.60 (_____) = $140,000
−$100,000

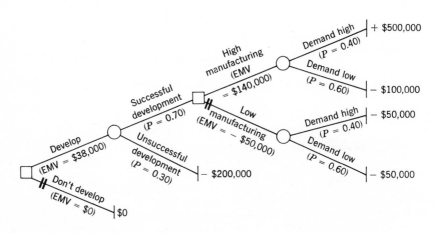

Figure 5.6 Decision tree for the sequential decision problem with expected
monetary values (EMV) included.

102 Therefore, given successful product development (and working right to left in terms of the
decision points in this problem) the two decision
acts available are to manufacture at a high level,

$140,000   with an associated EMV of $_____ , and to
manufacture at a low level, with an associated EMV

−$50,000   of $_____ . Therefore, given successful product development the best act is to manufacture at a

high   [high / low] level.

103 It is common practice to eliminate nonpre-
ferred acts on the decision tree by a double bar
(#) as is done in Figure 5.6. Now we move left to
the next decision point, which is in fact the initial

decision point in this problem. Because the monetary values associated with branches that are eliminated are ignored in any further analysis, we can observe that if we choose to develop the product then two economic consequences are possible: the product will be successfully developed, leading to an EMV of $140,000, or the product will not be developed, leading to a loss of $20,000. Therefore:

$140,000
–$200,000
$38,000

EMV (develop) = 0.70 (_____) + 0.30 (_____)
= _____

$38,000

$0

develop

104 In respect to the first decision point, then, we have the choice of developing the product, with an associated EMV of $_____ , or not developing the product, with an associated EMV of $_____. Therefore, the best act is to [develop / not develop] the product.

$200,000

high

105 Following this "best decision," if product development is in fact unsuccessful the decision process is terminated with a $_____ loss. If development is successful then the best decision in respect to the production level is to manufacture at a [high / low] level.

Review

goals (or
objectives)

106 The first step in OR analysis is the identification and quantification of the _____ of the system. (Frames 1 to 7)

variables

107 Following the identification and measurement of the goals of the system, the _____ that affect goal attainment are identified and measured. (Frames 8 and 9)

mathematical

108 Having identified and quantified all goals and variables in a decision-making situation, it is our objective (using the OR technique) to select or construct the appropriate _____ model   _____ to represent the system of relationships. (Frames 10 to 15)

109 Throughout, the orientation of operations

systemwide   research is [departmental / systemwide]. (Frames 1 to 4)

110 In general, on what basis is a mathematical technique chosen to solve an OR problem? (Frames 16 to 30)

Appropriateness to the situation; representativeness of the way the variables actually interact, etc.

_____

_____

_____

_____

111 Considering now the specific quantitative techniques we have discussed, the method that is appropriate when costs associated with idle capacity must be balanced against costs of waiting is

queuing theory   _____ _____ . (Frames 37 to 41, 56)

112 The total cost of detecting output of poor quality first decreases and then increases as personnel are added to a particular inspection department. The mathematical method that could be used to find the point of minimum cost in this case

calculus   is _____ . (Frames 27 to 30, 55)

113 The manager who attaches quantitative estimates of the likelihood of various events as an aid

probability   to decision making is utilizing _____

analysis   _____ . (Frames 31 to 36, 58)

114 An estimate of the probabilities that various numbers of employees will leave company employment during the coming year, based on probabilities of departure for each of several categories of reasons, might be determined by the application of

simulation   the _____ method. (Frames 50 to 53, 59)

game theory

115 Determining a decision-making strategy by anticipating what a major competitor will do involves the use of _____ _____ . (Frames 42 to 44, 54)

linear
programming

116 The mathematical method that would be appropriate when we want to determine how many units of each of a number of products should be manufactured within certain capacity limitations so as to maximize revenue is _____ _____ . (Frames 45 to 48, 57, 60 to 89)

constraints (or
restrictions)

117 The first step in the graphic solution to a linear programming problem is to construct a graph representing the quantities of the two variables and to chart, or enter, the _____ on this graph. (Frames 60 to 72)

feasible-solution

118 The area on the graph whose values satisfy the constraints in the problem is called the _____ area. (Frames 73 to 77)

optimum

119 Within the feasible-solution area, that combination of values for the two variables which results in the _____ solution is chosen. (Frames 78 to 84)

simplex

120 When we are involved in a linear programming problem which includes more than two variables, such as product quantities, the method of solving the linear programming problem which is more appropriate than the graphic solution is the _____ method. (Frames 85, 86, and 89)

transportation

121 A simplified version of the simplex method, which is applicable to such problems as minimizing shipment costs when several sources and destinations are involved, has been called the _____ method. (Frames 87 to 89)

decision act
state (either order)

122 When a decision table is used for the purpose of statistical decision analysis, each value in the body of this table represents the economic consequences associated with a particular _____ and a particular _____ . (Frames 90 to 93)

expected
monetary value
(EMV)

123 The "best act" in statistical decision analysis is the one which has the highest _____ . (Frames 94 to 96)

decision
tree

right

124 When sequential decisions are involved, the graphic device frequently used in conjunction with statistical decision analysis is the _____ _____ . The first decision point subjected to analysis is the decision point located in the extreme [left / right] portion of the diagram. (Frames 97 to 105)

Discussion Questions

1. What is the relationship between the managerial function of planning and the use of quantitative decision-making techniques?

2. Discuss the major steps included in operations research. Is there any importance to the sequence of these steps?

3. For what type of decision-making situations is the construction of a mathematical model feasible and worthwhile?

4. Give examples of problems to which calculus, queuing theory, game theory, and the simulation method could be appropriately applied.

5. Discuss linear programming from the standpoint of the major assumption of this technique and the type of decision-making situations in which it can be used.

6. At what level or levels in the organization should managers have familiarity with the concepts and techniques of operations research?

7. Describe the basic procedure followed in statistical decision analysis, in terms of what factors need to be identified, what values need to be determined, and the basis used for determining the "best decision."

8. In the case of sequential decision analysis, describe the logic of working from right to left in the decision tree analysis, rather than the left-to-right orientation that might seem to be more natural in terms of the actual sequence of decision acts and events.

9. Refer to the sequential decision problem illustrated in this chapter. If you were the manufacturer, would you choose to adopt the "best act"? In answering this question, consider the probabilities associated with the events which follow this decision as well as the EMV associated with the decision.

10. Some managers have argued that quantitative decision analysis may be appropriate in certain technical areas of decision making, but that it is inappropriate in the broader decision areas in which managerial ingenuity is important. In what respects may such an opinion be correct? In what respects is it incorrect?

Case Problem: Pliable Plastics Corporation

The Pliable Plastics Corporation is organized into four manufacturing departments with the process-time availability per month indicated in the table below. The company has just been presented with the opportunity to produce either a toy dump truck set or a doll to the extent of the company's full capacity, or to produce any combination of the two items, for a national distributor. The dolls and trucks are to be packed in boxes containing one dozen of either one or the other item. The manufacturing manager estimates that each box of one dozen dolls will require 1.5 hours of molding, 2.0 hours of assembly, 2.0 hours of artwork, and 1.0 hours of packaging. He estimates that each box of a dozen trucks will require 2.5 hours of molding time, 1.0 hours of assembly, 0.5 hours of artwork, and 1.0 hours of packaging. The distributor will pay $80 for each box of dolls and $50 for each box of trucks. How many boxes of dolls and/or trucks should be scheduled for production next month so as to maximize gross revenue? Why might company management decide not to take advantage of this opportunity?

DEPARTMENT	HOURS OF PROCESS TIME (PER MONTH)
Molding	2,000
Assembly	1,500
Art	1,000
Packaging	1,500

Case Problem: Choice of Investments

An individual wishes to invest $50,000 in one of three ways during the coming year: in an insured savings account, a mutual common-stock fund, or in common-stock warrants. If he puts the funds in a savings account he is assured of a $5\frac{1}{2}$ percent rate of return (ignore the compounding of interest for the purposes of this problem). The return on the other investment opportunities depends on the state of the economy during the coming year, however. After reviewing several economic forecasts, the investor decides that the probability that the economy will be in an expansion is 0.30, that it will be stable is 0.60, and that it will be in a recession is 0.10. The mutual fund investment will probably result in a gain of $7,500 if the economy is in an expansion, $2,500 if the economy is stable, and —$10,000 if there is a recession. Similarly, investments in warrants will result in an approximate gain of $50,000 if the economy is in an expansion, —$10,000 if the economy is stable, and —$30,000 if there is a recession. Construct the decision table and determine the best decision act for this investment situation. Consider any implications of adopting the "best act."

Case Problem: A Franchise Opportunity

An investor is considering placing a deposit of $10,000 to reserve a franchise opportunity for a new residential area for one year. There are two areas of uncertainty associated with this sequential decision situation: whether or not a prime franchise competitor will decide to locate an outlet in the same area and whether or not the residential area will develop to be a moderate or large market. Overall, then, the investor must first decide whether to deposit the initial $10,000 as a down payment for the franchise. Then during the one-year period the decision of the competing franchise system will be revealed, and the investor estimates that there is a 30 percent chance that the competing franchise system will also develop an outlet. After the decision of the competing system is known the investor must then decide whether or not to proceed with constructing the franchise outlet. If there is competition and the market is large the net gain during the relevant period is estimated as being $15,000; if the market is moderate this will be a net loss of $10,000. If there is no competition and the market is large the net gain will be $30,000; if the market is moderate there will be a net gain of $10,000. The investor estimates that there is about a 60 percent chance that the market will be large. Using decision-tree analysis, determine whether or not the initial deposit of $10,000 to reserve the franchise opportunity should be made.

Suggested Readings*

Arnoff, E. L.: "Successful Models I Have Known," *Decision Sciences,* vol. 2, no. 2, April 1971.

Braverman, J. D.: *Probability, Logic, and Management Decisions,* McGraw-Hill Book Company, New York, 1972.

Brown, R. V.: "Do Managers Find Decision Theory Useful?" *Harvard Business Review,* vol. 48, no. 3, May-June 1970.

Churchman, C.W., R. L. Ackoff, and E. L. Arnoff: *Introduction to Operations Research,* John Wiley & Sons, Inc., New York, 1957.

Horowitz, I.: *An Introduction to Quantitative Business Analysis,* 2d ed., McGraw-Hill Book Company, New York, 1972.

Kazmier, L. J.: *Statistical Analysis for Business and Economics,* 2d ed., McGraw-Hill Book Company, New York, 1973.

Levin, R. I., and C. A. Kirkpatrick: *Quantitative Approaches to Management,* 2d ed., McGraw-Hill Book Company, New York, 1971.

Miller, D. W., and M. K. Starr: *Executive Decisions and Operations Research,* Prentice-Hall, Inc., Englewood Cliffs, N.J., 1960.

Thierauf, R. J., and R. A. Grosse: *Decision Making through Operations Research,* John Wiley & Sons, Inc., New York, 1970.

Wagner, H. M.: *Principles of Management Science,* Prentice-Hall, Inc., Englewood Cliffs, N.J., 1970.

Williams, J. D.: *The Compleat Strategyst,* 2d ed., McGraw-Hill Book Company, New York, 1965.

Winkler, R. L.: *An Introduction to Bayesian Inference and Decision,* Holt, Rinehart and Winston, Inc., New York, 1972.

*Also see the cross-reference table in the Preface.

ORGANIZING

There are several facets to the function of organizing that need to be considered in any attempt to develop an overall understanding of this function and its importance in the process of management. In the first place, the formal organization structure needs to be considered, including the basis used for setting up departments, the type of organizational growth, the span of management in the structure, and the effect of managerial decentralization on the structure. These topics are covered in Chapter 6.

Furthermore, a formal set of organizational relationships that has considerable impact on how smoothly a firm functions is that involving line and staff. In Chapter 7, we consider the nature of line and staff activities and the types of authority that can be assigned to those carrying out staff activities.

An organization is not just a structure or a set of formal relationships; it is a social system as well. Accordingly, in Chapter 8 we consider the status and role implications of formal organizational assignments and the nature of the informal organization and its functions, including the use of power and politics.

Finally, an organization is a functional entity by the fact
that people are appointed to positions in the organization. Chapter 9 therefore is concerned with staffing the
organization, particularly in regard to managerial personnel. The topics covered include the determination of
executive needs and the selection, appraisal, and development of managerial personnel.

Chapter  **six**
ORGANIZATION STRUCTURE

The formal organization chart represents the division of activities within a firm, indicates who reports to whom, and serves to describe the vertical channels of communication which link the chief executive to the working, or operative, level in the organization. In this chapter we identify the factors which serve as bases for grouping activities in an organization, the difference between vertical and horizontal organizational growth, and the factors affecting the proper span of management. In the final section we discuss the philosophy of managerial decentralization and its effect on the functioning and formal structure of the organization.

A   DEPARTMENTATION

In the language of management theory, the process of grouping activities is referred to as *departmentation*. Thus, departmentation is the grouping of activities at any level in the organization, not just the "departmental" level alone. Because the organization chart represents the relationship among the formal groups of activities that have been defined, the process of departmentation is the first step in the managerial function of organizing.

departmentation

1   Several different bases for the grouping of activities, that is, for _____ , can be used. The basis of *number* simply involves assigning an equal number of people at random to each organizational unit.

2   Departmentation on the basis of number alone has fallen into disuse with the growth in complexity of organizations. Would this basis be compatible with the need to establish specialized organizational units? [Yes / No]

No

3   Since departmentation based on number is primarily useful when undifferentiated manpower is to be grouped, this basis for departmentation [was / was not] generally applicable in medieval armies.

was

4   The most important and most widely accepted practice is departmentation according to *function*, or work to be done. Departmentation by function [would / would not] be compatible with the need for occupational specialization.

would

5   Although a variety of work has to be accomplished in the modern enterprise, three categories of activity—production, sales, and finance —have been given special attention when departmentation is on the basis of _____ .

function

6 In manufacturing firms, the departments carrying out the functions of production, sales, and

finance

_____ have often been called the "major functional departments."

7 Although other departments are also important for the firm's continued existence, those departments whose functions are particularly vital to the operation and survival of the firm are called

major

the _____ functional departments.

8 The creation of utility in the form of goods or

production

services concerns the _____ functions,
the exchange of these goods or services for pur-

sales

chasing power constitutes the _____
function, and the allocation of funds in the firm

finance

concerns the _____ function.

9 No matter what level of the organization is involved, the grouping of activities by function is based on the work to be done. Therefore in large organizations. which include a wide variety of job

is

activities, the basis of function [is / is not] widely used.

10 Thus the purchasing and accounting departments within a firm are examples of the grouping

function

of activities according to _____ .

11 Similarly, the finishing, painting, and inspection departments in a manufacturing plant are ex-

function

amples of departmentation by _____ .

12 Thus far we have discussed the two bases for grouping activities in an organization: depart-

number

mentation based on _____ and

function

_____. In addition, activities can
also be grouped by *product,* or product line.

13 In departmentation based on product, a plant or division executive has extensive authority over

the manufacture, sale, and service of a given product. Whether the plant or division in question is
is not located near other company facilities [is / is not] necessarily relevant.

14 Two plants of the same company located side by side may have separate sales departments for their particular products. In General Motors, the Buick, Cadillac, and Chevrolet divisions are ex-
product amples of departmentation by _____ .

15 Full development of all product lines and the development of specialized product knowledge by engineering and sales personnel are [advan-
advantages tages / disadvantages] of departmentation by product, whereas coordination difficulties and possible undue growth in power of specific product
disadvantages divisions are [advantages / disadvantages].

16 Departmentation by *territory* is a fourth basis for grouping activities in an enterprise. In this
is case, physical or geographical location [is / is not] necessarily relevant.

17 When nearness to local conditions makes for economies of operation, either in producing or in
territory selling, departmentation based on _____ tends to be used.

18 The desire to adapt to local market conditions
good is generally a [good / poor] reason for departmentation by territory, whereas doing so because of difficulties in communication within the com-
poor pany is usually considered a [good / poor] reason.

19 Establishing sales districts, each headed by a local manager, is an example of departmentation
territory by _____ .

20 Thus far we have discussed four bases for
number departmentation: by _____ ,
function; product _____ , _____ , and
territory _____ .

21 Departmentation by *customer* is another basis for organizing activities. When the major emphasis is on being better able to serve different categories of buyers of the firm's products, departmentation by _____ deserves serious consideration.

customer

22 Catering to the specific needs of different types of customers is a(n) [advantage / disadvantage] of departmentation by customer, whereas possible underemployment of facilities because of the changing importance of different customer groups is a(n) [advantage / disadvantage].

advantage

disadvantage

23 The Teen Shop in a department store is an example of departmentation by _____.

customer

24 Finally, departmentation of a firm's activities may be based on the *process*, or type of equipment, involved. Grouping all punched-card keypunching machines in one area, even though several departments are served, is an example of departmentation by _____ .

process

25 Note that departmentation by process is really a special case of departmentation by function. In both cases, activities are grouped according to the _____ being done.

work

26 However, whenever work that would otherwise be done in several different locations in an enterprise is done in one place because of the special equipment being used, departmentation by _____ is involved.

process

27 Heavy specialized equipment, or a need for serial use of different types of equipment, makes departmentation by _____ desirable.

process

28 In all, we have discussed six bases for departmentation. The most important basis is by _____ . The basis of least importance

function

in modern organizations is departmentation by

number   _____ . Other bases are by

product; territory   _____ , _____ ,

customer; process   _____ , and _____ .

29 It is quite typical to find that a different basis for departmentation is used at different organizational levels in a firm. *Primary, intermediate*, and *ultimate departmentation* refer to the organization

levels   _____ involved.

30 *Primary departmentation* is the grouping of activities at the level immediately below the chief executive officer of the organization. Refer to Figure 6.1. The basis for primary departmentation in this

function   case is by _____ .

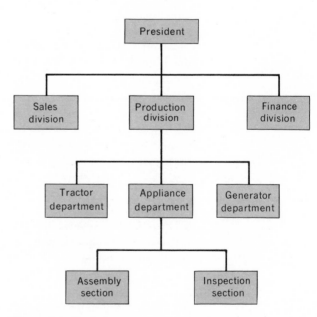

Figure 6.1 Partial organization chart.

31 *Intermediate departmentation* includes all the grouped activities in the organization structure

primary   below the _____ departments and above the departments at the base of the structure.

32 Because all activities below the primary level of departmentation and above the departments at the base of the organization structure are included, more than one organizational level can in fact be

intermediate

involved in _____ departmentation.

33 In Figure 6.1, what is the basis for intermediate departmentation in the production division?

Product

_____

34 *Ultimate departmentation* is departmentation at the base of the organization structure, that is,

primary

below the _____ and _____

intermediate

departments.

35 In Figure 6.1, what is the basis for ultimate departmentation in the appliance department?

Function

_____

36 Refer to Figure 6.2. What level of departmen-

Intermediate

tation is by territory? _____

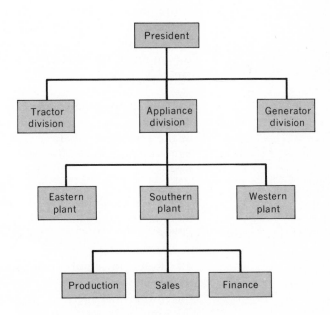

Figure 6.2 Partial organization chart.

37 In Figure 6.2, what level of departmentation is by product? _____

Primary

38 What level of departmentation is by function in Figure 6.2? _____

Ultimate

39 Compare Figures 6.1 and 6.2. At what level do the two organization charts follow a common departmentation basis, and what is that basis? In both charts, departmentation at the _____ level is based on _____ .

ultimate

function

40 As was the case in this example, it is almost invariably true that departmentation at the lowest, or ultimate, organizational level is on the basis of _____ .

Function (or occasionally process, which is a special case of departmentation by function)

B VERTICAL AND HORIZONTAL GROWTH IN THE ORGANIZATION

As an enterprise expands, the organization structure tends to grow both vertically and horizontally. Addition of levels to an organization structure is *vertical growth*, whereas the differentiation of functions or addition of positions without increasing the number of organization levels is *horizontal growth*.

41 Levels are added to the organization structure during _____ growth. A description of the relationship between and among the levels in an organization is often referred to as the *scalar process*.

vertical

42 Thus the delegation of authority and assignment of responsibility in the organization are part of the _____ process.

scalar

43 Refer to Figure 6.3, which identifies two stages in the growth of a small firm. Counting the owner-manager, at stage I there is (are) one

three

_____ [number] manager(s) in the firm whereas at stage II there are _____ [number] managers.

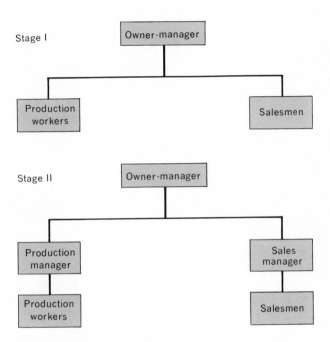

Stage I — Owner-manager — Production workers — Salesmen

Stage II — Owner-manager — Production manager — Production workers — Sales manager — Salesmen

two

44 In stage I there are _____ [number] levels in the organization (counting the owner-manager as a level), whereas at stage II there

three

are _____ [number] levels.

45 Stage II also represents a differentiation of activity as compared with stage I. Whereas the owner-manager directly supervised the operative employees in stage I, in stage II he has assigned supervisory authority to two subordinate managers. Therefore, changes in the scalar process result

vertical

in [vertical / horizontal] changes in the organization.

46 Just as the growth in the vertical dimension
scalar   concerns the _____ process. the *func-*
tional process affects developments in the horizontal
dimension of the organization.

47 Figure 6.4 represents a third stage in the development of a small firm. The difference from
stage II does not concern authority changes within
a particular functional area of work, such as
production or sales. Rather the change involves the
differentiation of an additional *function* at an established organization level. It is for this reason
that horizontal changes are associated with the so-
functional   called _____ process.

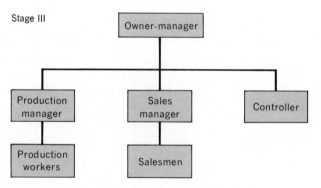

Figure 6.4 Horizontal organization growth.

48 At stage II, shown in Figure 6.3, there are
three   _____ [number] levels in the organi-
two (production   zation and _____ [number] separately iden-
and sales)   tified areas of functional activity.

49 At stage III, shown in Figure 6.4, there are
three   _____ [number] levels in the organi-
three (production, zation and _____ [number] separa-
sales, and   tely identified areas of functional activity.
controller)

50 Thus, functional differentiation, that is, the
establishment of a new functional department,

horizontal

typically results in [vertical / horizontal / both vertical and horizontal] organizational growth.

51 Overall, then, changes in the scalar process

vertical

are associated with changes in the [vertical / horizontal] dimension and affect the number of organ-

levels

izational [functions / levels]. On the other hand, changes in the functional process are associated

horizontal

with the _____ dimension and affect the

functions

number of organizational _____ that are separately identified.

C SPAN OF MANAGEMENT

The *span of management* is also called the "span of supervision" and the "span of control." The concept has to do with identifying the number of subordinates whose work a superior can effectively manage. Although early writers in management tried to identify the ideal span of management for all organizational circumstances, the results of studies in this area indicate that no universal ratio is meaningful. As part of the function of organizing, the characteristics of each situation have to be considered before determining the span of management that is appropriate.

52 The *organizational level*, the *kind of activity* being supervised, the *kind of personnel* being supervised, and the *kind of organization* are all factors that help determine the ideal span of _____

management (or
supervision, or
control)

applicable in a particular situation.

53 At the lowest organizational level, where responsibility is delegated for performing specific tasks, would you expect a relatively broad (many subordinates) or narrow (few subordinates) span

Broad

of management to be appropriate? [Broad / Narrow]

54 Although the differences in span of management at the various organizational levels have not been definitely determined, it is generally true that the span of management at the level of ultimate departmentation is broader than at either the

primary

intermediate

_____ or the _____ level.

55 The *kind of activity* supervised also affects the span of management. In general, the more varied the activities in the jobs being supervised, the

narrower

[broader / narrower] the ideal span of supervision.

56 Other things being equal, a greater variety of job activity necessitates closer supervision. On the other hand, jobs that follow a fixed routine allow

broad

for a [broad / narrow] span of management.

57 For example, as compared with a foreman on a continuous assembly-line operation, we would expect a foreman in a job shop to have

fewer

[more / fewer] subordinates.

58 Another factor that influences the span of management, in addition to the organizational

level

activity

_____ and the kind of _____ supervised, is the kind of personnel involved.

59 Aside from the amount of routine or varied activity involved, occupations in which individuals traditionally work independently tend to have a

broad

[broad / narrow] span of management.

60 For example, for professional salesmen, research scientists, and college professors one would

broad

expect a relatively [broad / narrow] span of management, even though the work may involve a great deal of variety.

61 Finally, the *kind of organization* helps to determine the span of management that is appropriate. The terms "centralized" and decentralized," or some degree of either in terms of delegation of authority, are descriptions of kinds

organizations

of _____ .

62 A *centralized* organization is one in which detailed and comprehensive planning is done by the chief executive or by a small group of key managers. Therefore, at what organizational levels are most decisions made in a centralized organization?

Higher

[Higher / Lower]

63 Centralized organizations tend to encourage close supervision of subordinates at every level in order to assure that established policies, procedures, and methods are followed. Therefore, the typical result of following the centralized philosophy is that the span of management is relatively

narrow

[broad / narrow].

64 On the other hand, in a *decentralized* organization operating decisions are pushed down to the lowest level possible. If a manager, by company policy, is to give greater "freedom of action" to his subordinates, should he have relatively more or

More

fewer subordinates? [More / Fewer]

65 Therefore, a company that is decentralized from the standpoint of delegation of authority

broad

tends to encourage a [broad / narrow] span of management.

66 In summary, then, we have considered four factors that influence the appropriate span of management for a particular situation: the organiza-

level

tional _____, the kind of

activity; personnel

_____, the kind of _____,

organization

and the kind of _____.

67 Work at the ultimate organizational level, routine activity, and a decentralized organization all tend to make the appropriate span relatively

broad

[broad / narrow].

centralized

narrow

68 On the other hand, higher organizational levels, varied activity, and a _____ organization all tend to make the appropriate span [broad / narrow].

69 In any particular managerial situation some factors may dictate a narrow span, whereas others indicate that a wide span is appropriate. Therefore a manager must consider and balance all relevant factors in deciding on the appropriate

span of
management

_____.

D DECENTRALIZATION AND THE OVERALL ORGANIZATION

Managerial decentralization affects not only the span of management, but also the number of managers and the number of levels in the organization structure. Thus the philosophy of encouraging the delegation of authority to the lowest level possible leads to overall organizational effects, and we shall discuss some of these in this final section of the chapter.

four

eight

70 Refer to Figure 6.5. In company A each manager has _____ [number] subordinates, whereas in company B each manager has _____ [number] subordinates.

Four

Three

71 What is the number of organization levels in company A (counting the chief executive as a level)? _____ [number]; in company B? _____ [number]

B

A

72 A *flat* organization structure is one that has relatively few levels and a large number of subordinates per level, whereas a *tall,* or *pyramidal,* structure has a greater number of levels. In Figure 6.5, company _____ appears to have a relatively flat organization structure, whereas company _____ has a tall structure.

Company A:

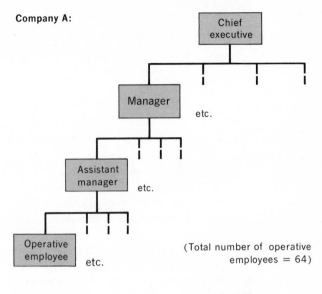

(Total number of operative
employees = 64)

Company B:

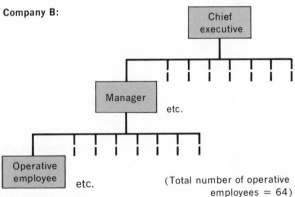

(Total number of operative
employees = 64)

Figure 6.5 Partial organization charts for two companies using different spans of management.

73 Because managerial decentralization encourages a broader span of management, it tends to lead to the development of a [flat / tall] organization structure.

flat

74 Once again, refer to Figure 6.5. In company A, a directive from the chief executive has to go

two   through _____ [number] intermediate lev-
           el(s) before reaching the operative employees,
one   whereas in company B it goes through _____
           [number] level(s).

           75 Thus the flat, or decentralized, organization
shorter   structure results in [longer / shorter] lines of com-
           munication in the organization.

           76 What is the total number of managers in com-
           pany A; that is, how many employees are above the
Twenty-one operative level in company A? _____
Nine   [number] In company B? _____ [number]

           77 Therefore, managerial decentralization leads
broad   to a [broad / narrow] span of management, a [flat
flat   / tall] organization structure, [longer / shorter]
shorter   lines of communication, and [more / fewer] execu-
fewer   tives.

           78 Conversely, managerial centralization leads
narrow   to a [broad / narrow] span of management, a [flat
tall   / tall] organization structure, [longer / shorter]
longer   lines of communication, and [more / fewer] execu-
more   tives.

           79 Which type of organization leads to a closer
           working relationship between supervisors and sub-
           ordinates and to tighter executive control?
Centralized [Centralized / Decentralized]

           80 Because of the opportunity to make manage-
           rial decisions (and mistakes) at lower organization
           levels, which type of organization is superior in
           providing the opportunity for executive develop-
Decentralized ment? [Centralized / Decentralized]

           81 Because of the success associated with the in-
           troduction of the managerial philosophy of decen-
           tralization at General Motors beginning in the
           1920s, this approach to management and organi-

zation has gained many adherents in American industry. In his testimony before the Senate Subcommittee on Anti-Trust and Monopoly in 1955, Harlow Curtice, then president of General Motors, gave major credit for the company's success to the

decentralization

application of the philosophy of _____.

82 In his testimony Mr. Curtice identified Alfred P. Sloan, Jr., who assumed the company presidency in 1921 when the company was in financial difficulty, as being the first executive to apply the concept in General Motors. Exhibit 6.1 is a brief excerpt from Mr. Curtice's testimony. As indicated, Mr. Sloan's organizational innovations led

a blend of
centralization and
decentralization

to [complete centralization / complete decentralization / a blend of centralization and decentralization].

EXHIBIT 6.1 *Excerpt from "The Development and Growth of General Motors," by Harlow Curtice.*

(From testimony before the subcommittee on Anti-Trust and Monopoly of the United States Senate Committee on the Judiciary, December 2, 1955, pp. 5–12.)

Even before the crisis of 1920 materialized, Mr. Sloan was very conscious of the need in General Motors for a new and clearly defined concept of management philosophy. He had observed that much time was being consumed in solving detailed administrative problems and in meeting the critical situations which were constantly arising. He recognized that too great a concentration of problems upon a small number of executives limited initiative, caused delay, increased expense, reduced efficiency and retarded development.

He realized that centralization, properly established, makes possible directional control, coordination, specialization, and resulting economies. He also realized that decentralization, properly established, develops initiative and responsibility; it makes possible a proper distribution of decisions at all levels of management, including the foreman—with resulting flexibility and cooperative effort, so necessary to a large-scale enterprise. His objective was to obtain the proper balance between these two apparently conflicting principles of centralization and decentralization in order to obtain the best elements of each in the combination. He concluded that, to achieve this balance so necessary for flexibility of operation, General Motors management should be established on a foundation of centralized policy and decentralized administration. Mr. Sloan's concept of the management of a great industrial organization, expressed in his own words as he finally evolved it, is "to divide it into as many parts as consistently as can be done, place in charge of each part the most capable executive that can be found, develop a system of coordination so that each part may strengthen and support each other part; thus not only welding all parts together in the common interests of a joint enterprise, but importantly developing ability and initiative through the instrumentalities of responsibility and ambition—developing men and giving them an opportunity to exercise their talents, both in their own interests as well as in that of the business."

---

83 Harlow Curtice also credited the growth of our country and of the automobile industry itself as factors contributing to the growth of General Motors. However, following Mr. Sloan's managerial innovations the company grew much more rapidly than its competitors, who tended to follow a highly centralized management philosophy. Whereas General Motors has consistently accounted for the largest percentage of new car sales in the United States in recent years, in 1921 its percentage of industry sales, as indicated in Figure 12 6.6, was about _____ percent.

84 Since the 1920s the large majority of firms in the United States have incorporated the philosophy of decentralization into their approach to management and organization. For example, Sears-Roebuck pioneered the application of this philosophy in the field of retailing during the 1930s. In noting the virtues of managerial decentralization, we should also note the principal

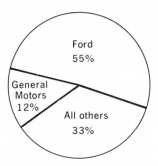

Figure 6.6 Percent of industry motor vehicle sales in 1921.

control (and
coordination)

danger associated with carrying it too far, which is possible loss of managerial _____ (refer to Exhibit 6.1 if you wish).

85 Before World War II most firms in the United States were relatively centralized and thus found that the benefits associated with more delegation of authority and assignment of responsibility to subordinate managers far outweighed the risks. The current problem in most firms, however, is that of finding the proper balance between the contrasting managerial philosophies of _____ and _____.

centralization

decentralization

Review

departmentation

86 The grouping of activities in order to form organizational units is called _____. (Introduction to Section A; Frame 1)

function

number

87 In all, six bases for departmentation were discussed. The most extensively used basis is departmentation by _____, whereas the basis that is of least importance when job specialization is involved is departmentation by _____. (Frames 2 to 12)

product; territory

88 The other four bases for departmentation are by _____, _____,

customer | _____, and _____.
process | (Frames 13 to 28)

89 Although all departments are established to help achieve organizational objectives, the activities of three departments are so vital to the survival of the firm that they have been called the "major functional departments." These are the departments performing the functions of

production; sales

finance | _____, _____, and _____. (Frames 5 to 8)

90 In terms of the organizational level involved, the grouping of activities at the level immediately below the chief executive is referred to as

primary | _____ departmentation, the grouping at the base of the organization structure is referred

ultimate | to as _____ departmentation, and the grouping at the level (s) in between is referred

intermediate | to as _____ departmentation. (Frames 29 to 37)

91 The basis for grouping activities at the level of ultimate departmentation is almost invariably by

function | _____. (Frames 38 to 40)

92 Levels are added to the organization structure

vertical | during _____ growth. The related delegation of authority and assignment of responsibility in the organization is referred to as the

scalar | _____ process. (Frames 41 to 45)

93 Just as the pattern of assigning authority in the vertical dimension of the organization chart is referred to as the scalar process, so the division of activities in the horizontal dimension is referred to

functional | as the _____ process. (Frames 46 to 51)

94 The number of subordinates for whose work a superior is responsible is referred to as the

span of | _____. (Introduc-
management | tion to Section C; Frame 52)

level
activity
personnel
organization

95 The appropriate span of management depends on the organizational _____ involved, the kind of _____ supervised, the kind of _____, and the kind of _____. (Frames 53 to 69)

centralized

decentralized

96 From the standpoint of delegation of authority, an organization in which top managers do detailed and comprehensive planning can be described as being _____, whereas the organization in which operating decisions are pushed down to the lowest level possible is _____. (Frames 61 to 64)

narrow

97 A managerial situation involving a higher organizational level, varied activity, and a centralized organization would tend to result in the appropriate span of management being [broad / narrow]. (Frames 65 to 69)

broad
flat
shorter
fewer

98 As compared with centralization, managerial decentralization leads to a relatively [broad / narrow] span of management, a [flat / tall] organization structure, [longer / shorter] lines of communication, and [more / fewer] executives. (Frames 70 to 78)

centralized

decentralized

99 Closer superior-subordinate relationships and closer executive control are typical in the [centralized / decentralized] organization, whereas greater opportunity for the development of management skills is typical in the [centralized / decentralized] organization. (Frames 79 and 80)

General Motors

100 The introduction of the managerial philosophy of decentralization in American business during the 1920s is generally credited to Alfred P. Sloan, Jr., who was at that time president of _____ _____. (Frames 81 to 85)

Discussion Questions

1. What are the advantages of constructing and using a formal organization chart in a company?

2. For each of the six bases for departmentation, give an example of its appropriate application in a business firm.

3. Why is it logical that departmentation at the ultimate level in the organization should be defined on the basis of function?

4. The direct result of adding people tends to be vertical growth in the organization, while adding functions tends to result in horizontal growth. Why? Why is it likely that both types of growth will occur as a firm expands in size?

5. What is the ideal span of management?

6. In practice, as contrasted to analyzing the factors discussed in this chapter, how is the span of management likely to be determined for a particular situation? Consider the implications of using the alternative approaches.

7. What is the relationship between geographic decentralization of a company and managerial decentralization?

8. What is the philosophy of, and what are the organizational implications of, managerial decentralization?

9. In considering the types of decisions that should be centralized as contrasted to those that should be decentralized, what developments during the past decade or so tend to make a higher degree of centralization possible, and perhaps even desirable?

10. It has been said that although a manager can delegate authority, the associated responsibility, or accountability, is assigned but not delegated. Discuss the implications of this statement.

Case Study: Lesner's Department Store

Although his department store is small compared with two large national chain stores located in the same city, Abe Lesner is proud of his ability to judge local demand and to merchandise a variety of goods through his varied promotional efforts. Over the years, he has probably used every promotional technique known in retailing. He has been in the business for thirty years and has seen the store develop to the point where he now has an assistant store manager and three department managers, each of whom is responsible for the buying and retailing of different categories of merchandise.

Mr. Lesner considers himself semiretired in that he no longer spends more than forty hours per week in the store. In fact, he'd like to cut down even more on the hours he spends at work but has concluded that it is just impossible. For one thing, the assistant store manager, who happens to be his son-in-law, makes no decisions without first consulting him, and so he finds that if he's not there, decisions affecting overall operations of the store are just not made. The department managers do tend to operate more independently, but even here he finds it necessary to prod them into the good merchandising practices that they otherwise seem to ignore. And if he had more time to review the department manager activities, Lesner is sure he could further improve performance and profitability. But since Mr. Lesner is approaching his seventieth birthday and feels that he has earned the right to slow down, he would really prefer to reduce the number of hours he spends in managing the business without jeopardizing its continued success.

1. What would happen if Mr. Lesner simply stopped coming to the store? Are his fears realistic?
2. To what extent has the concept of managerial decentralization been applied? How might its use be extended?
3. How might fuller development of his subordinate managers be achieved?
4. Can Lesner's Department Store, as Mr. Lesner knows it, really survive without his active management?

Case Study: A Question of Managerial Authority

Bill Chambers has worked for the Goodwin Manufacturing Company for a number of years, and for the last four years he has been general foreman in charge of the assembly line. His departments have always been rated high in respect to efficiency, cost, and schedules, and Bill is personally respected by his subordinate foremen and by members of the service organizations.

A week ago a new supervisor, Ed Whittaker, was transferred into the area from another division whose operations were discontinued. Ed had been a general foreman in the other division and carried the same title in his new assignment. When the superintendent introduced Ed Whittaker to Bill Chambers and the foremen in the department he made no mention of Ed's specific duties. However, in an earlier conversation in his office the superintendent informed Ed Whittaker that he would be responsible for all subassembly areas while Chambers would be responsible for the final assembly areas. The superintendent did not mention the details of this assignment to Bill Chambers because he was hard pressed to complete some overdue reports. He assumed that the two men could work things out, and in any event he planned to review their respective areas of responsibility again at the end of the week.

The day after his transfer into the area Ed Whittaker began making changes in the existing system and giving instructions to various supervisors in the subassembly areas in order to implement changes which he felt were desirable. The supervisors reacted with dissatisfaction to the proposed changes and immediately went to Bill Chambers to ask what was going on and to inquire who was in charge of the department. Chambers could not furnish any specific information but told the supervisors to do as Whittaker instructed until he could discuss the matter with the plant superintendent.

1. What did the plant superintendent do that was incorrect? How can he correct the situation?
2. When Ed Whittaker received his assignment, did he handle the situation correctly?
3. Do you think that Bill Chambers did the right thing in having the men do as Whittaker had instructed? Should Chambers talk to Whittaker before discussing the matter with the superintendent?
4. Overall, what kinds of reasons may be involved in the superintendent's decision to assign an additional general foreman in the assembly area? Should the reason be communicated to the supervisors in the area?

Suggested Readings*

Carzo, R., and J. N. Yanouzas: "Effects of Flat and Tall Organization Structures," *Administrative Science Quarterly*, vol. 14, no. 2, June 1969.

Dale, E.: "Centralization Versus Decentralization," *Advanced Management*, vol. 21, no. 6, June 1956.

———: *The Great Organizers*, McGraw-Hill Book Company, New York, 1960.

Ghiselli, E. E., and J. P. Siegel: "Leadership and Managerial Success in Tall and Flat Organization Structures," *Personnel Psychology*, vol. 25, no. 4, Winter 1972.

*Also see the cross-reference table in the Preface.

Golembiewski, R.: *Organizing Men and Power*, Rand McNally & Company, Chicago, 1967.

House, R. J., and J. B. Miner: "Merging Management and Behavioral Theory: The Interaction between Span of Control and Group Size," *Administrative Science Quarterly* vol. 14, no. 3, September 1969.

Hunt, R. G.: "Technology and Organization," *Academy of Management Journal*, vol. 13, no. 3, September 1970.

Jones, H. R., Jr.: "A Study of Organization Performance for Experimental Structures of Two, Three, and Four Levels," *Academy of Management Journal*, vol. 12, no. 3, September 1969.

Kegan, D. L.: "Organizational Development: Description, Issues, and Some Research Results," *Academy of Management Journal*, vol. 14, no. 4, December 1971.

Koontz, H.: "Making Theory Operational: The Span of Management," *The Journal of Management Studies*, vol. 3, no. 3, October 1966.

Lawrence, P. R., and J. W. Lorsch: *Organization and Environment*, Boston: Harvard Graduate School of Business Administration, 1967.

Litterer, J. A.: *The Analysis of Organizations*, John Wiley & Sons, Inc., New York, 1965.

Schollhammer, H.: "Organization Structures of Multinational Corporations," *Academy of Management Journal*, vol. 14, no. 3, September 1971.

Sherman, H.: *It All Depends: A Pragmatic Approach to Organization*, University: University of Alabama Press, 1966.

Steiglitz, H.: *Corporate Organization Structures*, Studies in Personnel Policy, no. 183, National Industrial Conference Board, Inc., New York, 1961.

Steiglitz, H., and A. R. Janger: *Top Management Organization in Divisionalized Companies*, Studies in Personnel Policy, no. 195, National Industrial Conference Board, Inc., New York, 1965.

Suojanen, W. W.: "The Span of Control: Fact or Fable?" *Advanced Management*, vol. 20, no. 11, November 1955.

Urwick, L. F.: "The Manager's Span of Control," *Harvard Business Review*, vol. 43, no. 3, May-June 1965.

Wolf, H. A.: "The Great GM Mystery," *Harvard Business Review*, vol. 42, no. 5, September-October 1964.

Woodward, J.: *Industrial Organization: Theory and Practice*, Oxford University Press, London, 1965.

Chapter **seven**
LINE
AND
STAFF
RELATIONSHIPS

The line activities in an organization are those that are directly concerned with attaining the company's product or service objectives, whereas staff activities are said to exist in order to help make line activities more effective. The authority relationships between those engaged in line activities and those engaged in staff activities, which can follow several patterns, is the major topic of this chapter. Near the end of this chapter we also consider some of the frictions that typically develop because of the need to use functional staff experts in organizations.

A   LINE AND STAFF FUNCTIONS

In a manufacturing firm, production, sales, and finance are typically considered to be line activities, whereas such areas of work as personnel relations and purchasing are examples of staff activities. Although the level of performance of line activities very quickly affects the overall success of a firm, this does not suggest that staff activities are therefore less important to the long-run survival of the firm.

objectives (or
goals)

1   Line activities in an organization are those activities that are *directly* concerned with attaining the firm's _____.

through

2   The function of staff activities, on the other hand, is to help attain organizational objectives [independently of / through] improved effectiveness of line activities.

Line

3   Insofar as organizational success is concerned, there is a time differential between the effects of line and staff activities. Which type of activity affects organizational success sooner? [Line / Staff]

immediate

longer

4   A failure in the production function has [immediate / long-run] implications in respect to a product objective, whereas a failure to provide effective work incentives affects overall organizational success in the [longer / shorter] run.

line

5   The particular activities that are considered to be line (as contrasted to staff) activities are dependent on the type of organization involved. In a manufacturing firm, production, sales, and finance are typically identified as _____ activities.

staff

6   In manufacturing firms, purchasing, personnel relations, and accounting are examples of _____ activities.

7 Would the line activities in a hospital or university be the same as those in a manufacturing firm? [Yes / No]

No

8 Once the activities that are directly concerned with attaining the organization's goals, that is, the

line
_____ activities, are identified, the staff functions that help make the line more effective are then established.

9 The relationship between line and staff activities in most organizations is quite complex. Contrary to what one might expect, for example, the

is not
staff [is / is not] invariably subordinate to the line organization.

10 There are two general categories of staff activity: *specialist* and *personal*. Whereas a specialist staff serves various components of the line organization, that staff which works only for a particular ex-

personal
ecutive is the _____ staff.

11 An "administrative assistant" or "assistant-to," who may help a particular executive by carrying out some of the routine functions of his office or by investigating special problems for him, belongs to

personal
the category of _____ staff.

12 On the other hand, a group of experts in a particular field who work with a number of line managers in order to promote greater organiza-

specialist
tional effectiveness constitute a [personal / specialist] staff.

13 The relationship between a specialist staff and line managers can be such that the staff may have *advisory, service, control*, or *functional* authority in respect to line activities. In the sections of this chapter that follow we consider each type of staff authority in turn, thus giving primary attention to

specialist
the role of the _____ staff in the organization.

B ADVISORY STAFF AUTHORITY

A staff group with advisory staff authority offers suggestions and prepares plans in its area of specialty for consideration by line managers, but as the name of this type of authority implies, line managers are in no way obligated to follow staff advice in this case.

14 A "management development department" that serves department managers in a company by investigating problems in supervisory development and recommending possible courses of action to requesting line managers can be described

advisory   as having _____ staff authority.

15 Is line authority in effect restricted by the existence of a specialist staff that has been assigned ad-

No   visory authority? [Yes / No]

16 It has been said that a good portion of an advisory staff manager's job is to sell, not tell. Since the line manager need not accept advisory staff recommendations, would this seem to be an accurate

Yes   description of the authority relationship? [Yes / No]

17 Approval or rejection of a complete recommended solution should be the staff man's goal. Often referred to as the concept of *completed staff work,* it makes development of the staff

more   man's own ideas [more / less] likely.

18 The pitfall in which a staff specialist simply "writes up" the ideas of line managers can be avoided by following the concept of completed

staff work   _____ _____.

19 On the other hand, does the concept of completed staff work suggest that the staff man should entirely refrain from discussing the problem or his own tentative solutions with line person-

No   nel? [Yes / No]

impractical

20 Staff solutions arrived at without consultation with affected line personnel are more likely to be [practical / impractical].

No

21 But does the staff man appropriately fulfill his function if he bases his written recommendations primarily on line-manager suggestions? [Yes / No]

completed staff
work

22 Thus the objective of having the advisory staff man submit complete proposals that reflect his own ideas is included in the concept of _____   _____   _____. To be practical, however, discussion with line personnel to be affected by the proposals is necessary.

advisory

23 In many multidivision companies, the central personnel staff conducts studies of the various personnel activities of the divisions, such as training and development, and submits proposals for program changes to the division managers. Of the four kinds of staff authority, this is an example of _____ staff authority.

major

24 Furthermore, in many companies the division requesting and receiving advisory staff service is billed for the cost involved in conducting the study. Under such circumstances, line managers are likely to request staff advice for relatively [minor / major] problems.

seriously

25 When a budgetary charge is made for utilizing the advisory staff, the staff recommendations are likely to be treated [lightly / seriously].

No

26 When line managers must pay for staff advice, is the size of the staff organization likely to increase beyond the value of its contribution to company effectiveness? [Yes / No]

27 Thus, imposing a charge for advisory staff recommendations ensures that (1) line managers

do not   [do / do not] request staff advice for every minor
are   problem, (2) the staff recommendations [are / are
not] seriously considered, and (3) advisory staff
is   size [is / is not] consistent with its contribution to
overall company effectiveness.

28 Of course, one hazard associated with imposing a budgetary charge for the advisory activities of
a specialist staff is that line managers may request

infrequently   needed advice too [frequently / infrequently].

29 Whether or not a budgetary charge is involved, one approach by which top management
tries to make certain that specialist advice is considered by line managers is that of *compulsory staff advice.* Since this refers to advisory authority, does
the word "compulsory" indicate that line managers
must follow the staff recommendations in this case?

No (continued in   [Yes / No]
next frame)

30 The word "compulsory" in the context of advisory staff authority indicates that the specialist
advice must be sought before a line decision in particular areas is made, *not* that the advice in question
must be followed. Again, this is a way of assuring
that specialist staff advice will at least be considered

line   by _____ managers.

C SERVICE STAFF AUTHORITY

As the name once again implies, a staff group with
service authority is one that carries out some area
of activity that has been separated from the line job
as a service to the line. However, unlike the situation for advisory staff authority, if the activity in
question is to be carried out, the line manager must
do it through the staff organization, and is not free
to do it himself.

31 Using the area of purchasing as an example,
does a line manager typically have the authority to

Yes

decide what items need to be purchased for his department? [Yes / No]

In most
companies, he is
obliged to work
through the
purchasing agent.

32 Once the line manager has identified the necessary purchases, must he work through the company purchasing agent, or is he free to negotiate purchases on his own, if he desires?

_____

_____

_____

service

33 Thus, a purchasing department typically can be described as having _____ staff authority.

Yes (The line must
use the staff
service.)

34 Is line authority restricted to some extent by the existence of service staff authority? [Yes / No]

No

35 On the other hand, is a line manager likely to do a better job in a particular area of work than the staff personnel specializing in that type of work? [Yes / No]

purchasing agent

36 For example, the person who is likely to know more about sources of materials and supplies is the [line manager / purchasing agent].

more

37 Furthermore, certain economies of centralized operation make it important that the service staff be used. In the case of the purchasing function, assigning this activity to a staff group makes the availability of quantity discounts [more / less] likely.

compulsory

38 Thus, uniformity in procedures, generally more effective work, and economies of centralized operation result from the [voluntary / compulsory] use of service staffs by line managers.

D   CONTROL STAFF AUTHORITY

A staff group with control staff authority actually has the responsibility for controlling certain aspects of line performance. The staff unit involved usually acts as an agent for a higher line manager.

39   In the preceding sections, we have discussed two types of specialist staff authority. They are

advisory
service

_____ staff authority and _____ staff authority.

40   In contrast to these types of staff authority, a department manager who assigns the departmental inspection function to one unit has in effect assigned _____ staff authority to that inspection unit.

control

41   Is operating line authority restricted by the existence of control staff authority? [Yes / No]

Yes (At least it is at
the organization
levels below the
control staff.)

42   On the other hand, higher-management control of operations is [helped / hindered] by the assignment of control staff authority.

helped

43   Control staffs also help achieve a higher caliber of performance by line units. For example, rejection of a marginal product is more likely to be done by [an employee of the department / a member of an "outside" inspection unit].

a member of an
"outside"
inspection unit

44   The operating supervisor may see himself as being in the position of receiving "control" instructions from a higher-level line manager as well as from one or more staff specialists or staff groups with control authority, thus resulting in apparent [compliance with / violation of] the classical management principle of *unity of command.*

violation of

45   But the violation of the unity-of-command

principle may be more apparent than real in this case, since the decisions being enforced by the specialists with control authority were made [by the specialists themselves / by a higher line manager].

by a higher line
manager

E   FUNCTIONAL STAFF AUTHORITY

Functional authority is said to exist whenever an individual is given decision-making authority outside the formal chain of command, and for specified activities only. The manager who is assigned functional authority is a specialist in the area of activity involved, but he may be either a line or a staff manager. As contrasted with control authority, the individual with functional authority has the authority to determine the appropriate standards in his area of speciality, as well as having the authority to enforce these standards.

46   The authority of the safety director to issue instructions regarding installation and use of safety equipment involves the assignment of

functional   _____ authority to a staff manager.

47   On the other hand, in addition to his departmental assignment, the finance manager in a company may be given authority to specify the format of financial records kept by other departments. This is an example of the assignment of functional

line   authority to a _____ manager.

48   Refer to the partial organization chart in Figure 7.1 on page 180. How many of the managers have been assigned functional authority for speci-

Two   fied activities? _____ [number]

49   Over how many managers does the safety di-

Five   rector have functional staff authority? _____
[number]

50   More than any other type of staff authority, the assignment of functional staff authority re-line   stricts the authority of the _____ managers affected.

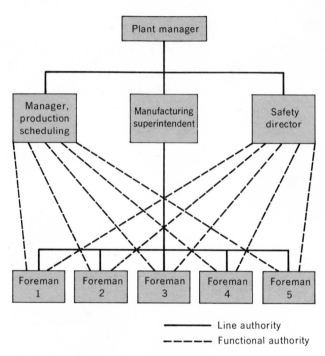

Figure 7.1 Partial organization chart illustrating functional authority as contrasted to line authority.

51 For example, in matters of personnel discipline, production scheduling, use of safety equipment, and the like, does the typical production manager have complete decision-making authority? [Yes / No]

No

52 When the company personnel manager requires plant managers to follow seniority in making layoffs, the authority of the plant managers has been [enhanced / diminished].

diminished

53 Similarly, when the controller requires periodic budgetary reports from company sales offices,

diminished

the authority of the company sales manager has been [enhanced / diminished].

enhanced

54 On the other hand, in the last example, the authority of the controller has been [enhanced / diminished] by the assignment of functional authority.

Three

55 Referring once again to Figure 7.1, from how many individuals does each foreman receive instructions? _____ [number]

violation of (since each foreman is getting directives from more than one person)

56 Again, the principle of unity of command states that every individual in an organization should receive instructions from just one superior. The use of functional authority tends to result in [compliance with / violation of] this principle.

Yes

57 Therefore, is it conceivable that extensive assignment of functional authority could seriously damage or destroy organizational departmentation and the basis for line authority? [Yes / No]

essential

58 On the other hand, the requirements of companywide coordination of activities and the necessity of common procedures because of governmental and labor-union influences make the assignment of functional authority [essential / unnecessary].

minimize

59 Because of the organizational effects of the extensive assignment of functional authority, it is considered good practice to [maximize / minimize] the assignment of functional authority.

60 One way of limiting the undesirable organizational effect of functional authority is by specifying that the functional authority of any manager shall not extend beyond one organizational level. Refer

to Figure 7.2. How many organizational levels are
there in all? _____ [number]

Five

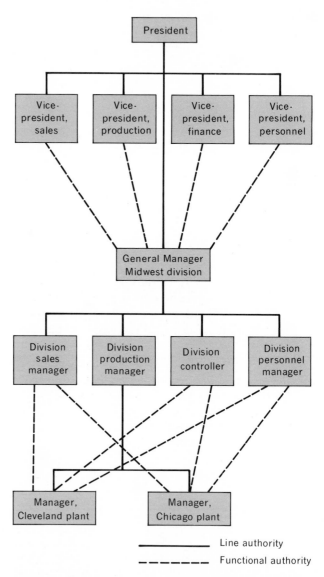

Figure 7.2 The limitation of functional authority to one organizational level.

61 How many organizational levels are affected by the functional staff authority of the vice president in charge of personnel? _____ [number]

One

62 How many organizational levels are affected by the functional staff authority of the division controller? _____ [number]

One

63 In summary, we have discussed four kinds of authority relationships between the specialist staff and the line organization: advisory, service, _____, and _____.

control; functional

64 List the four kinds of staff authority in order of the extent to which line authority is thereby restricted, beginning with the relationship involving the most effect on the line: _____, _____, _____, and _____ authority.

functional
control; service
advisory

65 When the staff serves the line by investigating problems and recommending courses of action for line-manager consideration, _____ staff authority is involved.

advisory

66 The situation in which the staff is assigned decision-making as well as enforcement authority over specific activities in its area of specialized competence is descriptive of _____ staff authority.

functional

67 A staff whose function it is to act as an agent of higher line management by supervising specific operations within the formal organization structure has been assigned _____ staff authority.

control

68 The situation in which a line manager has the authority to decide whether or not an activity should be done, and if it is, that it must be carried

service out by a staff unit, describes _____ staff
authority.

69 Is it possible for the same staff unit to be assigned different categories of authority for dif-
Yes ferent areas of activity? [Yes / No]

70 For example, a personnel department may
serve the function of advising managers in the
areas of executive department and of screening
applicants to fill personnel needs. In this case, the
advisory personnel unit has been assigned _____
service and _____ authority, respectively.

71 Overall coordination of company activities
and the formulation of procedures by functional
enhanced experts are [enhanced / impeded] by the growth
of staff authority in an organization.

72 Clear authority relationships in the organization and simplification of the organization struc-
impeded ture are [enhanced / impeded] by the growth of
staff authority.

F   LINE-STAFF FRICTION

Since the utilization of functional experts in organizations has resulted in the various authority relationships discussed in this chapter, it should not be
surprising to find that some degree of friction
often accompanies the necessary activities of technical staff units. In this section it is not our intention to propose solutions, but rather to identify the
source of such conflict by describing some of the
criticisms that each group directs toward the other
group. In part, the solution to such friction lies in
clearer authority assignments and in better communication, the latter being the topic of discussion
in Chapter 10. On the other hand, a certain
amount of intergroup friction and rivalry is normal in any organization and indicates that people
are at least interested enough to compete.

73 From the line point of view, staff people are often seen as *assuming too much authority, taking credit for good ideas, failing to keep line personnel informed,* and *seeing problems only from a specialized and narrow viewpoint.* The line manager who states, "The staff should realize that its job is to help us, not to tell us what to do," is in effect suggesting that staff people

authority   assume too much _____.

74 The line comment, "We get blamed for the problems in every new program until we get the bugs ironed out, after which every staff department claims it did the job," represents the line

credit   complaint that staff often takes _____ for successful programs.

75 The line observation, "Staff people keep significant facts to themselves so as to keep us off balance," is an example of the complaint that staff

line   personnel fail to communicate with _____ personnel.

76 "The directions I get from the quality assurance department take care of my quality problems all right, but at the expense of problems in scheduling and personnel assignment," illustrates

narrow   the point that a staff may have a [narrow / broad] conception of problems and solutions.

77 On the other hand, staff people perceive the source of difficulty in line-staff relationships quite differently. They feel, for example, that *the line doesn't make proper use of staff, the line resists new ideas,* and *the line doesn't give the staff enough authority.* When the line managers make decisions in specialized areas without consulting with them, staff peo-

are not   ple feel that their services [are / are not] being appropriately used.

78 The staff comment, "People in the line don't like to be involved with us because they'd rather do things as they always have," indicates that staff people see line personnel as resisting new

ideas (etc.)   _____.

79 "We have been hired to bring our specialized knowledge and skill into the organization, but we are then restricted to an advisory role only," suggests that staff people often feel that they have

authority   not been assigned sufficient _____.

80 Through this discussion we do not mean to suggest that line-staff conflict represents a serious problem in most organizations. For one thing, line and staff personnel frequently have broad areas of mutual and compatible interest, and for another, many organizational conflicts are not at all a matter of line versus staff. For example, friction between the manufacturing and sales divisions of a firm involves conflict between two groups typically consid-

line   ered as being [line / staff] in nature.

81 When people develop identifications with specialized work groups, some intergroup conflict is probably inevitable. Organizational action to reduce such frictions is desirable, however, when

disruptive   they become [competitive / disruptive] in nature.

G   THE PERSONAL STAFF

Whereas a specialist staff serves several components of the line organization, a personal staff, such as the assistant-to, works only with a single line manager.

82 Answering correspondence for the line manager, studying and recommending alternative courses of action, and acting as a liaison with other departments are typical duties of a member of a

personal   _____ staff.

83 Other titles in place of assistant-to include "staff assistant" and "administrative assistant." Would the title "assistant manager" also suggest

that a staff assistant position is involved?
[Yes / No]

No (This title would
usually be used for
a line executive
subordinate to the
manager.)

line

84 Therefore an "assistant manager" is typically a
[line / staff] manager.

85 In military organizations, a "general staff"
consists of a staff of experts who advise a particular
senior line commander. Therefore, a general staff

personal   is also an example of a _____ staff.

is not   **86** The authority of a line manager [is / is not]
diminished because of the existence of a personal
staff.

87 Through the assistance provided by one or
more staff personnel directly subordinate to him a
line manager is able to investigate organizational
problems and proposed solutions more

increasing   thoroughly, thereby [increasing / decreasing] his
ability to manage a broad scope of operations.

88 On the other hand, from the viewpoint of subordinate line managers, it may not be clear when a
senior executive's staff assistant is speaking "for
himself" as contrasted to speaking "for the boss."
Thus, a typical consequence of the extensive use of
staff assistants is that the decision-making authority

is not   of these individuals [is / is not] clearly understood
by others in the organization.

Review

89 Activities which are directly concerned with
attaining company objectives are regarded as

line   _____ activities, whereas those that are indirectly related to attaining company objectives are

staff   _____ activities. (Introduction to Section A;
Frames 1 to 9)

90   There are two general categories of staff activ-
specialist; personal   ity: _____ and _____.
(Frames 10 to 13)

91   What type of specialist staff authority leads to
the danger that staff recommendations will be al-
tered to please line managers and perhaps will
even amount to a "writing up" of line ideas?
Advisory   _____ (Introduction to Section B;
Frames 14 to 30)

92   That advisory staff personnel should submit
complete proposals for action, rather than partial
solutions,   is   called   the   concept   of
completed staff   _____ _____ _____. (Frames
work   17 to 22)

93   Once a manager has decided to take certain
action, such as hiring additional personnel, must
he do this through the unit having service staff au-
Yes   thority in that area? [Yes / No] (Introduction to
Section C; Frames 31 to 38)

94   A staff group, such as an inspection unit,
which acts as an agent for a higher line manager
control   has had _____ staff authority assigned
to it. (Introduction to Section D; Frames 39 to 45)

95   Whenever a manager is given decision-making authority outside the formal line structure, and
functional   for specified activities only, _____ authority is involved. (Introduction to Section E;
Frames 46 to 72)

96   Can functional authority be assigned to line as
Yes   well as to staff personnel? [Yes / No] (Frames 46
and 47)

97   The use of functional authority results in ap-
violation of   parent [compliance with / violation of] the principle of unity of command. (Frames 55 to 59)

one

98 In order to limit the undesirable organizational effects of functional authority, it is often specified that such authority shall not extend beyond _____ [number] organization level(s). (Frames 60 to 62)

service

control; functional

99 Of the four types of specialist staff authority we have discussed, list those that result in some restriction of line authority: _____, _____, and _____. (Frames 34, 41, and 50)

staff

100 From the line point of view, the cause of any friction between the line and staff components in an organization is ascribed to too much authority being given to the [line / staff]. (Introduction to Section F; Frames 73 to 81)

personal

101 In contrast to a specialist staff, the type of staff that works with a particular line manager rather than with a number of line components is the _____ staff. (Frames 82 to 88)

Discussion Questions

1. Since staff groups in a manufacturing firm do not directly produce or sell the product or arrange financing, why are they created?

2. Granted the need for staff advice and assistance, why should members of a staff group ever be given control or functional authority over line activities?

3. When a difference of opinion about how particular work should be done exists between a line manager, such as a production foreman, and a staff specialist, what advantages does the foreman have in this controversy?

4. In a controversy between a production foreman and a member of a specialist staff, what advantages does the staff man possess?

5. Contrast the organizational position and possible functions of a personal staff with those of a specialist staff.

6. Discuss the difference between control staff authority and functional authority, and describe the characteristics of the situation in which each would appropriately be used.

7. In a firm with geographically dispersed operations, consider the implications of your applying for a position entitled "assistant to the branch manager" as contrasted to "assistant branch manager."

8. If a large firm with production facilities located throughout the country tends toward a philosophy of managerial centralization, how is this likely to affect the formation of specialist staff groups in terms of (*a*) the location of such groups and (*b*) the extent of their development?

Case Study: Noncooperative Line Managers

As manager of personnel and industrial relations, Clyde Schoen was assigned principal authority and responsibility for personnel selection and training, and additional authority and responsibility to coordinate the company personnel practices in such areas as discipline and wage and salary management so as to assure a consistency throughout the company. In announcing Schoen's appointment to the newly established position several months ago, the company president indicated the advantages of a centralized personnel function at the present stage of the company's growth, and he urged all managers and supervisors to give the new department their full cooperation.

The president's directive notwithstanding, most line managers have failed to give Clyde Schoen very much cooperation. For example, when sending requests that new employees be hired, many supervisors are still not submitting associated job descriptions, which Schoen has requested be provided as a matter of routine. As a result, the personnel department cannot determine specific applicant qualifications in such instances but rather is forced to send the applicants to the department concerned for final selection. Of the eight employee dismissals that have taken place since Schoen assumed his duties, in only two instances did the supervisor request the action through the personnel department. In the other cases the supervisor simply sent a memo informing the personnel department of his action, with little, if any, explanation given. Realizing the necessity of working with rather than against line management, Clyde Schoen has tried to be diplomatic in reminding line managers of the necessity of clearing such actions with the personnel department, without much apparent success.

Most recently, Schoen spent several weeks devising a supervisory development program, originally suggested as an area of need by the company president at the time of Schoen's appointment. The program was scheduled for the last two working hours of each Monday, and the ten meetings were to be oriented toward a discussion of basic management principles. In his directive to the managers and supervisors Mr. Schoen emphasized the importance of the program and the president's expressed interest in it. When he entered the conference room for the first meeting, however, he found only nine of the company's thirty-eight management personnel in attendance.

Feeling both embarrassed and infuriated, Schoen has decided that the time for a confrontation with

line management has come. He believes that either
he must make an issue of this failure to comply
with his directive or see his departmental functions
degenerate. Accordingly, arming himself with a
copy of the memo that was sent to each supervisor
informing him of the supervisory development
program, he intends to present his case to the company president with the request that either line
managers be instructed to comply with such personnel directives or that the president accept his
resignation as manager of the personnel and industrial relations department.

1. Was line-management response to the actions
   and requests of the personnel department predictable? Why or why not?
2. How might Clyde Schoen have handled his relations with the managers differently?
3. What is the company president likely to do in
   response to Mr. Schoen's request? What should
   he do?

Case Study: A Choice of Job Offers

Walt Stander is scheduled to complete his bache-
lor's degree in business administration in June,
with a dual major in economics and finance. In his
course work he has particularly enjoyed the analy-
tically oriented courses, and included several
courses in statistics and accounting among his elec-
tives. By the end of March he was interviewed by a
number of companies at the placement center on
campus, and as a result of these interviews he has
three offers to which he has to respond by April 15.

One position which has been offered is as a labor
economist in the industrial relations department of
a large aerospace company. The general nature of
the position involves analysis of labor markets to
determine equitable wage rates, appropriate loca-

tion of new company facilities, and possible participation by the company in technical training.

The second position involves appointment to the management intern program of a large regional bank. In this program each participant spends the first year in various assignments in the central offices of the bank and is then assigned as the assistant manager in a branch bank in the second year.

The third position involves appointment to the finance staff of a large manufacturing company which is diversified in terms of products manufactured. The function of the group is to determine the methods by which the company's financing needs can be satisfied and to evaluate alternative investment opportunities. The entry salary level for each of the three positions is about comparable, considering differences in the cost of living at the respective places of work.

While Walt feels fortunate in having three good job offers, the existence of opportunities that are so diverse has created a decision-making problem for him at this point in time.

1. What professional, or type-of-work, factors should Walt Stander consider in comparing the three job offers?
2. What personal factors should Walt consider in comparing the three opportunities?
3. How could you describe the three positions in terms of line/staff activities?
4. If one of Walt Stander's objectives is to "get into top management some day," how do the three positions relate to this objective?

Suggested Readings*

Atchison, T. J.: "The Fragmentation of Authority," *Personnel*, vol. 47, no. 4, July-August 1970.

*Also see the cross-reference table in the Preface.

Baker, J. K., and R. H. Schaffer: "Making Staff Consulting More Effective," *Harvard Business Review*, vol. 47, no. 1, January-February 1969.

Belasco, J. A., and J. A. Alutto: "Line and Staff Conflicts: Some Empirical Insights," *Academy of Management Journal*, vol. 12, no. 4, December 1969.

Dale, E.: *Organization*, American Management Association, New York, 1967.

————— **and L. F. Urwick,** *Staff in Organization*, New York: McGraw-Hill Book Company, 1960.

Henning, D. A., and R. L. Mosely: "The Authority Role of a Functional Manager: The Controller," *Administrative Science Quarterly*, vol. 15, no. 4, December 1970.

O'Donnell, C.: "The Role of the Assistant: A Modern Business Enigma," *California Management Review*, vol. 2, no. 3, Spring 1960.

Chapter **eight**

THE ORGANIZATION AS A SOCIAL SYSTEM

A business organization is not made up of just a set of formal authority relationships, as the formal organization chart might suggest. On the one hand, the formal position that a person holds directly influences his status as an individual and the role he strives to fulfill in the organization. In addition, the existence of an informal pattern of relationships adds a new dimension to the organization that should be understood by a manager if the forces and efforts of these groups are to be directed toward company goals instead of away from them.

A STATUS

The term *status* refers to the relative standing of an individual compared with others in a group. Status is assigned by group consensus, and hence an individual living in isolation would not have a status position as such. Since many executive decisions directly affect the relative standing of specific individuals or groups in a firm, so-called "organizational problems" often are really status problems.

supported

resisted

1 We would generally predict that a decision that enhances the status of a group in the company will be [supported / resisted] by that group, whereas a decision that lowers the status of a group will be [supported / resisted] by that group.

more

2 There are several factors that determine the status of people in an organization. The most important factor in determining a person's status is his level in the managerial hierarchy, or *scalar status*. From this standpoint, a vice president generally has [more / less] scalar status than a department manager.

scalar

3 The authority to direct the activities of others is the essential feature of _____ status.

functional

4 As contrasted to scalar status, *functional status* is based on a person's job or area of activity in the organization. Although all the vice presidents in a company are equal in scalar status, they do not have equal amounts of _____ status.

functional

5 In a given organization, some work is bound to be considered more important than other work. The type of status based on the importance of one's area of work in the firm, as judged by others, is _____ status.

6 For example, in a manufacturing-oriented or-

higher

ganization the industrial engineer would probably have [higher / lower] functional status than a sales representative.

scalar

7 Thus, an individual's rank in an organization determines his _____ status, whereas the kind, or area, of work he does determines his

functional

_____ status.

8 In Figure 8.1, would you expect the overall status of the treasurer or the controller to be

Treasurer;
because he has
higher scalar
status

higher? Why?_____

_____

_____

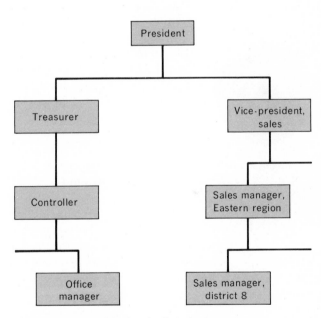

Figure 8.1 A partial organization chart.

9 In Figure 8.1, would a district sales manager or an office manager be higher in overall status?

Uncertain (See
next frame.)

_____

10 Thus, although scalar status can be inferred

functional

from the organization-chart structure, this is not the case for ＿＿＿＿＿＿ status, which also influences a person's overall status in a group.

11 *Status symbols* are used in all organizations as indicators of relative standing. Perhaps the most formalized use of such symbols takes place in military organizations, in which the insignias of rank directly indicate relative ＿＿＿＿＿＿.

status

12 However, even in nonmilitary organizations, there are numerous indicators of the relative standing of individuals. The size of an office, the presence or absence of carpeting, and the type of desk are all ＿＿＿＿＿＿ symbols among executives.

status

13 In many large companies, these status symbols follow a formalized system, so that all managers at a given organization level have similar offices, for example. Exhibit 8.1 presents a humorous but not entirely fictional description of a system of status symbols in business. Note that most of these "visible appurtenances" are such that they are arranged for, or supplied, by [the individual himself / the organization].

the organization

14 The fewer formal designators of rank that exist, the more important are the visible appurtenances, or status symbols. Thus, when the system of job titles used in a company quite clearly indicates the person's position in the management hierarchy, the status symbols are relatively [high / low] in importance.

low

15 Concern about status is not limited to the executive levels of an organization. Among operative employees, the location of the workplace, the type of clothing worn on the job, and whether or not a man owns his own tools can all be ＿＿＿＿＿＿ ＿＿＿＿＿＿.

status symbols

16 As organizations have become more complex and people have become more mobile in our society, the reliance on status symbols has generally [increased / decreased].

increased

17 Thus, many of the things we own are valued as much for their prestige value as for their utility. From this standpoint, high-priced cars, clothing that is "in style," and even certain foods all represent _____ _____.

status symbols

18 Even though the status system serves as a source of organizational problems, it also serves as a coordinating influence. Status systems facilitate cooperative behavior by conferring insignia and titles of office, thus making authority relationships [clear / ambiguous].

clear

19 Status systems also affect communication. The use of formal titles of office in business communication results in [more / less] disruption of communication channels with a personnel change in that office.

less

20 Furthermore, the existence of a status system can have motivational consequences in that the expectacy of attaining status can serve as an incentive for individuals in an organization, thus [encouraging / discouraging] higher productivity.

encouraging

21 On the other hand, undue concern regarding one's current status leads to *status anxiety*, or fear of lowered organizational status, which may have [positive / negative] effects on job performance.

negative

22 The failure of a manager to consider the significance of such "minor" factors as the office locations he assigns to his subordinates is likely to lead to status _____ for some of them.

anxiety (or
reduction, etc.)

23 Thus, by making authority relationships

EXHIBIT 8.1 *Status Symbols*

From Morris S. Viteles, "What Raises a Man's Morale?" *Personnel*, January 1954, p. 305. Reproduced with permission.

VISIBLE APPURTENANCES	TOP DOGS	V.I.P.'S	BRASS	NO. 2'S	EAGER BEAVERS	HOI POLLOI
Briefcases	None—they ask the questions	Use backs of envelopes	Someone goes along to carry theirs	Carry their own—empty	Daily—carry their own—filled with work	Too poor to own one
Desks, office	Custom made (to order)	Executive style (to order)	Type A, "Director"	Type B, "Manager"	Cast-offs from No. 2's	Yellow oak—or cast-offs from Eager Beavers
Tables, office	Coffee tables	End tables or decorative wall tables	Matching tables, type A	Matching tables, type B	Plain work table	None—lucky to have own desk
Carpeting	Nylon—1-inch pile	Nylon—1-inch pile	Wool-twist (with pad)	Wool-twist (without pad)	Used wool pieces—sewed	Asphalt tile
Plant stands	Several—kept filled with strange exotic plants	Several—kept filled with strange exotic plants	Two—repotted whenever they take a trip	One medium-sized—repotted annually during vacation	Small—repotted when plant dies	May have one in the department or bring their own from home

Vacuum water bottles	Silver	Silver	Chromium	Plain painted	Coke machine	Water fountains
Library	Private collection	Autographed complimentary books and reports	Selected references	Impressive titles on covers	Books everywhere	Dictionary
Shoe-shine service	Every morning at 10:10	Every morning at 10:15	Every day at 9:00 or 11:00	Every other day	Once a week	Shine their own
Parking space	Private—in front of office	In plant garage	In company garage—if enough seniority	In company properties—somewhere	On the parking lot	Anywhere they can find space—if they can afford a car

clearer, by minimizing the effects of changes in personnel, and by serving as incentives,

status symbols

_____ _____ facilitate the attainment of organization goals.

24 However, when people become worried and preoccupied about their current status, the result-

anxiety

ing status _____ can reduce their effectiveness in the organization.

B ROLE

The sociological concept of role concerns the set of behavioral expectations that apply to a particular position in a group. In a business organization, the formal position description is generally the most important, but not the only factor in determining the role. The informal organization and decisions made by the individual himself also have a hand in determining the role definition for a particular position.

25 The behavioral expectations that affect a particular position constitute the forces that deter-

role

mine the _____ for that position.

26 The individual is influenced by two major sources of role expectation in an organization:

formal

those spelled out by the company, or the [formal / informal] organization, and those determined by the groups with whom the individual is

informal

in contact, or the [formal / informal] organization.

27 As a result of these formal and informal influences, the individual attempts to structure the social situation and to define his place in it. This

role

process is called _____ definition.

28 Thus the expected behavior for a given position, as interpreted and defined by the person in role definition | that position, becomes the _____ for that position.

29 At least three factors, forces, influence the structuring of a role definition: the individual

formal

informal

himself, the expectations of the _____ organization, and the expectations of _____ groups.

30 *Role conflict* results when an individual is faced with two or more role expectations that are incom-

cannot

patible. The individual in question [can / cannot] satisfy both role expectations simultaneoulsy.

31 The nature of the situation and the personality of the individual involved both determine the

role

seriousness of _____ conflict.

32 From the standpoint of the situation, the more rigidly incompatible expectations are en-

more

forced, the [more / less] prevalent role conflict is likely to be.

33 From the standpoint of the personality of the individual, the greater his ability to ignore some of

less

the role expectations, the [more / less] severe his role conflict is likely to be.

34 Role conflict can have its source in any of the three forces that influence role definition, namely,

formal

informal

individual

the _____ organization, the _____ organization, and the _____ himself.

35 The foreman who faces incompatible demands for productivity from his line supervisor and for quality from a quality-control staff is in a

role

_____ -conflict situation stemming from expectations of different parts of the

formal

_____ organization.

36 A newly appointed supervisor who is faced

with incompatible behavioral expectancies both from his fellow foremen on the one hand and from his former coworkers on the other is faced with a

role-conflict

informal

_____ situation stemming from expectancies in the _____ organization.

37 On the other hand, the employee who must choose between satisfying management's expectations regarding his performance and alternative pressures from fellow employees is in a role-conflict situation which involves both the

formal; informal

_____ and the _____ organization.

38 A conflict between company job expectations and the individual's objectives regarding his occupational development involves a conflict between the expectancies of the _____

formal

individual

organization and the _____ himself.

39 In summary, a role-conflict situation is minimized and an individual's effectiveness maximized when there is compatibility in the role expectations of the _____ organization,

formal

informal

individual

the _____ organization, and the _____ involved.

C FUNCTIONS OF THE INFORMAL ORGANIZATION

In addition to the formal, or planned, pattern of relationships, there is a network of personal and social relationships among the people that make up any organization. Although activities in the informal organization are not under direct managerial control, they have an important influence on how well the organization as a whole functions.

positions

40 The emphasis of the formal organization is on the [people / positions] in the organization,

people

whereas the emphasis of the informal organization is on [people / positions] and their relationships.

41 Authority in the informal organization is given by those following the leadership of a particular individual, rather than by organizational assignment. Thus, it can be said that formal authority flows from [above / below], whereas informal authority flows from [above / below].

above
below

42 Since people generally prefer to maintain stable formal and informal group relationships, informal groups tend to [promote / resist] changes in either the formal or the informal organization.

resist

43 Accordingly, in fulfilling the function of *helping group members to attain specific personal objectives*, informal groups typically strive to [maintain / change] the status quo.

maintain

44 Therefore, managers who are planning to institute an organizational or procedural change need to consider the reactions to that change in the _____ organization.

informal

45 A second function of informal groups is that of *providing social satisfaction to group members*. Individuals who have little or no formal status in the organization may gain such _____ in the informal group.

status (recognition, social satisfaction, etc.)

46 For example, the informal group leader who is looked to for advice by other group members thereby attains a measure of _____ in the organization, although it may not derive from his formal job assignment.

status

47 A third function of the informal organization, in addition to helping individuals attain specific objectives and providing social satisfaction, is *communication*. The "grapevine" is made up of the

communication   channels of _____ that are
outside the formal system.

48 Because it often is successful in disseminating
information more rapidly or broadly than the for-
grapevine   mal communication system, the _____
is a phenomenon in all larger organizations.

49 *Rumor* is the content of the grapevine that is
not authenticated. In order to elimate all
grapevine   rumor, the _____ itself would have to
be eliminated.

50 Not only is elimination of the grapevine impossible, it is not even desirable. Although the
grapevine transmits invalid rumors, it also helps
rapidly (etc.)   to transmit valid information more _____,
thus making the organization more effective.

51 Futhermore, even though rumors may be
untrue, the content of these rumors provides
significant   information   regarding   employee
attitudes (or   _____ to the alert manager.
anxieties, etc.)

52 It has been found that attempting to eliminate
or track down informal communication channels
does little to dispel erroneous beliefs in the organization, but it may actually aggravate them. On the
other hand, prompt publication of relevant facts is
the most effective method of refuting invalid
rumors   _____.

53 It is generally preferable that the rumor itself
not be described when releasing facts to refute it.
Repeating the rumor can result in its being as well
refute   remembered as the facts that _____ it.

54 For example, if a recent company purchase of
land in another locality has led to inaccurate
rumors about production facilities being moved,

would

prompt release of the facts (involving, perhaps, company expansion plans) [would / would not] tend to dispel the rumor.

55 However, discussing the rumor along with the contradicting facts might [strengthen / weaken]

weaken

the effectiveness of the facts in refuting the rumor.

56 The fourth function of informal groups, in addition to helping individuals to attain specific

objectives; social

_____, providing_____

communication

satisfaction, and serving as a_____ medium, is *social control* of behavior.

social

57 The _____ control practiced by an informal group can be either internal or external in terms of the organizational location of those persons who are affected by such group pressures.

58 When group pressure is directed toward making members of the group itself conform to the

internal

group expectancies, _____ social control is involved.

59 On the other hand, in attempts to control the behavior of those outside the social group,

external social

_____

control

is involved.

60 The informal work-group activities designed to "keep the foreman in line" are an example of

external

_____ social control, whereas "kidding" a work-group member about the unsuitability

internal social

of his work clothes involves _____

control

_____ .

61 Essentially, we have in this case another example of the influence of the informal group on role definition. In our discussion of role, we concluded that the three forces that influence role definition are the _____ organization, the _____ organization, and the _____ himself.

formal
informal
individual

62 In summary, the four major functions of informal groups consist of helping individual group members attain specific _____, providing _____ satisfaction, serving as a _____ medium, and serving as the agency for _____ _____ of behavior.

objectives
social
communication
social control

D CHARTING THE INFORMAL ORGANIZATION

Company organization charts are used to depict the formal organization, but the informal organization typically is not charted in business firms. One reason is that the system of relationships among the members of an organization is always changing, so that any such chart would soon be too outdated for any managerial use. For those doing organizational research covering a particular span of time, however, it is useful to have a charting of both the formal and the informal organizations, in order to more fully understand the dynamics of the firm being studied.

63 There are two general methods of charting the informal relationships in an organization. The first, the *sociogram*, is based on analyzing the attraction among members of a small group. Therefore, the sociometric technique works best for studying the informal relationships within a [division / department / section].

section

64 Sociometric analysis is appropriate for studying informal relations in a small group. Typically, each person is asked for his preferences regarding assignment with work companions, or the actual pattern of contacts in the group is observed. The subsequent charting of these preferences results in the construction of a _____.

sociogram

65 Refer to Figure 8.2. How many people are there in the small group being studied? _____ [number]

Eight

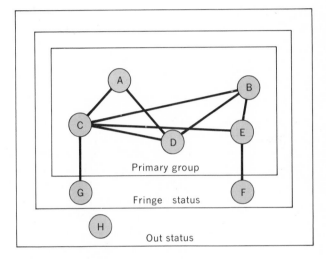

Figure 8.2 A sociogram.

66 Which person has the greatest number of direct relationships with others in the group and thus may be in the position of becoming the informal group leader, or group spokesman? _____

C

67 *Primary-group* membership involves being completely accepted by the other group members. How many individuals are in the primary group? _____ [number]

Five

68 The *fringe status* is unstable in that this is marginal membership which culminates in either membership in the primary group or complete separation. Identify the individual(s) who are in a fringe status in Figure 8.2. _____

G and F

69 Finally, the *out status* is made up of people, often called "isolates," or "loners," who are not members of the informal group, even though they are members of the formal organization being studied. How many isolates are there in this figure? _____ [number]

One

70 Fill in the answers without referring to the figure: The three categories of group membership from the standpoint of sociometric analysis are the _____ _____ , _____ _____ , and _____ _____ .

primary group
fringe status
out status

71 Research evidence indicates that small work groups assembled on the basis of sociometric choice are generally more productive than those assembled on an arbitrary basis. Would we generally expect within-group conflict to be higher or lower in sociometrically grouped sections than arbitrarily grouped sections? _____

Lower

72 Another approach to charting the informal organization is to diagram the pattern of informal interactions on the formal organization chart itself. Compared to the sociogram, would this method be appropriate for studying larger or smaller segments of the organizations? _____

Larger

73 Refer to Figure 8.3. The chart depicts both the _____ and the _____ patterns of relationships in the organization.

formal; informal

74 How many of the communication channels in the figure "violate" the formal pattern in that an individual has continuing contact with someone else's superior or subordinate? _____ [number]

Three (1–31, 22–33, and 23–35)

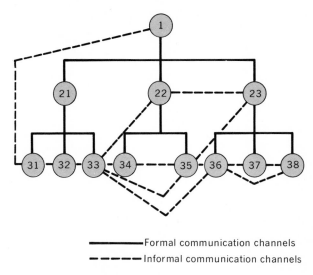

━━━━━Formal communication channels

━ ━ ━ ━Informal communication channels

Figure 8.3 Formal and informal patterns of relationship in part of an organization.

75 Would you expect that the organization with no deviation from the planned formal pattern of relationships would be more effective than one in which some deviation occurs? [Yes / No] Why or why not? _____

No; Too rigid (or slower communication, etc.)

_____

_____

E POWER AND POLITICS

From the standpoint of classical organization theory, the *power*, or influence, that an individual possesses in the organization should be directly equivalent to the amount and type of formal authority assigned to him. Upon inspection of the actual patterns of influence in all formal organizations, however, we would have to conclude that a number of other sources of organizational power exist. In this section we shall identify some of these additional sources of power and briefly consider their implications in company politics.

76   The total amount of influence that an individual has in an organization, that is, his total ability to influence the behavior of other people, is referred

power   to as his _____.

77   Whereas power is the total capacity to apply effective force and thus influence the behavior of others, one of the principal sources of this power is that which has been institutionalized and assigned

formal   by delegation of [formal / informal] authority.

78   However, in addition to the formal source of power a number of informal sources exist, such as *knowledge, ability to reward, place in the communication system,* and *uniqueness of skill.* For example, because of the information he possesses about salary levels at competing firms, a personnel manager is likely to have more influence than others as a member of the salary committee. In this case, the source of his additional authority is associated with his special-

knowledge   ized _____.

79   Indeed, it might well be said that "knowledge is power" in most organizations. In addition, a group with formal service authority may have additional organizational power because it can choose to give priority to some requests. The additional authority in this case is essentially related to the

ability to reward   group's [uniqueness of skill / ability to reward].

80   An employee who is difficult to replace because of a combination of talents particularly suited to the requirements of his position has a power source based principally on his [place in the

uniqueness of skill   communication system / uniqueness of skill].

81   The factor of *knowledge* as a source of power usually refers to information that the individual has collected or brought into the organization. On the other hand, when an individual is in such a position to selectively filter information passing through his office, he may gain power as a

communication
system

result of his place in the _____

_____ .

82 The informal sources of power that we have
mentioned have been given as examples and not as
an exhaustive listing. In addition to the relatively
impersonal factors that we have discussed, others
involving power gained through personal association might also be discussed. In that all such
sources of power are distinct from formal authority as such, they are classified as representing

informal   _____ sources of authority.

83 The term "playing politics" is often used to
refer to the use of informal sources of power for
the purpose of attaining certain objectives outside
the organization's standard operating procedure.
In addition, the term implies that the objective is
personal gain, although many writers in this area
would not limit the definition in this way. Thus, a
methods analyst who is able to "sell" a manager on
changing the work procedure in his department
through a combination of coercion, compromise,
and concession might be described as having
gained in his objectives by the use of informal

politics   sources of power, or playing _____ .

84 Unless a purely personal and selfish objective
is involved, political activity may well be constructive in nature. Whether organizationally constructive or destructive, the term "political" always indicates   that   objectives   are   being   attained

outside   [within / outside] planned organizational patterns.

85 Almost inevitably, patterns of alliances in the
organization develop in conjunction with the use
of political methods, with certain groups finding
themselves in a position of "natural" conflict. In a
manufacturing company, for example, those involved in the production and sales functions, re-

spectively, tend to find themselves in a position of

conflict
[alliance / conflict] with one another.

86 In addition to conflicts and alliances among the line functions, other areas of conflict and politics include competition between individual managers, between supervisors and subordinates, between line and staff, between staff activities, and between union and management. Should it be an organizational goal that all such conflicts be elimi-

No
nated, or at least minimized? [Yes / No]

87 The very existence of conflict can stimulate productive activity, and only when it becomes disruptive and destructive is it desirable to curtail such competition. Faced with the presence of conflicting views, political methods often provide the principal approach by which a manager can accomplish organizational objectives by the use of

informal
[formal / informal] sources of power.

Review

88 An individual's level in the managerial hierar-

scalar
chy determines the relative amount of _____ status attached to his position. (Frames 1 to 3, 8 to 10)

89 The importance of a person's area of work in a firm, as judged by others, determines the amount

functional
of _____ status attached to his position. (Frames 4 to 10)

90 Indicators of relative rank, such as the type of

status symbols
office and its location, are called _____ _____. (Frames 11 to 17)

91 Status symbols tend to make authority rela-

clear
tionships in an organization [clear / ambiguous],

fewer
lead to [more / fewer] disruptions in communication associated with personnel changes, and

encourage   when used as incentives, they [encourage / discourage] higher productivity. (Frames 18 to 20)

92   A continued concern regarding one's current status which tends to have disruptive effects is
status anxiety   called _____.
(Frames 21 to 24)

93   At least three forces influence the structuring
formal   of the role definition: the _____ or-
informal   ganization, the _____ organization,
individual   and the _____. (Frames 25 to 29)

94   When an individual is faced with two role
role conflict   requirements that are incompatible, _____
_____ results. (Frames 30 to 39)

95   Leadership authority in the formal organiza-
above   tion flows from [above / below], whereas leadership authority in the informal organization flows
below   from [above / below]. (Frames 40 and 41)

96   Informal groups help individuals in the group
objectives (etc.)   attain their _____, are a source of
social   _____ satisfaction, serve as a
communication   _____ medium, and are the agency
social control   for _____ _____ of behavior. (Frames 42 to 62)

97   The control that informal groups exert over
the behavior of members of the group itself is
internal social   called _____ _____
control   _____. (Frames 56 to 61)

98   A chart that depicts the informal set of relationships within a small group is called a
sociogram   _____. (Frames 63 to 71)

99   The other method of charting informal relationships, usually used for larger segments of the
formal   organization, makes use of the _____
organization   _____ chart. (Frames 72 to 75)

100 The total amount of influence that an individual has in an organization, whether formally or informally derived, is referred to as his level of
power   _____. (Frames 76 to 82)

101 The use of power to accomplish individual or organizational objectives outside the formal channels, often accompanied by alliances with some groups and conflict with others, is referred to
politics   as the use of _____. (Frames 83 to 87)

Discussion Questions

1. How is the sociological concept of "status" differentiated from the concept of "role"?

2. Why are status symbols important in organizations? What are some examples of such symbols in modern business enterprises?

3. Consider the statement, "An individual has many roles, depending on the situation in which he finds himself." Do you agree? Illustrate.

4. Why do informal groups exist in every organization? What functions do they fulfill for the individual and for the organization?

5. From the standpoint of sociometric analysis, three degrees of informal group membership can be described. What is there about the "fringe status" that tends to make this degree of membership unstable and short-lived? Exemplify.

6. When used in addition to a formal organization chart, what charting methods give a more complete picture of the organization? How are these techniques usually used?

7. Pressures from the formal organization have been blamed by some observers for a tendency toward overconforming behavior in corporations. Do you agree that the formal organization is the principal source of such pressures?

8. Should an executive be permitted to "get ahead" in a company by playing politics? Consider the pros and cons.

Case Study: Conflict Among Managers

The president of Amplex Mills sat at his desk in the hushed atmosphere so typical of business offices after the close of working hours. Again he had spent a great deal of his time with the managers of the purchasing and production functions, and he now tried to compare today's particular problem with others that had occurred in order to find a common thread. Yet the basic difficulty was not entirely obvious, unless it had to do with Dick Corbett, the manager in charge of purchasing, and his ability to work with other managers in the firm.

When the purchasing department was established two years ago, all managers concerned agreed with the need to centralize this function and place a specialist in charge. As George Morton, the manufacturing manager, saw it, it would free his supervisors from detailed ordering activities that could be better done by someone else. Wil Jorgesson, manager of marketing and sales, voiced the opinion that the flow of materials into the firm was important enough to warrant a specialized management assignment. Yet since the purchasing department began operation, it has been precisely these two managers—of production and marketing—who have had a number of confrontations with the new purchasing manager, and occasionally with one another, in regard to the way the purchasing function is being carried out.

From Morton's point of view, instead of simplifying his job as production manager by taking care of

purchasing for him, the purchasing department
has developed a formal set of procedures that has
resulted in as much time commitment on his part
as he had previously spent in placing his orders directly with vendors. Further, he is especially irri-
tated by the fact that his need for particular items
or particular specifications is constantly being
questioned by the purchasing department. When
the department was established, George Morton
assumed that the purchasing manager was there to
fill his needs, not to question them. After all, the
company's principal objective is the manufacture
of textile products, and all other activities within
the firm, including purchasing, should contribute
to this manufacturing objective, not detract from
it.

As Wil Jorgesson sees it, the purchasing function is
an integral part of the marketing function, and the
two therefore need to be jointly managed as a
unified process. Effective management of the
procurement function implies a concern with the
exchange function of buying and selling goods and
services and cannot therefore be separated from a
firm's overall marketing strategy. However, Dick
Corbett has attempted to carry out the purchasing
function without regard for this obvious relationship between his responsibilities and those of
Wil Jorgesson, thus making a unified marketing
strategy impossible.

In his previous position Dick Corbett had worked
in the purchasing department of a firm considerably larger than Amplex. Before being hired, he
was informally interviewed by all the top managers, including George Morton and Wil Jorgesson,
but it was the president himself who negotiated the
details of the job offer. As Corbett sees it, he was
hired as a professional to do a professional job.
Both Morton and Jorgesson have been distracting
him from this goal by presuming that he is some-
how subordinate to each of them, which he

believes is not the case. The people in the production department, who use the purchasing function most, have complained about the detail that he requires on their requisitions. But he has documented proof that materials are now being purchased much more economically than they were under the former decentralized system. He finds Jorgesson's interests more difficult to understand, since he sees no particular relationship between his responsibilities for efficient and effective procurement and Jorgesson's responsibilities to market the firm's products.

The president has been aware of the continuing conflict among the three managers for some time, but on the theory that a little rivalry is healthy and stimulating, he has felt that it was nothing to be unduly concerned about. With all three managers tending to be strong-willed by temperament, it would have been rather surprising if there were no conflict at all. But now that so much of his time is being taken up by much of what he considers to be petty bickering, the time has come to take some positive action.

1. Is George Morton's view of the situation realistic? Why? Why not?
2. How do you evaluate Wil Jorgesson's position?
3. How might this conflict be associated with factors in the formal organization? With power and politics?
4. What should the president of Amplex Mills do now?

Case Study: A Proposal for Product Redesign

Tom Malone is the Los Angeles field marketing representative for the Chicago Division of Acme Electronics, a multidivision aerospace firm. As a recently retired Army officer, he has many contacts in the military, and was hired to seek and develop markets for portable microwave equipment. In this capacity, he reports on a line basis to Bob Howard, division marketing manager, but on a staff basis to Tom Andrews, microwave product manager, whose products Malone is to market. Both Howard and Andrews are located in Chicago.

Malone approached his new civilian marketing assignment with enthusiasm. He contacted many of his former Army associates about portable microwave equipment. While these acquaintances were happy to see Malone when he visited them, only two had any need for microwave equipment. However, the equipment which they needed would require development. Malone believed that a catalog Acme microwave set could, with considerable redesign, meet the requirements for the two potential customers, and he prepared a report recommending that the division undertake the redesign. The report was replete with facts and sales projections indicating the redesign costs could be amortized and a high profit returned to the company in about eighteen months. This was based on a price of $30,000 per set, which Malone's contacts indicated would fit within their budgets. The funds for the redesign would have to be allocated from either the product manager's (Andrews') budget, or from funds under control of the division engineering department.

A meeting was arranged in Chicago at which Tom Malone presented his proposal to Howard, Andrews, and the manager of the division engineering department. These men, Malone learned, were at the same level in the organization. The following viewpoints were expressed at the meeting:

Bob Howard felt that the program should be pursued as proposed by Malone. (The business would fill a void in Howard's division sales forecast eighteen months from now. Howard's forecast was, he felt, a personal promise to management. The forecast had been prepared six months before.)

Tom Andrews was highly opposed to expending his funds for a project that would not generate sales in the current year. (Andrews' product sales for the current year were lagging behind his forecast to management made three months earlier.)

The manager of division engineering was in favor of developing a product, but not on the basis suggested by Malone. Engineering believed that a different, new-design approach incorporating integrated circuits should be adopted instead of redesigning a catalog item. The new design would employ the latest state-of-the-art techniques and would sell for $46,000. (Engineering had previously promised management that a new design incorporating integrated circuits would be released this year.)

As the meeting continued with no apparent progress toward a decision that would be acceptable to all three managers, Malone pondered whether he should have become involved with the proposal at all, or should have restricted his efforts to the sale of catalog items.

1. Should Tom Malone have restricted his efforts to catalog items, rather than developing a new product proposal?
2. How has the organizational position of each person in this situation affected his viewpoint?
3. How can, or should, the conflicting viewpoints be resolved? In what way may the present organizational design be inadequate in respect to such product decisions?

Suggested Readings*

Davis, K.: *Human Behavior at Work: Human Relations and Organizational Behavior*, 4th ed., McGraw-Hill Book Company, New York, 1972.

Filley, A. C.: "Committee Management: Guidelines from Social Science Research," *California Management Review*, vol. 13, no. 1, Fall 1970.

Graham, G. H.: "Interpersonal Attraction as a Basis of Informal Organization," *Academy of Management Journal*, vol. 14, no. 4, December 1971.

Greene, C. N.: "Relationships among Role Accuracy, Compliance, Performance Evaluation, and Satisfaction within Managerial Dyads," *Academy of Management Journal*, vol. 15, no. 2, June 1972.

Hilton, B. L., and H. J. Reitz (eds.): *Groups and Organizations*, Wadsworth Publishing Company, Inc., Belmont, Calif., 1971.

House, R. J.: "Role Conflict and Multiple Authority in Company Organizations," *California Management Review*, vol. 12, no. 4, Summer 1970.

Katz, D., and R. L. Kahn: *The Social Psychology of Organizations*, New York: John Wiley & Sons, Inc., 1966.

Miles, S. B., Jr.: "The Management Politician," *Harvard Business Review*, vol. 39, no. 1, January-February 1961.

Murray, J. A.: "A Sociometric Approach to Organizational Analysis," *California Management Review*, vol. 13, no. 1, Fall 1970.

Rizzo, J. R., R. J. House, and S. L. Litzman: "Role Conflict and Ambiguity in Complex Organizations," *Administrative Science Quarterly*, vol. 15, no. 2, June 1970.

Scott, W. G.: *Organization Theory: A Behavioral Analysis for Management*, Richard D. Irwin, Inc., Homewood, Ill., 1967.

Tusi, H.: "Organizational Stress as a Moderator of the Relationship between Influence and Role Response," *Academy of Management Journal*, vol. 14, no. 1, March 1971.

Whyte, W. F.: *Men at Work*, Richard D. Irwin, Inc., and the Dorsey Press, Homewood, Ill., 1961.

Zaleznik, A.: "Power and Politics in Organizational Life," *Harvard Business Review*, vol. 48, no. 3, May-June 1970.

*Also see the cross-reference table in the Preface.

Chapter **nine**
STAFFING
THE
ORGANIZATION

In the preceding chapters devoted to the function of organizing we have considered the structure of a business enterprise and the behavioral implications of the fact that people are involved in this structure. Our attention to the human element is incomplete, however, if some attention is not given to the process and methods by which people are selected for participation in the organization, how their performance is appraised, and the methods which can be used to develop higher-level skills. Indeed, some authors consider this process so important to managerial effectiveness that they classify "staffing" as a separate function of management, in addition to planning, organizing, directing, and controlling. Since this book is concerned particularly with the role of manager, the topics of selection, appraisal, and development are covered from the perspective of the operating manager, rather than from the perspective of the personnel manager. It is for this reason that such topics as the reliability and validity of personnel techniques and the use of personnel tests are not included in this chapter. Further, the discussion of staffing is restricted to the managerial positions in the organization, rather than all positions. For example, the discussion of developmental techniques is concerned specifically with management development. A more comprehensive development of these topics would require an entire textbook in itself, and several such textbooks are included in the suggested readings at the end of this chapter.

A ORGANIZATIONAL PLANNING FOR EXECUTIVE NEEDS

In order to provide the basis for determining what kinds of managers should be recruited and selected and the kinds of management development activities that should be carried on, it is necessary to identify the present status of managerial staffing and the projected need for additional managers. Therefore, in this section of the chapter we consider the general activities directed toward the objective of determining managerial needs and begin our coverage by describing the management inventory, which is a systematic procedure by which the present status of managerial talent can be assessed.

1 A *management inventory* should include not only a listing of presently assigned managerial personnel, but also their areas of professional interest and major accomplishments to date. In some companies, employees who already qualify for appointment to managerial positions are also included in the inventory. Thus, a management inventory [does / does not] need to be restricted only to those already occupying managerial positions.

does not

2 In fact, in some companies it is the practice to include all salaried employees above a designated income level in the management inventory. Given the nature of such an inventory, is it likely that the information contained therein would need to be updated periodically? [Yes / No]

Yes

3 In order to simplify the updating of the inventory and its use, a summary record is often prepared for each individual, as illustrated in Exhibit 9.1 on page 226. Of course, this information could also be entered on punched cards or magnetic tape, thereby facilitating computer analysis of the management data. As indicated in Exhibit 9.1, in addition to containing certain categories of personal data the record form is concerned with the type of _____ position that the individual can fill.

managerial

4 As indicated throughout the above discussion, the overall procedure by which the number and kinds of managerial personnel available in the organization can be determined is called the _____ _____ .

management inventory

5 Having established the current status of the managerial staffing situation through the development and maintenance of a management inventory, such needs can be projected for the future by considering the rate of *personnel loss* and the likely level of *organizational expansion* (or possibly contraction). Of these two factors, the one which is particularly related to the characteristics of present managers, such as their ages, is that of _____ _____ .

personnel loss

(Front Side)

James A. Miller

Birth date: 3/16/30   Service date: 9/15/65   Retirement: 4/1/95

Family status: Married, 2 children

Company experience: Assistant controller, 1970–present
                      Cost analyst, 1965–1970

Previous employment: Cost analyst, Hays & Co., 1960–1965
                       Financial analyst, Ford Motor Company,
                       1957–1960

Military service: Ensign and Lt. (J.G.), U.S. Navy Supply Corps,
                    1952–1955

Education: M.B.A., University of Michigan, 1957
             B.S. (accounting), Wayne State University (Detroit),
             1951

(Back Side)

James A. Miller

Professional interests: Financial analysis, budgeting, long-range plan-
                          ning, formulation of control systems

Outside interests: Boy Scouts, Kiwanis, professional groups in financial
                     administration

Health: Excellent

Summaries of recent appraisals:
   1972   Exceptional technical performance; some human relations
          training recommended
   1971   Has mastered fundamentals of the position of assistant con-
          troller and performing at acceptable level
   1970   Exceptional performance as analyst; promotion recommended
   1969   Exceptional performance as analyst; qualified for promotion
   1968   Above average performance in the analyst group

EXHIBIT 9.1   *Sample Management Inventory Record*

6 Personnel losses due to retirement and because of known physical disabilities can be predicted with fairly good accuracy. On the other hand, losses of managerial personnel due to resignations or because of individual desires to transfer to nonmanagerial positions are not as predictable on an individual basis. Therefore, for the latter types of losses an analysis of [personal / historical] data would be most appropriate.

historical

7 Overall, then, personnel losses due to such factors as retirement can be determined by reference to the personal data in the management inventory. On the other hand, the rate of loss due to resignations can be determined by reference to historical data in the company. Of course historical experience is not necessarily predictive of future losses due to such reasons as resignations, terminations, transfers, leaves, and deaths, but such data provide the foundation for a judgment about the future loss rate. In formulating such a judgment, such industry studies as the projected market demand for various categories of managerial personnel [should / need not] also be considered.

should

8 The projection of the need for managerial personnel should be based not only on personnel losses but also on the predicted expansion of the organization. Again, an analysis of historical data provides information of value for this purpose. Should such a forecast also include consideration of long-range organizational plans that have already been formulated but not yet implemented? [Yes / No]

Yes

9 Thus, we have indicated that two principal factors should be considered in projecting the need for managerial personnel in an organization. One is the anticipated rate of personnel _____ and the other is the predicted _____ of the organization.

loss
expansion (or
growth)

10 Most major corporations attempt projection of managerial needs at least several years into the future, with five-year projections being quite common. It is important that managerial needs be forecast as far in advance as can reliably be done because of the relatively [short / long] time period required for management development.

long

11 In considering managerial positions as contrasted to managerial personnel, the development of *position descriptions* for all such positions would be used for all three personnel functions of selection, appraisal, and development. As contrasted to the job descriptions prepared for operative positions in the organization, one difficulty associated with managerial position descriptions is that such positions are [more / less] structured.

less

12 Because managerial positions do not have the repetitive ingredient associated with most operative positions, the traditional basis of describing jobs in terms of physical activities is not applicable. For this reason, some firms hold the view that such positions cannot really be described by a formal and standardized position description. However, it is the viewpoint in this text that such positions can be described in terms of the responsibilities associated with the principal *management functions*, these being the functions of _____ , _____ , _____ , and _____ .

planning
organizing
directing
controlling

13 In addition to identifying managerial responsibilities, such a position description should also include the specific organizational objectives associated with the position and should identify any areas of technical skill or knowledge that are required. As indicated by the "common elements" included in Table 9.1, therefore, at least _____ [number] areas of information should be included in any managerial position description.

six

Table 9.1 Common Elements to Be Included in all Managerial Position Descriptions

1. Organizational objectives. What are the principal objectives of the organizational unit associated with this management position?
2. Planning. What are the areas of planning activity in terms of scope and time?
3. Organizing. To what extent is the person in this position involved in restructuring work groups, and what are the personnel selection, appraisal, and development responsibilities associated with this position?
4. Directing. How many employees are supervised directly and what types of motivational situations are involved?
5. Controlling. What kinds of control systems are associated with this position? To what extent are they a part of centralized control systems and to what extent do they need to be locally developed?
6. Technical responsibility. What technical areas of responsibility are included in this position, including technical knowledge required for successful management of the organizational unit?

14 In summary, the managerial position description provides the basis for carrying out the personnel functions of _____, _____ , and _____ for such positions. In addition to describing the type and extent of managerial responsibilities in respect to the functions of planning, organizing, directing, and controlling, each position description should include an identification of the organizational _____ associated with the position and the areas of _____ knowledge or skill that are required.

selection
appraisal
development

objectives (or
goals); technical

B USE OF INTERVIEWING IN SELECTION

Particularly from the standpoint of the manager as contrasted to that of the personnel department, a primary basis for selecting individuals for an organizational unit is the personal interview. Of course, such factors as previous job experience, previous levels of performance and present availability serve as the basis for determining who will be interviewed in respect to a position opening. In this section we consider the objectives of the selection interview, the principal types of interviewing methods which can be used, and common pitfalls in using interviews for the purpose of selection.

15 A selection interview is a conversation between two (or more) persons oriented toward possible job placement. Though it might thus appear that *personnel selection* is the only objective of such an interview, in the broader sense it is one of three general objectives. In addition to the employer choosing an employee, the prospective employee is also choosing an employer. To do so the prospective employee needs appropriate *information*, and therefore the second objective of a personal interview is that of providing _____ about the organization and its policies.

information

16 Whether or not a mutual job commitment is made, it is to the long-run benefit of the organization that the candidate leave the interview with a positive attitude toward the organization. *Developing a positive attitude* toward the organization and its personnel practices is the third objective of a selection interview. Whereas a description of the organization's promotion policies and fringe benefits would be associated with the objective of _____ , sincere attention devoted to the applicant's skills and potential would be associated with the objective of _____.

providing
information

developing a
positive attitude

17 Thus, the three principal objectives of selection interviewing are _____ _____ , and _____ .

personnel
selection;
providing
information;
developing a
positive attitude

18 The four types of interviewing methods which we now consider are the patterned interview, the depth interview, the nondirective interview, and the stress interview. We choose to use the terminology "types of interviewing methods" rather than "types of interviews" because of the fact that [only one / several] of these methods can be used within a single interview.

several

19 The *patterned interview method* is one in which the specific areas of information which the interviewer is to obtain are identified beforehand and usually are listed on a form. The interviewer uses this written form as a guide during the interview. Exhibit 9.2 on page 232 presents the first page of a standardized patterned interview form which has been widely used in conjunction with office positions. As indicated by the contents of this exhibit, such standardized forms are useful mainly for
nonmanagerial   [managerial / nonmanagerial] positions.

20 For managerial placement, the type of detailed information obtained by means of a patterned interview should already be available in the completed application form or in the personal resume. In contrast, the *depth interview method* is directed toward an in-depth exploration of the applicant's skills and the personal motives underlying his interest in the particular position and in the organization. For example, when a sales manager questions a prospective employee about his opinion of certain types of marketing and pricing practices in order to determine the extent of his knowl-
depth   edge, he can be described as using a _____ interview method.

21 Thus far we have considered the patterned and depth interview methods. A third type is the *nondirective interview method*. As used in the context of selection interviewing, a nondirective interview is one in which the interviewer asks very broad questions and leaves it up to the applicant to choose the direction of the answer. *What* the applicant chooses to talk about can be very informative in judging his motives and deciding how he will fit into the organization. "What have you learned or gained in your present position?" would be an example of the type of question used in the
nondirective   _____ interview method.

EXHIBIT 9.2 *A Form Which Can Be Used in Conjunction with a Patterned Interview (first page only).* Published by the Dartnell Corportion, Chicago. Reproduced with permission.

| 1 | 2 | 3 | 4 |

See page 4 for explanation

PATTERNED INTERVIEW FORM

Name_____For what position_____Date_____

How did you come to apply for this position?_____

What is your understanding of its responsibilities?_____
  Is his understanding of duties and responsibilities correct?

Its compensation and opportunities?_____
  Are his expectations realistic?

What are your principal qualifications for it?_____
  Does he omit ability to handle any important responsibilities of the job?

How soon would you be available?_____What are your salary requirements?_____

MILITARY SERVICE

Service in the Armed Forces? ☐ Yes, ☐ No. Present status_____

If rejected or exempted, reason_____Dates of service: From_____to_____

Branch_____; Rank at entering_____; at leaving_____; Overseas (how long, where?)_____

Combat (how long?)_____; Hospitalized (how long?)_____Reason_____

Degree of recovery_____; Eligibility for disability pay $_____. 52-20 Compensation_____(If yes) How long?_____

Type discharge_____. What do you think of service?_____As a career?_____

WORK HISTORY: Are you now employed?_____(If no) How long unemployed?_____What are you doing?_____

How are financing yourself?_____Unemployment compensation drawn?_____

LAST OR PRESENT POSITION: Company_____Dates: From_____19____to_____19____

Kind of business_____Where hired?_____Where now located?_____

How was job obtained?_____Work at start_____Subsequent duties_____
  Did he show self-reliance? Stability of interests? Does the work require energy and industry?

	Earnings:	Base	Incentive
_____Was progress made? Any indications of strong motivation?_____	To start	_____	_____
_____Indications of industry? Acceptance of responsibility? Leadership? Self-reliance?_____ Work at leaving	At leaving	_____	_____

_____Serious illnesses or leaves of absence_____
  Is he regular in job attendance? Indications of outside interests?

Last superior_____Title_____Age_____. Frequency contacted: In person_____by phone_____
  How close is supervision?

Authority delegated to you_____No. supervised_____
  How well structured is his job?

What supervisory problems have you had?_____How did you handle them?_____
  Is he an autocrat? Laissez-faire type of leader? Harsh? Fair-minded?

Compatibility with superior: Very much_____moderate_____not much_____. Why?_____
  Indications of loyalty? Hostility?

Most-liked features of job_____Least enjoyed_____
  Has he been happy in his work? Did he get along well with people? *Inclined to be critical? Justified in dislikes?*

Why leaving?_____Why at this time?_____
  Are reasons adequate and realistic? Does he give up in the face of difficulties?

Gainful employment on the side_____Activities between this and preceding job_____Unemployment compensation?_____
  Does this indicate financial need? Lack of loyalty? *Did he support himself? Did he want steady employment?*

NEXT TO LAST POSITION: Company_____Dates: From_____19____to_____19____

Kind of business_____Where hired?_____Where last located?_____

How obtained?_____Work at start_____Subsequent duties_____
  Did he show self-reliance? *Stability of interests? Did the work require energy and industry?*

Form No. EP-312-R-2

Copyright, 1968, The Dartnell Corporation, Chicago, Ill. 60640. Printed in U.S.A.
Developed by The McMurry Company

22 Finally, the *stress interview method* is a type of procedure designed to place the applicant under planned stress and, logically, a stress situation with ingredients common to the stresses included in the position itself. An example of using such a method would be to say to a sales applicant "So you want to be a salesman. Let's see you sell me this desk pen." Recall the three objectives of a selection interview. The objective that might be well served by this

personnel selection

method is that of _____.
The one which might be particularly adversely af-

developing a positive attitude

fected is that of _____
_____.

23   Thus, the type of interview procedure which is designed to put the applicant "on the spot" and which requires skillful use so as not to create ill will

stress

toward the organization is the _____ interview.

24   Overall, the four types of interviewing methods that have been discussed are known as the

patterned; depth
nondirective
stress

_____ , _____ ,
_____, and   _____
methods.

25   Having considered the objectives of selection interviewing and the principal types of interviewing methods which can be used, we now consider some common pitfalls in selection interviewing. These include the halo effect, bias, and the failure to listen. The *halo effect* describes the situation in which a single prominent characteristic of the applicant influences the interviewer's entire judgment of him. Thus, a neat and alert appearance

positive

can lead to a [positive / negative] halo effect while arriving late (or even arriving too early) for an in-

negative

terview can lead to a _____ halo effect.

26   It is of course entirely appropriate to consider specific characteristics of the applicant as being either positive or negative factors in respect to the requirements of the position. But when the interviewer allows some one characteristic to dominate

halo

his entire evaluation of the applicant, then a
_____ effect is said to have occurred.

27   Somewhat related to the halo effect is the factor of interviewer *bias*, in that the accuracy of the
interviewer's perception of the applicant is again
involved. Bias, however, is concerned with the interviewer allowing his personal preferences rather
than the position requirements to determine the
standards by which applicants are evaluated. When
an interviewer has a conversation with an applicant
whose interests and values are similar to his own,

positive

he is more likely to make a [positive / negative]
evaluation.

28   The implicit (rather than explicit) nature of
personal preferences and their role in selection can
be so pervasive that if managerial attention is not
directed toward this factor the organization can
come to be staffed only with people who have similar backgrounds and values. The resulting organizational homogeneity can be stifling to diversity
and creativity and is certainly contrary to the philosophy of staffing the organization on the basis of
skills rather than extraneous factors. For these
reasons, interviewers should be particularly con-

bias

cerned about the problem of _____ in the
selection process.

29   Finally, a third pitfall in interviewing is the
failure to listen. Many a manager who is supposed to
be conducting an interview finds it only too easy to
do almost all the talking himself. If the manager
identifies areas of information to be obtained
before the interview, he is more likely to ask questions which require the applicant to respond and
which consequently require the interviewer to

listen

_____ to the applicant.

30   We have identified and discussed three common pitfalls which an interviewer should be aware

of in the interview process. These are the

halo effect; bias
failure to listen
_____, _____, and the
_____.

C APPRAISAL OF MANAGERIAL PERFORMANCE

Once individuals have been placed in an organization their continued performance and progress should be monitored in some systematic way. Performance appraisal occurs whether or not a formal system is established for such a purpose. However, the validity of appraisals and their usefulness for making retention decisions, determining who is best qualified for promotion, and determining training needs is dependent on establishing a planned program for appraisal. In this section we first consider several traditional systems of appraisal and then consider recent trends in appraisal systems, including the so-called "goal-oriented approach."

31 The term "merit rating" is the traditional term used to describe the process by which employees are evaluated. Although the term is still used, there has been a general shift toward rating or appraising the "performance" of an individual, rather than his "merit" as such. Therefore the term
performance
_____ appraisal generally has come to
merit rating
be preferred to the term   _____.

32 Three possible approaches can be used to evaluate performance, as follows:

a. An unplanned and casual appraisal
b. The traditional and systematic evaluation of (1) employee characteristics or (2) employee performance
c. The goal-oriented approach emphasizing involvement of the person being rated in the overall process.

As indicated in the introduction to this section, the results of an appraisal program are not only useful for the obvious purposes of determining employee retention and promotion, but should also be useful for determining _____ needs in the organization.

training

33 An *unplanned and casual appraisal* may be adequate for determining employee retention, but it is certainly not analytical enough to yield reliable data useful for promotion and training decisions. On the other hand, a formal and planned appraisal system should yield such data. Further, we can also observe that a systematic plan also yields the type of data whereby the performance of individuals [can / cannot] be more readily compared.

can

34 Most appraisal systems used today are based on the *traditional approach* to appraisal. Within this approach, the emphasis may be on the individual per se (employee characteristics) or on what the individual does (employee performance). The traditional methods have shifted over the years toward greater emphasis on evaluating the employee against job standards and requirements, and therefore have increasingly emphasized the evaluation of [employee characteristics / employee performance].

employee performance

35 Table 9.2 lists several traditional methods of performance appraisal that have been developed and used. The first method listed, that of *ranking*, is the oldest and simplest system of appraisal. As implied, by this approach a manager ranks his subordinates according to their level of worth and their performance in the organization. Suppose that a manager observes that different subordinates have distinctly different areas of strength and weakness. From this standpoint he would find it [easy / difficult] to rank the individuals in terms of their performance.

difficult

Table 9.2 Some Traditional Methods of Performance
Appraisal

Ranking
Forced distribution
Graphic scales
Checklist
Critical incidents method

36 Other than the difficulty involved in ranking
individuals who have different areas of strength
and whose jobs may also be somewhat different, we
can also observe that the results of such an apprais-

do not provide   al system [provide / do not provide] data relevant
to determining individual training and develop-
ment needs.

37 Because of the weaknesses associated with the
ranking method of appraisal, another approach
developed was the *forced distribution method*. By this
approach, several categories of worth are established in advance, such as quality of work, punc-
tuality, and dependability. The "forced distribution" aspect of the system stems from the fact that
five grade levels are established for each characteristic, and a designated percentage of employees are
to be assigned to each grade level. Typically, 10 percent are to be placed in the top grade for each characteristic, followed by percentages of 20, 40, 20, and
10 for the remaining grades. Therefore, the subordinates   being   rated   are   essentially   being

ranked   [ranked / independently evaluated] in respect to
each characteristic.

38 If all employees happened to be very competent in respect to a particular characteristic, would
the forced distribution system indicate this fact?

No   [Yes / No] Would the results of such a rating program be useful for determining training needs?

No   [Yes / No]

39 The forced distribution rating system is predicated on the assumption that the subordinates being rated are approximately normally (symmetrically) distributed in regard to each characteristic. Therefore, to the extent that the system is useful at all it is more suitable for relatively [small / large] work groups.

large (With small work groups the percentage assumptions are difficult to apply.)

40 Thus, the appraisal system which is more analytical than a simple overall ranking, and by which the individual's general ranking in respect to each of several characteristics is indicated by the rater, is the _____ _____ system.

forced distribution

41 Because of inherent weaknesses associated with the ranking and forced distribution methods of appraisal, neither type of system is now used very much. The most widely used system of performance appraisal is that of establishing scales for each identified factor to be rated, that is, the *graphic scales system*. Figure 9.1 presents an example of a graphic rating scale factor. In this example, note that each individual who is rated would be [ranked / independently evaluated] in relation to other individuals.

independently evaluated

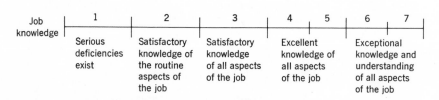

Figure 9.1   An example of a graphic rating scale factor.

42 Unlike the ranking and forced distribution methods, the evaluations entered on a graphic rating scale represent evaluations in respect to job standards, rather than in respect to other people as such. Thus, if the majority of those being rated are

would

relatively weak in some factor, such as "organization of work," such a situation [would / would not] be obvious as a training need in the appraisal results.

43   A graphic rating scale can be made up of a series of boxes or as a continuous scale, as is the case in Figure 9.1. One of the problems with graphic scales is that most ratings tend to be clustered toward the higher end, thus resulting in poorer capability of differentiating the performance levels of different people. Notice that in Figure 9.1 an attempt to gain better discrimination is made by "splitting" the rating categories at the

higher

[lower / higher] end of the scale.

44   It is the general practice to sum the ratings for the several factors being rated and to use this total as an indicator of the general level of performance for the person being rated. However, the meaning of such a total is questionable, since being rated high on "dependability," for example, does not really counterbalance being rated low on "job knowledge." Therefore, it is our viewpoint in this text

the rating on each
individual
characteristic

that the useful part of a graphic rating is [the rating on each individual characteristic / the sum of the ratings].

45   Though the graphic scales appraisal method appears very analytical and exact, it is rather difficult to use because it requires that many judgments be made by the rater. There is, therefore, the danger that the rater may simply "fall back" on rating a given employee consistently above (or below) average on all factors without regard to their individual meanings. As far as determining training needs is concerned, the resulting ratings

be of little value

would [still be of value / be of little value].

46   Because of the problem cited above, the *checklist method* was developed as an alternative to the use of graphic scales. A checklist is made up of a series of descriptive statements about the performance of the employee, and the rater checks (or indicates a "yes") for those statements that apply to the person being rated, as indicated in Figure 9.2. Therefore, from the rater's standpoint the checklist requires that the rater [describe / evaluate] the individual's performance.

describe

		Yes	No
28.	Completes reports on schedule.	____	____
29.	Follows through on areas of administrative difficulty.	____	____
30.	Tends to seek advice too soon when new problems develop.	____	____
31.	Does an appropriate amount of planning.	____	____
32.	Anticipates and corrects difficulties in achieving organizational objectives.	____	____
33.	Has a positive attitude toward the organization.	____	____
34.	Frequently needs to be motivated.	____	____

Figure 9.2 Sample items from a checklist appraisal form.

47 Even though the descriptive statements imply an evaluation, the rater's task is simply to determine whether each statement applies or does not apply to the person being rated. He can of course still choose to bias the rating. But since the levels for a factor are not "lined up" along a scale he is [more / less] likely to introduce rating bias because of a failure to read the individual items carefully.

less

48 The items included in a checklist are weighted with preestablished values in order to arrive at a total rating. This indicates that the relationship of each descriptive statement to overall performance is determined [before / after] such a form can be used.

before

49 Therefore, a considerable amount of effort is required to develop a valid checklist form. In terms of using the results of the appraisal for a postappraisal discussion between supervisor and employee, of the following appraisal methods the one that lends itself best to a constructive interview is the [graphic rating scale / checklist].

graphic rating scale

50 Thus, whereas the checklist is generally easier to use than the graphic scale, it tends to [increase / reduce] costs associated with the development of the appraisal system and to [increase / reduce] the bias included in the appraisals, and it is [more / less] useful for appraisal interview purposes.

increase

reduce
less

51 Finally, the last of the traditional methods of appraisal which we discuss is the *critical incidents method*. By this approach, instead of working with predesignated factors or statements the manager is required to be alert to particular areas of performance (or nonperformance) on the part of each employee on a continuing basis. These "critical" incidents are recorded by the rater and serve as the basis for the appraisal interview. Thus the critical incidents method is principally oriented toward [employee characteristics / job performance].

job performance

52 Further characteristics of the critical incidents method are that it [does / does not] readily provide an overall quantitative rating for each employee and that it [is / is not] useful for identifying needed areas of training or development.

does not

is

53 Since the identification and timely recording of critical incidents is crucial to the success of such a rating system, some training and motivation of the managers who are to use the system is required. Whereas use of the technique requires more of the rater's time, as compared with a standard graphic rating form, the performance areas

more (This is the
key idea in
identifying
"critical"
incidents.)

included by this approach are [more / less] likely to be those that are important in the particular job situation.

54 In this section we have discussed the ranking, forced distribution, graphic scales, checklist, and critical incidents methods as examples of traditional approaches to performance appraisal. Note that in describing the strengths and weaknesses of

have not

each system we [have also / have not] identified one of the systems as being the best one for all circumstances.

55 A relatively recent development in the area of performance appraisal is *goal-oriented appraisal*. From the standpoint of this approach, all the traditional appraisal methods are viewed as placing the rater in the role of evaluating and criticizing individuals from a position of superiority. The main feature of the goal-oriented approach is the mutual establishment of job-oriented goals and a performance review directed toward how these goals have or have not been achieved. Because the establishment of the goals is a cooperative endeavor, the approach is predicated on the assumption that

is

the employee being appraised [is / is not] oriented toward organizational achievement and that the

individualized

appraisal is made on a(n) [standardized / individualized] basis.

56 The characteristics of the goal-oriented approach are such that it is more appropriate for use

managerial

with employees in [operative / managerial] positions.

57 A primary strength of the goal-oriented approach to appraisal is that of [obtaining standard-

stimulating
self-improvement

ized evaluations / stimulating self-improvement] while a principal weakness of this approach is that

obtaining
standardized
evaluations

of [obtaining standardized evaluations / stimulating self-improvement].

58 Any appraisal system which does not provide a comparative evaluation thereby provides less information for decisions involving retention, merit increases, and promotion. But in positions which are not tightly structured, and in which self-improvement and personal commitment are important factors, the _____

goal-oriented

approach has been found to be useful as the basis for performance appraisal.

59 No matter what approach to appraisal is used, the appraisal interview is a typical aspect of most such systems. When the traditional approach to appraisal is used, the appraisal interview tends to be oriented toward [job objectives / evaluation]. When the goal-oriented approach is used the interview tends to be oriented toward [job objectives / evaluation].

evaluation

job objectives

60 The formal meeting and discussion between the rater and the employee, which is held in conjunction with a periodic appraisal of performance, is called the _____.

appraisal interview

61 Over the years, there have been systematic trends and shifts in performance appraisal. As indicated in Table 9.3 on page 244, such appraisals have increasingly come to be used for [promotion decisions / self-development], they have increasingly focused on [performance / personal traits], and they have come to involve [more / less] emphasis on quantitative comparisons.

self-development

performance

less

D   MANAGEMENT DEVELOPMENT

In this final section of the chapter we are concerned with two categories of activities associated with training and development: those that take

Table 9.3 Changing Emphasis in Performance Appraisal over
the Years

ITEM	FORMER EMPHASIS	PRESENT EMPHASIS
Terminology	Merit rating	Employee appraisal Performance appraisal
Purpose	Determine qualification for wage increase, transfer, promotion, layoff	Development of the individual; improved performance on the job
Application	For hourly paid workers	For technical, professional, and managerial employees
Factors rated	Heavy emphasis upon personal traits	Results, accomplishments, performance
Techniques	Rating scales with emphasis upon scores; statistical manipulation of data for comparison purposes	Appraisal by results, mutual goal setting, critical incidents, group appraisal, performance standards, less quantitative
Post-appraisal interview	Supervisor communicates his rating to employee and tries to sell his evaluation, seeks to have employee conform to his views	Supervisor stimulates employee to analyze himself and set own objectives in line with job requirements; supervisor is helper and counselor

SOURCE: Reprinted with permission of The Macmillan Company, New York, from *Personnel: The Management of People at Work*, 2d ed., p. 334, by Dale S. Beach. Copyright © 1970 by Dale S. Beach.

place on the job and those that take place off the job. The on-the-job methods which are described are coaching, position rotation, special projects, and committee assignments. Off-the-job activities include special training courses, management games, role playing, and sensitivity training. These are not all the methods and activities that are used, but they represent a sampling of the more important techniques. The off-the-job activities can be carried out within or outside the organization, as in university-sponsored management seminars. Formal courses that are specific to an organization, such as courses in organization policies and personnel practices, are appropriately conducted as in-house programs.

62 *Coaching* is the most frequently used method of on-the-job development. This approach is based on the viewpoint that day-to-day performance, with the aid of expert guidance, is a proper foundation for self-development as a manager. The use of this method of development places a particular responsibility for training on [the personnel manager / every manager] in the organization.

every manager
(since each
manager is
responsible for
"coaching" his
subordinates)

63 Of course, every supervisor is responsible for guiding and evaluating the performance of his subordinates in any event. But as compared with the guidance included in performance appraisal, for example, the term "coaching" implies a guidance that is [more / less] frequent and [more / less] formal.

more
less

64 One difficulty associated with coaching as a method of on-the-job development is one in which the manager may neglect the area of responsibility in favor of matters that seem more urgent. Thus the success of coaching as a training method is particularly dependent on the attitude of the

manager ——————————.

65 Another on-the-job developmental method is known as *position rotation*. Whereas coaching implies the development of knowledge and skill in [one / several] job(s), rotation implies a development of skill and knowledge in [one / several] job(s).

one
several

66 Generally, position rotation is used with relatively younger employees as part of a management development program. One of the advantages of

broad

position rotation is that by experiencing managerial responsibilities in several areas of the organization the junior-level manager has an opportunity to develop a [specialized / broad] understanding of the organization.

67 Two weaknesses of position rotation are the possibility of disruptive effects associated with transferring a number of people on a periodic basis and the attitude of the individual towards a job that represents a temporary assignment. One way of minimizing the latter problem is to ascertain

specific

that the individual is assigned [specific / general] responsibilities in conjunction with each position.

coaching
position rotation

68 Thus far we have discussed two on-the-job methods of development: _____ and _____ _____.

in addition to

69 A third method of on-the-job training is assignment to *special projects*. A special project involves an assignment outside the scope of the person's routine areas of responsibility. In order to avoid any disruptive organizational effects, such projects usually are assigned [in lieu of / in addition to] the routine areas of responsibility.

should not

70 Of course, when the special project is assigned in addition to the regular job responsibilities, the regular responsibilities [should / should not] be such that they require full-time attention.

position rotation

71 By participating in a special project, as for example studying the reliability and validity of a personnel selection procedure used in the organization, the individual has the opportunity to develop various areas of knowledge and to demonstrate his analytical ability in a variety of situations. In this respect the developmental experience has some similarity to [coaching / position rotation].

72 For projects that are particularly extensive,

several individuals may be assigned from different functional areas to form a task group, and the assignment may even be on a full-time basis for the life of the project. Such interaction would help the participants develop a [specialized / broad] understanding of the organization.

broad

73   The last method of on-the-job development we discuss is *committee assignments.* Such assignments have a similarity to the special projects discussed above, but differ in that such committees usually exist on a continuing basis and require less time commitment than special projects. For example, a cost control committee might include members of several departments in the organization and meet periodically to coordinate cost control efforts. In order to stimulate meaningful participation on such committees it [is / is not] desirable that member contributions be made known to each person's supervisor.

is

74   Unless it is clear that contribution to the committee's assigned objectives is a part of each member's job responsibility, such participation will be neglected in favor of the person's "regular" job assignment. Again, active participation in interdepartmental problems contributes to the development of a _____ understanding of the organization.

broad

75   We have discussed four methods of on-the-job development. The one which is concerned with the development of specialized skills in a particular job is _____, and the method which involves formal job transfers within the organization is _____.

coaching

position rotation

76   The on-the-job method of development which involves temporary, and usually part-time, assignment to work on a particular task is _____, while the method which includes meeting with a group com-

special projects

posed of individuals from several departments on a continuing but part-time basis is _____ _____ .

committee
assignments

77 The four off-the-job developmental methods which we now discuss are special training courses, management games, role playing, and sensitivity training. *Special training courses* is the broadest of these categories and such courses are usually concerned with specific areas of knowledge or skill. Thus, the required knowledge and skill to use a new budgeting procedure might be developed by means of a _____ .

special training
course

78 The method of instruction used in a special training course would depend on the areas of knowledge and skill being developed. If the course is concerned with informing managers about specific budgetary procedures, then the [lecture / case method] is likely to be used. If the course concerns the development of general problem-solving ability, then the [lecture / case method] is likely to be used.

lecture

case method

79 As is true for all the off-the-job methods, special training courses can be offered within the organization or employees may participate in outside programs, such as those sponsored by the colleges. For such areas as the study of employee motivation it is often felt that awareness of what other companies are doing is better developed by participation in a program [within / outside] the organization.

outside

80 The second method of off-the-job training which we consider concerns the use of *management games*. A management game, or simulation, typically involves the assignment of individuals to teams which interact as competing companies in a simulated industry. Each team makes decisions concerning such factors as production level, capital allocation, and marketing expenditure for each simulated time period. Thus, the training objectives of business games are principally concerned with the development of [human relations / deci-

decision-making   sion-making] skills.

81 Although the development of decision-making skills based on analysis is a predominant feature of business games, the interaction of individuals within each team and the necessity of "selling" team members on the appropriateness of certain decisions also has relevance for the development

human relations   of _____ skills.

82 The calculations which are carried out to determine the success of each team are quite complex in that they are based on assumed mathematical relationships among such factors as marketing efforts, price, and competitor's strategies. Therefore, the results in each simulated period of play are generally determined by [the teams them-

a computer   selves / a computer program].
program

83 What is learned by the experience of participating in a business game is also related to the type of debriefing discussion which follows the last simulated period of decision making. Rather than being preoccupied with "who won," particular management practices should be given attention. For example, it has been observed that teams which make specialized job assignments for team members (such as production manager) frequently perform better because of the resulting division of labor. Such an observation provides the opportunity for highlighting the importance of the mana-

organizing   gerial function of _____ in team success.

84 Whereas business games are concerned principally with the development of decision-making skills, *role playing* is concerned principally with the development of human relations skills, that is, the

people (etc.) skills involved in dealing with _____.

85 As the name of the method implies, in role playing each of two or more individuals is asked to assume a particular role and to interact verbally in a human relations problem situation. In effect, the method gives participants a chance to try out prob-

laboratory lem-solving methods in a [real / laboratory] situation.

86 For example, one participant might take the part of an employee whose work has been slipping lately while another takes the part of the manager in an appraisal interview. While the two participants interact based on their assigned positions (but placing *themselves* in the roles, rather than following stereotypes) other participants observe the appraisal interview and then discuss its strengths and weaknesses. Such a training session would be

role-playing called a _____ session.

87 Because a participant in a role-playing session has an opportunity to learn how his behavior affects other people, this technique, as contrasted to the techniques of lectures and discussions, can have a particular influence on the participant's

attitudes toward
people [attitudes toward people / knowledge about human relation concepts].

88 The last of the off-the-job methods which we consider is *sensitivity training*. Whereas role playing may have an effect on an individual's attitudes toward other people, sensitivity training is particularly concerned with self-awareness and self-knowledge as the key to developing social sensitivity. Therefore, of the training methods which we have considered this method is the most

psychologically [skills / psychologically] oriented.

89 A complete description of sensitivity training is beyond the scope of this text. In general, it involves participation in a small group—called a T (training) group—within an unstructured social situation and with an open and frank discussion of the behavioral traits of the participants. In general, therefore, the trainer acts more like [an observer / a teacher].

an observer

90 Although the trainer plays an outwardly passive role, he needs a thorough knowledge of human behavior so as to introduce subtle guidance to the group's activities during the several days in which such a group typically interacts. Furthermore, because of the nature of the interaction it is desirable that the trainer be an experienced [manager / psychologist].

psychologist

91 The psychological aspects of sensitivity training and the personal nature of the involvement have resulted in considerable controversy regarding its use. We include this method in our discussion not because of the extent of its use, which is rather limited, but because of the attention that has been given to this technique in recent years. Because of the type of involvement required in sensitivity training, such sessions are generally held [within / outside] company premises and are carried out on a [one-evening-per-week / live-in] basis.

outside
live-in

92 Of the four methods of off-the-job training which we have considered, the method best suited to covering specific areas of knowledge is _____, and the method which places the participants in a simulated and competitive business environment is _____.

special training
courses

business games

93 The training method which is concerned with developing human relations skills by providing the opportunity to practice such behavioral skills is _____, and the method which has been designed to help an individual to

role playing

sensitivity training

"know himself," and thereby also to know others better, is _____.

Review

94 The listing of present and potential managers, along with an identification of their areas of interest and organizational achievements to date, is called a _____. (Frames 1 to 4)

management
inventory

95 The two principal factors which should be considered in projecting the need for managers into the future is the anticipated rate of personnel _____ and the predicted _____ of the organization. (Frames 5 to 10)

loss (or turnover)
growth

96 A managerial position description should include an identification of the organizational _____ associated with the position and the technical skills required. Beyond this, the activities in the position might very well be described in terms of the four managerial functions, these being the functions of _____, _____, _____, and _____. (Frames 11 to 14)

goals (or
objectives)

planning
organizing
directing
controlling

97 The three main objectives of selection interviewing are _____, _____ and _____. (Frames 15 to 17)

personnel
selection;
providing
information;
developing a
positive attitude

98 The type of interview method which is concerned with obtaining specific areas of information is the _____ interview, while the one by which particular matters are explored and discussed in some detail is the _____ interview. The method by which the applicant has

patterned

depth

considerable latitude in choosing what to discuss is
the _____ interview, while the method
by which the applicant may feel he is being put
under duress is the _____ interview
method. (Frames 18 to 24)

nondirective

stress

99 Three common pitfalls in interviewing which
we discussed are the situation in which the interviewer allows a single prominent characteristic to
lead to a _____ effect, allowing personal preferences to influence the evaluation in terms of interviewer _____, and the tendency of some interviewers to do most of the talking and thereby
failing to _____ to the applicant.
(Frames 25 to 30)

halo

bias

listen

100 The traditional method of appraisal whereby
the rater lists the employees according to level of
performance is called _____. The
method in which the relative percentage ranking
of each employee is indicated in respect to each
factor, rather than on an overall basis, is the
_____ system.
(Frames 31 to 40)

ranking

forced distribution

101 The method of appraisal in which the employee is rated in respect to a quantitative scale
for each factor is the _____
method. The method in which the rater indicates
which statements in a prepared list are descriptive of the employee or his performance is the
_____ method. (Frames 41 to 50)

graphic scales

checklist

102 The method of appraisal in which the rater is
required to keep a record of notable instances of
job success and failure for each employee during
the rating period is the _____
method. (Frames 51 to 54)

critical incidents

103 A relatively recent development in the area

of performance appraisal by which the performance review is oriented toward mutually est-
tablished job objectives, and which is therefore
particularly useful as a way of stimulating self-
goal-oriented   improvement, is the _____
approach. (Frames 55 to 58)

104 The formal discussion between the rater and
subordinate which takes place in conjunction with
the performance appraisal is called the
appraisal interview   _____. (Frames 59
to 61)

105 Of the on-the-job methods of development,
the method which is most widely used and which
concerns the development of knowledge and skill
coaching   in a particular job is _____. The
method in which there is a planned series of assignments to different positions in the organization
position rotation   is _____. (Frames
62 to 68)

106 The on-the-job method of development
which involves assignment to additional research
studies or tasks that are not part of the usual job
special projects   routine is called _____.
The method which involves periodic group meetings with personnel from other functional areas in
committee   the organization is _____.
assignments   (Frames 69 to 76)

107 Of the off-the-job methods of training and
development, the method most frequently used to
convey specific areas of knowledge is known as
special training   _____.
courses   The method in which the participants are placed in
a simulated competitive environment and operate
business games   as executive teams is _____.
(Frames 77 to 83)

108 The developmental method in which partici-

role
playing

pants have the opportunity to learn human relations skills in a laboratory setting is _____

_____. The method in which participants meet as a group for a relatively extended period for the purpose of achieving better self-knowledge and awareness of social interaction is _____.

sensitivity training

(Frames 84 to 93)

Discussion Questions

1. What are the advantages of including all personnel above a given salary level in a management inventory, as contrasted to including in it only those who have actually been assigned to management positions? What are the disadvantages?

2. Position descriptions for operative positions are frequently concerned with the physical activities performed on the job. How does this relate to the appropriate content for a managerial position description?

3. Describe some of the interviewing methods that can be used by a manager and indicate the principal use of each method.

4. Differentiate the occurrence of a halo effect in an interview from that of interviewer bias.

5. What is implied by the term "merit rating" as contrasted to "performance appraisal"? What are the general advantages associated with using the latter term?

6. What are the basic differences between the traditional approach to performance appraisal and the goal-oriented approach? Which approach is most widely used today?

7. What off-the-job developmental methods are

likely to be found most useful for the purpose of upgrading technical skills?

8. In what ways are role playing and sensitivity training similar? In what ways do these training methods differ?

Case Study: A Management Development Program

The Roscoe Company began an extensive management development program several years ago. Supervisors at all levels participated in the in-company program, and in addition they were also encouraged to improve their skills by taking night courses at local colleges and universities at company expense. At the time the program was initiated and at subsequent management development meetings, the supervisors were advised by top management that the management development program was designed to improve the supervisors as managers and to qualify them for future promotions within the company.

Art Davis, a section supervisor, has been with the company for over ten years. He has diligently participated in the company management development program and has completed several night courses at a university in order to improve his knowledge of his job functions and the functions of his superior. However, twice during the last two years the company has hired outsiders to fill supervisory vacancies within Art's department. In each case Art and other section supervisors in the department had applied for the vacancy and felt that their experience with the company plus the additional knowledge gained through the management development program made them better qualified than the outsider who was hired. Art and his fellow supervisors question whether the management development program is worthwhile if vacancies are filled by outsiders.

At a recent appraisal interview Art brought up the problem for discussion with his department manager. He was told that in many cases no supervisor within the company is considered to be qualified for the managerial opening. Art expressed the opinion that the company management development program is a waste of time for the supervisors if the knowledge and experience gained are not recognized by higher-level management. Art's supervisor explained that it takes time to develop the supervisor for higher-level responsibility, but that individuals are rewarded for their self-improvement efforts by extra merit salary increases associated with the annual performance appraisals.

1. Should the company have given emphasis to the promotional opportunities which are to be associated with participation in the management development program?
2. How might the placements of the two managers who were hired from outside the company have been handled differently?
3. What is likely to be the effect of the response which Art's supervisor gave to his complaint?
4. What else might Art's supervisor have said as a more complete or appropriate response to his complaint?

Case Study: An Irresistable Job Offer

Ted Mason graduated from a large California university with a B.S. degree in marketing. He was interviewed on campus by a dozen or more national firms and received firm offers from several of them. Ted also talked to the owner-manager of a local San Diego food manufacturing company and was very impressed with both the owner and the work, as it was described to him. The owner of the firm seemed impressed with Ted and invited him to visit their plant and office facilities. After seeing the business plant site and talking with a number of the management people Ted decided that the offer to begin with the company as a sales management trainee was just what he wanted. The fact that his career with the company would keep him permanently in San Diego was important in his decision, since Ted's father operated a number of sports fishing boats with which Ted helped his father on some of his weekends, mainly because he enjoyed boats and deep-sea fishing. Also, living in San Diego would assure his staying close to his fiancee while she completed her studies at a local college.

Before Ted had given the San Diego firm his final decision, a large national food manufacturer with headquarters in New York called Ted and asked him to fly there to discuss further the offer they had made to him on campus. Ted had never been to New York and so, although he did not have a high level of interest in their offer, he saw no reason why he should not accept an all-expense-paid trip to see the big city. When he arrived, he was entertained and interviewed by the top sales executives of the company, which impressed him greatly. The sales department offices on the thirty-second floor of their world headquarters building gave an expansive view of the city and were quite impressive. The vice president of marketing for the firm made Ted an offer to begin in their management training program at a salary fully 30 percent higher than the San Diego offer. He would be in a trainee category for about six months, after which he would be guaranteed a sales management position at the beginning management level of sales supervisor. The vice president asked that Ted give them an answer to the offer as quickly as possible because they had other candidates for the job whom they did not want to take a chance of losing. Ted was highly flattered at the offer and the attention they had given him, and accepted the position. The vice president further explained that while there were two training slots open, one in Los Angeles and one in Pittsburgh, they wanted him to go to Pittsburgh because that slot had been open for the longest period.

Ted found conditions in Pittsburgh to be quite different from what he had expected. The style of life and types of outdoor activities in the area did not correspond to the things he liked to do. Ted was a good salesman and by working hard he struggled through the six-month training period with no problems being apparent to his superiors. His promotion to sales supervisor placed him in charge of the recruiting, interviewing, hiring, training, and supervising for five sales territories.

Ted first became frustrated and then quite discouraged when after only four months in his new job he found that his sales team was operating below the efficiency of all of the other four supervisory sales teams in the Pittsburgh district. Everything seemed to be falling apart. He couldn't keep his people, he had difficulty finding good replacements, and the morale of his men showed in the poor sales record they were establishing. In addition, Ted hated the ice and snow of the cold winters, to which he was not accustomed, and he missed the boats and deep-sea fishing of San Diego.

The real clincher came when he received a letter from his fiancee breaking their engagement and telling him she was interested in someone else. Not only did Ted Mason become disenchanted with his job but his superior, the Pittsburgh district manager, was also displeased with Ted and his lack of performance since his promotion to sales supervisor. As a result, the district manager passed up an opportunity to give Ted an anticipated merit increase hoping that this would shake Ted into realizing his need to shape things up. To Ted this was the final blow. The following day Ted wrote

his resignation and delivered it to his district manager.

1. What might be the cause of the low level of performance of Ted's sales team?
2. Basically, where did the problem begin? How
   could it have been averted?
3. Should the district manager accept Ted Mason's
   resignation? Are there any other alternatives?

Suggested Readings*

Beach, D. S.: *Personnel: The Management of People at Work*,
2d ed., The Macmillan Company, New York, 1970.

Brown, R. S.: "A Systems Approach to Management Development," *Financial Executive*, vol. 38, no. 4, April
1970.

Byham, W. C., and R. Pentecost: "The Assessment
Center: Identifying Tomorrow's Managers," *Personnel*, vol. 47, no. 5, September–October 1970.

Coleman, B. P.: "An Integrated System for Manpower
Planning," *Business Horizons*, vol. 13, no. 5, October
1970.

Finkle, R. B., and W. O. Jones: *Assessing Corporate Talent*,
John Wiley & Sons, Inc., New York, 1970.

Flippo, E. B.: *Principles of Personnel Management*, 3d ed.,
McGraw-Hill Book Company, New York, 1971.

Koontz, H.: *Appraising Managers as Managers*, McGraw-
Hill Book Company, New York, 1971.

Labovitz, G. H.: "More on Subjective Executive Appraisal: An Empirical Study," *Academy of Management Journal*, vol. 15, no. 3, September 1972.

Luthans, F., J. W. Walker, and R. M. Hodgetts: "Evi-
dence on the Validity of Management Education,"
Journal of the Academy of Management, vol. 12, no. 4,
December 1969.

McMurry, R. N.: "Avoiding Mistakes in Selecting Executives," *Michigan Business Review*, vol. 22, no. 4, July
1970.

Pigors, P., and C. A. Myers: *Personnel Administration: A
Point of View and Method*, 7th ed., McGraw-Hill Book
Company, New York, 1973.

*Also see the cross-reference table in the Preface.

Rowland, V. K.: *Evaluating and Improving Managerial Performance*, McGraw-Hill Book Company, New York, 1970.

Sheridan, A. J., and R. E. Carlson: "Decision-Making in a Performance Appraisal Situation," *Personnel Psychology*, vol. 25, no. 2, Summer 1972.

Thompson, P. H., and G. W. Dalton: "Performance Appraisal: Managers Beware," *Harvard Business Review*, vol. 48, no. 1, January–February 1970.

IV
DIRECTING

One of the most complex of the management functions is directing, or providing leadership. Effectively communicating with people and understanding what motivates their behavior are essential to achieving success in this function. In addition, studies of leadership success and supervisory effectiveness have enhanced our understanding of the personal and procedural factors that make successful management direction likely.

Chapter 10 is concerned with the communication process from the standpoint of the basic concepts involved, the types of symbols, organizational barriers to communication, the structure of communication networks, and the possible patterns of communication in small groups. The last two topics are related to the process of organizing, as well as to that of directing.

Some of the basic findings of psychologists regarding human motivation are summarized in Chapter 11. Included is a discussion of the categories of human motives, motivational conflict, and reactions to personal frustration. On the other hand, in Chapter 12, we turn to industrial applications of motivation theory. In addition to discussing the often misunderstood relationship between morale and productivity, we report the results of studies of motivation in industry.

Chapter 13 is concerned with some of the approaches that have been used in studying leadership success and the role of the leader in terms of various organizational climates and leadership styles. Included also is the leader's use of power through disciplining inappropriate actions. The contents of Chapter 14 are more specifically oriented toward the work of the first-level supervisor in terms of his role in the organization and the supervisory methods that have been found to be effective. Particular attention is also given to employee resistance to change and how such resistance can be overcome.

Chapter **ten**

ADMINISTRATIVE COMMUNICATION

The process of communication, that is, the passing of information and understanding, is a prerequisite for attaining desired changes in the behavior of subordinates and others in the organization. In previous chapters we have indicated the relationship between the organization chart and the formal chain of communication on the one hand, and the informal organization and its associated grapevine on the other. In this chapter, we begin by defining the communication process in general and identifying the four major elements involved in this process: the *sender*, the *receiver*, the *com-*

munication channel, and the *symbols*. The rest of the chapter builds upon these elements. The section on symbols in communication is concerned with some of the semantic problems in verbal communication, the section on barriers to communication is concerned with some of the factors that impede communication in administrative situations, and the sections on communication networks and communication patterns are concerned with communication channels from the interpersonal and organizational points of view.

A BASIC CONCEPTS

"Communication" is defined as the passing of information and understanding from one person to another. It is, therefore, an active process involving at least one sender and one receiver. Information and understanding are passed to the receiver, and knowledge of its effect is passed back to the sender in the form of feedback.

1 Of the two persons involved in the communication process, the *sender* is the one who typically initiates the contact for the purpose of passing _____ and _____ to the *receiver*.

information
understanding

2 Two other elements are necessary if communication is to take place: the *communication channel* and the *symbols*. These provide the basis for contact between the _____ and the _____.

sender
receiver

3 In an organization, the various contacts among organizational units and/or individuals can be represented by a system of _____ channels.

communication

4 *Symbols* can be of various types. However, in administrative communication, information and un-

derstanding are typically conveyed by the use of
symbols   verbal _____.

5 There would be no information flow in the
channel connecting the sender and receiver with-
symbols (or words) out the use of _____.

6 We have established, then, that the purpose of
information   communication is to pass _____ and
understanding   _____ from one person to another.

7 Would a discussion between a used car salesman and a prospective customer be a com-
Yes (The situation munication situation? [Yes / No]
conforms to the
definition of
communication.)

8 The four elements necessary for communication to take place are the sender, the
receiver   _____, the _____,
communication   _____, and the _____.
channel; symbols

9 The success of the communicative effort is
based on the extent of new information or under-
receiver   standing achieved by the _____. Can
we *directly* observe the information or understand-
No (That kind of ing achieved by another individual? [Yes / No]
X-ray machine
hasn't been
invented yet!)

10 Since the information or understanding
within another person cannot be directly observed,
the receiver's *behavior* provides the basis for judging the success of a sender's attempt to
communicate   _____.

11 The verbal explanations that the receiver can
give and the skills that he can exhibit are both as-
behavior   pects or examples of his _____.

12 Even changes in the receiver's facial expres-

sion or bodily gestures can be considered as
_____ effects.

behavioral (or
behavior)

13 *Feedback* is the observation by the sender of
the effect of his actions on the _____
of the receiver.

behavior (or
actions)

14 Consider an executive discussing a new procedure with one of his subordinates. Is feedback
available to him in this situation? [Yes / No]

Yes

15 Consider a lecture at a professional meeting.
Is any feedback available to the speaker in this situation? [Yes / No]

Yes (though not as
much feedback as is
available in other
situations)

16 Consider a political candidate speaking to an
audience via television. Is immediate feedback
available to him in this situation? [Yes / No]

No (although
delayed feedback
can be available)

17 In a sense, the passing of information and understanding in the reverse of the usual direction,
that is, from receiver to sender, is a description of
_____.

feedback

18 The sender's efforts to communicate can
result in one of three effects, in terms of the
receiver's behavior. A *desired change* may occur, an
undesired change may occur, or *no change* may occur.
Successful communication involves the occurrence
of a _____ change.

desired

19 Like successful communication, miscommunication involves an effect in the receiver's behavior, but in this case it is a(n) _____
change.

undesired

20 On the other hand, *no communication* involves
_____ change in the receiver's action from the
behavioral point of view.

no

21 Thus, when the desired effect occurs in the receiver's behavior, successful communication has taken place; when an undesired effect occurs,

miscommunication _____ has taken place; the absence of any effect on the receiver's behavior sig-

no nifies that _____ communication has taken place.

22 A supervisor reprimands a woman employee, and as a result she leaves the workroom in tears.

miscommunication The immediate effect signifies that [successful communication / miscommunication / no communication] has taken place.

23 A salesman makes a desired sale. This is an ex-

successful ample of [successful communication / miscom-
communication munication / no communication].

24 A supervisor gives instructions to accounting machine operators on how to prevent machine jamming. The following week he notices that the incidence of machine trouble has not changed. This is an example of [successful communica-

no communication tion / miscommunication / no communication].

25 The sender has no way of knowing what effect, if any, his efforts to communicate have had on the receiver unless he provides for

feedback _____ in some form.

26 The presence of feedback provides the basis for the sender to modify his efforts in various

successful ways in order to achieve _____
communication _____.
(etc.)

27 Since the success of communication efforts cannot be evaluated without providing for

feedback _____, we shall refer to this concept on several occasions in the remaining sections of this chapter.

B SYMBOLS IN COMMUNICATION

The very words that we use can be a source of strength or weakness in our attempt to communicate. *Semantics*, which is the science of language and meaning, concerns itself with the study of communication symbols and their meaning. Not surprisingly, it has been found that words do not necessarily have commonly understood meanings. Certain types of words are especially likely to have ambiguous meanings, and thus they lead to difficulties in communication.

semantics

28 The study of communication symbols is included in the science of _____.

No

29 Words have been viewed as cognitive maps. From this standpoint, would the map be identical from person to person? [Yes / No]

disagree

30 Consider the words "grievance," "management," and "work standards." It has been found that union stewards and foreman [agree / disagree] on the meanings of these words.

words (or symbols)

31 A staff man from the quality control department has experienced a great deal of difficulty in "getting his message across" to shop foremen. It is possible that the _____ he uses do not have a commonly understood meaning.

abstract

concrete

32 One of the factors related to the certainty with which a word can be defined is the degree to which it is *abstract*, as contrasted to *concrete*. A word that represents a concept is a(n) _____ word, whereas a word that stands for an object with a physical reality is a(n) _____ word.

concrete

abstract

33 "Table," "car," and "bolt" are _____ words; "struggle," "power," and "progress" are _____ words.

34 Successful communication is more likely when a relatively large number of _____ words are used in a message.

concrete

35 However, not all abstract words have equally ambiguous meanings. *Connotative* words point inward and signify aspects of personal experience, which leads to the greatest degree of ambiguity. Abstract words that express an individual's feelings or reactions are thus _____.

connotative

36 *Denotative* words have a strong reference to external events. Therefore, abstract words that refer to factors outside the individual are _____.

denotative

37 Connotative words, then, are directed _____, whereas denotative words point to _____ events.

inward (etc.)
external (etc.)

38 The abstract words "beautiful," "stimulating," and "fearful" are _____ words, whereas the abstract words "contract," "manage-ment," and "profit" are _____ words.

connotative

denotative

39 Rank the following situations from highest to lowest (ranks 1, 2, and 3), in terms of the amount of semantic difficulty likely to occur:

3   _____ Message with a high number of con-crete words

1   _____ Message with a high number of ab-stract, connotative words

2   _____ Message with a high number of ab-stract, denotative words

40 When the meaning of a word is uncertain, the *context* provides a *frame of reference* that helps define the word. Semantic difficulty is thus reduced when words or phrases are presented in _____.

context

41 As the number of abstract, and especially abstract connotative, words in a message is increased, the length of the message should be [increased / decreased] to provide more _____ as a frame of reference to give the words their intended meanings.

increased
context

C BARRIERS TO COMMUNICATION

Thus far we have considered the behavioral concepts underlying the communications process and the semantic factors that enhance or impede this process. In addition to taking note of such concepts and factors to improve organizational communication, we should also observe that there are a number of barriers in administrative communication that may have an adverse effect on the process. In this section we consider five such barriers: the pressure of time, psychological distance, filtering, premature evaluation, and the failure to listen.

42 The *pressure of time* is perhaps often used as an excuse for not communicating with others in the organization, but it is also a real factor affecting the opportunity to communicate. Take, for example, the relationship between a manager and a subordinate. Should every organizational decision made by the subordinate be communicated by him to the manager? [Yes / No]

No

43 The delegation of authority and assignment of responsibility to an individual would suggest that the subordinate should not really try to communicate every detail. However, suppose that certain actions represent exceptions to usual procedures. In order to keep the manager informed such actions [should / need not] be communicated.

should

44 If a subordinate were not to communicate such exceptions then the coordination of activities in the organization would thereby suffer and the stage would be set for potential embarrassment for the manager or for his subordinate. Thus, the principle of exception can be used as the basis for dealing with the fact that the pressure of

time   _____ affects the opportunity to communicate in an organization.

45 In addition to the pressure of time, another barrier to communication in formal organizations is *psychological distance*. From this standpoint, it is suggested that an engineer in the research and development department and an operative employee

are   in the production department [are / are not] likely to have some difficulty in communicating.

46 Although psychological distance is to some extent inherent in the different jobs, or roles, occupied by different people, the distance can be exaggerated by unwarranted use of status symbols. The more such symbols of office as private dining rooms, private receptionists, and differing office

more   furniture are used, the [more / less] difficulty is likely in communications between people at different hierarchical levels in the organization.

47 Therefore, the minimal use of status symbols tends to improve organizational communication by

psychological   reducing the barrier of _____ .
distance

48 The third barrier to effective communication which we consider is *filtering*. The process of filtering involves a biased choice of what is communicated, on the part of either the sender or the receiver. For example, if a subordinate "tells the boss what he wants to hear" filtering is said to have

sender   been done by the [sender / receiver]

49 If a subordinate identifies several factors affecting the productivity in a department, but the manager seems to hear and to respond only to those factors that fit his preconceived view of the

situation, then filtering is said to have been done by
the [sender / receiver].

receiver

50 Thus, the barrier in the communication process by which "selective telling" or "selective listening" takes place, with bias being inherent in the
selectivity, is called _____.

filtering

51 The three barriers to effective communication
which we have thus far considered are the pressure
of _____ the _____
_____ between sender and receiver,
and the use of _____ by either
the sender or the receiver.

time

**psychological
distance;**

filtering

52 Another barrier to effective communication is
the tendency that most people have, when listening, toward *premature evaluation.* Unlike filtering,
premature evaluation does not imply selective listening as such. Rather, it implies a tendency to
form an evaluation based on [excess / insufficient]
input.

insufficient

53 Although premature evaluation is done by the
listener, or receiver, the way that a sender organ-
izes his message may influence the tendency
toward premature evaluation. For example, if a
sender first states that there are four factors affecting department productivity and then discusses all
four in greater detail, the initial identification of
the number of factors tends to [increase /
decrease] the likelihood that the listener will form a
premature evaluation before all relevant factors are
discussed.

decrease

54 Thus, the tendency that most listeners have to
form a judgment before sufficient information has
been presented is called _____
_____.

**premature
evaluation**

55 Finally, the fifth barrier to effective communication which we consider is the *failure to listen*. Although this factor may seem to be an extension of the barriers associated with the pressure of time, filtering, and premature evaluation, what we have in mind in the present context is the attention that a listener should give to *all* content of a message, both emotional as well as factual. From this standpoint, a manager who responds to the facts included in a grievance and ignores an employee's

is not

obvious anger [is / is not] really listening to everything the employee is saying.

56 By the very nature of the complexity of the two types of content included in a message, the content which is more likely to be overlooked is

emotional

that which is [emotional / factual].

57 Overlooking emotional content would be bad enough in itself, in terms of the effectiveness of the communications process. However, such omission is particularly serious because the emotional content may be the only "real" content of the message. This observation suggests that a supervisor who restricts his attention to the "facts" surrounding a

wasting his time

grievance may be [acting appropriately / wasting his time].

58 In situations in which emotional content is prevalent, the listener's strategy should be similar to that employed in nondirective interviewing, as discussed in Chapter 9 on staffing the organization. Essentially, by encouraging an employee to elaborate further on his problem and to broaden the topic being considered, the listener is more likely

emotional

to gain an understanding of the [emotional / factual] content of the sender's original message.

59 The term "empathetic listening" refers to the hearing and understanding of emotional content.

Thus, the failure to use empathetic listening is what we have in mind when we indicate that the fifth barrier to effective communication in the organization is the _____.

failure to listen

D   COMMUNICATION NETWORKS

Whereas a communication channel is the medium by which information and understanding are passed from a sender to a receiver, a communication network on the organizational level is the pattern of contacts among decision centers. Along with the behavioral and semantic factors, the appropriateness of this network affects communication success.

60   The communication situation involving just two persons is the *circuit communication model.* In addition to the sender and the receiver, the circuit communication model includes not only the flow of information to the receiver but also the flow of

feedback

_____ to the sender.

61   Because the model forms a closed circuit, it has been called the _____

circuit
communication

_____ model.

62   Construct a diagram for the circuit communication model in the space below, including the sender, receiver, flow of information, and feedback in the diagram.

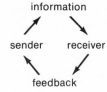

63   Because there are several senders and several receivers, an organization can be viewed as a

communication

_____ network. From this standpoint the organization is represented as a *sys-*

tem of decision centers that are *interconnected by communication channels.*

64 A system of decision centers interconnected by a communication channels is a _____ _____ .

communication
network

65 A communication network has two important elements: a system of _____ centers, and a number of _____ channels.

decision
communication

66 In Figure 10.1 on page 278, the communication network portrays [all of / part of] an organization.

part of

67 How many communication channels are in the figure? _____ [number]

Five

68 How many decision centers are in Figure 10.1? _____ [number] Which decision center has the greatest number of outgoing channels? _____ _____

Five

Sales department

69 How many feedback loops might there conceivably be in all? _____ [number]

Five (one for each
communication
channel)

70 If we were to study the relationship between just two of the decision centers in the figure, say between the quality control department and the production department, ours would be a study that would conform to the _____ _____ model.

circuit
communication

71 On the other hand, the diagraming of the total pattern of contacts in an organization, which can be used to evaluate or analyze communication flow in an organization is called a _____ _____ .

communication
network

72 As is true for the simpler circuit com-

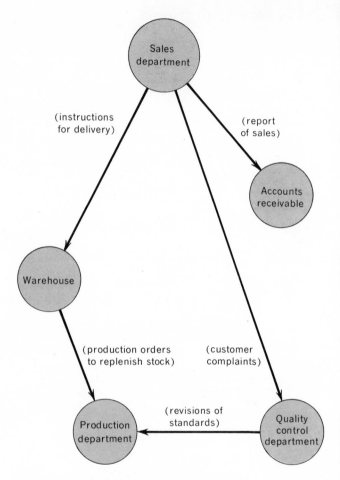

Figure 10.1 A partial communication network.

munication model, the sending unit has no way of knowing the effects of its communication efforts

feedback   unless it provides for _____ .

73 In organizational terms, *control action* on the part of decision centers is dependent on the avail-

feedback   ability of _____ .

74 Without feedback, the organizational effect of

unknown   earlier decisions would be [known / unknown], and effective control action would not be possible.

75 A delay of feedback to communications efforts within an organization leads to less effective

control _____ action on the part of decision centers.

76 A sales manager issues new instructions governing expense-account spending. When he obtains the consolidated reports at the end of the month, he realizes that his instructions were inappropriately followed. In this case, the

delay _____ in feedback has led to slower discovery of the miscommunication.

77 A supervisor follows the practice of asking subordinates to give their interpretation of assignments that he has made. He is thus attempting to

feedback hasten _____ for the purpose of more

control effective _____ action.

E COMMUNICATION PATTERNS IN SMALL GROUPS

In most of the coverage included in this chapter we have concentrated on the two-person communication situation, particularly as it is represented by the circuit communication model. Even the communication network itself was viewed largely in the context of studying one channel at a time, along with the associated feedback. In this section of the chapter we describe the results of classic research aimed at evaluating the organizational consequences of different communication patterns, or networks, in small-group problem-solving situations.

78 Figure 10.2 portrays three of the principal communication patterns used by Bavelas and others in investigating problem-solving behavior by five-person groups; these are the *circular, chain,* and *centralized* patterns. The pattern in which every person has someone "to each side of him" with whom he can communicate is the

circular _____ pattern.

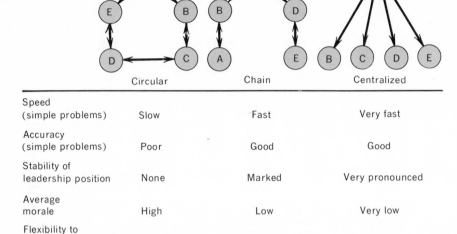

	Circular	Chain	Centralized
Speed (simple problems)	Slow	Fast	Very fast
Accuracy (simple problems)	Poor	Good	Good
Stability of leadership position	None	Marked	Very pronounced
Average morale	High	Low	Very low
Flexibility to problem change	High	Low	Low

Figure 10.2 The influence of different communication patterns on problem-solving performance of small groups. (Adapted from Alex Bavelas and Dermot Barrett, "An Experimental Approach to Organizational Communication," *Personnel,* vol. 27, no. 5, pp. 366-371, March 1951. Reproduced with permission.)

79 The pattern that is similar to the circular, except that two people find themselves "at the end" of the communication network and therefore can communicate with only one other person, is the

chain _____ pattern.

80 The pattern in which one person is in a key position because all communications must be with him or must pass through him is the

centralized _____ pattern.

81 Using these patterns, groups of people were assigned problem-solving tasks in which the information needed to solve the problem was distributed among all members of the group. As indicated in Figure 10.2, the communication pattern which was generally fastest and most accurate for

centralized simple problems was the _____ pattern.

82 On the other hand, the pattern in which the average morale level was the highest and for which adaptability to a change in the problem was most rapid was the _____ pattern.

circular

83 Since none of these small-group patterns can represent the full complexity of formal communication networks in organizations, the findings need to be interpreted with some caution. However, as examples of "pure" types of patterns the results indicate that the problem-solving objectives of "speed," as well as "flexibility," [can / cannot] be achieved by the same pattern.

cannot

84 Rather, the results indicate that speed can be achieved at the expense of flexibility, and vice versa, and that communication patterns should be designed with reference to the objective that is considered most important. In the case of these experiments we might note that the pattern with the highest speed has the [largest / smallest] number of active participants in the final decision process.

smallest
(Essentially, there are four transmitters of information and one decision maker.)

85 The pattern which results in the highest average morale level and greatest flexibility in the face of changed conditions is the one with the [largest / smallest] number of active participants in the decision process.

largest

86 As is also indicated in Figure 10.2, a person's position in a communication pattern can determine his leadership role. Of the three patterns, the one in which the leader emerges most rapidly is the _____ pattern, and he emerges specifically at the position identified by the letter _____ .

centralized

A

87 The pattern for which the position of the leader is entirely unpredictable is the _____ pattern.

circular

88 As another example of the importance of position in a communication network, refer to Figure 10.3. This could represent a senior corporate officer, A, who communicates with corporate officers C, D, and E only through his assistant, B. Viewed as a communication pattern, the key organizational position in this case is at the one identified by the letter _____.

B (He is the only one with direct access to all information.)

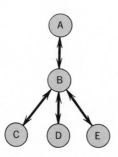

Figure 10.3 A communication pattern in a small group.

Review

89 Communication is defined as the passing of _____ and _____ from one person to another. (Frames 1 to 6)

information
understanding

90 The four elements that are necessary for communication to take place are the _____, _____, _____, and _____. (Frames 2 to 8.

sender;
receiver; channel
symbols

91 The ultimate success of a communicative effort depends on the effect it has on the receiver's _____ . (Frames 9 to 17)

behavior (or
actions)

92 When the desired change occurs in the receiver's behavior, _____ communication has taken place. When an undesired

successful

miscommunication

no communication

change occurs, _____ has taken place. Finally, the absence of a change signifies that _____ has taken place. (Frames 18 to 27)

semantics

93 The science of language and meaning is called _____ . (Frames 28 to 31)

concrete

abstract

94 Words that stand for objects with a physical reality are _____ , whereas words that stand for concepts are _____ . (Frames 32 to 39)

connotative

denotative

95 Words that point inward, or describe inner experiences of the sender, are _____ , whereas words that refer to externally oriented concepts or objects are _____ . (Frames 35 to 39)

abstract

connotative

96 The words that are most difficult to define precisely are those that are both _____ and _____ . (Frames 32 to 41)

time

psychological

distance

97 Among the barriers to communication which were discussed, the opportunity to communicate is limited because of the pressure of _____ . The extensive use of status symbols is not conducive to enhancing communication because of the associated increase in _____ _____. (Frames 42 to 47)

filtering

premature

evaluation

98 The "selective telling" or "selective listening" that may take place during communication describes the barrier called _____ . The tendency that listeners have to arrive at judgments before all relevant information has been presented is called _____ _____ . (Frames 48 to 54)

99 The barrier referred to as the failure to listen identifies the failure to use empathetic listening during the communications process. In turn, this indicates that in addition to the factual content of a message the listener should also be alert to the

emotional

_____ content. (Frames 55 to 59)

100   A sender, a receiver, a flow of information to the receiver, and a flow of feedback to the sender

circuit
communication

are included in the _____

_____ model. (Frames 60 to 62)

101   "A system of decision centers interconnected by communication channels" defines a

communication
network

_____ _____ .

(Frames 63 to 71)

102   Timely and effective control action on the part of the decision centers in an organization is

feedback

dependent on the availability of _____ to their communicative efforts. (Frames 72 to 77)

103   The small-group communication pattern which has been found to be the fastest and most accurate for simple problems is the

centralized

_____ pattern, whereas the one with the highest average morale, as well as the most flexibility in the face of changing conditions, is the

circular

_____ pattern. (Frames 78 to 88)

Discussion Questions

1.   From the so-called cognitive point of view, communication results in a change in understanding; from the behavioral point of view, it results in a change in performance. Compare these two approaches as ways of explaining what "really" happens during communication.

2.   Why is filtering particularly troublesome as a barrier in administrative communication? What can a manager do to reduce this barrier?

3. During the discussion of barriers to communication it was suggested that not only may an orientation toward the "facts" in a supervisory situation be an incomplete approach, but it may also be misdirected. Do you agree or disagree? Elaborate.

4. What types of words tend to lead to the most semantic difficulty? Why?

5. Comment on the statement, "The circuit communication model is the basic structural element that is included in all complex communication situations."

6. Referring to the major elements that are necessary for communication to take place (sender, receiver, channel, and symbols), give examples of communication failures that can be traced to each of these elements.

7. Describe an organizational situation in which something like the centralized communication pattern might be most appropriate and compare it with a situation in which the circular pattern might be better.

8. From the behavioral point of view, the availability of feedback to the sender is considered to be a key factor affecting the success of communication. In this context, what is feedback and why is it important?

Case Study: A Problem in Listening

In the Beaver Falls Power Company, two of the sessions in the fifteen-session supervisory development program are concerned with the topic of communication and its importance in managerial success. Near the end of the first session, Jim Crane, foreman in the maintenance department, volunteered the comment that even though he found the topic to be interesting and agreed that it was important, something vital was missing in the company's training program. "As a supervisor, my problem is that people just don't know how to listen," he said. "With a lot of my men, after I spend a great deal of effort instructing them as to exactly what to do, they're just as likely to be doing something entirely different when I check on their progress later. What we should do is set up a course in good listening and have all our employees take it."

1. Do you agree with Jim Crane that communication can be improved by having people develop better listening skills? Should such a course be offered in the company?
2. In any communication situation, who has ultimate responsibility for communication success or failure? Why?
3. Do you think Mr. Crane is effective as a communicator? How might he improve?

Case Study: The Misinformed Supervisor

Mr. Henry Macon, president of the Food Processing Corp., was regarding with acute distress a summary given to him by John Haeningsen, director of personnel. The facts in the summary follow.

Three of the senior staff members in the research and development department have announced their intention to leave the company within thirty days. Further, in the course of a confidential survey conducted by Jack Haeningsen, four more have indicated that they are looking for other positions, and three others have expressed serious dissatisfaction with "the way things are going around here."

The Food Processing Corp. was founded in 1933 by Mr. Macon's father as a marketing organization for disposing of excess and surplus food products, mainly potatoes, which constituted a glut on the market during the depressed period of the thirties. The imaginative Senior Macon, realizing the need for new areas to develop in marketing, had hired a research chemist who developed an economical process for converting potatoes into low-cost industrial alcohol. Convinced of the profits to be gained through the sound application and marketing of research, father and son had persevered until, by 1968, they were principal stockholders of a substantial organization which was involved in the production of a large variety of food products with the emphasis still on potatoes, and with marketing activities encompassing military and commercial customers over the entire United States.

The firm employs 1,200 people, of whom sixty-five are chemists, engineers, and technicians involved in research and development. William Parsons is assistant general manager in charge of R&D, with over twenty-five years of experience in food-processing research.

Three months earlier, Parsons had promoted Kenneth Bullitt to the position of R&D section chief on military and government contracts. Bullitt was known as a hard-working, hard-driving research chemist who had participated in and directed a series of programs which were brought to successful and profitable conclusion. This was his opportunity to perform as the section chief responsible for an entire group of programs. The promotion of Bullitt, while based on meritorious past performance, was motivated in part by a substantial decrease in government business due to the recent congressional economy wave. Bullitt's new section was staffed by eighteen professional chemists and engineers and twelve support technical workers. The data embodied in Haeningsen's report concerned an incident in this section. It appears that at a regular weekly staff meeting with his people Bullitt made the comment, "When this contract we now have for irradiating flake potatoes for the Air Force is completed in six months, I don't know what we'll do around here to keep you people busy." An early result of this comment was the resignation of three of the staff members, with the additional consequences detailed at the beginning of this case description. Worse, the three engineers who had resigned were well known and respected in the company, and had disclosed the reason for their actions to a number of selected friends. The effect on morale, as well as on productivity, has developed to the point that immediate action is required if further and even more serious consequences are to be averted.

Macon's first reaction was to call Parsons, the assistant general manager of R&D, into his office and order him to reprimand Bullitt and then to have Bullitt either dismissed or at least demoted. Even though the government programs are being reduced, the board of directors of the company has recently decided on increased activity in certain commercial areas, with the result that more research personnel will be needed for the new projects.

1. Was Bullitt correct in communicating his judgment about the prospects for future employment to the people in his section? Why or why not?
2. What should Mr. Macon do about the belief that has developed among many employees regarding the future prospects of the company?
3. What should Mr. Macon do about Kenneth Bullitt and perhaps William Parsons?
4. Are there any changes that Mr. Macon should make in respect to the overall communications system in the company?

Suggested Readings*

Athanassiades, J. C.: "The Distortion of Upward Communication in Hierarchical Organization," *Academy of Management Journal,* vol. 16, no. 2, June 1973.

Davis, K.: "Success of Chain-of-Command Oral Communication in a Manufacturing Group," *Academy of Management Journal,* vol. 11, no. 4, December 1968.

———: *Human Behavior at Work: Human Relations and Organizational Behavior,* 4th ed., McGraw-Hill Book Company, New York, 1972.

Gelfand, L. I.: "Communicate through Your Supervisors," *Harvard Business Review,* vol. 48, no. 6, November–December 1970.

Geneen, H. S.: "The Human Element in Communications," *California Management Review,* vol. 8, no. 2, Winter 1966.

Hayakawa, S. I.: *Language in Thought and action,* 2d ed., Harcourt, Brace & World, Inc., New York, 1964.

Lesikar, R. V.: *Business Communication,* Richard D. Irwin, Inc., Homewood, Ill., 1972.

Schwartz, M. M., H. F. Stark, and H. R. Schiffman: "Responses of Union and Management Leaders to Emotionally-Toned Industrial Relations Terms," *Personnel Psychology,* vol. 23, no. 3, Autumn 1970.

Wickesberg, A. K.: "Communications Networks in the Business Organization Structure," *Academy of Management Journal,* vol. 11, no. 3, September 1968.

*Also see the cross-reference table in the Preface.

Chapter **eleven**
HUMAN
MOTIVATION:
BASIC
FINDINGS

Whether in a small informal group or in a large organization, people work cooperatively and enthusi-
astically because of the personal satisfaction associated with such activity. What kinds of satisfactions do people strive for? Are individuals consistent in what they want? What happens when a person must choose between conflicting goals? What
are the different types of individual reactions to
frustration and conflict? These are the kinds of
questions that we investigate in this chapter.

A INTRODUCTION

Human behavior is seldom random in nature; rather, it is directed toward specific goals, or incentives, in the environment. However, this does not mean that goals control behavior. The goals are attractive only because of the motives they satisfy, which reside within an individual. Therefore, an individual's behavior is guided by his motives, whereas goals, which are external to the individual, provide him with the opportunity for satisfying his motives.

goals (or incentives)

1 As illustrated in Figure 11.1, people direct their energies toward the attainment of _____ in the environment.

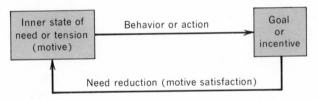

Figure 11.1 The process of motivation.

motives

2 However, goals as such are important to an individual only because they provide him with the opportunity to satisfy his _____ .

motives

3 For example, an art exhibit does not automatically attract all passersby, nor does an appetizing meal appeal to someone who has just eaten. The effectiveness of a goal or incentive depends on the _____ of the individuals involved.

motives

4 Therefore, it is not the incentives as such that serve to guide behavior; rather, it is the _____ within a person that guide his behavior.

within the person

in the environment

5 Motives are [within the person / in the environment], whereas goals are [within the person / in the environment].

6 In organizational situations involving adults, the behavior of people is typically guided by well-developed motives; that is, their behavior is directed toward the attainment of specific

goals (or
incentives)

_____ in the environment.

7 Which motives would be most important in guiding a person's behavior at a particular time, those that are satisfied or those that are unsat-

Unsatisfied

isfied? [Satisfied / Unsatisfied]

8 On the other hand, the motives that would have the least influence on a person's behavior are

satisfied

those that are _____ .

9 In summary, we can say that motivated behav-

goals (or
incentives)

ior is always directed toward specific _____ .

10 The motives which are most important in guiding an individual's behavior are those that are

least

[most / least] satisfied at the time.

B CATEGORIES OF MOTIVES

Since motives exist within individuals and cannot therefore be directly observed, psychologists are forced to make inferences regarding the number and kinds of motives that are associated with human behavior. Because of this difficulty, those working in the area of motivation theory have often come to different conclusions regarding the classification of motives. Based on the observable goals for which people strive, there are three basic categories of motives: *physical, social,* and *psychic.*

11 When we categorize motives as being in the physical, social, or psychic dimension, we are doing so by inference, because we are actually describing goals   the kinds of observable _____ for which people strive.

12 The dimension, or category, of motives related to underlying biological needs, such as hunger, thirst, sexual drive, and the preference for certain conditions of temperature and humidity, is

physical   the _____ dimension.

13 In the organizational situation, anything that adds to the physical comfort and security of people is related to motive satisfaction in the

physical   _____ dimension.

14 Which three of the following conditions of work are most closely related to the satisfaction of

1,   the physical dimension of motives? _____ ,

3, 5   _____ , and _____ [indicate by number]

1. Controlled temperature and humidity
2. Pleasant work companions
3. Absence of physical hazards
4. Opportunity to apply new ideas
5. A cafeteria serving good food

15 Since the influence of motives depends on the extent to which they are already satisfied, we would expect that in our society physical motive satisfac-

less   tion has become relatively [more / less] important during the last fifty years.

16 For which socioeconomic group of people would the physical dimension of motivation be most important? [Upper income / Middle income

Lower income / Lower income]

17 Those motives, other than physical, whose satisfaction depends on association with, and accept-

social   ance by, other people belong to the _____ dimension.

18 For example, being an accepted member of a

social   congenial work group results in _____
            motive satisfaction.

            19 Furthermore, other things being equal, an in-
            dividual will choose to have membership in a
            group in which his social status is relatively
high   [high / low]

            20 Which three of the following conditions of
            work are most closely related to satisfaction of the
2, 3,   social dimension of motives? _____, _____,
5   and _____ [indicate by number]

            1. Controlled temperature and humidity
            2. Pleasant work companions
            3. A friendly supervisor
            4. Opportunity to apply new ideas
            5. Holding a job considered important by others

            21 Particularly in determining the influence of
            an individual's social motives on his behavior, we
            have to consider not only the level of such satisfac-
            tion as *he* perceives it, but also his *level of aspiration*.
            In other words, the deprivation of social motive
            satisfaction is the difference between an individu-
aspiration al's level of _____ and his perceived
satisfaction _____ .

            22 For example, it is generally difficult for a poli-
            tician accustomed to a high level of social motive
            satisfaction to readjust his level of aspiration fol-
defeat   lowing an election [victory / defeat].

            23 What is important is not just the perceived
            amount of social motive satisfaction, but the
            amount of such satisfaction compared to the indi-
aspiration vidual's level of _____ .

            24 When a level of social motive satisfaction as
            perceived by the individual is below that indivi-
            dual's aspiration, he tends to work actively to-

goals (or
incentives or
things)

ward _____ in the environment that include such satisfaction.

25 Beginning in the 1930s, the human relations approach to management was in part a reaction against the assumption that workers strive for economic satisfaction alone. Instead, human relationists have emphasized the importance of interpersonal relationships and informal groups. From the motivation theory point of view, the human relations approach has stressed the importance of

social

the _____ dimension of motivation as a factor influencing worker productivity.

26 The two dimensions, or categories, of motives that we have considered thus far are the

physical
social

_____ and _____ motives. We shall now turn our attention to the *psychic* motives.

27 Whereas the behavior of all animals exhibits the influence of the most basic, or

physical

_____ , dimension of motives and some of the higher animals appear to be in-

social

fluenced by _____ motives, the category of motives that is peculiar to man is that con-

psychic

taining the _____ motives.

28 Goals that are attractive because they add to an individual's self-worth, even though they may not lead to any physical or social satisfaction as

psychic

such, are concerned with the _____ dimension of motives.

29 Consider, for example, the person who anonymously contributes his money or services to a charitable cause. He receives neither physical motive satisfaction nor social esteem, yet he finds such action personally satisfying. Such satisfaction in-

psychic

volves the _____ dimension of motivation.

30 The employee who corrects a deficiency in a product component because "it is the right thing to do," and not because he expects anyone to know about or reward him for his action, is responding

psychic in terms of the _____ dimension of motivation.

31 Which three of the following conditions of work are most closely related to the psychic dimen-

1, 3, sion of motivation? _____ , _____ , and

4 _____ [indicate by number]

1. The opportunity to help others
2. A conveniently located place of work
3. The opportunity to accomplish something worthwhile
4. The opportunity to work independently
5. The opportunity to hold a position of social eminence

32 In recent years, some writers have reacted against the classical human relations emphasis in management because of its main orientation to-

social ward the _____ category of motives. From the motivation theory point of view, writers who emphasize the importance of developing men who act on the basis of personal *values*, even when this makes them unpopular, are highlighting the

psychic importance of _____ motives in managerial behavior.

33 In this section we have considered three dimensions, or classifications, of motives:

physical; social _____, _____, and

psychic _____ .

34 As we emphasized at the beginning of this sec-

cannot tion, since motives [can / cannot] be directly observed, the classification of motives described here does not represent the only possibility; we have worked with the minimum number of categories possible.

35 An analysis of human motives that includes more than three categories, and which is frequently cited in management literature, is that developed by A. H. Maslow. As depicted in Figure 11.2, Maslow has differentiated _____ [number] categories of motives.

five

36 As depicted in Figure 11.2, Maslow suggests that human needs follow a certain order or priority, and we shall discuss this idea further in the next section of this chapter. For the present, we might observe that his two categories, the basic physiological needs and the safety and security needs, are included in the one dimension that we have called the _____ dimension of motives.

physical

37 Similarly, Maslow's belonging and social activity as well as esteem and status needs are included in our _____ dimension of motives.

social

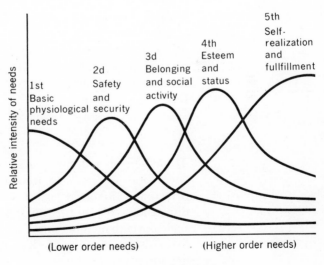

Figure 11.2 Maslow's hierarchy of needs. (Adapted.)

38 Finally, a category of Maslow's that is essentially equivalent to our psychic dimensions of motives is named _____

self-realization and fulfillment

_____.

C MULTIPLE MOTIVATION AND THE CONFLICT OF MOTIVES

We have been referring to examples of motives as if they exist one at a time. Of course, this is hardly the case. The complexity of human nature is reflected in the fact that a variety of motives operate simultaneously to influence an individual's behavior. Furthermore, the fact that some of these motives are incompatible with one another forces an individual to assign priorities and to make choices among these competing motives.

39 Seldom is it the case that a goal is considered desirable because of a single motive alone. Rather,

motives

several different _____ from different dimensions may be active when a person works

goal (or incentive)

toward a particular _____ .

40 For example, although financial incentives are often thought of as being related to the physical dimension of motives, they could represent satis-

three

faction in any or all of the _____ [number] categories of motives that we have discussed.

41 When an employee uses his income to buy "necessities of life," the dimension of motivation

physical

principally involved is the _____ dimension. When he purchases status symbols, such as a club membership, _____ mo-

social

tive satisfaction is involved. Contributing to charities and providing for the education of his children

psychic

exemplifies the _____ dimension of motives.

42   Furthermore, it has been found that an individual may himself not be aware of the motives that are guiding his behavior; that is, *unconscious* motives may be involved in addition to those that

conscious (or   are _____ .
known to him, etc.)

43   Motives of which the person is at the moment unaware, even though they are active in guiding

unconscious   his behavior, are said to be _____ motives.

44   A person who professes no interest in being noticed by others, yet continually wears clothes and does things that attract public attention, may be

unconscious   influenced by [conscious / unconscious] social motives.

45   When incompatible motives are simultaneously active within an individual, he may be forced   to   choose   between   or   among   the

goals (or   _____ available in the environment.
incentives, or
objects, etc.)

46   Thus, a person who is having difficulty in choosing personal goals may be affected by incom-

motives   patible _____ .

47   The presence of incompatible motives that are more or less equally influential results in an internal situation that psychologists have called *motivational conflict*. Thus, motivational conflicts always

within himself   concern   an   individual's   conflicts   [within himself / with those around him].

48   Considering the simplest situation of just two conflicting motives, psychologists have described three kinds of *conflict* situations, as illustrated in Figure 11.3 on page 300: the approach-approach,

avoidance-   approach-avoidance,   and   _____
avoidance   situations.

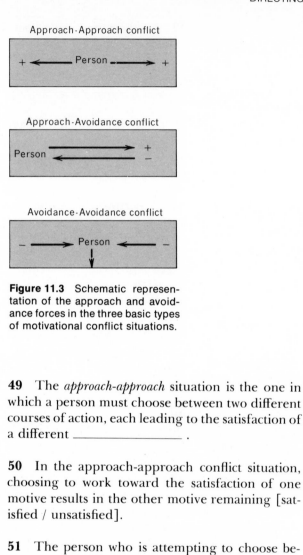

Figure 11.3 Schematic representation of the approach and avoidance forces in the three basic types of motivational conflict situations.

49 The *approach-approach* situation is the one in which a person must choose between two different courses of action, each leading to the satisfaction of a different _____ .

motive

50 In the approach-approach conflict situation, choosing to work toward the satisfaction of one motive results in the other motive remaining [satisfied / unsatisfied].

unsatisfied

51 The person who is attempting to choose between two job offers, one of which is in a part of the country he prefers and the other closer to his job interests, is involved in an _____ _____ conflict.

approach-approach

52 On the other hand, in *approach-avoidance* conflict the person is both attracted to, and wants to avoid, the same object or activity in his environment. Thus approach-avoidance conflict involves personal deliberation about whether or not to work toward a particular _____ .

object (or goal, or activity, etc.)

53 There is only one object, or goal, involved in the approach-avoidance conflict situation, but there are two antagonistic _____ involved.

motives

54 When a person cannot "make up his mind" about a job offer, even though no other job opportunity exists, _____ conflict can be said to exist.

approach-avoidance

55 Finally, the *avoidance-avoidance* conflict occurs when a person is forced to choose between two alternatives, both of which are considered undesirable by him. Being figuratively "between a rock and a hard place" represents an _____ _____ conflict.

avoidance-avoidance

56 Because two undesirable alternatives are present in the avoidance-avoidance conflict situation, would you conclude that an individual would choose to remain in such a situation, given a choice? [Yes / No]

No

57 Unlike both the approach-approach and approach-avoidance situations, in which the possibility of personal satisfaction may cause an individual to remain in a conflict situation, in the avoidance-avoidance situation there [is / is not] typically a desire to *escape*, either physically or psychologically.

is

58 The student faced with the prospect of either failing in a course in which he has no interest or doing more studying is in an _____ _____ conflict. His temporary avoidance of the problem by going to a movie represents an attempt to _____ from the situation.

avoidance-avoidance

escape

59 We have discussed three kinds of conflict situations in this section: _____
_____ , _____
and _____
situations.

approach-approach
approach-avoidance
avoidance-avoidance

60 The conflict in which only one environmental object or goal is involved and which results in indecision about whether or not to work toward the goal is _____
conflict.

approach-avoidance

61 On the other hand, the regional sales representative who is faced with the choice of spending more time on the road or losing some of his accounts is in an _____
conflict situation.

avoidance-avoidance
(He wants to avoid
having to accept
either alternative.)

62 An executive who must decide whether to accept a promotion that necessitates having to move with his family to another city is involved in an _____ conflict.

approach-avoidance
(The promotion
has both positive
and negative
features.)

63 Having established that an individual's motives are not necessarily compatible with one another, we shall now consider the question as to whether there is any pattern in the kind of motives that "win out" in the resulting _____ ; that is, is there a tendency for the dimensions of motives to follow a hierarchy in terms of their strength?

conflict

64 A. H. Maslow, whom we discussed in Section B of this chapter in regard to his analysis of five categories of motives, has suggested that motives develop in a certain order and that those categories developed earlier tend to have more strength in situations concerning motivational conflict than those developed later. In terms of his assumption and system, the category illustrated in Figure 11.2 (repeated), which carries the most strength in motivational conflict situations is that containing the _____ needs,

basic physiological

whereas the most vulnerable category contains the

self-realization and
fulfillment

_____

needs.

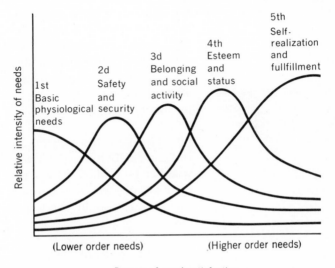

Figure 11.2 Maslow's hierarchy of needs. (Adapted.)

65 In terms of the three dimensions of motives we have identified and discussed in the preceding section of this chapter, if Maslow's conclusion is correct, the most basic and influential motives

physical

would be those included in the _____ dimension, followed by those included in the

social; psychic

_____ and _____ dimensions, respectively.

66 From the hierarchical point of view, the development of a higher motive is dependent on the prior satisfaction of those motives below it. Thus, we would expect social motive satisfaction to

physical

become important only after the _____ motives have been substantially satisfied.

67 Furthermore, we would expect the satisfaction of psychic motives to become important to an

social

individual only after his _____ motives have been reasonably satisfied.

68 Similarly, the hierarchical theory suggests that under conditions of stress the satisfaction of motives higher in the hierarchy is given up first. In other words, under conditions of physical threat the category of motive satisfaction that would be

psychic
social

given up first is the _____ , followed by abandonment of _____ motives.

69 The hierarchical theory would predict that for the extremely hungry person, the questions as to whether he is liked, whether he has status among his associates, and whether he has satisfied his per-

little

sonal ideals would carry [much / little] importance.

70 In a study of conditions in hunger-ridden postwar Germany,[1] it was found that the incidence of psychoneurosis was very low. Since the development of neurotic behavior has been associated with frustrated attempts to satisfy social motives, this

consistent

finding is [consistent / inconsistent] with the hierarchical theory of motivation.

71 On the other hand, we can observe many apparent exceptions to the hierarchical theory. The artist who puts artistic creation above all else, including physical comfort and social satisfaction,

---

[1]Kilby, Richard W., "Psychoneurosis in Times of Trouble: Evidence for a Hierarchy of Motives," *Journal of Abnormal and Social Psychology*, 1948, vol. 43, pp. 544–545.

inconsistently

is behaving [consistently / inconsistently] with the hierarchical theory.

psychic

72 A person who is willing to give up everything, even his life, for the sake of his values exhibits a behavioral pattern dominated by the _____ dimensions of motives.

motives (or
motivation)

73 Thus, even though motives may generally follow a particular hierarchy, observation indicates that any one of the dimensions of _____ may be dominant in a particular person.

physical; social

74 Just as some people are most responsive to incentives that satisfy psychic motives, others may be principally oriented toward the satisfaction of the _____ or _____ dimension of motives.

D REACTIONS TO FRUSTRATION AND CONFLICT

Frustration indicates the failure to satisfy personal motives because of barriers to goal attainment. Because personal motives are also not satisfied during motivational conflict, the reactions to conflict are often similar to those observed under externally imposed frustration. One possible reaction to frustration is that the individual will work toward eliminating the barriers to goal attainment. However, a number of other reactions which are not quite so rational are also possible, especially in the face of long-term frustration or conflict. In this section of the chapter we discuss the *aggressive, withdrawal,* and *compromise* types of reactions, or defense mechanisms, that are often substituted for effective problem-solving behavior.

75 The nonrational ways of behaving to be discussed in this section have often been referred to as *defense mechanisms* by psychologists because they serve to protect the individual's feeling of self-worth in the face of continued motivational [satisfaction / frustration].

frustration

76 Thus, ways of thinking and behaving in circumstances of frustration which are not effective problem-solving approaches, are self-deceptive, and serve to protect an individual's self-concept are referred to as _____ mechanisms.

defense

77 The explanation of just how the defense mechanisms protect the self-concept is psychologically complex and beyond the scope of this text. However, the fact that employees (including managers) frequently experience on-the-job frustrations suggest that various defense mechanisms [are / are not] likely to be used in organizations.

are

78 Our listing and description of the defense mechanisms will not be exhaustive, but it will include some examples of the aggressive, withdrawal, and compromise types of mechanisms. As indicated by its title, the *aggressive* type of reaction in response to frustration involves some kind of attack directed [inward / outward].

outward

79 The aggressive reaction may be either direct or displaced. *Direct aggression* is involved when the aggressive response is directed at the barrier to goal attainment or something closely associated with it. As with all defense mechanisms, this behavior does not represent an effective problem-solving strategy. For example, the foreman who "gets mad" at an inspector for rejecting parts manufactured in his department thereby exhibits a [direct / displaced] aggressive response.

direct

80 In *displaced aggression* the aggression is directed toward a scapegoat which (or who) has no direct relation to the reasons for frustration. For example, an employee who develops into an agitator on the job because of marital problems at home

job (etc.)

has displaced his aggressive response from home to _____ .

81 Thus the first category of defense mechanisms we have discussed thus far includes the

aggressive

direct; displaced

_____ reactions, which may be either _____ or _____.

82 The second category of reactions has been called the *withdrawal* type. Withdrawal can be a symptom of a serious psychological problem. However, in the context of the relatively milder defense mechanisms we are discussing, two examples are *regression* and *emotional insulation*. When an individual withdraws from the kind of problem-solving effort of which he is capable and turns to less ma-

regression

ture behavior instead, _____ can be said to take place.

83 A woman employee who "breaks down and cries" when reprimanded and a repairman who hits a sensitive mechanism with a wrench because he's unable to loosen it both illustrate the with-

regression

drawal reaction called _____ .

84 As a withdrawal reaction, *emotional insulation* is somewhat more subtle. By not "exposing" himself emotionally, an individual can often protect an unrealistic self-concept. Thus, the manager who is always very correct in his dealings with others in the company but never extends himself personally and never engages in informal contacts or activities

emotional

insulation

may be engaging in a form of _____ _____ .

85 Thus the second category of defense mechanisms we have discussed, the withdrawal reactions, includes the reactions (among others) of

regression

emotional

insulation

_____ and _____ _____ .

86 The third category of defense mechanisms includes the *compromise solutions,* so named because they are neither simply of the aggressive nor of the withdrawal type. Of the several reactions included in this category, we shall briefly discuss *compensation* and *rationalization.* Achieving a feeling of satisfaction by substituting a different goal for the one that is really desired describes the compromise

compensation   reaction called _____ .

87 The manager who prides himself on having his section reports submitted before those of all other sections may be substituting this form of achievement for others that are more meaningful, and thereby he may be indulging in a form of

compensation   _____ .

88 On the other hand, rationalization describes the tendency to give related but irrelevant reasons to excuse or "explain away" below-par performance. The employee who always has numerous excuses ready for his failure to achieve job objectives may thus be practicing a form of

rationalization   _____ .

89 Two particular forms of rationalization have been described in popular form: the *sour-grape* and *sweet-lemon* rationalizations. The sour-grape rationalization describes the tendency we have to conclude that a goal we failed to achieve really wasn't worthwhile, whereas the sweet-lemon rationalization represents an attempt to identify something good about a situation involving failure. A project manager who says, "It's just as well that we failed to meet the schedule last week, because now we might be able to get some overtime approved,"

sweet-lemon   may be indulging in the _____ form of rationalization.

90 The manager who fails to achieve quality objectives and then proceeds to claim that they are re-

sour-grape

ally unrealistic and therefore unimportant as objectives may be indulging in the _____ _____ form of rationalization.

91 In summary, we have given two examples of the compromise type of defense mechanisms: the

compensation
rationalization

reactions of _____ and _____ .

92 Two particular forms of rationalization that have been popularly described have been called

sour-grape
sweet-lemon

the _____ and _____ rationalizations.

Review

93 Behavior that is directed toward specific goals in the environment is guided by the individual's

motives

_____ . (Frames 1 to 6)

94 At a particular time, the motives that are most important in guiding behavior are those that are

least

relatively [most / least] satisfied. (Frames 7 to 10)

95 Organizations in which camaraderie and esprit de corps are high provide a high amount of

social

motive satisfaction in the _____ dimension for their members. (Frames 11 to 25)

96 Achievement for its own sake and sacrifice of personal comfort for the good of someone else or

psychic

for a cause typify the _____ dimension of motivation. (Frames 26 to 38)

97 When a person doesn't seem to fully understand or be aware of his own motives, we can describe the situation as including the activity of

unconscious

_____ motives. (Frames 39 to 44)

98 When a person has trouble in choosing between two possible job assignments because of the

different type of personal opportunity each represents, we can describe the situation as involving

approach-approach   _____ _____ conflict.
(Frames 45 to 51; 59)

99 An employee working under a financial incentive system, who would like to produce more in
order to earn more money but would thereby lose
the friendship of those in the work group, faces an

approach-avoidance   _____ _____ conflict.
(Frames 52 to 54, 60, 62)

100 The junior executive who faces the choice of
either working in the evenings or missing a due
date for a job assignment is involved in an

avoidance-avoidance   _____ _____ conflict situation. (Frames 55 to 58, 61)

101 According to the hierarchical theory, the
most basic of the three dimensions of motives that

physical   we have discussed is the _____ dimension. (Frames 63 to 74)

102 We have described three general categories
of defense mechanisms as types of unrealistic reac-

aggressive   tions to frustration: the _____ ,
withdrawal   _____ , and _____ types.
compromise   (Frames 75 to 78)

103 An example of an aggressive reaction is

direct (or   _____ , an example of a withdrawal
displaced)   reaction is _____ , and an example of
aggression;   the compromise type of defense mechanism is
regression (or
emotional insulation);   _____ . (Frames 79 to 88)
compensation (or
rationalization)

104 Two forms of rationalization that have been
popularized because they are so frequently used

sour-grape   are the _____ and
sweet-lemon   _____ rationalizations.
(Frames 89 to 92)

Discussion Questions

1. It has been said that "man does not live by bread alone." What other kinds of objects or events serve to satisfy his motives?

2. Taylor's "scientific management" has been criticized because of its emphasis on economic incentives. In what ways is this criticism legitimate? What factors may have made Taylor's emphasis more appropriate in his time than it is now?

3. The "human relationists" of the thirties and forties demonstrated the importance of noneconomic incentives in the workplace. In their emphasis on social motives what other dimension of motives did they tend to neglect? What was the general nature of the early studies that made such an omission likely?

4. In what respects may managerial indecision be indicative of motivational conflict?

5. What is the general evidence that supports a hierarchical view of human motives? On the other hand, what kind of evidence contradicts this theory?

6. Since "rationalization" may include the construction of rational excuses for failure, how can a manager determine whether an employee is rationalizing or presenting valid reasons for failure?

7. Since motivational conflict represents some kind of conflict between (or among) the internal motives of an individual, in general how can such conflicts be resolved?

8. A department manager suggests to a section supervisor that the supervisor will have to learn how to motivate his people. What is the general approach by which a supervisor can "motivate" his subordinates?

Case Study: Professional Employee Motivation

The Monroe Company is a company in the machine tool industry whose management group has always prided itself on the high level of employee relations in the company. The company's philosophy primarily reflects the belief of the founder of the firm, since passed away, that the firm's success had to be based on thorough employee commitment to its objectives. The fringe benefits paid by the company are the highest in the industry, and the employee suggestion system has provided a generous financial incentive for suggestions that result in improvements in the company's products or reductions in manufacturing costs. The profit-sharing program, by which the company contributes a fixed percentage of its profits to an employee investment and retirement fund, has also been credited as a major factor in promoting a high level of esprit de corps in the company.

Within the context of this organizational climate, Ron Ohlmann found that in his job as manager of the manufacturing methods department, employee motivation had never been a problem. During the past two years, however, the machine-tool industry has experienced a decline in sales, and the Monroe Company has shared in this decline. In response to market conditions and competitive factors in the industry, personnel reductions have been made in staff groups as well as in manufacturing departments, and merit increases have been largely curtailed. Since company profits were low last year, so was the contribution to the employee profit-sharing fund. Furthermore, the value of the investment fund has itself declined because of falling stock prices.

The general economic "tightening of the belt" within the company has meant that frequently fewer people are available to do the same work. For example, the work load of the manufacturing methods department is not particularly reduced because of lower production schedules but is often increased in certain respects. Ron Ohlmann was gratified at the response of departmental employees during the first several months of economic turndown. A majority of the supervisory and professional employees began putting in extra hours during evenings or on weekends in order to meet departmental commitments and deadlines. Recently, however, Mr. Ohlmann has detected other employee attitudes that he believes are indicative of a developing problem. On three specific occasions he has heard of employee complaints about the overtime work necessary to complete assigned projects. As one of the engineers expressed it, "The company is getting a lot of free labor under the present arrangement, and I don't see any end in sight." Although it is not clear whether the two are related, several engineers have also left the department recently in order to accept job offers with other companies, even though this meant forfeiture of company contributions in their investment fund accounts and even though the salaries they received in their new jobs were not significantly higher.

1. Before the economic turndown, what were the factors, or influences, that led to a high level of employee effort to accomplish organization objectives?
2. In what ways was the motivational climate changed by the turndown in company sales?
3. Should Ohlmann be particularly concerned by the fact that a few of his professional personnel have recently left the company?

4. In the context of the present economic situation what can the company do to improve the motivational climate? What can Ron Ohlmann do?

Case Study: The Reluctant Supervisor

As part of the company's management development program, a group of managers from various functional areas has devoted several class sessions to a study of motivation theory and the relevance of such knowledge to the manager's responsibility for directing and controlling the operations of his organizational unit. One of the participants in the program is George Schaeffer, who has been a supervisor in the production department for about a year. During the discussion session, George made the observation, "Motivation theory makes sense in general, but there is really no opportunity for me to apply these concepts in my job situation. After all, our shop employees are unionized and have job security and wage scales that are negotiated and are not under my control. The study of motivation concepts has given me some ideas about how to get my sons to do their chores and their homework, but it hasn't given me anything I can use on the job. Furthermore, in a working situation we're all dealing with adults, and it seems to me this reward and punishment thing smacks of personal manipulation that just won't go over with people."

1. In what respect is George Schaeffer correct in his comment about not having any opportunity to apply motivational concepts in his job situation?
2. What types of incentives for effective performance may George be overlooking?
3. What do you think about his concern that the application of motivational concepts leads to the manipulation of people?

Suggested Readings*

Atkinson, J. W., and D. Birch: *The Dynamics of Action*, John Wiley & Sons, Inc., New York, 1970.

Chung, K. H.: "A Markov Chain Model of Human Needs: An Extension of Maslow's Need Theory," *Academy of Management Journal*, vol. 13, no. 1, March 1970.

Dichter, E.: *Motivating Human Behavior*, McGraw-Hill Book Company, New York, 1971.

Lewin, K.: *A Dynamic Theory of Personality*, McGraw-Hill Book Company, New York, 1935.

Logan, F. A.: *Fundamentals of Learning and Motivation*, W. C. Brown Company Publishers, Dubuque, Iowa, 1970.

Maslow, A. H.: *Motivation and Personality*, Harper & Row, Publishers, Incorporated, New York, 1954.

Munn, N. L.: *Introduction to Psychology*, 3d ed., Houghton-Mifflin Company, Boston, 1972.

*Also see the cross-reference table in the Preface.

Chapter **twelve**

MOTIVATING
PEOPLE AT
WORK

Whereas the preceding chapter presents the principal findings regarding human motivation, conflict, and frustration in general, in this chapter we address our attention to motivational factors in the job situation as such. We begin by considering the relationship between morale and productivity and indicate why the existence of high morale in an organization does not necessarily mean that people in that organization will be productive. We then describe Theory X and Theory Y as two contrasting assumptions about the nature of human nature which have direct impact on methods of carrying out the managerial function of directing. Finally, we discuss the motivation-maintenance theory, a theory of motivation based directly on industrial research, which suggests that high employee satisfaction is not the opposite of employee dissatisfaction but is based on entirely different factors in the job situation.

A MOTIVATION, MORALE, AND PRODUCTIVITY

Since the discovery of the importance of nonmonetary incentives in the Hawthorne studies, discussed in Chapter 1, particular interest in employee morale has developed. As a result, a number of techniques concerned with morale appraisal have been used in business firms, and the results of these surveys provide a basis for evaluating the effectiveness of a company's human relations efforts. Underlying much of this interest and activity is the implicit assumption that high morale leads to high productivity, and thus to achieve one is virtually to achieve the other. In this section we suggest that individual productivity does not directly result from having the opportunity to satisfy personal motives on the job. Rather, productivity results only when the organizational and personal goals can be integrated, so that accomplishing one type of objective also results in the accomplishment of the other. The general viewpoint presented here will be expanded in the following sections of this chapter, which will give greater consideration to how personal satisfaction *and* productivity can be achieved in an organization.

1 High morale typically has been found to be related to the opportunity a person has to satisfy his motives in a situation. Therefore, providing the means for satisfying personal motives in the work

morale   situation leads to high employee _____.

2 High productivity refers to successful attainment of organizational goals. In some early research in this field, it was found that employees who were satisfied with their job situations tended also to be more productive. Therefore, it was assumed that high morale leads to high _____.

productivity

3 However, later research findings, which contradicted the earlier evidence, led to skepticism about the assumed relationship between _____ _____ and _____.

morale
productivity

4 Two general motivational methods can be observed in supervisory techniques—*positive* and *negative* motivation. Providing the opportunity for satisfying employee motives is the basis for [positive / negative] motivation, whereas threatening punishment for inappropriate behavior is the basis for [positive / negative] motivation.

positive

negative

5 Control of human activity through the threat of decreased motive satisfaction involves the _____ motivational method.

negative

6 In the diagram below, *P* stands for the person and *OG* for the organization goal. The person is in effect "pushed" toward the organizational goal by the application of the external force associated with [positive / negative] motivation.

negative

7 Because of the threat of reduced satisfactions, in the organization in which negative motivational methods predominate employee morale is typically [high / low].

low

8 Provided that there are some kinds of barriers that keep people in the organization, however, productivity *may* be high in an organization in

negative

which _____ motivational techniques predominate.

9 For example, even though he considers conditions poor, the employee who is within ten years of

unlikely

retiring is [likely / unlikely] to leave an organization.

10 However, when negative motivational techniques predominate, individuals with other lucra-

leave

tive job offers will tend to [stay in / leave] the organization, thus depleting the organization's human resources and long-run success.

11 Therefore, even though the long-run effects result in depletion of personnel resources and human talent in an organization, in the short run the low morale associated with negative motivation

productivity

may be accompanied by high _____ .

12 Turning now to positive motivation, that is, leadership based on reward rather than threat, we see that such methods generally have the *direct*

morale

result of raising _____ .

13 If the work situation is such that the individual is able to satisfy his own motives even though organizational goals are not achieved, then high

productivity

morale, but not high _____, will result.

14 In the diagram below, *P* stands for person, *OG* stands for organizational goal, and *PG* stands for

positive

personal goal. In this situation involving [posi-

would not

tive / negative] motivation, we [would / would not] expect high morale to lead to high productivity.

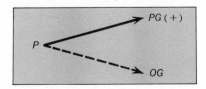

15   For example, a job situation in which the person is able to enjoy financial security and the company of pleasant working associates independently of his job efforts (at least within certain limits) may *not* result in high productivity, even though his
morale _____ may be high.

16   On the other hand, if personal motive satisfaction can be attained only in conjunction with, or as a result of, achieving organizational goals, then
high; high [high / low] morale *and* [high / low] productivity will tend to result.

17   In the diagram below, *P* again stands for the person, *OG* for the organizational goal, and *PG* for the personal goal. In this situation involving posi-
morale tive motivation, *both* high _____ and
productivity high _____ are likely.

18   For example, if a person perceives his long-range occupational plans to be consistent with his
high present job assignment, [high / low] morale and
high [high / low] productivity will tend to result.

19   Through this introduction, then, we have suggested that high morale tends to develop in
positive conjunction with a [positive / negative] motivational climate.

20   However, a positive motivational climate does not necessarily result in high productivity. The two are related when the personal goals of an employee are attained *through* the accomplishment of
organizational _____.
goals (or
objectives)

21   Furthermore, in the short run, high productivity can also result from the use of negative motivational methods. However, over a period of time this approach results in the tendency for skilled people to [join / leave] the organization.

leave

22 Of course, "real life" situations [usually / seldom] conform closely to just one of the three situations that we have described. However, the relative balance of the motivational factors will be predictive of the kind of employee response that is likely.

seldom

23 Only in the positive motivational method does the manager give active consideration to the motives that are guiding the employee's behavior and the _____ in the job situation that might serve as incentives.

goals (or factors or objectives, etc.)

24 Because conditions of work and financial arrangements are relatively fixed in many working situations, successful employee motivation on the part of the supervisor typically involves incentives that relate mainly to the [basic physical / higher-order] needs.

higher-order

25 The greater success a manager has in "tying together" organizational goal attainment and personal goal attainment, the higher will be both _____ and _____ .

morale; productivity

B McGREGOR'S THEORY X AND THEORY Y

In his book entitled *The Human Side of Enterprise* (McGraw-Hill Book Company, New York, 1960), Douglas McGregor describes two contrasting sets of assumptions that managers use in attempting to motivate their subordinates toward higher productivity. Called *Theory X* and *Theory Y*, these assumptions are widely regarded as being a convenient and effective way of describing the implications of a manager's motivation theory. Theory X represents the traditional view of direction and control, whereas Theory Y represents the integration of the goals of the individual and those of the organization. The focus of Theory Y, therefore, is much the same as that of our discussion on morale and productivity in the preceding section. However, in this section we highlight the strategy by which this integration of objectives can be achieved.

26 The manager who uses the Theory X approach assumes that the average human being has an inherent dislike of work and will avoid it if he can. Therefore, in order to achieve organizational

coerce objectives it is necessary to [challenge / coerce] most people.

27 In fact, the theory does not directly imply that only punishment or the threat of it will result in effective performance, since positive rewards attached to the job itself could also be motivating. But since the work itself is not considered motivating, the available rewards are assumed to be prin-

physical cipally associated with [physical / higher-order] needs.

28 In other words, Theory X suggests that the positive reasons for working are associated with the physical satisfactions purchased away from the job. In a society with a relatively low subsistence level and shortage of employment opportunities this "carrot-and-stick" theory of management

well would tend to work rather [well / poorly].

29 However, with the higher standards of living and variety of job opportunities in societies that are technically advanced, the physical needs of people are usually fairly well satisfied. In effect, then, this leaves the organization based on Theory X man-

negative agement with only the [positive / negative] motivational approach.

30 Some further assumptions associated with Theory X are that the average human being prefers to be directed, wants to avoid responsibility, has relatively little ambition, and wants security above all. Again, the implication of these assumptions is that a person [can / cannot] be motivated by the contents of the job itself.

cannot

31 In the diagram below, S represents the supervisor, P represents the person in a job situation, and J represents the job to be performed. According to Theory X, the job can be described as having a negative valence from the worker's point of view, and thus he tends to avoid job commitment and job responsibility in various direct and/or indirect ways. As indicated in the diagram, the "push" needed to accomplish job goals comes from the

supervisor

_____ .

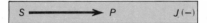

32 Although Theory X purports to describe human attitudes toward work, McGregor suggests that instead it describes the consequences of the managerial assumption that work is inherently [attractive / repugnant].

repugnant

33 McGregor suggests that when people are deprived of the opportunity to satisfy higher-order needs that have become important to them, they react in a number of different but predictable ways that are all indicative of personal frustration. Thus, he suggests that the real source of the motivational problems associated with Theory X can be directly related to the nature of the [people / situation].

situation

34 In the past, organizations have attempted to handle the consequences of this frustration without addressing themselves to its cause. Thus a "tough" management attitude represents an orien-

negative

tation toward the [positive / negative] motivational approach.

35 On the other hand, a management strategy based on a "soft" or "human relations" orientation attempts to gain employee commitment by making the job situation pleasant and providing fringe benefits, thus primarily increasing the opportunity physical   to satisfy [physical / higher-order] needs.

36 Of course, the weakness of the soft approach in the absence of any other managerial action is that increased opportunity is given to satisfy needs independent of   [through / independent of] job performance as such.

37 Thus, McGregor suggests that management by direction and control—regardless of whether it is hard or soft—relies on motivational methods ineffective   that are relatively [effective / ineffective].

38 In summarizing the first theory described by McGregor, we can state that the assumption that people are primarily interested in the satisfaction of physical needs, and that the average person dislikes work as such, is descriptive of Theory

X   ——————— .

39 Under Theory X the motivational techniques used can be either positive or negative. However, because basic physical needs are relatively well satisfied in our society today, the motivational techniques actually available by this approach are prenegative   dominantly [positive / negative] in nature.

40 In his book, McGregor argues that the solution to industry's motivational problems is not hard or soft management as such, but the acceptance of a new set of motivational assumptions that gives prominence to man's higher-order needs. He refers to this alternative set of assumptions as Y   Theory ——————— .

41 Theory Y suggests that work is as natural as play or rest, and that the average human being does not inherently dislike it. Rather, if a man is committed to the objectives associated with that work, his performance can be effectively guided on internal the basis of [internal / external] control.

42 But how is this commitment to job objectives achieved? McGregor suggests that since the higher-order needs are now the relevant ones for many people, commitment to jobs is increased when the methods and procedures [are carefully allow individual prescribed / allow individual judgment and judgment and choice].
choice

43 Similarly, Theory Y further suggests that under the conditions of modern industrial life the intellectual potential of the average human being is only partially being [only partially / fully] utilized.

44 McGregor recognizes that complete restructuring of job situations is not possible, and thus we cannot expect to achieve perfect integration of organizational requirements and individual goals. However, to the extent that jobs can be made more meaningful, motivational problems will be less [less / more] severe.

45 The supervisor who follows the Theory Y approach to management encourages his people to develop and utilize their capacities, knowledge, skills, and ingenuity in accomplishing organizational objectives. This very encouragement provides the opportunity for satisfaction of . higher-order [physical / higher-order] needs.

46 As described in the preceding frames, then, the Theory Y approach implies that the management method should be [hard / soft / not necesnot necessarily sarily either hard or soft].
either hard or soft

47 However, since the higher-order needs of employees are typically far from being satisfied, under Theory Y there is greater opportunity for

positive   utilizing   [positive / negative]   motivational methods.

48 Acceptance of the Theory Y approach does not imply complete absence of external direction and control. It does imply that greater reliance

internal   should be placed on [external / internal] control.

49 Under certain circumstances, such as those for unskilled employees in highly integrated production procedures, the opportunity to apply Theory Y may be limited. Such situations tend to breed motivational problems because there is limited opportunity on the job to satisfy [physical /

higher-order   higher-order] needs.

50 Even with such difficulties, however, the application of Theory Y is enhanced by defining job responsibilities that are relatively [nar-

broad   row / broad] in scope.

51 A particular company experience serves as a classic example to support McGregor's thesis along these lines. The concept of *job enrichment* (originally called *job enlargement*), first applied in the Endicott plant of International Business Machines in 1943, is based on the premise that many jobs have been made too narrow and should be enlarged in scope and complexity so that the person's overall area of

increased   job responsibility is [increased / reduced].

52 Specifically, whereas milling-machine operators in the Endicott plant had previously been responsible only for operating the machine as such and setup men had the responsibility of making adjustments for new operations, responsibility for both operating the machines and performing routine adjustments was assigned to the operators. With the increased responsibility, the wage rate for operators was increased, but this cost was more

setup men

than offset by the reduction in the number of
_____ _____ that were required.

53 In 1943 IBM's Endicott plant had 3,351
machine operators and 207 setup men, compared
with 4,411 operators and 4 setup men ten years
later. Furthermore, management found that employees became more interested in their work,
were absent less, did less complaining, and made
fewer mistakes after application of the concept of

job _____ enrichment.

54 In recent years there has been considerable
interest in applying the concept of job enrichment
to automobile assembly operations in this country
and especially in Sweden. Job enrichment provides
greater opportunity for the satisfaction of higher-
order needs and is thus a particular example of the

Y application of Theory _____ in management.

C THE MOTIVATION-MAINTENANCE THEORY

Another development in motivation theory that
has led to a reassessment of the basic assumptions
underlying the motivational methods presently
used in industry is Herzberg's description of two
independent sets of factors that influence job satisfaction and performance. The original research
study that led to the formulation of this theory is
described by Frederick Herzberg, Bernard
Mausner, and Barbara Snyderman in their book,
The Motivation to Work (John Wiley & Sons, Inc.,
New York, 1959). In a more recent book entitled
Work and the Nature of Man (The World Publishing
Company, Cleveland, 1966), Herzberg includes
results of later tests of the theory and considers
implications of the findings for psychological
growth and mental health, as well as for industrial
motivation. Essentially, the motivation-maintenance theory suggests that two separate sets of
factors influence the worker's attitude toward his

job. The factors that lead to high job satisfaction and goal-oriented effort—called the *motivational factors,* or *motivators*—are different from the factors that lead to dissatisfaction and discontent—called the *maintenance factors.* The maintenance factors were originally referred to as the "hygiene factors." In order to give greater meaning to these conclusions, we shall first describe Herzberg's method of research and the data that led to his theory and then consider the implications of the motivation-maintenance theory to the managerial function of directing.

55 In their original research study Frederick Herzberg and his associates at Western Reserve University interviewed 200 engineers and accountants in the Pittsburgh area. They first asked each employee to think of a time during which he felt especially good about his job, to describe the conditions which led to these feelings, and to give an estimate of the duration of time during which these feelings affected his job performance. Of course, in this case the effects on job performance would generally be [positive / negative] in nature.

positive

56 Each employee was then asked to think of a time during which he had developed negative feelings about his job, and again to describe the conditions which led to these feelings and to give an estimate of the duration of time during which these feelings had a [positive / negative] effect on his job performance.

negative

57 In these interviews the researchers found that the employees identified basically different types of conditions for the positive as contrasted to the negative feelings, rather than naming conditions that were basically opposites. Thus, whereas recognition was identified as one of the factors that led to positive feelings toward the job, lack of recognition [was / was not] generally identified as a factor leading to negative feelings toward the job.

was not

58 Similarly, whereas poor company policy and administration was a factor often underlying negative job feelings, good company policy and administration [frequently / seldom] was cited as a reason for positive job feelings.

seldom

59 Therefore, Herzberg concluded that the factors that lead to positive job feelings and associated job commitment and the factors that lead to negative job feelings and dissatisfaction are basically [the same / different].

different

60 The factors leading to positive feelings are the *motivational* factors, and in the original study here described they were found to be the factors of *achievement, recognition, work itself, responsibility*, and *advancement.* The presence or absence of these motivational factors, then, was found to be related to [job satisfaction and commitment / job dissatisfaction].

job satisfaction
and commitment

61 On the other hand, the maintenance factors included *company policy and administration, supervision, salary, interpersonal relations*, and *working conditions.* Herzberg found that a high level of organizational performance in these areas did *not* result in a high level of satisfaction and positive feelings. However, a low level of organizational concern about these factors resulted in _____.

dissatisfaction (or
negative feelings)

62 Figure 21.1 on page 331 shows the percentage frequency with which each factor was associated with positive and negative feelings toward the job in Herzberg's studies. As indicated in the figure, the factor with the highest percentage frequency as a motivator is _____ , whereas the factor with the highest percentage frequency as a maintenance factor is _____
_____ .

achievement

company policy
and administration

63 Furthermore, in Figure 12.1 we can also note that although each factor we have discussed is

predominantly either a motivator or a maintenance factor, there is some overlap in factors being
identified with both positive and negative feelings
toward the job. For example, the motivational factor with the highest percentage of mention as a
source of negative feelings is _____ .

recognition (in this
case, the failure to
receive
recognition)

64 Similarly, the maintenance factor with the
highest percentage frequency of mention as a
source of positive feelings is _____ .

salary

65 Although the identification of factors associated with positive versus negative feelings was
thus not entirely mutually exclusive, the percentage frequencies reported in Figure 12.1 indicate
[relatively little / considerable] overlap.

relatively little

66 Previous to Herzberg's findings, it was generally assumed that employee satisfaction and job
commitment were the opposite of employee dissatisfaction and negative feelings toward the job.
However, the results of Herzberg's studies indicate
that the two [are / are not] essentially opposites.

are not

67 Thus, managerial attention focused on one of
these sets of factors reduces negative feelings
toward the job but has little affect on the development of job commitment as such. Herzberg refers
to these as the _____ factors.

maintenance (or
hygiene)

68 Herzberg originally used the word "hygiene"
in this context as an analogy to the medical use of
the term "preventative and environmental." Thus
noncontaminated water [does / does not] prevent
disease. It [does / does not] cure disease.

does

does not

69 So also, the hygiene, or maintenance, factors
prevent negative job feelings and dissatisfaction,
but managerial attention given solely to these fac-

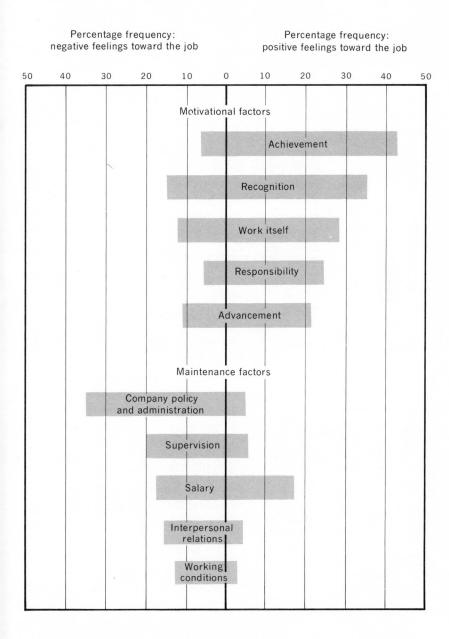

Figure 12.1 Comparison of factors associated with positive and negative feelings toward the job. (Modified from Frederick Herzberg et al., *The Motivation to Work*, John Wiley & Sons, Inc., New York, 1959, p. 81. Used with permission.)

job satisfaction
and commitment
(etc.)

tors does not result in _____

_____ .

70 Job satisfaction and commitment can be achieved only by directing managerial attention to the _____ factors.

motivational

71 As we mentioned previously, each employee interviewed was also asked to estimate the period of time during which the positive or negative feelings affected his job performance. Although the results were a bit mixed, three factors particularly stood out as resulting in lasting changes of attitude: *work itself, responsibility,* and *advancement.* Thus, the factors associated with lasting changes were all [motivational / maintenance] factors.

motivational

72 Thus far, we have simply named the five principal motivational factors and five principal maintenance factors identified in Herzberg's study. Now, let us consider the types of factors included in each group. Have you noticed anything about the factors that generally differentiates the motivators from the maintenance factors? [Yes / No]

(Optional answer;
discussion
continues below.)

73 Referring again to Figure 12.1, note that one set of factors is primarily concerned with things that might be said to "surround" the job; that is, they define the environment, or context, of the job. These are the [motivational / maintenance] factors.

maintenance

74 On the other hand, the second set of factors are primarily concerned with job content and are job-centered. They are oriented toward what happens in the job itself, rather than toward what happens in the job environment. These are the [motivational / maintenance] factors.

motivational

75 Interestingly, when people talk about the

job itself

sources of satisfaction associated with their jobs, they tend to identify factors in the [job environment / job itself].

76 However, when people talk about the sources of dissatisfaction and the negative factors associated with their jobs, they tend to identify fac-

job environment
(etc.)

tors in the _____ _____ .

77 The study originally conducted by Herzberg and his colleagues has now been repeated a number of times with a variety of professional and nonprofessional industrial work groups. Some differences in the specific factors have been found, but the maintenance factors have consistently been environmental in nature, whereas the motivational factors have consistently been in the job itself, thus

supporting

[supporting / refuting] Herzberg's two-factor theory.

78 For example, in 1964, M. Scott Myers reported the results of an extensive test of the motivation-maintenance theory at Texas Instruments, Incorporated.[1] During the 1950s the company increased annual sales from $2 million to $200 million while the total number of employees grew from 1,700 to 17,000 people. With the growth in the size and complexity of the organization they found that motivational problems become rela-

more

tively [more / less] important.

79 Accordingly, a random sample of 282 employees was selected and asked the two questions oriented toward job satisfiers and dissatisfiers, respectively. Employees in five job categories were represented in the sample: scientists, engineers, manufacturing supervisors, technicians, and assemblers. As compared with the original study by Herzberg, the sampled employees at Texas In-

[1]M. Scott Myers, "Who Are Your Motivated Workers?" *Harvard Business Review*, January–February, 1964, pp. 73–88.

broader

struments represented a [more specialized / broader] sampling of occupational groups.

80   Exhibit 12.1 presents sample "favorable" and "unfavorable" responses to the interview questions by incumbents in the five job categories sampled. In this exhibit, the kinds of factors that lead to *satisfaction* for employees in different types of jobs are similar (all   quite [similar / different].
job-oriented)

EXHIBIT 12.1   *Sample "Favorable" and "Unfavorable" Responses to Interview Questions by Incumbents in Five Job Categories*

(From M. Scott Myers, "Who Are Your Motivated Workers?" *Harvard Business Review*, January–February, 1964, pp. 74–75. Reproduced with permission.)

Scientist — Favorable

About six months ago I was given an assignment to develop a new product. It meant more responsibility and an opportunity to learn new concepts. I had to study and learn. It was an entirely different job. I always enjoy learning something new. I had been in basic research where it's difficult to see the end results. Now I'm working much harder because I'm more interested. I'm better suited for this type of work.

Scientist — Unfavorable

In the fall of 1961 my group would find problems which needed work. We presented them to our supervisor, and he would say, "Don't bother me with details; we are in trouble in this area and need one person for guidance and I am the person." He assigns the problems. He said, "Do what I say whether you think it will work or not." I wouldn't come in Saturday. Made me want to go home and work on my yard. Negative attitude. Killed my initiative because no matter what I came up with my supervisor wouldn't accept it. At first we tried to convince him but finally gave up. Very few gains made in this environment.

Engineer — Favorable

In 1959 I was working on a carefully outlined project. I was free to do as I saw fit. There was never a "No, you can't do this." I was doing a worthwhile job and was considered capable of handling the project. The task was almost impossible, but their attitude gave me confidence to tackle a difficult job. My accomplishments were recognized. It helped me gain confidence in how to approach a problem. It helped me to supervise a small number of people to accomplish a goal. I accomplished the project and gained something personally.

Engineer — Unfavorable

In December 1961 I was disappointed in my increase. I was extremely well satisfied with the interview and rating. I was dejected and disillusioned, and I still think about it. I stopped working so much at night as a result of this increase. My supervisor couldn't say much. He tried to get me more money but couldn't get it approved.

Manufacturing Supervisor — Favorable

In September of 1961 I was asked to take over a job which was thought to be impossible. We didn't think TI could ship what had been promised. I was told half would be acceptable, but we shipped the entire order! They had confidence in me to think I could do the job. I am happier when under pressure.

Manufacturing Supervisor — Unfavorable

In the fall of 1958 I disagreed with my supervisor. We were discussing how many of a unit to manufacture, and I told him I thought we shouldn't make too many. He said, "I didn't ask for your opinion ... we'll do what I want." I was shocked as I didn't realize he had this kind of personality. It put me in bad with my supervisor and I resented it because he didn't consider my opinion important.

Hourly Male Technician — Favorable

In June 1961 I was given a bigger responsibility though no change in job grade. I have a better job, more interesting and one that fits in better with my education. I still feel good about it. I'm working harder because it was different from my routine. I am happier ... feel better about my job.

Hourly Male Technichian — Unfavorable

In 1962 I was working on a project and thought I had a real good solution. A professional in the group but not on my project tore down my project bit by bit in front of those I worked with. He made disparaging remarks. I was unhappy with the man and unhappy with myself. I thought I had solved it when I hadn't. My boss smoothed it over and made me feel better. I stayed away from the others for a week.

Hourly Female Assembler—Favorable

About two weeks ago I wire-welded more transistors than anyone had ever done—2,100 in nine hours. My foreman complimented me, and I still feel good. Meant self-satisfaction and peace of mind to know I'm doing a good job for them. Once you've done it, you want to do it everyday, but you can't. It affected my feelings toward everyone. My old foreman came and talked to me. I didn't think I could ever wire-weld.

Hourly Female Assembler — Unfavorable

For a while the foreman was partial to one of the girls on the line. She didn't work as hard as the other girls and made phone calls. It got to the point where we went to the man over her foreman and complained. We were all worried since we are afraid of reprisals ... The girls don't act the same toward each other now because they are afraid. It affects everyone's work. It has been going on for such a long time it's uncomfortable. It is being stopped now by the foreman's supervisor and that girl has been moved.

---

81 M. Scott Myers summarized the findings at Texas Instruments by concluding that "... work rules, lighting, coffee breaks, titles, seniority rights, wages, fringe benefits, and the like..." were representative of the factors associated with [avoiding dissatisfaction / improving productivity].

avoiding
dissatisfaction

82 He also concluded that "...a challenging job which allows a feeling of achievement, responsibility, growth, advancement, enjoyment of work itself, and earned recognition..." were associated with [avoiding employee dissatisfaction / motivating employee productivity].

motivating
employee
productivity

83 The results of these studies do not suggest that maintenance factors are unimportant. The motivation and maintenance factors have different influences in the job situation. Since a person's decision about whether to accept and stay in a job is considerably influenced by such factors as pay and fringe benefits, this type of decision is particularly influenced by _____ factors.

maintenance

84 On the other hand, given that he finds himself in a particular job situation, an individual's commitment, or *productivity* decision, is particularly influenced by _____ factors.

motivational

85 Any particular job situation can be described in terms of the motivational and maintenance factors operative in that situation. As illustrated in Figure 12.2, each of these sets of factors [is either present or absent / can be present in varying degrees].

can be present in
varying degrees

86 Although most job situations include a mixture of the two groups of factors, a consideration of some "pure types" would help to summarize the implications of the motivation-maintenance theory. For example, a high rate of personnel turnover *and* a low level of job commitment would be typical when motivational factors are represented to a [high / low] extent and maintenance factors are represented to a [high / low] extent.

low
low

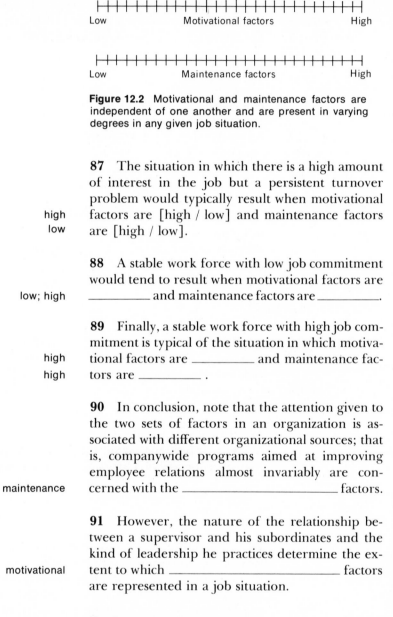

Figure 12.2 Motivational and maintenance factors are independent of one another and are present in varying degrees in any given job situation.

87 The situation in which there is a high amount of interest in the job but a persistent turnover problem would typically result when motivational factors are [high / low] and maintenance factors are [high / low].

high
low

88 A stable work force with low job commitment would tend to result when motivational factors are _____ and maintenance factors are _____.

low; high

89 Finally, a stable work force with high job commitment is typical of the situation in which motivational factors are _____ and maintenance factors are _____ .

high
high

90 In conclusion, note that the attention given to the two sets of factors in an organization is associated with different organizational sources; that is, companywide programs aimed at improving employee relations almost invariably are concerned with the _____ factors.

maintenance

91 However, the nature of the relationship between a supervisor and his subordinates and the kind of leadership he practices determine the extent to which _____ factors are represented in a job situation.

motivational

Review

92 The approach to motivating individuals which relies on the use of rewards can be described as in-

positive

morale (but not
necessarily high
productivity)

volving [positive / negative] motivation. This approach almost invariably results in high [productivity / morale]. (Frames 1 to 4, 12 to 15)

93 Negative motivational methods, based on threat or coercion, result in morale that is [high / low] and in short-run productivity that [is high / is low / can be either high or low]. (Frames 5 to 11)

low

can be either high
or low

94 Both high morale and high productivity can only result in the situation in which there is _____ motivation and an integration of _____ and _____ goals. (Frames 16 to 25)

positive

organizational

personal

95 The managerial assumption that people basically dislike work, prefer to be directed, and want to avoid responsibility has been called Theory _____. Proponents of this theory assume that man is motivated primarily by [physical / higher-order] needs, and they tend to use [positive / negative] motivational methods. (Frames 26 to 33)

X

physical

negative

96 In considering the hard, or punitive, versus the soft, or human relations, reactions to handling the consequences of Theory X, McGregor suggests that the best alternative is _____. (Frames 34 to 39).

neither of these

97 The assumption that work is as natural as play or rest, and that higher-order needs are the ones particularly relevant to successful motivation, is called Theory _____. (Frames 40 to 50)

Y

98 A procedure first applied in the Endicott Plant of IBM which tends to support McGregor's claims for the advantages of Theory Y is called _____. (Frames 51 to 54)

job enrichment

99   In their interviews with accountants and engineers in the Pittsburgh area Herzberg and his colleagues found that two separate sets of factors affected job attitude. The factors associated with positive job feelings were called _____ factors, whereas the factors associated with negative job feelings were called _____ factors. (Frames 55 to 65)

motivational

maintenance (or
hygiene)

100   Managerial attention directed at the maintenance factors results in reducing sources of employee _____. Attention directed toward the motivational factors tends to result in higher _____. (Frames 66 to 71)

dissatisfaction

job satisfaction
(and commitment)

101   A distinguishing feature of the two groups of factors is that whereas the motivational factors tend to be concerned with the [job environment / job itself], the maintenance factors are concerned with the [job environment / job itself]. (Frames 72 to 76)

job itself
job environment

102   Other studies, such as the one at Texas Instruments, have tended to [support / refute] the principal findings incorporated in the motivation-maintenance theory. (Frames 77 to 82)

support

103   Another way of considering the implications of the motivation-maintenance theory is to observe that the decision to join and perhaps remain in an organization is particularly influenced by the _____ factors, whereas the decision to be productive is particularly influenced by the _____ factors. (Frames 83 to 89)

maintenance

motivational

104   From the standpoint of the motivation-maintenance theory, company personnel policies and practices are for the most part oriented toward _____ factors, whereas the

maintenance

motivational

leadership techniques of individual managers are directed toward the _____ factors. (Frames 90 and 91)

Discussion Questions

1. Describe the conditions under which positive morale can be associated with low rather than high productivity.

2. Why is the combination of low morale and high productivity generally an unstable or temporary condition?

3. What do you think are the typical employee reactions to Theory X management?

4. What do you think are the typical employee reactions to Theory Y management?

5. Theory X and Theory Y are concerned with the nature of people. How does the nature of the job situation affect the application of these respective theories? What are the implications?

6. Comment on the statement, "When you come right down to it, people will always choose the so-called maintenance factors in preference to the motivational factors, when given a choice."

7. Within the context of the motivation-maintenance theory, how is it possible for an employee to be both "satisfied" and "dissatisfied" at the same time? What are the implications?

8. What can a manager do to increase the number of motivational (as contrasted to maintenance) factors operative in a work situation? What can an organization do along these lines?

Case Study: Junior Managers at Universal Motors

Tom Miller completed his college work with a major in business administration eighteen months ago. During his last semester at college he was interviewed by a number of company recruiters and was in the fortunate position of being able to choose from among four specific job offers. Based on the opportunity he saw for professional growth, salary level, and company location, he accepted the offer from Universal Motors.

One of the factors that particularly impressed him during his job deliberations was the Junior Management Program (JMP) at Universal Motors. During their first two years of employment the college graduates in this program are placed sequentially in four different but related job areas for about six months in each location. Based on Tom Miller's interests, it was agreed that his four areas of work experience during this period would be in personnel selection, technical training, supervisory development, and labor relations. Additional features of the JMP included a monthly dinner meeting for program participants which included talks by members of top management and a planned progression of salary increments during program participation.

With eighteen months and three of his four job assignments completed, Tom Miller now feels considerably disenchanted about the program. Further, he feels that he is not alone in his reaction, since a number of the graduates with whom he began the program have either dropped out of it to accept a full-time appointment in one of the areas of their rotational experience or have left the company entirely. He has no complaint with the overall administration of the program, since he has to admit that the company followed through on all commitments made at the time of employment. Rather, his complaint is directed toward the kind of experience, or lack of it, in his specific job assignments.

As an example, the six-month assignment that he just completed was in supervisory development. For the first two months he was given the assignment of compiling information for certain reports required by the personnel and industrial relations division. Since he was aware that the job was previously done by clerical personnel in the department, he was not particularly impressed by the assignment. He discussed the matter with the department manager, who explained that since Tom would be leaving shortly he could not be assigned the kind of responsibility that would require later follow-through. However, the supervisor did reassign him as assistant to two of the professional people in the department, one of whom was a conference leader and the other a program evaluator. As a result, during his last four months in the department he was at least able to get closer to the professional work being done, but he still felt like a "fifth wheel."

1. How would you describe the overall assumption underlying the Junior Management Program?
2. What have been the inadvertent motivational factors included in the program?
3. Can the program of sequenced job assignments be modified to correct its motivational deficiencies? How?
4. What are some alternatives to this type of program?

Case Study: Transfer to Another Department

Ralph Lentini is an electronics engineer who has been with Midvale Electronics since completing graduate studies in engineering eight years ago. During this time he has been employed in the research and development department and has progressed from junior project engineer to project supervisor. In his work as project supervisor he developed the reputation of being an outstanding supervisor in terms of the motivational climate he was able to develop in his project teams. Basically, he set objectives in collaboration with each team member and worked in a consultative capacity with the people in the project, but he avoided specifying the detailed procedures to be followed. Knowing the tendency of research people to get carried away with their own interests, however, collaboration in respect to weekly objectives was the strategy Ralph Lentini followed to keep activities directed toward intended goals. In fact, Ralph was well aware that much of the work being done represented personal interests of various project personnel. But on the other hand, these same people frequently skipped coffee breaks and remained after hours on their own in order to achieve project objectives.

With the phasing out of much of the research and development work in the company, a number of people were transferred to other types of positions. Because of his success in motivating exceptional performance in the project group, Ralph Lentini was assigned as supervisor in the section concerned with assembly of hand-held calculators. Ralph approached his managerial responsibilities with the same philosophy as in the previous position. That is, he informed each person that he was not concerned about the detailed procedure by which work was done, but that he was holding each person accountable for achieving production goals. Further, he indicated that he would briefly review operations with each individual on a weekly basis, but was always available to answer any questions.

Ralph was surprised at some of the employee reactions during his first week on the job. One man indicated that he was glad that Ralph wasn't going to be such a stickler for production as the last supervisor had been, and said that the other supervisor was too rigid about always wanting to see everybody on the job.

The production figures at the end of the week were something of a minor disaster, and Ralph now pondered about what his course of action should be to correct the situation.

1. How would you describe Ralph Lentini's approach to management from the standpoint of Theory X and Theory Y management?
2. What is there are about the two work situations which he supervised which made for the difference in the responses to his approach as a supervisor?
3. What possible differences are there between the people involved in the two work situations which was related to the difference in their responses?
4. What should Ralph Lentini do now?

Suggested Readings*

Ford, R. N.: *Motivation Through the Work Itself,* American Management Association, New York, 1969.

Herzberg, F.: *Work and the Nature of Man,* The World Publishing Company, Cleveland, 1966.

————, **B. Mausner, and B. Snyderman:** *The Motivation to Work,* John Wiley & Sons, Inc., New York, 1959.

House, R. J., and L. A. Wigdor: "Herzberg's Dual-Factor Theory of Job Satisfaction and Motivation: A Review of the Evidence and a Criticism," *Personnel Psychology,* vol. 19, no. 2, Summer 1966.

Judson, G.: "Blue-collar Blues on the Assembly Line," *Fortune,* vol. 84, no. 7, July 1970.

Macarov, D.: "Work Patterns and Satisfactions in an Israeli Kibbutz: A Test of the Herzberg Hypothesis," *Personnel Psychology,* vol. 25, no. 3, Autumn 1972.

Morse, J. J., and J. W. Lorsch: "Beyond Theory Y," *Harvard Business Review,* vol. 48, no. 3, May-June 1970.

*Also see the cross-reference table in the Preface.

Roche, W. J., and N. L. Mackinnon: "Motivating People with Meaningful Work," *Harvard Business Review,* vol. 48, no. 3, May-June 1970.

Starcevich, M. M.: "Job Factors Related to Satisfaction and Dissatisfaction across Different Occupational Levels," *Journal of Applied Psychology,* vol. 56, no. 6, December 1972.

Chapter  **thirteen**
LEADERSHIP

The phenomenon of leadership has been investigated by social scientists for a number of years. Most of the studies have directed attention to the leader's characteristics and behavior. In recent years, however, researchers have become interested in the group and other organizational influences that affect the leader and his success. From the standpoint of overall leadership style, on the other hand, managers differ in the motivational methods they use and the extent to which they delegate authority. The first three sections of this chapter are concerned with the research approaches that have been followed in studying leadership success, whereas the last two sections are concerned with overall leadership style and the use of managerial power in disciplining.

A   LEADER-ORIENTED APPROACHES TO STUDYING LEADERSHIP

Historically, attempts to explain the basis for successful leadership have focused on the characteristics of the leader himself. This is, of course, the logical place to begin searching for the factors that affect leadership success. Over the years, the "great-man" approach, the trait approach, and the behavioral approach have been developed as ways of studying the leader. Of these, the great-man approach is least sophisticated, since it suggests that the successful manager is an innately competent leader who is "born rather than made," and that the basis for his success cannot really be uncovered by studying him or his methods.

great-man

1 The assumptions that a leader and/or his behavior cannot be analyzed and that "a leader is a leader" are consistent with the _____ _____ approach to studying leadership.

Executive selection (since they assume that leaders are "born and not made")

2 Would companies following a great-man approach tend to emphasize executive selection, executive development, or both in their personnel programs? _____

3 In contrast to the great-man approach, the *trait approach* assumes that successful leadership is correlated with the personality characteristics of the appointed leader, and that these can be systematically studied. Thus the trait approach offers a basis for discovering the factors underlying _____success.

leadership (or
managerial, etc.)

4 Analyzing such personal characteristics as integrity, promptness, and dependability and attempting to relate these characteristics to executive success involve the _____ approach to studying leadership.

trait

5 The number of traits studied may vary from as few as a half dozen to twenty or more. Would this diversity in the number of traits investigated make it easier or more difficult to compare different studies that have been done from the trait point of view? [Easier / More difficult]

More difficult

6 The absence of a commonly agreed-upon set of executive traits makes comparison between and among studies difficult. Another difficulty is the definition of traits. For example, the trait "honesty" can relate to truth telling or to the property rights of others and hence has [only one / more than one] possible meaning.

more than one

7 A few years ago *Fortune* magazine asked seventy-five high ranking executives for definitions and opinions of various executive qualities. The definitions given for "dependability" included 147 different descriptive statements. Exhibit 13.1 on page 350 presents the categories of meanings represented by these statements. As indicated, there were _____
[number] different definitions given for the trait of dependability.

twenty-five

8 In addition to the absence of a uniform set of traits to be studied and ambiguity in the _____ of traits, difficulties in *measuring* the traits have also been encountered.

definition (or
meaning)

9 Traits are measured by quantifying the opin-

EXHIBIT 13.1 *Categories of Meanings Given by Executives for the Trait "Dependability"*

Adapted from Perrin Stryker, "On the Meaning of Executive Qualities," *Fortune,* June 1958, p. 189. Reproduced with permission.

1. Is thorough, steady, reliable, consistent
2. Does complete successful job, gets results
3. Follows orders, seeks approval, carries out assignments
4. Uses good judgment in decision making
5. Is honest, trustworthy, conscientious; keeps promises
6. Needs little or no checking up
7. Is punctual; meets schedules
8. Overcomes obstacles and pressures
9. Accepts full responsibility, does job
10. Is frank, unevasive, courageous
11. Behaves predictably
12. Inspires confidence
13. Is cooperative
14. Is devoted to duty and company
15. Considers others
16. Does more than he has to
17. Does his best
18. Is adaptable to leadership
19. Has good personal habits
20. Asks help if needed
21. Learns from mistakes
22. Has satisfactory substitute
23. Works like his superior
24. Uses initiative
25. Is self-disciplined

---

trait

ions of other people. There is a long history of rating-scale development that parallels the development of the _____ approach to studying leadership.

inconsistent

10 People's opinions are not entirely objective but contain an element of *bias*. This tends to make different descriptions of the same individual [consistent / inconsistent].

11 Accordingly, contemporary developments in rating-scale techniques have been focused on distilling the valid part of a rater's description while attempting to eliminate the part representing his

bias _____.

12 Although the discovered importance of specific personality traits has varied from study to study, three general trait areas—intelligence, communication skill, and the ability to assess group goals—have been found to be related to

leadership _____ success in a variety of situations.

13 Thus, in comparison with other members of the group they lead, leaders tend to be more intelligent, have better

communication _____ skill, and have a higher ability to assess group goals.

14 It is important that the general leadership characteristics occur in combination in order to be associated with leadership success. All three of the trait areas have to be involved: _____,

intelligence
communication _____ skill, and ability to assess group goals.

15 Thus a leader's low communication skill, for example, [can / cannot] be offset by his being of

cannot higher intelligence.

16 To have a high likelihood of leadership success, the person must be high in the three trait areas compared with [people in general / other

other group
members group members].

17 To summarize these findings, the three general trait areas that have been found to be related to leadership success in a variety of situations are

intelligence
communication _____, _____
group goals skill, and ability to assess _____.

18 Thus far we have discussed two leader-oriented approaches to studying the basis for leadership success: the _____

great-man

trait

approach and the _____ approach.

19 A third leader-oriented approach, the *behavioral approach*, shifts the emphasis from an analysis of the leader's characteristics to an analysis of

what he does (how he leads, his behavior, etc.)

_____.

20 Observing the relative amount of executive time spent on such activities as planning, motivating, and communicating is consistent with the

behavioral

_____ approach to leadership analysis.

21 Observing executive activities yields information about what they do. Does it necessarily yield information about what they *should* be doing?

No

[Yes / No]

22 In order to pinpoint the executive activities that differentiate the successful leader, the activities of the two following kinds of leaders, or executives, need to be compared: those executives considered to be successful and those executives con-

unsuccessful (etc.)

sidered to be _____.

23 Although identifying the most and least successful executives appears to be a relatively straightforward task, in practice the existence of other factors that affect organizational success makes it difficult to assess the relative influence of

leader (manager, etc.)

what the _____ does on organizational success.

24 Most writers have based their descriptions of successful leader behavior on their general observations and experiences in a variety of managerial situations. It is only recently that carefully planned

activities (or
behavior, etc.)

and quantified observations of executive
_____ have been carried out.

25 In order to relate differences in executive behavior to differences in executive success, we need
to have reliable measurement of their behavior on
the one hand and reliable measurement of their
success _____ on the other hand.

B THE ORGANIZATIONAL CLIMATE

Although most studies aimed at discovering the
basis for leadership success have focused on the
leader himself, attention has also been directed at
the organizational climate in which the leadership
position exists. Research evidence indicates, for example, that the one person who most influences a
leader's pattern of behavior is his direct organizational superior.

superior

26 The way that a manager leads is most importantly influenced by how his _____
leads.

leadership
(managerial, etc.)

27 In a study of first-level supervisors at International Harvester,[1] for example, it was found that
the supervisor's leadership style was influenced
more by his own organizational superior than by a
comprehensive training program in
_____ methods.

28 The general purpose of the leadership training course at International Harvester was to help
develop a higher level of a human relations orientation at the foreman level in the company. The
results of a questionnaire administered at the
beginning and end of the course indicated a signif-

[1]Edwin A. Fleishman, "Leadership Climate, Human Relations
Training, and Supervisory Behavior," _Personnel Psychology_, vol.
6, no. 2, pp. 205–222, 1953.

icant increase in human relations attitudes, thus
success   providing evidence of program [success / failure].

29 However, because the researchers wanted to
determine the effects of the program back in the
plant, they conducted follow-up studies with those
foremen who had completed the course earlier.
Figure 13.1 summarizes the results of the studies
in the plant in terms of both human relations
attitudes; behavior   _____ and _____.

30 As indicated in Figure 13.1, in comparison
with the untrained foreman those who had completed the human relations course were
lower   [higher / lower] in both human relations attitudes
and behavior.

31 Thus, based on the results in the plant, the
unsuccessful   training program appeared to be generally [suc-
cessful / unsuccessful].

32 On the basis of further analysis of the results
the researchers concluded that "...if the old way
of doing things in the plant situation is still the
shortest path to approval by the boss, then this is
what the foreman really learns." In other words,
the primary influence on the foreman's attitudes
his immediate   and behavior was that exerted by [the training
superior   course / his immediate superior].

33 Thus, this would suggest that in order to
change a "leadership climate" in an organization,
we need to *begin* such development and modifica-
top management   tion at the [supervisory / top management] level.
(and then work
with each level
below)

34 We need to begin at the top of an organization
in attempting to change leadership climate because
the influence on leadership methods extends from
above   [above / below].

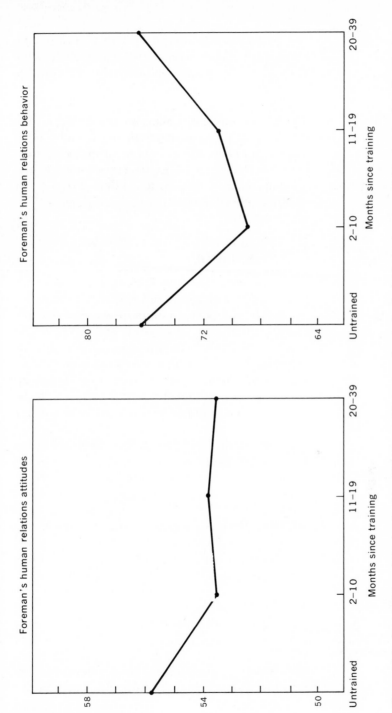

Figure 13.1 Comparison of the leadership attitudes and behavior of untrained and trained groups of foremen back in the plant. (Modified from Edwin A. Fleishman, "Leadership Climate, Human Relations Training, and Supervisory Behavior," *Personnel Psychology*, vol. 6, no. 2, 1953, p. 214. Used with permission.)

35 In addition to the leader's relationship with his own superior, his relationship with other managers and staff specialists also affects his

leadership (etc.) _____ behavior.

36 For example, if a manager has had previous difficulty with a particular staff department, he is likely to supervise the work of those of his subordinates who have extensive contact with that department in a manner [similar to / different from] that

different from

of other subordinates.

C THE SITUATIONAL APPROACH TO LEADERSHIP

The preceding discussions about the leader, the group, and the organization suggest that successful leadership is dependent on more than the leader's traits or behavior. Successful leadership is the result of the interaction between the leader and his subordinates in a particular organizational situation. Accordingly, a single pattern of leadership behavior used without discretion is unlikely to be successful in a variety of managerial situations.

37 Successful leadership is the result of the in-

leader

teraction between the _____ and his

subordinates

_____ in a particular organizational situation.

38 Therefore, a particular pattern of leader be-

is not

havior, or a particular pattern of traits, [is / is not] likely to lead to successful leadership in every situation.

39 For one thing, there frequently are important differences in leadership requirements according

organizational (or

to the _____ level in a firm.

managerial)

40 Would you expect to find important differences in leadership requirements between different functional groups, such as supervision of production employees as contrasted with supervision of staff personnel? [Yes / No]

Yes

41 Even given the same organizational level and functional area, the requirements associated with successful _____ may change over time.

leadership

42 For example, the production foreman who supervises employees in the same manner today as he did twenty years ago is likely to be [more / less] effective today than he was twenty years ago.

less

43 Thus, the successful leader is not a blind follower of particular leadership methods but chooses the leadership methods that he considers appropriate for a particular _____.

situation

44 The situational approach to leadership does not imply that every situation is unique in every respect. It does imply that every situation is somewhat different, thus making somewhat different leadership _____ appropriate.

methods
(behavior, etc.)

45 In the situational approach to leadership, the leader begins by [analyzing the overall situation / choosing a leadership method].

analyzing the
overall situation

46 Only after analyzing the overall situation, including a consideration of the followers and their objectives, should the leader decide upon a particular _____.

leadership method
(etc.)

47 As we indicated in the first section of this chapter, at least three general traits are correlated with leadership success: _____, _____ skill, and the ability to assess _____.

intelligence
communication
group goals

48 These traits [do / do not] suggest that the

do not

do

successful leader tends to behave in a particular way; they [do / do not] suggest that he has the capability of studying situational requirements and selecting from possible leadership strategies.

D LEADERSHIP STYLES

Overall leadership style can be considered from several points of view, two of which are covered in this section. From the standpoint of the motivational method used, leadership can be positive or negative. From the standpoint of the delegation of authority, leadership can be centralized or decentralized. In a classical study of leadership methods, the authoritarian method was extremely centralized, the free-rein method was extremely decentralized, and the democratic method was between the two in terms of the amount of authority delegated to members of the group. Following this discussion, we conclude this section of the chapter by describing a recent approach to describing leadership style that includes consideration of the motivational method used as well as the extent of shared authority.

negative

49 From the standpoint of motivational methods used, positive leaders emphasize the use of positive motivational methods, and negative leaders tend to use _____ motivational methods.

increased

decreased

50 As you no doubt recall from the chapter on motivating people at work, positive motivation involves the possibility of [increased / decreased] motive satisfaction, whereas negative motivation involves the possibility of [increased / decreased] motive satisfaction.

positive

51 The manager who motivates people by offering them greater satisfaction of their own motives when they work toward the organization's goals is utilizing _____ leadership.

negative

52 The manager who motivates people by explicitly or implicitly threatening punishment of some kind for noncooperation is using _____ leadership.

Negative

53 In which leadership climate would the employee tend to "look for a way out" of the situation?

_____

positive
negative

54 Of course, seldom is an actual leadership style completely _____ or completely _____. However, the relative balance between the two determines the motivational climate operating in an organizational unit.

55 Another dimension of leadership style or pattern is the extent to which the leader centralizes or decentralizes his decision-making authority. The leader who shares his authority with his subordinates tends toward [centralized / decentralized] leadership.

decentralized

56 In a classical study of leadership style,[2] *authoritarian, democratic*, and *free-rein* methods were compared in their effects on group behavior. Which style represents the extreme of centralized decision-making authority? _____

authoritarian

57 The studies being described concerned different leadership styles of adult leaders in boys' clubs. Would the effect of the leadership styles on the boys' behavior have any relevance to leadership in adult organizations? [Yes / No]

Yes (to the extent that people in general tend to respond similarly to leadership methods)

[2]Kurt Lewin, Ronald Lippitt, and R. K. White, "Patterns of Agressive Behavior in Experimentally Created Climates," *Journal of Social Psychology*, vol. 10, no. 2, pp. 271–299, 1939.

58 Which leadership method would involve complete freedom for group or individual decision making, with little or no leader participation? [Authoritarian / Democratic / Free-rein]

Free-rein

59 In which leadership method would all policies be a matter of group discussion and decision, but with the active assistance of the leader? [Authoritarian / Democratic / Free-rein]

Democratic

60 The leadership method in which the leader determines all policy himself and assigns specific work tasks to each group member is the [authoritarian / democratic / free-rein].

authoritarian

61 Of the three leadership methods studied, maximum centralization of authority was represented by the _____ method, maximum decentralization of authority was represented by the _____ method, and considerable, but not complete, decentralization of authority was represented by the _____ method.

authoritarian

free-rein

democratic

62 Although all the results of these studies cannot be completely presented here, several of the differences in the boys' behavior are worth noting. In terms of both quality and quantity of work, the free-rein leadership method was inferior to both the _____ and _____ methods.

democratic
authoritarian

63 On the other hand, the highest level of productivity per se was not found under the democratic leadership method but rather under the _____ method.

authoritarian (Thus research findings may not always conform to our personal biases.)

64 Because there is considerable freedom of group expression, but with the coordinating presence of leader authority, the greatest amount of originality in work was found under the _____ method.

democratic (not free-rein, as many would expect)

65 Perhaps because of the high degree of control over individual behavior, the greatest amount of discontent was expressed under the _____ form of leadership.

authoritarian (which, finally, would be expected on the basis of "common sense")

66 Submissive behavior, with some loss of individuality, was most marked in the strongly centralized _____ situation.

authoritarian

67 The leadership style that resulted in the greatest number of group-oriented remarks and the greatest degree of friendliness was the _____.

democratic

68 Summing up, a greater degree of aggression, submission, and productivity characterized the _____ group; a greater degree of friendliness and originality in work characterized the _____ group; and a greater degree of disorganization, nonproductivity, and play-oriented behavior characterized the _____ group.

authoritarian

democratic

free-rein

69 The conclusion that when a leader ceases to lead, disorganization in group behavior results is suggested by the findings associated with the _____ method.

free-rein

70 The conclusion that strong centralized leadership can promote high productivity is suggested by the findings that are associated with the _____ method. It should be added, however, that all the boys who dropped out of club activities during these experiments did so while they were in the authoritarian climate.

authoritarian

71 The conclusion that participative leadership methods are especially valuable when innovation or creativity is one of the "products" desired of the work group is suggested by the findings associated with the _____ leadership style.

democratic

72 Do these findings suggest that supervisory methods, or leadership style, should be the same in a shop situation as contrasted with a research staff, for example? [Yes / No]

No

73 Similarly, recent research regarding leadership style indicates that the decentralized, or democratic, leadership methods are most successful in [research / production] departments, whereas centralized methods are more appropriate in [research / production] departments.

research

production

74 As an example of recent interest in leadership style, Exhibit 13.2 on pages 364 and 365 is adapted from a technique developed by Rensis Likert, director of the Institute of Social Research at the University of Michigan, to help businessmen analyze the management style used by their companies. Of the styles described in this exhibit, the one in which managers have the lowest level of confidence in subordinates is the _____ _____ style.

exploitive
authoritative

75 The management style in which upward communication tends to be "censored for the boss" is the _____ style.

benevolent
authoritative

76 The management style in which goals are established by orders from above, but after discussion with subordinates, is the _____ style.

consultative

77 Finally, the management style in which control data are used for self-guidance rather than for external control is the _____ style.

participative

78 In using the chart in Exhibit 13.2, each answer is regarded as a rating on a continuous scale from the left to the right of the chart. Likert has found that most executives with whom he has consulted rate their companies in terms of the descriptions in the second and third categories, that is, in terms of

benevolent authoritative; consultative

the _____ and the _____ styles.

79 Executives who have used this chart have also indicated belief that companies do best when they have profiles well to the right on this chart, that

participative

is, in the direction of the _____ style, and that companies do worst with profiles positioned to the left, that is, in the direction

exploitive authoritative

of the _____ style.

E MANAGERIAL POWER AND DISCIPLINING

Managerial power includes the ability that a manager has to provide rewards and to inflict punishment. Whereas the discussion in Chapter 7, in the section on power and politics, was concerned with the degree of influence that a person has to "get things done" in an organization, in this section we consider the concept of power as it is applied in the context of disciplining subordinate personnel in an organizational unit.

80 As indicated in the introduction given above, the ability to provide rewards or to inflict punishment is included in the concept of managerial

power

_____ .

81 Although the use of power can have a positive (reward) or negative (punishment) connotation, in this section we give attention to several principles that should be followed when disciplinary action on the part of a manager becomes necessary. Thus, the material in this section is concerned with how

	EXPLOITIVE AUTHORITATIVE	BENEVOLENT AUTHORITATIVE	CONSULTATIVE	PARTICIPATIVE
LEADERSHIP How much confidence is shown in subordinates?	None	Condescending	Substantial	Complete
How free do they feel to talk to superiors about job?	Not at all	Not very	Rather free	Fully free
Are subordinates' ideas sought and used, if worthy?	Seldom	Sometimes	Usually	Always
MOTIVATION Is predominant use made of (1) fear, (2) threats, (3) punishment, (4) rewards, (5) involvement?	1, 2, 3 occasionally 4	4, some 3	4, some 3 and 5	5, 4, based on group set goals
Where is responsibility felt for achieving organization's goals?	Mostly at top	Top and middle	Fairly general	At all levels
COMMUNICATION How much communication is aimed at achieving organization's objectives?	Very little	Little	Quite a bit	A great deal
What is the direction of information flow?	Downward	Mostly downward	Down and up	Down, up, and sideways
How is downward communication accepted?	With suspicion	Possibly with suspicion	With caution	With an open mind
How accurate is upward communication?	Often wrong	Censored for the boss	Limited accuracy	Accurate
How well do superiors know problems faced by subordinates?	Know little	Some knowledge	Quite well	Very well

EXHIBIT 13.2 *A Rating Form for Analyzing Management Style*

DECISIONS	At what level are decisions formally made?	Mostly at top	Policy at top, some delegation	Broad policy at top, more delegation	Throughout but well integrated
	What is the origin of technical and professional knowledge used in decision making?	Top management	Upper and middle	To a certain extent, throughout	To a great extent, throughout
	Are subordinates involved in decisions related to their work?	Not at all	Occasionally consulted	Generally consulted	Fully involved
	What does decision-making process contribute to motivation?	Nothing, often weakens it	Relatively little	Some contribution	Substantial contribution
GOALS	How are organizational goals established?	Orders issued	Orders, some comment invited	After discussion, by orders	By group action (except in crisis)
	How much covert resistance to goals is present?	Strong resistance	Moderate resistance	Some resistance at times	Little or none
CONTROL	How concentrated are review and control functions?	Highly at top	Relatively highly at top	Moderate delegation to lower levels	Quite widely shared
	Is there an informal organization resisting the formal one?	Yes	Usually	Sometimes	No-same goals as formal
	What are cost, productivity, and other control data used for?	Policing, punishment	Reward and punishment	Reward, some self-guidance	Self-guidance, problem solving

(Adapted from *The Human Organization: Its Management and Value* by Rensis Likert. Copyright 1967 by McGraw-Hill, Inc. Reproduced by permission of McGraw-Hill Book Company. No further reproduction authorized.)

punish   the manager uses his power to [reward / punish].

82   One of the principles associated with the use of disciplinary power is that such actions by the manager should be consistent. This implies that if an area is designated as a "no smoking" area any employee observed to be smoking there should be

regardless of
previous infraction
(but the specific
disciplinary
actions may vary)

disciplined [regardless of previous infractions /only if he has violated rules before].

consistency

83   Thus, the principle of disciplining which indicates that organizational rules should apply to all employees, regardless of their status, is the principle of _____.

should not

84   Another principle associated with disciplinary action is that such action should be taken only when there has been *forewarning*. In this respect, a relatively new employee who has violated operating rules unknowingly [should / should not] be disciplined.

forewarning

85   The principle which makes it necessary that the manager inform each employee of all operating rules and practices so that the employee is in a position to know which actions are appropriate and which are inappropriate is the principle of _____.

unfair

86   In addition to consistency and forewarning, the concept of *fairness* indicates that the penalty included in a disciplinary action should be equitable in respect to the nature of the offense. From this standpoint, discharging an employee with several years of good service because he failed to call in that he was sick would probably be considered [fair / unfair].

87   Because all employees in the organizational unit will judge whether a penalty was equitable, and not just the individual employee being disciplined, it is particularly important that the princi-

fairness

ple of _____ be adhered to in such actions.

88 Thus far we have considered three principles that should be followed in conjunction with using managerial power for disciplining inappropriate

consistency
forewarning
fairness

behavior or performance: _____, _____, and _____.

89 A fourth principle that should be followed in applying disciplinary action is *promptness*. If an infraction of organizational rules has occurred, the effectiveness of the disciplinary action in terms of influencing employee behavior is enhanced if the

days

action is taken within several [days / weeks].

90 However, the principle of promptness does not necessarily indicate that the disciplinary action should be "immediate." Consider the emotional states of the manager and of the employee in a disciplinary situation. The principles of consistency and fairness are more likely to be followed if dis-

after a "cooling
off" period

ciplining action occurs [immediately / after a "cooling off" period].

91 Finally, when reprimanding an employee the manager should strive to arrange for some degree of *privacy*. In general, congratulations and rewards should be given publicly and reprimands should be discussed in private. Of course, the main reason for this is the psychological effect of being reprimanded in front of one's fellow employees. That is, an employee is more likely to acknowledge his mistakes and to change his behavior in the future if the reprimand and the associated disciplinary ac-

private

tion are discussed in [private / public].

92 In addition to the principles of consistency, forewarning, and fairness, two other principles which should be used when disciplinary action is

promptness
privacy

necessary are the principles of _____ and _____.

93 The principles we have discussed are summarized in Table 13.1. The attention here devoted to disciplining is not to suggest that a manager should rely on his power to discipline as a primary basis for improving organizational effectiveness. But any manager, and particularly one who is newly appointed, is likely to be "tested" by subordinate personnel in his enforcement of organizational policies and may therefore find it necessary

discipline (or
punish)

to use his power to _____ with appropriate awareness of the principles involved.

Table 13.1 Principles Associated with Taking Disciplinary Action

Consistency
Forewarning
Fairness
Promptness
Privacy

94 In reference to the discussion in the preceding section of this chapter, primary reliance on disciplinary power in an organizational unit would result in a motivational climate that is predomi-

negative

nantly [positive / negative].

95 The use of discipline can help to prevent or discourage repetition of undesirable patterns of behavior if applied in conformance with the principles discussed in this section. However, the appropriate behavior is more likely to replace the undesirable pattern, and to do so more rapidly, when

rewarded (etc.)

the desired behavior is _____.

96 Further, we also noted some consequences of authoritarian leadership methods in the preceding section of this chapter. If the desired job performance should include individual initiative and creativity then the motivational climate must be pre-

positive

dominantly [positive / negative].

Review

97 The leader-oriented approach to studying leadership which suggests that the successful executive is a man of outstanding ability who would have been successful in any situation is the great-man _____ approach. (Frames 1 and 2)

98 Difficulties in defining and measuring personality characteristics of leaders are problems encountered in conjunction with the trait _____ approach. (Frames 3 to 11)

99 In comparison with other group members, successful leaders tend to be high in all three general trait areas of _____, intelligence; _____, and communication skill; ability to _____. assess group goals (Frames 12 to 18)

100 Shifting the emphasis from what the leader is to what the leader does is consistent with the behavioral _____ approach to studying leadership. (Frames 19 to 25)

101 In the evaluation of the leadership training course at International Harvester it was found that the most important influence on the foreman's attitudes and behavior came from _____ his superior (etc.) _____. (Frames 26 to 32)

102 A comprehensive study of leadership would include not only consideration of the leader himself, but also the organizational _____ climate (or _____ in which leadership is taking situations, etc.) place. (Frames 33 to 36)

103 That a particular set of executive traits or use of a particular style will not invariably lead to success in different leadership positions is the conclusion of the situational _____ approach to leadership. (Frames 37 to 48)

104 In terms of overall leadership style as related to motivational methods, the use of rewards is
positive emphasized by the _____ leader,
whereas the use of threat or coercion is empha-
negative sized by the _____ leader. (Frames 49 to 54)

105 Another facet of leadership style is the extent of centralization or decentralization of deci-
authority (etc.) sion-making _____. (Introduction to Section D, Frame 55)

106 In a classic study of leadership style, the three following leadership methods were used in
authoritarian boy's club groups: _____,
democratic _____, and
free-rein _____. (Frames 56 to 61)

107 In this study of leadership styles, a greater degree of disorganization, nonproductivity, and play-oriented behavior are characteristics of the
free-rein _____ group; a greater degree of aggression, submission, and productivity are char-
authoritarian acteristics of the _____ group; and a greater degree of friendliness and originality in work are characteristics of the
democratic _____ group. (Frames 62 to 73)

108 In a more recent approach to describing leadership style Likert has devised a rating chart in which the most highly centralized method is called
exploitive the _____
authoritative and the most highly decentralized method is called
participative the _____ method. (Frames 74 to 79)

109 The process by which managerial power is used to enforce conformance to organizational rules by punishing inappropriate performance is
disciplining called _____. (Frames 80 and 81)

110 Of the principles that are to be followed in conjunction with taking disciplinary action, the one which is an indication that the rules should apply to all personnel regardless of rank or status is _____, the one which is an indication that the rules should be made known is _____, and the one which is an indication that the punitive action should be equitable is _____. (Frames 82 to 88)

consistency

forewarning

fairness

111 The principle of disciplinary action which indicates that such action should come as soon as possible after the violation of rules is _____, and it has been found that a reprimand is most effective when it is discussed [publicly / privately].

promptness

privately

112 In general, the managerial power to discipline should be used sparingly, because desired behavior and performance are best encouraged, or reinforced, by the use of _____. (Frames 93 to 96)

rewards

Discussion Questions

1. In what sense are the trait and behavioral approaches to studying successful leadership "two sides of the same coin"? How are the two approaches essentially different?

2. In addition to the characteristics of a particular leader, what factors in an organization influence the way in which a manager attempts to lead his subordinates?

3. What are the implications of the situational approach to leadership?

4. What are some implications of the classical study of leadership style conducted by Lewin, Lippitt, and White? What are the limitations of the study?

5. As indicated by the analysis in Exhibit 13.2, the results of a number of studies tend to favor the participative management style. By reviewing the contents of the chart in respect to this management style, identify the reasons why this style would not be considered desirable by some managers.

6. Using the chart devised by Likert, describe the managerial climate in the organization in which you now work or have recently worked. Do you think the climate could be improved? How?

7. Why should a manager minimize his reliance on his power to discipline? What are the alternatives in a situation in which many infractions of the rules are taking place?

8. In general, why is it best to "praise in public but reprimand in private?" Under what circumstances would it be best not to follow this rule?

Case Study: A Change of Supervisors

As Supervisor of the communications section in Aero-tech, Inc., Ralph Jones had the reputation of being a hard-nosed boss who demanded strict adherence to his instructions and placed great emphasis on the use of formal, as well as informal, control methods. When he was first appointed as supervisor two years ago, a considerable amount of discord developed in the communications section as a result. As a matter of fact, during the first six months of his appointment eight of the fourteen engineering and technical personnel in the section either transferred to other jobs in the company or left the company itself because of dissatisfaction with his methods. However, just about the time that John Dorfman, manager of the research and development department, was considering removing Jones as supervisor, the problems in the section subsided as the remaining members and those he hired accepted his style of leadership. Although he encouraged participation of his subordinates during the planning stage of a project or program, once he made procedure and scheduling decisions, he expected strict compliance on the part of the communications section personnel.

During his tenure as supervisor Ralph Jones reduced project personnel costs associated with the communications section by 10 percent while meeting all time schedules for program completion set by the manager of research and development and by the project managers. He had the reputation of running a tight and efficient operation. Largely because of this record of accomplishment he was offered what he described as an irresistible managerial opportunity with a competing firm in the aerospace industry, and after two weeks' notice left the company to accept that position three months ago.

At first John Dorfman assumed that he would promote someone from within the communications section. However he found that no one had really been Jones' assistant or understudy, and that no one in the section seemed particularly desirous of going into supervision. After two weeks of search, the research and development manager was able to arrange the transfer of Tom Yarborough, then supervisor of the command systems section, to the vacated position. In turn, Yarborough had one of his subordinates take over supervision of the command systems section. Yarborough was regarded as a highly competent supervisor, and although this transfer did not represent a promotion for him, he saw it as an opportunity to gain a greater diversity of experience.

Tom Yarborough was a strong proponent of management by objectives. He believed in making all task assignments in terms of the objectives to be accomplished and leaving it up to the personnel involved to formulate the necessary procedures and methods. He was available for consultation regarding job problems, but the personnel in the communications section found that he avoided becoming involved in the detail of the work. After his first month as supervisor, it was obvious to John Dorfman that things were not going well in the communications section. Two scheduled completion times for tasks assigned to the section had been missed, and the progress on one or two others was possibly also behind schedule. In discussing the situation with two or three of the key employees in the section during a coffee break, the department manager learned that it was the consensus of the men in the section that Tom Yarborough didn't understand the work he was supervising and was not acting as a supervisor. He refused to specify how goals were to be accomplished and then held individual employees responsible when specific tasks were not completed on time. As a result, the personnel in the section were frustrated by the very absence of direction on his part and doubted that Yarborough was capable of providing the direction even if he wanted to do so.

1. How would you describe Ralph Jones' approach to management in terms of leadership style?
2. Was the employee reaction to Jones' methods predictable? Why?
3. How would you describe Tom Yarborough's approach to management in terms of leadership style?
4. Was the employee reaction to Yarborough's methods predictable? Why?
5. What should Mr. Dorfman do about the present situation in the communications section?

Case Study: A Matter of Overtime

As was typically the case during the closing of the

books at the end of the fiscal year, it was necessary to have a number of the employees in the accounting department work beyond the usual office hours so that the end-of-year reports could be prepared on time. As the 5 o'clock hour approached, John Zayle, the chief accountant, noticed that two of the employees got ready to leave the office to go home. He therefore called them over to his desk.

Zayle: "You are supposed to be working overtime tonight until about 9:00 P.M."

First employee: "Why, no one notified me that I was supposed to work."

Zayle: "I told both of you the first day of the week about working tonight."

Second employee: "This is the first I have heard of it. I received no written information."

Zayle: "No written message is necessary. The fact that I told you is sufficient."

The men returned to their desks and started working. At 6:30 P.M. John Zayle stated that he was going to the coffee shop down the street for a quick dinner and asked the two men if they wanted to join him. They indicated that they did not, so he went to the restaurant alone. When Zayle returned about forty minutes later he found the office deserted.

When the two employees reported for work the next morning John Zayle told them they were fired. They went to the industrial relations department and appealed his action. Based in part on the lack of a written record of the assignment to work overtime, the industrial relations manager reduced the firing decision to a two-week layoff. John was fuming. Not only had he wasted much of the day in the appeal proceedings but he was now in the position of having two vacant positions for which he could not hire replacements during this particularly busy time period.

1. At what point did the problem described in the case description really begin?
2. Was the disciplinary decision to fire the two men appropriate? Why or why not?
3. Should the industrial relations manager have the authority to overrule a manager's decision regarding disciplinary action? In this respect, what mistake did John Zayle make?
4. What is likely to be the nature of the relationship between John Zayle and the two employees when they return from the two-week layoff?

Suggested Readings*

Cummins, R. C.: "Leader-Member Relations as a moderator of the effects of Leader Behavior and Attitude," *Personnel Psychology*, vol. 25, no. 4, Winter 1972.

Evans, M. G.: "Leadership and Motivation: A Core Concept," *Academy of Management Journal,* vol. 13, no. 1, March 1970.

Fiedler, F. E.: *A Theory of Leadership Effectiveness,* McGraw-Hill Book Company, New York, 1967.

Filley, A. C., and R. J. House: *Mangerial Process and Organizational Behavior,* Scott, Foresman and Company, Glenview, Ill., 1969.

Hand, H. H., M. D. Richards, and J. W. Slocum, Jr.: "Organizational Climate and the Effectiveness of a Human Relations Training Program," *Academy of Management Journal,* vol. 16, no. 2, June 1973.

Richards, S. A., and J. V. Cuffe: "Behavioral Correlates of Leadership Effectiveness in Interacting and Counteracting Groups," *Journal of Applied Psychology,* vol. 56, no. 5, October 1972.

*Also see the cross-reference table in the Preface.

Schneider, B.: "Organizational Climate: Individual Preferences and Organizational Realities," *Journal of Applied Psychology*, vol. 56, no. 3, June 1972.

Wickert, F. R., and D. E. McFarland: *Measuring Executive Effectiveness*, Appleton-Century-Crofts, Inc., New York, 1967.

Chapter **fourteen**
EFFECTIVE
SUPERVISION

In this final chapter concerned with the management process of directing we discuss some selected topics and present research findings particularly relevant to the first-level supervisor in the organization. We begin by considering the supervisor's position in the organization and several conflicting viewpoints concerning his proper role. In the second section of this chapter we review the supervisory approach used in high-productivity units as contrasted to that used in units that are low in productivity. This discussion is then extended to a consideration of the managerial grid, a device that has been considered very useful for describing the organizational implications of various supervisory styles. We conclude the chapter by describing some research results in an area of increasing supervisory responsibility, that of managing job and organizational changes.

A THE ROLE OF THE FIRST-LEVEL SUPERVISOR

The first-level supervisor is in a unique position in the organization in that he is the only manager who supervises the work of nonmanagers. Since the ultimate attainment of organizational goals depends on what happens at the operative level, this makes the first-level supervisor's position particularly important. The success of plans and strategies determined at the top management level depends on his ability to translate them into action at the working level. In this section we identify several different views concerning the supervisor's appropriate role and consider their implications as factors affecting his performance.

1 Throughout this chapter we use the word "supervisor" to designate the first level of management in the organization. Whereas top executives and middle managers in the organization supervise other members of the company management team, the supervisor has responsibility for directing the work of _____ .

operative employees (or nonmanagers, etc.)

2 In the following list, underline the identifying letters of those position titles that designate supervisory positions.

a; b; c (All these titles designate first-line supervisory positions.)

a. section head, accounts receivable
b. supervisor, research and development
c. foreman, paint shop

3 Therefore, first-level supervisors are located in all the functional areas of work in the organization, including staff, as well as line, components. From this standpoint, both the manager responsible for the work of a group of financial analysts in the company and the foreman on the assembly line are

supervisors
considered to be _____.

4 Most of the studies concerned with the supervisor's work have been done with the first-level supervisor in manufacturing, that is, the foreman. Because he has certain assigned responsibilities for planning, organizing, directing, and controlling,

is
the foreman appropriately [is / is not] considered a member of management.

5 Although the supervisor is now considered a member of management, historically there have been a number of different views concerning his proper role in the organization, and the influence of these views is still felt. The first of these views (identified in Figure 14.1), which particularly indicates the importance of his position in the organ-

key man
ization, identifies him as the _____ _____ in management.

6 In terms of the *key-man* concept, from the worker's point of view the supervisor is the direct

top
management
face-to-face representative of _____
_____ .

7 In the other direction, top management's views of the operative employees is largely based on the kind of information passed on to them by the

supervisor (or
foreman)
_____.

8 Thus, because of his unique position in the chain of authority and in the communication system, the supervisor has been considered to be the

key man
_____ _____ in management.

9 However, based on the same facts concerning

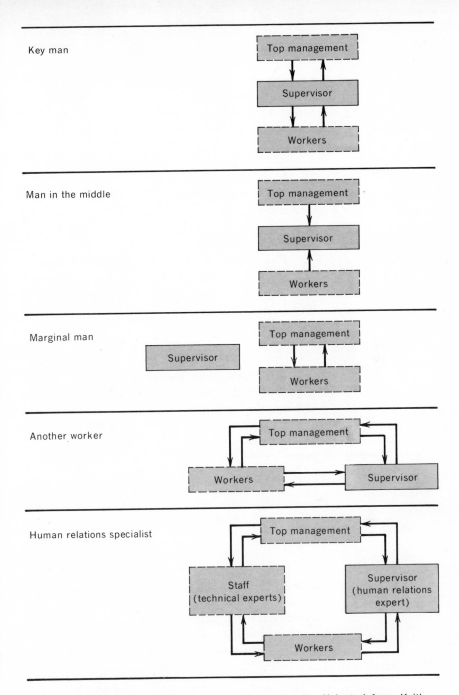

Figure 14.1 Different viewpoints of the supervisor's role. (Adapted from Keith Davis, *Human Behavior at Work: Human Relations and Organizational Behavior*, 4th ed., McGraw-Hill Book Company, New York, 1972, p. 121. Reproduced with permission.)

his position in the organization, another view of the supervisor's position is that he's the *man in the middle*, caught between the expectations and demands of _____ _____

top management

workers

and _____.

10 In contrasting the key-man view with the man-in-the-middle view, the one that sees him in a strategic position of strength is the _____

key-man

_____ view.

11 The view that takes cognizance of his vulnerability to the pressures of competing groups and also his inability to completely satisfy the differing expectations of these competing groups is

man-in-the-middle

the _____ view.

12 Considering the possible implications of his organizational position from a sociological point of view, the supervisor also finds himself to be a *marginal man;* i.e., he may not be a fully accepted

management

worker

member of either the _____ group or the _____ group.

13 As is typical of a person with marginal group membership, the supervisor may find that both top

do not

management and the workers [do / do not] fully confide in him.

14 Furthermore, whereas top management and staff specialists have extensive contact with one another and a common set of interests, and workers have a pattern of informal groups and perhaps a union, the supervisor's infrequent contact with other supervisors further adds to his posi-

marginal man

tion as a _____ _____.

15 Thus far we have discussed three viewpoints concerning the supervisor's role in the organiza-

key-man
man-in-the-middle
marginal-man

tion: the _____ ,
_____ ,
and _____ viewpoints.

16   Another view of the supervisor not so prevalent today is that he belongs to *another worker group*,
rather than to management. Until the Labor Management Relations (Taft-Hartley) Act of 1947,
supervisors were legally considered to be employees with collective bargaining rights, thus enhancing the likelihood that they would think of them-

workers

selves as [managers / workers].

17   Although their legal status has changed, many
supervisors still think of themselves as being more
like workers than managers. Along these lines,
both the foreman's previous experience as an operative employee and centralized planning and

reinforce

scheduling   in   a   company   tend   to   [rein-
force / change] this viewpoint.

18   Both managerial decentralization, by which
more authority is delegated to first-level supervisors, and participation of supervisors in management development programs increase the likelihood that the supervisor will identify himself as a

management

member of the _____ group.

19   In addition to the key-man, man-in-the-middle, marginal-man, and another-worker views, the
supervisor has been considered as the *human relations specialist* in the organization. From this point
of view, he is not particularly the key man in the
operations, but rather one of the many specialists
contributing to the organization's effectiveness. His

human
relations

specialty is that of dealing with _____
_____ problems.

20   The view that the supervisor is primarily a

centralized (since
other types of
problems—such as
scheduling—are
handled by staff
specialists)

human relations specialist is particularly likely in the organization that is highly [centralized/decentralized].

21 Regardless of the type of organization, however, when supervisors are asked to identify their most important job problems, they almost invariably name such problems as employee motivation and conflicts among people, thereby acknowledging their necessary role as _____ _____ specialists.

human
relations

22 In most organizations the supervisor needs some level of technical knowledge in the areas of work being supervised. However, particularly when detailed schedules and procedures for his department are prepared by technical specialists in the organization, his principal remaining responsibility is that of being the _____ _____ specialist.

human
relations

23 In our review of the different viewpoints of the supervisor's role, both historical and presently held, we have identified five principal views: the _____, _____, _____, _____, and _____ views.

key-man
man-in-the-middle
marginal-man
another-worker
human relations
specialist

24 To some extent, all these views apply to the supervisor's position today. However, in order to improve the supervisor's opportunity to do an effective job, the top management of a firm should strive to make his predominant role that of a _____ _____ in management.

key man

25 From this standpoint, any organizational action that seems to treat him like a nonmanager or like a member of a "special" group (i.e., neither management nor worker) should certainly be avoided, since these two types of actions would

another-worker

marginal-man

tend to reinforce the _____ and _____ views of the supervisor's role, respectively.

26 Being a member of management who is in a key position in respect to his work with operative employees, he also needs to develop as a human relations specialist and will often find himself in the position of being the man in the middle. In spite of that, his opportunity to do an effective job and to develop self-confidence is reinforced when top management treats him as a fully accepted

management

member of the _____ group.

27 The particular strategy or practices that a firm should follow in order to accomplish this objective is, of course, entirely dependent on the company situation. What is required is true top management acceptance of the supervisor as a manager, rather than the use of any given set of techniques. That thousands of first-level supervisors joined a union—the Foreman's Association of America— before they were redefined as members of management by the Labor Management Relations Act of 1947 indicates that up to that time, at least,

unsuccessful

many firms were [successful / unsuccessful] in integrating foremen into the company management group.

B SUPERVISORY EFFECTIVENESS

Of course, all the preceding chapters in this part of the book on the management function of directing are relevant to developing effective supervisory practices. Since a large number of supervisory problems concern motivation, Chapter 12 on motivating people at work is particularly applicable.

In this section we briefly review the results of an extensive series of studies of supervisory practices conducted by Rensis Likert and his colleagues in the Institute for Social Research at the University of Michigan.[1] Their findings are consistent with the motivational principles discussed in both Chapters 11 and 12. They contribute to our understanding of motivation and supervision by describing actual patterns of supervision associated with high-production and low-production units in industrial organizations.

28   The studies of supervisory practices which we discuss were conducted in several public utilities, an insurance company, an automobile manufacturing company, a heavy-machinery factory, a railroad, an electric appliance factory, and several government agencies, thus representing a rela-
broad   tively [narrow / broad] industrial sample.

29   In evaluating supervisory effectiveness two major criteria were used: (1) the productivity per man-hour or some similar measure of the organization's success in achieving its productivity goals, and (2) the job satisfaction and other personal satisfactions derived by employees. The very fact that these two criteria are separately stated suggests that the researchers began with the premise that
might be   they [are closely related / might be independent of
independent of   one another].
one another

30   And as a matter of fact, in comparing high-productivity and low-productivity sections within companies, Likert found little relationship between employee attitude toward the company and productivity as such, although absenteeism and turnover may have been affected. As indicated by

[1]The results of the original series of studies are reported in detail in Rensis Likert, *Motivation: The Core of Management*, Personnel Series, no. 155, American Management Association, New York, 1953.

40;

20

the data in Table 14.1, whereas 37 percent of the employees in the high-productivity sections had a high level of satisfaction with the company and 24 percent had a low level of satisfaction, in low-productivity sections the percentages for high and low levels of satisfaction were _____ percent _____ percent, respectively.

Table 14.1 Attitude toward the Company and Section Productivity

ATTITUDE TOWARD COMPANY	HIGH-PRODUCTIVITY SECTIONS	LOW-PRODUCTIVITY SECTIONS
High	37%	40%
Average	39%	40%
Low	24%	20%
	100%	100%

do not

31 Until these studies were completed, it had been a common managerial assumption that developing a favorable employee attitude toward the company will result in increased productivity. The findings reported in Table 14.1 [do / do not] support this assumption.

32 An indirect measure of employee attitude toward the company which is sometimes used is the extent of participation in company recreational activities. To the extent that there is any relationship at all, Table 14.2 on page 388 indicates that the absence of participation in company recreational activities may be associated with the section being [high / low] in productivity.

high (Seventy-two percent of those in high-productivity sections never participated.)

33 In contrast to these findings, Likert found a marked relationship between the kind of supervision received and productivity, as well as per-

Table 14.2 Participation in Company Recreational Activities and Section Productivity

PARTICIPATION	HIGH-PRODUCTIVITY SECTIONS	LOW-PRODUCTIVITY SECTIONS
Frequently	8%	7%
Occasionally	20%	34%
Never	72%	59%
	100%	100%

sonal satisfaction. In this phase of the studies, supervisors who emphasized work-oriented planning and control procedures in describing their jobs were designated as being [employee- / production-] centered, whereas supervisors who emphasized the interpersonal nature of their jobs were designated as [employee- / production-] centered.

production-

employee-

34 For example, a supervisor might describe his job by saying: "I try to consider each man's strengths and weaknesses and how the men work together before I make any job assignments. When possible, I try to assign a man to the kind of jobs he likes best." This pattern of supervision would be considered _____ centered.

employee-

35 Another supervisor might indicate: "I have to get employees to produce, and my main tool is the efficiency chart. With this chart I am able to plan ahead and hit the work areas that are behind." This pattern of supervision would be considered _____ centered.

production

36 When the approach to supervision was compared with the associated employee productivity, as indicated in Table 14.3, the high-production sections tended to have supervisors who were _____ centered.

employee-

37 Rather surprisingly, then, the supervisors who

Table 14.3 Approach to Supervision and Section Productivity

APPROACH TO SUPERVISION	HIGH-PRODUCTIVITY SECTIONS	LOW-PRODUCTIVITY SECTIONS
Production-centered	14%	70%
Employee-centered	86%	30%
	100%	100%

indicated that they gave primary emphasis to production tended to be in charge of sections that

low

were [high / low] in productivity.

38 Further evidence along these lines, as well as an indication of the reasons behind these results, is given by the observed relationship between closeness of supervision and section productivity. As reported in Table 14.4, high-production sections were inclined to have supervisors who employed

general

_____ supervision.

Table 14.4 Closeness of Supervision and Section Productivity

SUPERVISION	HIGH-PRODUCTIVITY SECTIONS	LOW-PRODUCTIVITY SECTIONS
Close	10%	67%
General	90%	33%
	100%	100%

39 Likert found that production-centered supervisors tended to supervise closely, that is, in terms of specific procedures to be followed rather than in terms of goals to be achieved. Based on the results of these studies, this pattern of supervision is as-

low

sociated with [high / low] section productivity.

40 However, we might well challenge this conclusion by asking whether "cause" and "effect" might not have been reversed. After all, is it not possible that supervisors of low-production units find it necessary to be production-centered and to employ close supervision because their people are not productive, rather than the other way around? In terms of the results we have presented thus far, might this conclusion be equally valid? [Yes / No]

Yes (The data do not indicate direction of causation.)

41 Because of this question of cause and effect, in one of the companies participating in this research project the supervisors of several high- and low-productivity sections were switched to see whether the supervisory approach or productivity would change. The result was that the basic supervisory approaches associated with the two types of supervisors did not change, but the productivity of the sections did change. The former low-productivity sections showed marked improvement with the employee-centered supervisors, whereas the former high-productivity sections slipped somewhat, indicating that [supervisory style affects productivity / productivity affects supervisory style].

supervisory style affects productivity

42 The employee-centered approach with its general, or goal-oriented, supervision does not imply a lack of concern about productivity. Rather it indicates that the supervisors of high-productivity sections recognize that productivity is accomplished by [procedures / people].

people

43 On the other hand, supervisors of low-productivity sections tended to look at employee-centered methods as being a luxury and something to be indulged in [before / after] achieving high productivity.

after

44 Thus far, we have considered the effect of supervisory methods on productivity. The other criterion of supervisory effectiveness in these studies was the level of employee morale. Again, the supervisory approach used did influence employee morale, and, as for the productivity findings, morale was highest in sections with _____ centered supervisors.

employee-

45 Figure 14.2 on page 392 reports the activities of the supervisors of high- and low-morale groups as seen by their subordinates, in terms of percentage frequency of mention. For the relatively impersonal functions of enforcing rules, arranging work, and supplying material, the supervisors of high-morale groups, as contrasted to low-morale groups, [did / did not] differ substantially.

did not

46 As for the findings regarding productivity, it wasn't so much what the supervisors of low-morale groups did, but what they didn't do that influenced the morale of their sections. What they failed to do was to give adequate attention to the _____ elements in the work situation.

human (or
employee, etc.)

47 As an example, whereas only 11 percent of the employees of low-morale groups reported that their supervisor informs the men about what is happening in the company, in high-morale groups the percentage of employees mentioning this was _____ percent.

47

48 Although there were other results of the University of Michigan studies not directly relevant to our present discussion, one of their principal findings was that both high productivity and high morale of work groups is more likely when the supervisor's approach to his job is _____ centered.

employee-

49 In the research report, employee-centered supervisors gave attention to individual employee needs [instead of / in addition to] the impersonal planning and control responsibilities inherent in their positions.

in addition to

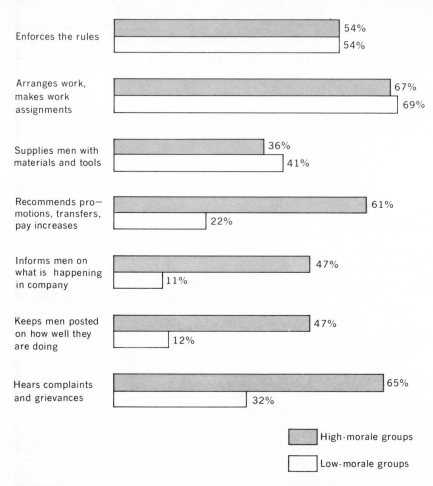

Figure 14.2 Descriptions of supervisors' activities by members of high-morale and low-morale groups. (Adapted from Rensis Likert, *Motivation: The Core of Management*, Personnel Series, no. 155, American Management Association, New York, 1953, p. 9. Used with permission.)

C THE MANAGERIAL GRID

In the University of Michigan studies it was found that the effective supervisor did not make a choice between giving attention to production as contrasted to people but was able to combine an interest in both of these factors. In order to clarify the several types of supervisory orientations that are possible in regard to the production and people factors in the job, the *managerial grid* has been used to represent the varying degrees of emphasis that a supervisor can give to these two factors. The grid was developed by Robert R. Blake and Jane S. Mouton and is described in their book, *The Managerial Grid* (Gulf Publishing Company, Houston, 1964). The general characteristics of this grid and the number designator system associated with it are described in this section.

50   Figure 14.3 on page 394 presents the managerial grid we discuss in this section, with a description of five supervisory approaches entered on the grid. The two numbers identifying each approach indicate the extent of concern for production and people, respectively. Thus a "2,7 managerial style" would represent a relatively [high / low] concern for production and a [high / low] concern for people.

low

high

51   Of the five managerial approaches described on the grid, the one that would most likely lead to a high level of production, *as well as morale*, is the _____ style.

9,9

52   After discussing the characteristics of the other four approaches briefly described on the grid, we consider the implications of the grid and its use in developing a 9,9 supervisory approach. We begin by discussing the 9,1 supervisory style, in which there is a high concern for _____ but a low concern for _____ .

production

people

53   Under the 9,1 style people are regarded as instruments of production, and emphasis is given to the use of formal authority. As a result, the full development of employees generally [is / is not] attained, and employee morale is typically [high / low].

is not

low

54   However, employee reaction to the 9,1 approach is not universally negative. The approach is

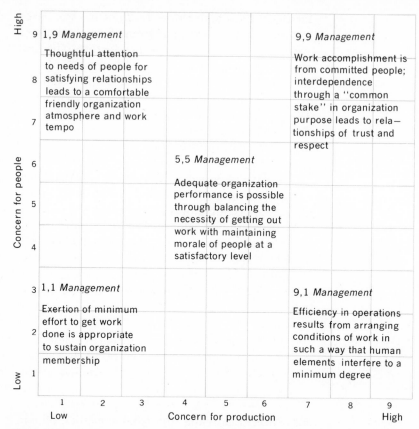

Figure 14.3 The managerial grid. (From Robert R. Blake and Jane S. Mouton, *The Managerial Grid*, Gulf Publishing Company, Houston, 1964, p. 10. Copyright Gulf Publishing Company; reproduced with permission.)

low
submissive

most likely to be effective when the educational level of subordinates is [high / low] and the employees are generally [aggressive / submissive].

55 In contrast, the 1,9 supervisory style describes a low concern for production coupled with a high concern for people. As applied to Likert's studies, described in the preceding section of this unit, this

neither (The employee-centered supervisors in those studies also displayed concern for production.)

describes [employee-centered / production-centered / neither] type of supervision.

56   Under the 1,9 approach production standards are generally described as being ["demanding" / "reasonable"] and individual and group conflict is [encouraged / discouraged].

"reasonable"
discouraged

57   Furthermore, under the 1,9 approach there is a tendency for goals (as well as procedures) to be set by [the supervisor / the work group].

the work group

58   The 1,1 management style describes a lack of concern for both production and people. Overall, it implies that the supervisor has a [high / low] level of involvement in his job.

low

59   The supervisor who uses this approach tends to see himself as a message carrier between managerial levels and among the individuals at his organizational level. By this approach, the likelihood that an error in decision making will be attributed to him is [high / low].

low (One way of avoiding mistakes is not to make decisions.)

60   Consistent with his tendency to avoid situations in which he might expose himself, the supervisor who follows the 1,1 approach tends to [welcome / avoid] contact with higher-level managers.

avoid

61   Of the three managerial styles we have discussed thus far, the one in which the supervisor has decided that "people come before production" is the _____, the one in which "production comes before people" is the _____, and the one in which the supervisor avoids any true managerial commitment is the _____.

1,9
9,1

1,1

62   In the middle of the grid, the 5,5 managerial style identifies the supervisor who has moderate concern for both production and people. However, his attitude is that optimum production and optimum morale [are / are not] possible simultaneously.

are not

63 Therefore, the 5,5 supervisor finds it necessary to combine a level of concern for people with that for production so that a kind of workable balance is achieved—one that results in [optimum / acceptable] productivity and [optimum / acceptable] morale.

acceptable
acceptable

64 Historically, the hostile and antagonistic reactions to 9,1 management produced an overreaction toward the 1,9 direction in many organizations. The subsequent swing of the pendulum has frequently resulted in the search for a *balance* by adopting the _____ approach.

5,5

65 Finally, of the several managerial approaches identified in Figure 14.3, the one that assumes that there is no necessary and inherent conflict between the organization's production requirements and the needs of people is the _____ approach.

9,9

66 Since the 9,9 supervisory approach assumes that people have a need to be involved and committed to productive work, employee participation in work planning is [encouraged / discouraged].

encouraged

67 Put the other way, this means that through individual and group contribution and accomplishment both high _____ and high _____ are achieved in the organization.

productivity
morale

68 Of the five supervisory approaches we have discussed, four of them implicitly or explicitly assume that there is an inherent conflict between productivity and morale. The extreme approach oriented entirely toward productivity because "that's what people are paid for" is the _____ method. The extreme approach oriented entirely toward human relations because "satisfied people in a friendly group will be productive" is the _____ method.

9,1

1,9

69   The approach by which the supervisor tries to "balance" his pressure for production with a consideration for morale is the _____ method. A supervisor accustomed to a 9,1 approach who runs into employee resistance on the one hand and increased staff control on the other may finally adopt the passive managerial attitude described by the _____ method.

5,5

1,1

70   The approach that presumes a high level of employee maturity and results in his involvement and participation in job planning within the context of established objectives is the _____ approach.

9,9

D   OVERCOMING RESISTANCE TO CHANGE

In addition to his organizational responsibility for achieving high production with and through a high level of employee morale and motivation, the supervisor has seen the pace of technological progress add an important ingredient of another sort to his job. Technological improvements frequently necessitate changes in work organization, methods, and procedures, and thus they have a disruptive effect on the social organization at the workplace. A common group reaction to this threat of disruption is resistance to the change. Although this resistance is occasionally overt, as in organized restriction of production, more often it involves a subtle withholding of effort, perhaps to "prove" that the change won't work and should be abandoned. In this section we summarize the results of the now classic study by Coch and French[2] which is concerned precisely with this type of supervisory problem.

[2]Lester Coch and John R. P. French, "Overcoming Resistance to Change," *Human Relations*, vol. 1, no. 4, pp. 512–532, 1948.

71   The studies by Coch and French were done in the main plant of the Harwood Manufacturing Corporation, a garment manufacturer located in Virginia. One of the most serious problems faced on the supervisory level was the resistance of sewing-machine operators to necessary changes in methods and jobs. From the standpoint of organizational objectives, this resistance led to lower levels of _____.

production

72   For jobs in which a significant change had occurred, management found that only 38 percent of the sewing-machine operators recovered to the standard of sixty units per hour. The other 62 percent either became chronically substandard operators or quit employment after the job change. Furthermore, the experienced operators took longer to recover their original level of production than the time required for new employees to reach the same level. The factor directly associated with this depressing effect on production was the job _____.

change

73   Despite special monetary allowances and discussions with the union the problems associated with the job changes continued. The purpose of the research by Coch and French was to find out (1) why people resist change and (2) what can be done about it. Thus, the first necessary step in the study was to devise a tentative explanation, or theory, for [the reason for the productivity problems / the way of solving the productivity problems].

the reason for the
productivity
problems

74   One possible explanation for the depressed productivity following a change was that the eight-week period required to recover standard levels represented an unavoidable learning phenomenon. Would the fact that new operators achieved standard production more rapidly than those experiencing the change contradict this explanation? [Yes / No]

No (Discussion continues next page.)

75 If previous job habits tended to interfere with new job requirements, resulting in "negative transfer" from the standpoint of learning theory, we would expect experienced operators to require [more / less] time than new operators.

more

76 To test this possible explanation, employees whose jobs had been changed were interviewed, and time-and-motion studies were conducted. The changed operators rarely complained of "wanting to do it the old way," and the time-and-motion studies showed very few false moves after the first week of change, indicating that negative transfer [was / was not] the principal factor in the recovery problem.

was not

77 It was also found that the level of the operators' productivity before the change was unrelated to the extent of difficulty following the change, further suggesting that the principal problem might be one involving [learning / motivation].

motivation

78 Therefore, Coch and French devised a motivational explanation for the difficulties associated with the job changes. They suggested that the individual's desire to quickly recover the standard production level and incentive pay interacts with the perceived difficulty of the task during the first stage of change, resulting in a condition of frustration. This condition of frustration shared by a number of individuals then leads to several possible outcomes. When the work group is highly cohesive (i.e., the members are psychologically close to one another) and in addition has negative attitudes toward management, the most likely result is [continued effort to recover / group restriction of production / individual employee terminations].

group restriction
of production

79 When the work group is highly cohesive and has positive attitudes toward management, the most likely result is [continued effort to recover / group restriction of production / individual employee terminations].

continued effort to
recover

80 When the people in the work group are not particularly friendly with one another, i.e., when the group is not cohesive, the most likely result of the job change is [continued effort to recover / group restriction of production / individual employee terminations].

individual
employee
terminations

81 Therefore, the divergent results of successful recovery on the one hand and organized restriction of production on the other hand are both associated with work groups that are _____.

cohesive

82 However, Coch and French suggested that *two* factors were necessary to attaining a high proportion of successful recovery: the work group has to be _____and has to have _____ attitudes toward management.

cohesive
positive

83 With this tentative explanation in mind, the researchers suggested that the extent of individual and group *participation* in planning the job change would affect both cohesiveness and attitudes. At this point in the research, then, Coch and French were addressing themselves to [why people resist change / what could be done about resistance to change].

what could be
done about
resistance to
change

84 Although they studied a number of work groups under varying conditions, three basic types of conditions were designated in order to test the effects of participation. In the *no-participation* condition employees did not participate in planning the job change, but an explanation of the change and the reasons for it were given to them. In the *participation-through-representation* condition, selected operators from the group worked with supervisory personnel in planning the necessary changes. In the *total-participation* condition all members of the group participated in planning the change. In terms of their underlying theory, the researchers predicted that the condition most successful in achieving recovery in productivity was

total-participation

the _____ condition.

85 Figure 14.4 summarizes the results of these studies. Note that production figures are indicated for periods both before and after the job change. Before the change, production levels for the three

about the same

types of groups were [about the same / markedly different].

86 After the change, however, employees work-

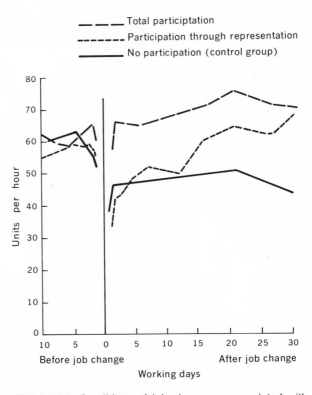

Figure 14.4 Conditions of job change as associated with productivity after the change. (Adapted from Lester Coch and John R. P. French, "Overcoming Resistance to Change," *Human Relations*, vol. 1, no. 4, p. 523, 1948. Reproduced with permission.)

ing under different conditions of participation differed markedly in productivity. The most successful groups were those working under conditions of

total participation

_____ _____.

87   Still in Figure 14.4, we see that the least successful group, and the one in which there is an apparent restriction of production at about fifty

no-participation

units per hour, is the _____ group.

88   The researchers also assigned the same people to different conditions of job change and found the results to be the same as those reported in Figure 14.4, thus conclusively demonstrating that dif-

do not (Rather, the conditions of change accounted for the differences.)

ferences among the people [do / do not] account for the observed differences in recovering productivity.

89   Overall, the studies at the Harwood Manufacturing Corporation demonstrated that one solution to the employee resistance often encountered during job change is that of providing more op-

participatior

portunity for employee _____ in planning the change.

90   Of course, this approach cannot be applied as an isolated technique, but, rather, it must be applied as part of a management philosophy oriented

more

toward assigning [more / less] authority and responsibility to employees at the operative level.

91   However, note also that in the studies at the Harwood Manufacturing Corporation employees working under the total-participation condition

how the changed objectives were to be achieved

had the authority to determine [what the changed objectives should be / how the changed objectives were to be achieved].

Review

92 Of the several viewpoints regarding the supervisor's appropriate role, the one that considers his position particularly important because it represents the link with operative employees in the organization is the _____ view. The viewpoint that this organizational position makes him vulnerable to pressures from "both sides" is the _____ view. (Frames 1 to 11)

key-man

man-in-the-middle

93 The viewpoint that the supervisor's position results in his being accepted neither as a manager nor as a worker is the _____ view. To the extent that a supervisor identifies himself more as an operative employee than as a manager, he is in fact expressing a belief in the _____ view. (Frames 12 to 18)

marginal-man

another-worker

94 The view suggesting that the supervisor's primary role is that of being a specialist in handling "people problems" is the _____ _____ view. (Frames 19 to 27)

human relations

specialist

95 In the studies of employee productivity and morale conducted by the University of Michigan researchers, the effects of two kinds of supervisory approaches were studied. These were the _____ centered and _____ centered approaches. (Frames 28 to 35)

production-

employee-

96 One of the principal findings of the studies was that low-productivity sections tended to have production-centered supervisors. Further, in terms of the direction of cause and effect, it was concluded that [productivity affected the super-

visory approach / the supervisory approach affected productivity]. (Frames 36 to 41)

97 As defined in the University of Michigan studies, employee-centered supervisors gave attention
to the [human / impersonal / human and imper-
sonal] components of their jobs. (Frames 42 to 49)

98 In the managerial grid, the approach by which
the supervisor gives full attention to production
rather than to people is designated _____
management, whereas giving extensive attention to
people rather than to production is designated
_____ management. (Frames 50 to
57)

99 The supervisor who fails to stress either
production or human relations and regards himself as a kind of communication link rather than as
a decision maker is practicing _____ management, whereas the attempt to balance a concern for
production with that for people is designated as
_____ management. (Frames 58 to 64)

100 Of the supervisory approaches described on
the managerial grid, the only one that presumes no
inherent conflict between the goals of achieving
optimum production and optimum morale is the
_____ approach. (Frames 65 to 70)

101 In their studies of employee resistance to
change at the Harwood Manufacturing Corporation, Coch and French concluded that the relevant
explanation primarily concerned employee [learn-
ing / motivation]. (Frames 71 to 78)

102 Further, they suggested that two conditions
had to exist to make successful adjustment to job
change most likely: the work group has to be
_____ and the group members need
to have _____ attitudes toward management. (Frames 79 to 82)

103 In testing their proposed solution to the resistance-to-change problem, Coch and French designated three conditions under which the job change took place; the employees that were consistently superior in adapting successfully to the change were those working under the so-called

total participation

_____   _____

condition. (Frames 83 to 91)

_____

Discussion Questions

1. In your view, how has the role of the first-level supervisor in manufacturing firms changed in the past twenty-five years?

2. Do you think that the foreman is or should be considered the key man in management? Why?

3. In what type of organization is the first-level supervisor most likely to be thought of as being primarily a human relations specialist? Why?

4. What's all this nonsense about encouraging supervisors to be employee-centered? After all, aren't they (and other employees) being paid to get out the production?

5. In Likert's studies, production-centered supervisors were concerned about production as such, whereas employee-centered supervisors combined an interest in people and production. Why do you suppose Likert does not report any finding for supervisors with a concern for people but not production?

6. How has the managerial grid helped to identify the implications of various types of supervisory practices?

7. Discuss the key elements associated with

achieving a successful change in procedures of work, assuming technical feasibility.

8. In terms of the objectives of the respective studies, how did the studies conducted by the University of Michigan group and those carried out at the Harwood Manufacturing Corporation differ? In what respects are the results of the two series of studies similar?

Case Study: A Change of Supervisory Philosophy at Triflex

Following a series of executive-level conferences aimed at defining the company's human relations outlook and policies at the Triflex Manufacturing Company, manufacturer of home appliances, a committee of top company officers decided that the supervisory implications of the program should be communicated through the company's management development programs. To ascertain that both foremen and middle managers interpret the new policies in a similar manner, they have directed the coordinator of management development to include at least two levels of management in all conference sessions.

Generally, the new company philosophy emphasizes the acceptance of employee-oriented motivational methods as an addition to the production-oriented philosophy that has been typical of the company's operations. Accordingly, the management development conferences have included a review of motivation theory, summaries of industrial motivation studies, and the implications of these findings to the effective supervision of personnel.

After two months of scheduled weekly conferences, the top management objective of achieving a consensus at both the first-level and middle management levels does not appear to be materializing.

Whereas most resistance had been anticipated at the foreman level, it is actually the superintendents in factory operations who appear most resistant. Although the foreman's commitment to the new methods is still largely at the "lip-service" level, they have at least indicated willingness to give the employee-oriented motivational methods a try. The superintendents, on the other hand, do not believe that the methods are even relevant to their jobs.

As the superintendents and certain other middle managers see it, the company's interest in employee-oriented methods has the objective of avoiding certain labor relations difficulties which are developing in some of the company's plants. Because of this, both the new human relations policies and the supervisory methods derived from them are oriented toward the operative level, rather than having implications for the supervision of managers. They believe that top management should acknowledge the fact that the foreman is in a basically different supervisory situation from that of higher-level managers, and that it is not only wasteful of time but also ineffective to require managers at higher levels to use methods oriented toward operative employees. They agree that employee-oriented methods are useful as motivational methods, but they believe that anyone in a management position should not need to be motivated as such.

1. Do you agree with the superintendents' point of view? Why or why not?
2. Given the present division of opinion between foremen and superintendents, what is likely to be the level of success in implementing the new company philosophy at the worker level?
3. In what respects did the top management proceed correctly in attempting to redefine the company human relations policies?
4. What additional things could have been or should be done to achieve acceptance of the

philosophy at all levels? Should the same philosophy be applicable at all managerial levels?

Case Study: An Analysis of Operating Procedures

Bill Rauch, in charge of the billing department, was called by the controller one morning and was informed that the company was considering some changes in the accounting and finance activities in conjunction with the planned installation of a new computer system. Therefore, some systems people from the hardware manufacturer wished to study the present procedures and methods being used in a number of departments, including the billing department. Further, the schedule called for the analysis in the billing department to be performed on Monday through Wednesday of the following week. After the call Mr. Rauch informed the three office supervisors of the planned visit by the systems analysts and also posted a notice on the bulletin board which indicated that the visit was related to the planned installation of the new computer system.

Promptly at 8:30 A.M. on the following Monday two computer systems analysts arrived in the department and introduced themselves to Mr. Rauch. They spent a few minutes with him having coffee and generally discussing the improvements and economies which can result from a more comprehensive use of the capabilities associated with recent technological advances in computers. Bill Rauch then introduced the analysts to the supervisors in the department, and they began their work by talking with the supervisors as well as with senior personnel in the department about the procedures and methods being followed. Mr. Rauch did not pay much attention to the analysts during the remainder of the day, particularly because of some additions to the billing procedure which he needed to implement.

Just after lunch on the second day of their visit in the department the two systems analysts stopped at Bill Rauch's office and asked if they could meet privately with him. After the office door was shut, one of the analysts explained the reason for their meeting with him by saying, "We're having quite a problem with our analysis in your department. Either we're having difficulties communicating with your supervisors and senior personnel or else they are deliberately trying to foul up our analysis. The two of us discussed the situation at length during lunch today, and we believe that the confusion is deliberate on their part. The people we have talked with have tried to make the procedures more complicated than they really are by always dwelling on the exceptions instead of describing the typical procedures used. For this reason, we think it would be best for us to terminate this analysis until we can get better cooperation from your people."

1. Assuming that the analysts' diagnosis of the source of confusion is correct, why might the supervisors have reacted as they did?
2. What might Bill Rauch have done differently to avoid the problem which developed?
3. Did the controller follow an appropriate procedure in the way he informed Bill Rauch of the study to be made by the systems analysts?
4. What should Mr. Rauch do now?

Suggested Readings*

Bennis, W. G.: *Changing Organizations,* McGraw-Hill Book Company, New York, 1966.

Blake, R. R., and J. S. Mouton: *The Managerial Grid,* Gulf Publishing Company, Houston, 1964.

Boyd, B. B., and J. M. Jensen: "Perceptions of the First-Line Supervisor's Authority: A Study in Superior-Subordinate Communication," *Academy of Management Journal,* vol. 15, no. 3, September 1972.

*Also see the cross-reference table in the Preface.

Coch, L., and J. R. P. French: "Overcoming Resistance to Change," *Human Relations,* vol. 1, no. 4, August 1948.

Davis, K.: *Human Behavior at Work: Human Relations and Organizational Behavior,* 4th ed., McGraw-Hill Book Company, New York, 1972.

Glueck, W. F.: "Organization Change in Business and Government," *Academy of Management Journal,* vol. 12, no. 4, December 1969.

Likert, R.: *Motivation: The Core of Management,* Personnel Series, no. 155, American Management Association, New York, 1953.

———: *New Patterns of Management,* McGraw-Hill Book Company, New York, 1961.

Powell, R. M., and J. L. Schlacter: "Participative Management: A Panacea?" *Academy of Management Journal,* vol. 14, no. 2, June 1971.

V
CONTROLLING

The management functions of planning and controlling are closely related in that whereas planning is concerned with the formulation of objectives, controlling is concerned with ascertaining that the specified objectives are achieved. In this sense, activities in a firm are set into motion as the result of managerial planning and they are "kept on the right track" by means of the control process.

In Chapter 15 we identify the general steps included in any control process and consider several types of managerial devices, and particularly the budget, that are used for the purpose of controlling. Possible types of human reactions to control procedures are also considered, along with a positive strategy for gaining employee acceptance of control procedures.

Chapter 16 covers Program Evaluation and Review Technique in some detail as an example of a system-oriented control device which has had relatively widespread application in industry. As is true for most control devices, PERT is used as a planning tool as well as a control device.

Chapter **fifteen**
THE CONTROL PROCESS

Once any system, be it a mechanical process or a business organization, is set into motion toward specific objectives, events occur which tend to pull that system "off target." A successful control process is one which effects corrections to the system involved before the deviations become serious. In this chapter we consider the basic steps included in any control process, the budget and other control devices that are used in conjunction with the process, and the human problems associated with achieving effective organizational control.

A   GENERAL CONCEPTS

Three essential steps make up the control process in organizations. These are establishing standards, comparing actual results against the standards, and taking corrective action. Of these, the first step, establishing standards, is dependent on the identification of organization objectives, which is done as part of the planning process. The measurement of results is then done according to the standards which have been established.

1   In the control process, the translation of enterprise goals into specific measurable outcomes, which then become the basis for evaluating performance, constitutes the step of establishing

standards   _____.

2   Thus, the number of sales within a department in a retail store is an example of a performance

standard   _____ .

Yes (And this
should be more
than a subtraction
from total sales,
because of the
extra expense
involved.)

3   In addition to total sales, should the quantity of returned merchandise be considered in defining a performance standard? [Yes / No]

Yes

4   Should the satisfaction of the customer and his tendency to buy other merchandise in other departments of the store be considered in the standard? [Yes / No]

Yes (In this case,
there may be a
tendency to carry
too much or too
little stock.)

5   Should the quantity of merchandise held in stock be part of the standard used to evaluate departmental performance in the store? [Yes / No]

Yes

6 Should the standard take into consideration not just the volume of sales but the kind of merchandise sold? [Yes / No]

several

7 Thus, in defining performance standards we typically find that [one / several] major facet(s) of performance must be considered.

control (or
observation, etc.)

8 Standards can be applied at the level of policies, procedures, or methods. Since entire operations cannot be observed, however, it is necessary to choose certain *points* for the purpose of _____.

control

9 By definition, a strategic point in an operation that is chosen to be the focal point of control action is called a strategic _____ point.

more

10 The earlier in a process that a strategic control point is located, the [more / less] likely it will be that deviations can be corrected before the attainment of the organization's goals is affected.

goals (or
objectives, etc.)

11 Strategic control points should be chosen so that the comparisons with the standards at these points are directly reflective of the success in attaining the organization's _____.

strategic control

12 The standards which are often defined at the _____ _____ points can be of several types. We shall briefly discuss *quantity, time use,* and *quality* standards.

quantity

13 Defining expected production volume, sales volume, or the number of people to be employed all involve _____ standards.

cost

14 Specifying the amount of money to be spent for raw materials or for advertising involves a _____ standard.

15 Setting up a schedule to be followed, or ad-

hered to, in the completion of certain activities
time use   involves a _____ _____ standard.

16 The first three types of standards, that is, the
quantity; cost; time   _____, _____, and _____
use   _____ standards, are relatively straightforward in that they readily lend themselves to specific measurement. On the other hand, the quanti-
quality   tative basis for a _____ standard may
be more difficult to specify.

17 Whereas the necessary tolerances for a physical product can be specified in measurable terms,
the objective that the credit department should
achieve "good public relations," which is also a
quality   _____ standard, is harder to specify in
quantitative terms.

18 Once the standard of performance is established, the measurement of results at the strategic control points is based on the type of stand-
quantity;   ard involved. Thus, measurement of _____,
cost; time use;   _____, _____ _____,
quality   and _____ may be included.

19 In the measurement of organizational performance, as well as in the definition of standards
in the first place, the less tangible quality measurements tend to be relatively [overemphasized / un-
underemphasized deremphasized].

20 For example, measuring the monthly sales
volume achieved by a district sales manager is relatively easy. Measuring his progress in achieving
professional development of his sales personnel is
[more / less] difficult.
more

21 Along these lines, developing specific cost limitations for travel expenses, for example, but failing to develop any standards for measuring the
need or value of the travel in the first place

suggests an underemphasis on the measurement
of _____.

quality (or the
value of the travel)

22 Not every item at a strategic control point is
necessarily measured. The method of *sampling* is
often applied in choosing what should be

measured   _____.

23 To the extent that only a portion of the output
at the control point is checked and this portion is
assumed to be representative of the entire output,

sampling   the method of _____ is involved.

24 At the strategic control point, a follow-up is
made just for those situations that are [in line / out

out of line   of line] with the standard. Focusing managerial attention on those situations that deviate from the
standard represents the *principle of exception*.

25 The restaurant manager who makes a point of
checking at random the quality of food being served

sampling   is applying the method of _____ in carrying
out his control activity.

26 The restaurant manager who investigates the
method of food preparation whenever he finds
anything wrong or when a specific complaint has
been made is following the principal of

exception   _____ in carrying out his control activity.

27 The application of sampling [increases / re-

reduces   duces] the number of observations, or measurements, that need to be made at a strategic control
point.

28 Application of the managerial principle of ex-

reduces   ception [increases / reduces] the number of detailed reviews of procedures that a manager makes
in carrying out his control responsibilities.

29 Thus, the amount of time spent measuring results at strategic control points is minimized by

sampling applying the method of _____ , whereas managerial time spent in reviewing how results were attained is minimized by applying

exception the managerial principle of _____ .

B   BUDGETARY CONTROL

Though the process of preparing budgets is associated with the management function of planning, their use is particularly associated with the function of controlling. In order to provide the basis for financial control within the organization, separate budgets are usually prepared for each organization unit within the enterprise for the designated time period. In this section of the chapter we first consider the general characteristics of budgets and then describe five specific types of budgets that can be used: operating budgets, cash budgets, appropriation budgets, balance sheet budgets, and variable budgets.

30 It has been stated that a budget is a type of plan expressed in quantitative terms. The "quantitative terms" in which budgets are expressed are

monetary (or units that can be converted into dollar amounts, such as man-hours or machine-hours) usually _____ amounts.

31 As indicated in the preceding section, three essential steps in the control process include establishing standards, comparing results with standards, and taking corrective action. In terms of these steps, the preparation of budgets is, in ef-

establishing standards fect, the step of _____ _____ .

32 The use of budgets to check and correct ongo-

control

planning

ing expenditures is thus directly a part of the _____ process, whereas setting up the budgets in the first place is part of the _____ process.

cost

33 In terms of the four types of standards described in the preceding section (quantity, cost, time use, and quality), the budgeting process typically involves the use of _____ standards.

monetary (or cost, or financial)

34 The use of budgets makes it possible for a manager to compare different organizational units, such as the sales and engineering departments, because of the common basis used for measuring performance, namely, the _____ basis.

weaknesses

35 However, the observation that budgetary controls may result in an overemphasis on cost reduction and an underemphasis on quality improvement is one of their major [strengths / weaknesses].

planning
controlling

36 A general advantage associated with formulating and using budgets is that organizational attention is thereby directed toward the management functions of _____ and _____.

revenue

37 The first specific type of budget we now consider is the *operating budget.* An operating budget includes a budget for anticipated revenues and another budget for anticipated expenses. In this context a "sales budget" would be a(n) [revenue / expense] budget.

expense

38 In contrast, a budget including an itemization of expected costs would be a(n) _____ budget.

revenue

39 Thus, the types of budgets which compose the operating budget are the _____ expense   budget and the _____ budget.

40 Many products or services are such that something of a seasonal influence occurs in respect to sales. Therefore, the budgeted revenues for different months of the year would be at [the

different   same / different] monetary level(s).

41 For firms that are involved in several products and in several geographic areas, sales budgets by

are   product and by territory [are / are not] required for the purpose of subsequent control action.

42 Similarly, in respect to the expense budget, the several categories of costs are budgeted individually in order to provide the basis for identifying areas of required control action. Thus, such costs as materials costs, direct labor, indirect labor, overhead, inventory costs, and general administra-

shown separately   tive costs are generally [consolidated / shown separately].

43 The type of budgeting procedure we have been considering, which is concerned with budgeting for anticipated revenues and anticipated ex-

operating   penses, is called the _____ budget.

44 Another type of budget used in business firms is the cash budget. Such a budget can be developed on the basis of the revenues and expenses identified in the operating budget, but with particular attention being given to the anticipated amounts of cash needed during the budgeted period. From this standpoint, a cash budget is principally concerned with the point in time at which merchan-

paid for   dise is [sold / paid for].

45 A cash budget is necessary to assure that an organization will be able to pay bills as they become due. How would it be possible for a company to be operating profitably—that is, for sales to be exceeding costs—and yet not have sufficient cash to pay current liabilities? _____

_____

_____

_____

_____

_____

_____

The sales may result in receivables, in the short run, rather than cash. Also, additional funds may be needed to increase inventories or for additions to capital equipment.

46 If a company anticipates a shortage of cash during an operating period, then early arrangements for short-term borrowing should be made. Along these lines, the condition of the money market should be considered. During the "cash squeeze" accompanying the 1969–1970 recession, for example, short-term loans were difficult to obtain. In any case, short-term loans generally carry a [high / low] rate of interest as compared with long-term financing.

high

47 On the other hand, if a company anticipates an excess cash position, the financial officer should explore the possibility of obtaining cash discounts from suppliers or consider the use of the funds in short-term investments. Thus, the financial officer generally should try to maintain a [positive / negative] cash balance and should strive to [maximize / minimize] the amount of this balance.

positive

minimize (since excess funds should be "put to work")

48 The type of budget which is concerned with planning for the availability of adequate funds and for the profitable use of any "excess" funds is the _____ budget.

cash

49 In addition to the operating budget and the cash budget, another type of budget is the *appropriation budget*. Such a budget is not concerned with short-term revenues and expenses as such. Rather, an appropriation budget is concerned with the commitment of funds to improve productivity and profitability in the long run. Thus, planned capital expenditures for facilities and equipment [would / would not] be included in such a budget.

would

50   In addition to investments in capital, other expenditures which would be included in an appropriation budget include research and development, institutional advertising, management development programs, and new market development. The feature that all such expenditures have in common is that they are oriented toward improving profitability [within the budget period / in the long run].

in the long run

51   The long-term nature of appropriation expenditures and the fact that limited funds are available for such investments indicates that a careful review of such proposed expenditures is warranted. For this reason, the items to be included in an appropriation budget are usually reviewed at the [departmental / top-management] level in the organization.

top-management

52   Thus far, we have considered three types of budgets used in organizations: _____, _____, and _____ budgets.

operating
cash; appropriation

53   The fourth type of budget which we now consider is the *balance sheet budget*. Essentially, such a budget represents the intended financial status at the end of the budget period, which is generally the close of the fiscal year. Since attention is directed toward the financial position at a particular point in time, rather than on transactions during a period of time, the items that are included in the projection are [assets and liabilities / receipts and expenditures].

assets and
liabilities

54 When the actual balance sheet is prepared at the end of the budget period, a comparison with the balance sheet budget serves to identify needed areas of increased managerial attention and, possibly, the need for special budgets to improve control. For example, such assets as finished goods inventory may be deemed to be [too low / too high / either too low or too high].

either too low or
too high

55 The type of budget which can be used to compare actual financial position with intended financial position in respect to a number of specific assets and liabilities is the _____ _____ budget.

balance
sheet

56 Our discussion of the operating budget was based on the assumption that all expenses should be planned beforehand, and that they should be consistent with a specific sales or production level. If the actual level of operations should differ from that which was anticipated, the use of such an operating budget would lead to organizational [flexibility / inflexibility].

inflexibility

57 As one approach to combating such inflexibility, the *variable budget* has been developed. By this budgeting method the exact amount budgeted is not specified, but rather it is made dependent on the level of operations during the budgeting period. Thus, with increases in production volume in a manufacturing plant such a budget would specify [increasing / decreasing] dollar amounts allocated to direct labor.

increasing

58 Would you also expect that the variable budget would identify varying amounts of depreciation on plant and equipment according to production level? [Yes / No]

No

59 Therefore, the budgetary method in which planned expenditures or charges in respect to *vari-*

variable

able costs, but not fixed costs, are tied to the level of operations is called the _____ budget.

60 Figure 15.1 is an example of a variable budget chart that can be used as a planning device and also as a control device. Note that on this chart the fixed costs are at the same level regardless of monthly output, namely, at $_____.

20,000

61 On the other hand, for the range of possible production volumes identified in Figure 15.1 the budgeted *total cost* can vary from a low of $20,000 to a high of $_____.

43,000
(approximately)

62 In addition to perhaps forcing management to study the actual relationships between levels of operation and costs, the principal advantage of the variable budget is that it [reduces uncertainty in costs / allows greater flexibility in the use of budgets].

allows greater
flexibility in the use
of budgets (The
uncertainty is still
there, but it can be
planned for.)

63 In all, we have discussed five types of budgets in this section. The type of budget concerned with anticipated revenues and expenses during a particular period is the _____ budget, while the type of budget concerned with planning for the adequacy of funds during the period is the _____ budget.

operating
cash

64 Allotted funds for long-term investments are involved in the _____ budget, while the intended financial status at the conclusion of a fiscal period is indicated by the _____ budget. Finally, budgetary flexibility, particularly in regard to the direct costs that vary with the level of operations, is enhanced by the use of a _____ budget.

appropriation
balance
sheet
variable

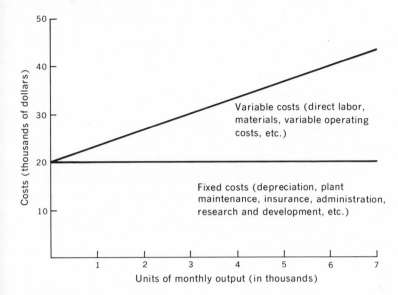

Figure 15.1 Variable budget chart.

C OTHER CONTROL DEVICES

In addition to the budget, several other types of formal control devices can be used for detecting the need for preventive or corrective action in organizations. In this section we consider statistical control reports, break-even-point analysis, special control reports, and internal audits.

65 In addition to the budgetary methods, statistical control reports are used as control devices in larger organizations. Would you expect that statistical control reports would also tend to emphasize those performance variables that are more readily measurable? [Yes / No]

Yes

66 For example, a periodic report which gives an analyzation of the employee turnover rate is a statistical _____ _____.

control report

67 Because statistical control reports have little

meaning unless compared with similar data for previous periods, it is important that they be prepared on a [continuing / noncontinuing] basis.

continuing
(weekly, monthly,
etc.)

68   *Break-even-point analysis* is a second additional type of control _____ used in business firms.

device

69   Break-even-point analysis involves the use of a chart to depict the overall volume of sales necessary to cover costs. Refer to the break-even chart in Figure 15.2. At what volume of sales will the revenue exactly cover the costs?

3,000 units   _____

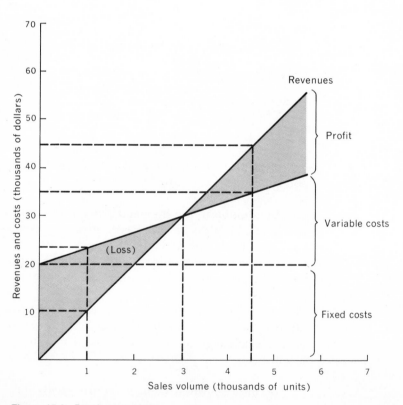

Figure 15.2   Break-even chart.

70 Therefore, in this particular case 3,000 units

break-even   is the _____ point.

71 As you have no doubt noted, the break-even chart is very similar in appearance to the variable budget chart. However, whereas the variable budget chart is used to plan budgets, the break-even chart is used to anticipate the amount of profit (or loss) associated with various levels of

sales   _____.

72 Thus, whereas the horizontal axis of Figure 15.1 identifies units of output, in Figure 15.2 it

sales   identifies units of _____. Whereas the vertical axis of Figure 15.1 identifies only categories of costs, in Figure 15.2 it identifies costs and

revenues   _____.

73 To exemplify use of the break-even chart, what is the total revenue associated with a sales vol-

$10,000   ume of 1,000 units in Figure 15.2? _____

74 What are the total costs associated with a sales

$23,000   volume of 1,000 units? _____
(approximately)

75 Therefore, at a sales volume of 1,000 units we

loss   would expect an overall [profit / loss] in the
$13,000   amount of _____.

76 Similarly, at a sales volume of 4,500 units we

profit   would expect an overall [profit / loss] in the
$10,000 ($45,000 in   amount of _____.
revenue minus
$35,000 in costs)

77 Thus, by directly comparing revenues and costs at various sales levels, a break-even chart

profit   identifies the expected amount of _____
loss   or _____.

78 So far, we have discussed two additional types

statistical controls   of control devices: _____

reports
break-even-point
analysis

_____ and _____

_____ .

79 *Special control reports* are a third additional category of control devices. These reports may or
may not contain statistical data, but the distinction
from other devices is that particular operations are
investigated at a particular time for a particular
purpose; that is, these reports are done on a [con-

noncontinuing   tinuing / noncontinuing] basis.

80 The great value of special control reports is
that operations appearing to deviate from expected standards are given additional executive attention. This is a direct application of the manage-

exception   rial principle of _____ .

81 A report reviewing present procedures in a
particular work area, such as the handling of cus-

special control   tomer complaints, is an example of a _____

report   _____ .

82 Finally, the *internal audit* is a fourth additional

control device   type of _____ _____ used
in business firms.

83 In addition to an audit of accounts, an evaluation of the application of policies, programs, and
methods and the attainment of objectives in a fairly
broad area of operations is included in the

internal   _____ audit.

84 For example, the central training department
of a large company that directs all subsidiary training units to appraise their own operations annually,
following a standard checklist of variables is, in ef-

internal audit   fect, conducting an _____ _____ .

85 Although the internal audit report may be

similar to the special control report, the principal distinctions are that the internal audit report is typically prepared on a [continuing / noncontinuing] basis and is also [more / less] extensive in its area of coverage.

continuing
(monthly, annually,
etc.); more

86 In addition to the budget, we have discussed four kinds of devices used in conjunction with the management function of controlling. Included were: _____ ,

statistical control
reports;
break-even-point
analysis; special
control reports;
internal audit

_____ ,

_____ ,

and the _____ .

87 Other than the budget, the type of control device that bears most directly on monetary analysis or the flow of funds is _____ .

break-even-point
analysis

88 The control device that is directly related to the managerial principal of control by exception is the _____ .

special control
report

89 The control device that is typically used on a continuing basis, and which can be directed at qualitative, or less tangible, results, as well as those that are easily quantifiable, is the _____ .

internal audit

90 Would you expect that an executive can come to a complete understanding of ongoing activities in an enterprise and institute appropriate control action through the use of the formal control devices alone? [Yes / No]

No

91 In any organizational situation, personal involvement of the manager with other key people in the enterprise, in addition to the use of formal _____ _____ , is necessary

control devices

to prevent the manager from becoming isolated from the ongoing operations.

D HUMAN REACTIONS TO CENTRALIZED CONTROL PROCEDURES

Ultimately, the success of a control system is determined by its effectiveness in getting people to make necessary modifications in their own performance. Although the classical approach to control systems assumes that people will automatically act to correct their own behavior when directed to do so, this does not necessarily happen. Individuals may resist formal control systems for a variety of reasons, some of which are discussed below.

92   One reason why a control procedure might be disliked is that it tends to disrupt a person's self-image; that is, the focal point of most control reports is to highlight the things that a person has
poorly done [well / poorly].

93   In terms of the influence of reward on behavioral change, it is not surprising that an unpleasant situation, or unpleasant involvement, tends to be
avoided [approached / avoided] by an individual.

94   Assuming that a person accepts the necessity of finding out about, and correcting, his inadequacies, the goals of the control system [need to /
need to need not] be accepted as worthwhile by him.

95   Thus, a failure to accept the organization's
goals _____ is a second reason why a control system may be resisted by an employee.

96   For example, a junior executive who feels that his job is "above the time-clock level" [would /
would would not] probably resist using a departmental sign-in sheet.

97   Even when the employee agrees with the

necessity of knowing unpleasant facts and considers the goals of the control system worthwhile, he may feel that the expected standard of performance is too high and [accept / reject] the control system on this basis.

reject

98   In situations in which it is possible to custom-fit performance standards for each person and this is accomplished, would there be a better chance of reducing resistance to controls? [Yes / No]

Yes

99   For example, as compared with a standard sales quota applied to all personnel, regardless of experience, individual sales quotas based on previous performance are [more / less] likely to be accepted.

more

100   On the other hand, a person may not consider the standard too high but may consider it to be irrelevant to, or at least an incomplete measurement of, attaining the organization's _____.

goals

101   For example, a control device that emphasizes only the importance of current sales volume may be [accepted / resisted] by the sales representative convinced of the importance of developing long-term good will with customers.

resisted

102   Thus far we have considered four reasons why individuals in an organization might resist controls: a tendency to _____ unpleasant facts, a failure to accept the organization's _____, a belief that the expected standard of performance is too _____, and a belief that the defined standards are a(n) [complete / incomplete] measurement of the attainment of organizational objectives.

avoid

goals

high

incomplete

103   The fifth reason for resistance to controls is that a person may object not to the controls themselves, but to the assignment of control authority to particular groups in the organization. Does an individual typically tend to object to control procedures which are carried out by his own superior?

No   [Yes / No]

104   On the other hand, it is more likely that control procedures administered by an outside staff

resisted   group will be [accepted / resisted] by line personnel.

105   Finally, just as there are two organizational systems in any firm—the formal and the informal—so also are there two sets of control systems. This implies that a person's work associates are an

control   important source of _____ over his work.

106   When informal group norms are consistent with company control objectives, we would expect

acceptance of   a high degree of [acceptance of / resistance to] the control devices; when group norms are contradictory to control objectives, we would expect a high

resistance   degree of [acceptance / resistance].

107   When the influence of the informal organization is an important factor underlying resistance to control procedures, the problem is best approached by considering how the [individual /

group (since the   group] point of view can be changed.
group is the source
of the resistance)

E   TOWARD EFFECTIVE CONTROLS

Each of the reasons for resisting controls has its counterpart in a line of action that a manager might take to reduce that source of resistance. In addition to this, however, there is a general point of view which, when applied, enhances the likelihood that people will work toward the goals of a control system.

108   First, let us consider that there are three possible focal points in the operation of a control system: *centralized control, personal control,* and *self-*

control _____ .

109 Control of a departmental budget by a finance staff is an example of [centralized / personal / self-] control.

centralized

110 The "checking up" and correcting that a supervisor does in his relationship with his subordinates is an example of [centralized / personal / self-] control.

personal

111 The individual who institutes changes in his own work methods after learning that he has failed to achieve desired objectives is practicing [centralized / personal / self-] control.

self-

112 In terms of the personal acceptance of control procedures, it is typically the case that the more intimately a person is involved in the control decisions, the [more / less] likely is it that he will accept them and put them into effect.

more

113 Thus, in terms of the three focal points of control systems, people in our society generally like _____ control best, _____ control least, with _____ control occupying an intermediate position.

self-
centralized
personal

114 From the standpoint of classical organization theory, the emphasis has been on the centralized flow of control data toward [top management / the lowest organizational level possible].

top management

115 In terms of the behavioral view of organizational performance, on the other hand, the importance of getting control information to that of the _____ _____

lowest organizational level possible (etc.)

is emphasized.

116   From the behavioral point of view, the circuit communication model, discussed in Chapter 10 on administrative communication, can be directly applied to control procedures as well. From this standpoint, direct feedback of information about results to the person actually doing the work leads to the most timely _____ action.

control

117   In regard to organizational philosophy and structure, an emphasis on self-control is consistent with the organizational philosophy of [centralization / decentralization].

decentralization

Review

118   A performance standard for a particular area of operation is typically made up of [one major / several] facet(s) of performance. (Frames 1 to 7)

several

119   A point in an operation that is chosen as a focal point for control activity is called a

strategic control
point

_____.

(Frames 8 to 11)

120   Several types of standards can be defined at a strategic control point in terms of the kind of measurment involved. There are _____,

quantity
cost; time use

_____ , _____ ,

quality

and _____ standards. (Frames 12 to 18)

121   A general problem in defining standards and measuring actual results is that the less tangible

quality

_____ standards and measurements tend to be underemphasized. (Frames 19 to 21)

122   When just a portion of the output at the strategic control point is checked with the assumption that this portion is representative of the entire output, the process of _____ is involved.

sampling

(Frames 22 to 25)

123 The amount of follow-up associated with the control process can be reduced by applying the management principles of _____.

exception

(Frames 26 to 29)

124 The quantitative units in which budgets are expressed are _____ units. The process of formulating and using budgets concerns the management functions of _____ and _____. (Frames 30 to 36)

monetary (or
dollar)
planning
controlling

125 Of the specific types of budgets considered in this chapter, the type which is concerned with anticipated revenues and expenses during a particular period is the _____ budget. (Frames 37 to 43)

operating

126 The type of budget concerned with planning for the availability of adequate funds is the _____ budget, while the type concerned with long-term expenditures and investments is the _____ budget. (Frames 44 to 52)

cash

appropriation

127 The type of budget which represents the intended financial status at the end of the budget period is the _____ _____ budget. The budgeting method which results in planning and control flexibility by allowing different budgeted amounts for different levels of operation is the _____ budget. (Frames 53 to 64)

balance sheet

variable

128 In addition to the budget, two other control devices that are entirely oriented toward the use of quantitative information, including the flow of funds, are _____ and _____.

statistical control
reports
break-even-point
analysis

(Frames 65 to 78)

129 Of the two types of control devices that may

be oriented toward nonquantitative standards, the one which is more limited in scope and is used on a noncontinuing basis is the _____, whereas the one that is more extensive and used on a continuing basis is the _____. (Frames 79 to 91)

special control
report

internal audit

130 Six reasons for individual resistance to control systems were discussed. Name three of these. (Frames 92 to 107)

(Refer to frames
indicated.)

_____

_____

_____

131 The three possible focal points, or directions, in the operation of a control system are _____ control, _____ control, and _____ control. (Frames 108 to 113)

centralized

personal; self-

132 Which focal point in the operation of control systems has the classical approach to organization theory tended to emphasize? _____ _____. (Frame 114)

Centralized
control

133 Which focal point in the operation of control systems does the behavioral point of view emphasize? _____. (Frames 115 to 117)

self-control

Discussion Questions

1. Describe the basic steps included in any control process and indicate how the steps are related to one another.

2. What is the relationship between the management functions of planning and controlling? Between organizing and controlling? Between directing and controlling?

3. Give examples of each of the four types of standards that may be used at a strategic control point. What kinds of measurement problems are associated with each?

4. Discuss the role of budgeting in an organization. What are its strengths and weaknesses?

5. Of the several types of budgets discussed in this chapter, which two would be of greatest use in a small business enterprise? Why?

6. Discuss the advantages and possible disadvantages of the variable budget. Can it be "overused"?

7. List some specific actions that a manager can take to counteract the various reasons for employee resistance to a control system.

8. Comment on the statement, "People prefer to have control over their own behavior." Do you agree? What are the implications of this statement for the management process of controlling?

Case Study: Western Office Equipment and Supply Company

The Western Office Equipment and Supply Company is in fact more than a supplier of office equipment and supplies. Upon completing his college studies shortly after World War II, Clyde Mueller, principal owner of the firm, was convinced that existing firms selling office equipment in the area in which his firm is now located were not providing essential services desired by the customer. As he saw it, in order to make an intelligent decision about office equipment, an organization needs an analysis of existing office procedures and recommendations for improvement. Accordingly, he established his firm on the premise that an office systems analysis is an integral part of a proposal for equipment purchase. The success of his approach is attested to by the fact that the firm now employs twenty people and grossed over $1 million in sales last year.

Mr. Mueller is general manager of the firm and himself acts as an office systems analyst for selected accounts. In addition, the activities of five other systems analysts are supervised and coordinated by George Hammond, who is the assistant manager and also part owner. Mrs. Betty Huntington supervises the typing pool, which is responsible for typing the recommendations that result from the systems analysts' work in client firms, in addition to performing other clerical services for the organization.

Several months ago the company's scope of operations was broadened to include new geographic areas, and since then a number of problems affecting the preparation of customer recommendations have developed. Previously, Mrs. Huntington had proofread all recommendations before sending them to George Hammond for subsequent distribution to the systems analysts concerned, but with the increase in work load she has had to rely on each typist doing her own proofreading, while she has tried to spot-check the figures included in the recommendations. Of course, questions regarding the accuracy of figures often have to be referred back to the originating analyst. However, with many of the analysts absent from the office for prolonged periods of time because of the expanded territories, confirmation of the figures has been difficult to accomplish.

The analysts have complained to Mr. Hammond both about the increase in the number of typographical and factual errors in their customer recommendations and about the apparent inability of the typing pool to have them prepared when requested. To check on the seriousness of the problem, Hammond kept a tally of the number of customer recommendations sent back to the typing pool for corrections during the past month and found that 80 percent of the recommendations were returned. He also found that the recommendations were being prepared by the day requested, but that their subsequent return for corrections was the principal cause of the delay.

Mr. Hammond has described the situation to Clyde Mueller during their lunch at the club and warned that equipment sales are already being lost because of the delays in the preparation of accurate customer proposals. Mueller expressed surprise, since he has not experienced any difficulty with the customer recommendations prepared for him, which are typed by Mrs. Huntington herself. As George Hammond sees it, the scope of the firm's operations has obviously outgrown Mrs. Huntington's ability to supervise and control the work performed in the typing pool. He suggests that she be designated as private secretary to Mr. Mueller and that a new supervisor with experience in a larger office be hired to replace her in the typing pool.

1. Would adoption of Mr. Hammond's suggestion probably take care of the difficulties being experienced in the typing pool? Why or why not?
2. What specific changes have taken place in the typing pool as the result of the expansion in the geographic area of the firm's activities?
3. Within the context of the present system, what changes might be made to improve the control system?
4. What organizational changes might be considered to improve the control system?

Case Study: Control of In-Process Inventory

The Rhibler Manufacturing Company is a relatively small firm manufacturing automobile parts and accessories for the replacement market. The company can be described as being highly centralized, in that specialist staff personnel issue quality specifications, cost specifications, and scheduling instructions to each manufacturing department in the company. There are three manufacturing plants, with the largest being located adjacent to the company's corporate office building.

For some time, the controller had noticed that the financial resources devoted to the in-process inventory seemed to be out of line with the known processing and assembly times required for the various items of equipment being manufactured. Essentially, the amount of material being processed seemed excessive in comparison with the amount that could in reality be in an in-process status in the company's facilities. He brought the matter up for discussion at one of the semiweekly sessions of the company's executive committee, and the reaction of the vice president in charge of production was that the controller was "playing around with assumptions and figures that are hypothetical and would only apply to a perfect situation." Further, the vice president for production indicated that the inventory control data show that all the input into the manufacturing plant can be accounted for in terms of the output. During the discussion the controller agreed that there was no question being raised about material being stolen; rather, it just seemed to be taking too long for the material to work its way through the plants. The discussion on the matter concluded with the company president suggesting that the vice president of production review the controller's analysis and take any appropriate action.

Several months after the meeting the company president took a major retail distributor on a tour of the main company plant. In one of the departments the president noticed several crates placed in a corner, which had obviously been there for some time. He walked over to see what they were, and to his surprise he found that they contained a large number of the components assembled in the department. When he questioned the foreman about the crates and why the material had not been shipped out of the department, he obtained a rather hesitant admission that the foreman kept a stock of the various items assembled in the department as a matter of routine. "This way," he explained, "whenever we have a machine breakdown I can use this stock to meet the production schedules, and that helps keep everything moving smoothly down the line."

After the visitor left, the company president called the controller and the vice president in charge of production, and the three of them went through all of the manufacturing and assembly departments in the main plant. In every department they visited they found an inventory of partially or fully assembled components being "held back" by individual foremen. "So that's where the stuff's been hiding," observed the controller. "It looks like we've got some housecleaning to do around here."

1. Assuming that the vice president in charge of production did not in fact know that manufactured items were being "held back," what does this suggest about the adequacy of his control system?
2. In what respects is the practice that the foremen followed appropriate, in terms of achieving organizational objectives? In what respects is the practice that the foremen followed inappropriate?
3. What inadequacy was there, if any, in the overall control system of the company?

Suggested Readings*

Adam, E. E., Jr., and W. E. Scott, Jr.: "The Application of Behavioral Conditioning Procedures to the problems of Quality Control," *Academy of Management Journal,* vol. 14, no. 2, June 1971.

*Also see the cross-reference table in the Preface.

Argyris, C.: "Human Problems with Budgets," *Harvard Business Review*, vol. 31, no. 1, January 1953.

Burdeau, H. B.: "Variable Budgets and Direct Costing," *Managerial Planning*, vol. 19, no. 4, January-February 1971.

Emch, A. F.: "Control Means Action," *Harvard Business Review*, vol. 32, no. 4, July 1954.

Ivancevich, J. M.: "An Analysis of Control, Bases of control, and Satisfaction in an Organizational Setting," *Academy of Management Journal*, vol. 13, no. 4, December 1970.

Jerome, W. T., III: *Executive Control: The Catalyst*, John Wiley & Sons, Inc., New York, 1961.

Strong, E. P., and R. D. Smith: *Management Control Models*, Holt, Rinehart and Winston, Inc., New York, 1968.

Vatter, W. J.: *Operating Budgets*, Wadsworth Publishing Company, Inc., Belmont, Calif., 1969.

Chapter **sixteen**

PROGRAM
EVALUATION
AND REVIEW
TECHNIQUE
(PERT)

Closely related to the quantitative decision-making techniques discussed in Chapter 5, new procedures have been developed as aids in the management functions of planning and controlling. In this chapter, we present the structural elements and application of the most important of these new procedures from the standpoint of the extent of its use: the program evaluation and review technique. Unlike the principal traditional control devices, this method is oriented toward the control of time and thus is particularly applicable to situations involving uncertainties in time requirements.

A NEW TECHNIQUES IN CONTROLLING

As is typical of the methods associated with operations research, the new techniques in controlling have a systemwide rather than a departmental orientation. Thus, rather than focusing upon the formal components of the organization, system-oriented control techniques highlight the relationship among the activities and events which culminate in attaining the objectives of a project or program.

1 The newer techniques do not markedly overlap the established control devices, but they provide the kind of information not readily available with the traditional methods. Therefore, when the recently developed control techniques are used, it is usually [in place of / in addition to] the control devices discussed in the last chapter.

in addition to

2 Specifically, most of the recently developed control techniques emphasize control of *time*, whereas budgeting, which is the most important traditional control device, is directed toward the control of _____.

cost (or money, etc.)

3 One of the most significant of the newer control techniques, and one that has had extensive application in the defense and aerospace industries, is the Program Evaluation and Review Technique. Consistent with many other recently developed control procedures, it is primarily directed toward the control of _____.

time

4 The Special Projects Office of the U.S. Navy first introduced the use of the Program Evaluation and Review Technique in the Polaris project in 1958. The Navy has stated that because of the use of PERT in this project, the Polaris missile submarine was brought to combat readiness about two years ahead of the original scheduled date, thus

dramatically illustrating the value of PERT in the
control of _____.

time (or
scheduling, etc.)

5 At about the same time that the Navy was developing PERT in cooperation with the management consulting firm of Booz, Allen & Hamilton,
the DuPont Company was concerned with the time
and cost required to bring new products from
research to production and independently developed a similar technique known as the Critical Path
Method (CPM). Like PERT, CPM is primarily
oriented toward achieving better managerial con-

time   trol in respect to _____.

6 Although the principal traditional control devices, particularly budgeting, are cost-oriented,
some of the early methods of production scheduling can be considered as forerunners of PERT aŋd
CPM. Of these, the most important is the *Gantt
milestone chart.* Henry L. Gantt was a contemporary
of Frederick W. Taylor, and thus he is generally

scientific   identified with the _____ management movement discussed in Chapter 1.

7 Figure 16.1 on page 446 illustrates the general
form of the Gantt milestone chart. As indicated, the
width of each bar in this chart identifies the total

task   time commitment planned for each _____.

8 Furthermore, overlapping bars on this chart indicate which tasks can be worked on simultaneously, whereas absence of overlap indicates that
a task has to be completed before the next task can
begin. In Figure 16.1, for example, the work on

A (On the other   task C cannot begin until task _____ is com-
hand, tasks B and   pleted.
C can overlap to
some extent.)

9 The word "milestone" refers to the point of
completion of a significant phase of a task. Since
these are points at which results can be measured,

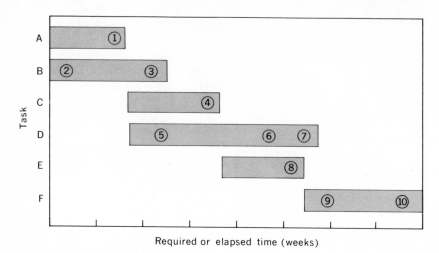

Figure 16.1 General form of the Gantt milestone chart.

control they are similar to the strategic _____ points discussed in Chapter 15.

10 Of course, in this case the milestones are used as a basis for evaluating the project schedule, rather than product quality as such. In Figure 16.1, the milestones within each task are indicated numbers by the _____ entered in the circles.

11 Furthermore, a milestone cannot be reached until all preceding milestones *within a given task* are completed. Thus, progress toward milestone 3
2 cannot begin until milestone _____ is completed.

12 However, the Gantt milestone chart does *not* indicate the sequential relationship between milestones in separate tasks. As we shall see, such interrelationships *are* indicated by the PERT network. In Figure 16.1, however, is progress toward milestone 8 dependent on milestone 6 being
Uncertain completed? [Yes / No / Uncertain]

13 As contrasted to the limited analysis of interrelationships in Gantt charting, PERT involves the identification of the entire network of activities and associated milestones, or events, which culminate in attaining the _____ of the system.

objectives (or goals)

14 Refer to the sample PERT network in Figure 16.2 on page 448. The first event in the sequence is called "_____" and the last is "_____ _____."

order received

complete unit
assembled and
tested

15 In this chapter, we present a fairly detailed coverage of the elements and computational procedure used in PERT. However, the examples will be much simpler than those encountered in actual managerial situations. The typical application of PERT in industry involves hundreds, and even thousands, of events in the PERT network, whereas our sample network in Figure 16.2, for example, has just _____ [number] events.

eight

16 In the following section of this chapter, we present the elements of the PERT network. Thus we shall first cover the [structural / functional] aspects of this technique.

structural

17 In the final section of this chapter we illustrate the use of PERT in decision making and control, thereby emphasizing its [structural / functional] properties.

functional

B   ELEMENTS OF THE PERT NETWORK

As we have just briefly indicated, a PERT network is made up of a sequence of events connected by the necessary activities. In Figure 16.2, as in all PERT network diagrams, the events are located within the circles whereas the activities are indicated by the arrows connecting the circles.

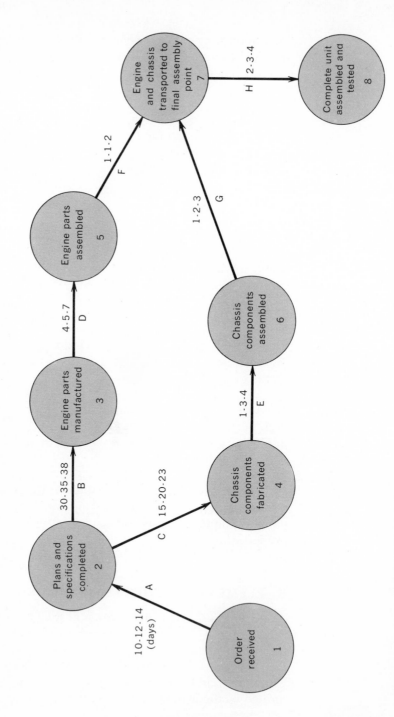

Figure 16.2 A simplified PERT network.

18 In PERT terminology, an *event* signifies the start or completion of a significant step in a project. Notice the kinds of events included in Figure 16.2. Since an event is always the start or completion of some work, does an event as such consume any time or resources? [Yes / No]

No

19 Thus, in PERT analysis an event is distinguished from an *activity*, which *does* involve the use of _____ or resources.

time

20 Events are typically represented by numbers, whereas activities may be represented by letters. Thus, the events in Figure 16.2 are identified by the [numbers / letters] _____ through _____ , and the activities are identified by the [numbers / letters] _____ through _____ .

numbers; 1

8

letters   A

H

21 Rather than using letters, we frequently identify activities by the numbers of the two events that they connect: "Activity 3–5" is an alternative way of identifying activity _____ in Figure 16.2.

D

22 Similarly, an alternative label for activity E in the figure would be activity _____.

4–6

23 Thus the basic structure of a PERT network consists of a series of _____ connected by the necessary _____ .

events

activities

24 "A time-consuming and resource-consuming element in the PERT network" describes an _____ .

activity

25 "A meaningful accomplishment in the program, recognizable as a particular instant in time and not in itself consuming time or resources" describes an _____ .

event

26 In a PERT diagram, the events are identified by _____ in the circles, whereas the ac-

numbers

letters (or pairs of numbers)

tivities are identified by _____ associated with the arrows.

27 The numbers used to indicate the events in a network are not necessarily in a sequential order; rather, the numbers simply serve as labels. From this standpoint, the following diagram [is / is not] a valid example of a PERT network:

is

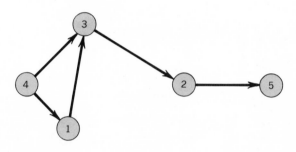

28 As we indicated, PERT is primarily concerned with control over time. Accordingly, three estimates for time use—*optimistic, most likely,* and *pessimistic*—are made for each [event / activity].

activity (An event does not consume any time.)

29 The time estimate which is based on the assumption that everything will go right and has about one chance in a hundred of being realized, is the _____ time.

optimistic

30 The time estimate which would be correct most often if the activity could be repeated many times under exactly the same conditions is the _____ _____ time.

most likely

31 The time estimate based on the assumption that everything short of a catastrophe goes wrong, and which also has about one chance in a hundred of happening, is the _____ time.

pessimistic

32 Accordingly, of the three time estimates given by the supervisor of an activity, the longest time estimate is _____ time, the shortest time estimate is _____ time, and _____ _____ time is between the two.

pessimistic
optimistic; most
likely

33 The three time estimates are sometimes written over the arrows that represent the activities in the PERT network. For activity 2–3 in Figure 16.2 on page 452 (repeated), the optimistic time is _____ days, most likely time is _____ days, and pessimistic time is _____ days.

30; 35
38

34 Generally, the three time estimates for each _____ are combined into a weighted average, called *expected activity time*, which is designated t_e.

activity

35 Where optimistic time is designated by a, most likely time by m, and pessimistic time by b, the formula used to compute t_e is

$$t_e = \frac{a + 4m + b}{6}$$

This is an estimate of the average time the activity would take if it were repeated many times. The time estimate which is most heavily weighted in the formula is the _____ time.

most likely

36 Given the following values for a, m, and b, compute the t_e for each activity, using decimals (to two places), rather than fractions, in your answers:

	Activity	a	m	b	t_e
7.00	A	4	7	10	_____
3.17	B	1	3	6	_____
4.17	C	3	4	6	_____

where

$$t_e = \frac{a + 4m + b}{6}$$

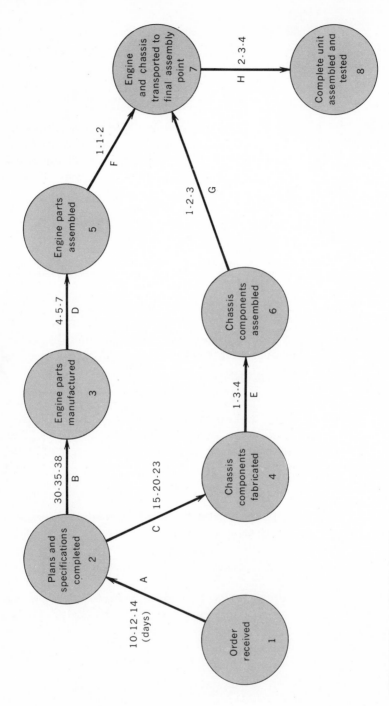

Figure 16.2 A simplified PERT network.

37 Using the formula given above, compute the expected time t_e for each of the following activities in Figure 16.2 and post the results below:

	Activity	t_e
12.00	A	_____
2.83	E	_____
3.00	H	_____

38 Suppose the following information is given for two activities in a PERT network:

Activity	a	m	b	t_e
K	1	4	7	4.00
L	3	4	5	4.00

K

Which activity has more uncertainty associated with its expected completion time t_e? [K/L]

39 As you may have observed in the last frame, the wider the spread (range) between the optimistic and pessimistic time estimates, the greater the degree of [certainty / uncertainty] associated with the expected time for the activity.

uncertainty

40 Because the degree of uncertainty, or *variance*, associated with the expected time for each activity is also important in PERT analysis, it is calculated using the following formula, in which v stands for variance:

$$v = [(b - a)/6]^2$$

Compute the variance for the expected time t_e when the optimistic time is 1 day and the pessimistic time is 7 days. Do your computations below:

$[(7 - 1)/6]^2 = 1$ $v = $ _____.

41 Given the formulas $t_e = (a + 4m + b)/6$ and $v = [(b - a)/6]^2$, complete the following table, carrying out your computations to the second decimal place:

t_e	v	Activity	a	m	b	t_e	v
6.00	0.11	1–2	5	6	7	_____	_____
6.00	0.44	1–3	4	6	8	_____	_____
14.67	4.00	2–5	10	14	22	_____	_____

42 For the data in Frame 41, in which of the expected time values would you, as a manager, have the greatest confidence? The expected time for activity _____. Why? _____

1–2
Because the
expected time for
this activity has the
smallest variance
associated with it.

43 For the data in Frame 41, in which expected time value would you have the least confidence? The expected time for activity _____. Why?

2–5
Because this
expected time
value has the
largest variance
associated with it.

44 Given the formula

$$v = [(b - a)/6]^2$$

complete the following table for the data in Figure 16.2.

	Activity	a	m	b	v
0.44	A	10	12	14	_____
0.25	D	4	5	7	_____
0.03	F	1	1	2	_____

45 We now turn our attention to events rather than activities. The T_E of an event is the expected time for that event to be reached, given the expected activity times in a network. For the network below, what is the value of T_E for event 3; that is, how soon can we expect to arrive at event 3? _____ days.

10 (the sum of the
t_e values for
activities 1–2 and
2–3)

46 There are often several "paths" through a

network that culminate at the final event of the
network or at particular events along the way. For
example, in Figure 16.3, the three paths that lead
to the attainment of event 7 are made up of events

1, 3, 4, and 7   _____, events _____, and
1, 2, and 7   events _____.
1, 5, 6, 8, and 7

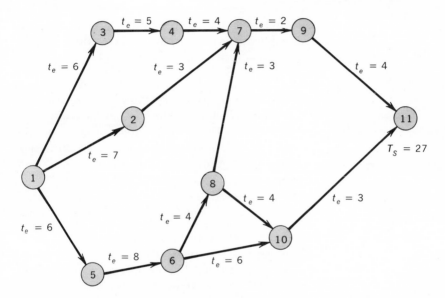

Figure 16.3 A simplified PERT network.

47 All the necessary preceding events *must* be
completed before an event can itself be completed.
For example, event 7 in Figure 16.3 can be
completed only after *all* the events in the three
paths that you just identified have been completed.
Therefore, when there are two or more paths that
lead to an event, the T_E for that event is equal to

most   the T_E in the [least / most] time-consuming path.

48 Compute the value of the expected time T_E
21 (the addition of   for event 7 in Figure 16.3 $T_{E(7)} =$ _____.
the t_e's in the
largest time-
consuming path)

49 Complete the following table for the events in Figure 16.3:

Event	T_E
3	_____
5	_____
9	_____
11	_____

6
6
23 (via 1–5–6–8–7–9)
27 (via
1–5–6–8–7–9–11)

50 Whereas the expected activity time is represented by the symbol t_e, the expected time to reach an event is represented by the symbol _____.

T_E

51 There are two other types of values associated with events. T_S, the *scheduled time*, is the contractual obligation date for the whole project, or the scheduled completion time for certain major events within the project. Refer to Figure 16.3. What is the scheduled time T_S for event 11, which is the culmination of the project? $T_S = $ _____.

27

52 T_L, on the other hand, is the *latest allowable completion time* for an event so that an entire project is kept on schedule. The T_L for each event must be so established that if every event in a network is completed by this time, then the scheduled time for the project, T_S, will be met. In Figure 16.3, what must the T_L for event 11 be? _____

27 (same as T_S, since this is the final event in the network)

53 In computing the T_L for an event, you must work back from the scheduled completion time of the final event in the network. For the network below, given that the project must be completed in 15 days and that the last activity in the network (Activity 3–4) has an expected time usage of 4 days, in how many days must event 3 be reached for the project to be on schedule at that point? Insert your answer on the diagram.

$T_{L(3)} = 11$

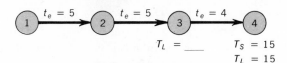

$T_L = \underline{\quad}$ $T_S = 15$
$T_L = 15$

54   Thus, to compute the latest allowable completion time T_L for any event, subtract the value of the t_e following it from the value of the T_L of the succeeding event. Fill in the rest of the latest allowable completion times in the following network.

$T_{L(1)} = 1$
$T_{L(2)} = 6$

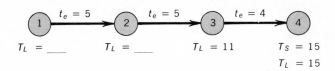

$T_L = \underline{\quad}$ $T_L = \underline{\quad}$ $T_L = 11$ $T_S = 15$
$T_L = 15$

55   Of course, whether or not the latest allowable completion time for each event will be met depends on the value of T_E, the expected completion time, for each event. In the diagram below, insert the value of T_E for each event.

$T_{E(2)} = 5$
$T_{E(3)} = 10$
$T_{E(4)} = 14$

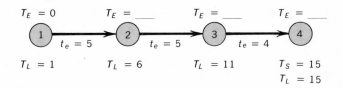

$T_L = 1$ $T_L = 6$ $T_L = 11$ $T_S = 15$
$T_L = 15$

56   Referring to the diagram above, for the entire project to remain on schedule, event 3 must be completed by _____ days from now, whereas the expected completion time for event 3 is _____ days from now.

11

10

57 In computing the T_E for an event, we follow all paths from the beginning of the network to the event in question and choose the addition of the t_e's in the most time-consuming path. In the diagram below, for example, the expected completion time for event 4 is _____ days from now.

4

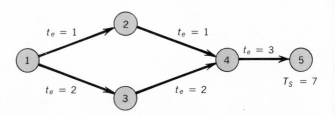

58 Similarly, we use the t_e's in the longest time-consuming path in computing the value of T_L by working back from the final event in a network. Thus, for the diagram above, the latest time for event 1, which is the formal beginning of the project, is _____ days from now.

0 (That is, work on the project should begin immediately.)

59 For the last frame, note that unless event 1 is accomplished immediately ($T_L =$ _____), the project will be behind schedule at event 3.

0

60 Complete the following table for the events in Figure 16.3 (repeated):

Event	T_L
11	_____
7	_____
5	_____
3	_____

27
21
6
12

61 In this section of the chapter we have discussed the computation of the expected activity time (t_e), the variance associated with the expected

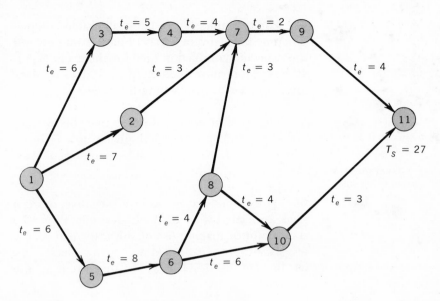

Figure 16.3 A simplified PERT network.

activity time (v), the expected completion time for

T_E an event (_____), the latest allowable comple-

T_L tion time for an event (_____), and the
scheduled, or contractual, completion time for an

T_S event (_____).

C   USING THE PERT NETWORK

In this section we demonstrate how the values
calculated for individual activities and events are
used in overall network analysis and managerial
control action.

62   The *slack* of an event is a measurement of the
excess time available to reach that event. Since it is
the number of days (or weeks, etc.) by which the
latest allowable completion time exceeds the expected time for an event, the appropriate formula
to find the slack for an event would be

$T_L - T_E$ $[T_L + T_E \ / \ T_L - T_E \ / \ T_E - T_L]$.

63 For example, if the latest allowable completion time for an event (T_L) is 14 days from now and the expected completion time for the event (T_E) is

2

12 days from now, then _____ days of slack are associated with reaching the event.

64 On the other hand, suppose that the two values just given were reversed, giving us a T_L of 12 and a T_E of 14. What would be the amount of slack

− 2 days (two days behind schedule)

associated with this event? _____

65 Thus there can be positive, negative, or zero slack associated with reaching an event. From the standpoint of making use of this information, the less slack there is (or the more negative slack there

more

is), the [more / less] *critical* is that event in the project.

66 Compute the value of the slack associated with attaining each event in the following table:

	Event	T_L	T_E	Slack $(T_L − T_E)$
2	1	2	0	_____
0	2	5	5	_____
5	3	13	8	_____
− 1	4	18	19	_____

67 Referring to the table that you just completed, which event has the most slack time and thus may have excess resources applied to it? Event

3

_____.

68 Referring to the table in Frame 66, which

4

event is most critical? Event _____.

69 Applying the concept of slack to entire paths, rather than just to individual events, the *critical path* in a PERT network is the one that has the

least

[most / least] slack.

70 To put it another way, the path from the first event to goal attainment which consumes the most

critical

time is the _____ path.

71 For the network below, the critical path is the one connecting events _____.

1–3–4–5

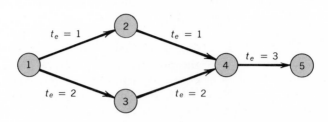

72 Refer to Figure 16.3 on page 459. The critical path for this network is the one connecting events

1–5–6–8–
7–9–11

_____.

73 As the name implies, the critical path is critical because a delay in the completion of any of the events in it can result in a delay in achieving the project objective, unless resource or personnel changes are made. Is it possible for there to be two or more equally critical paths in a PERT network? [Yes / No]_____

Yes
Several paths
might be at the
same minimum
slack level.

74 In the following network, both path _____ and path _____ can be considered critical paths.

1–4–5

1–2–3–5

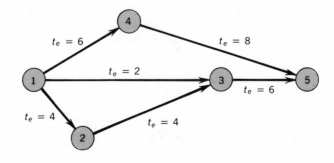

75 Because it directs the manager's attention to those events and activities that are most likely to delay the completion of a project, critical

path

_____ analysis is valuable as a control technique.

76 The final calculation in PERT analysis, and the one that has considerable significance for the control function, is the determination of the probability P_R of meeting a scheduled completion date for a project. Since it focuses on the completion of the project as a whole, the P_R value is typically

for the final event
in the network

calculated [for each event in the network / for the final event in the network.]

77 The first step in the calculation of P_R, which is the probability of _____

completing the
project on
schedule (etc.)

_____ is to compute the value of z.

78 The formula used to compute Z is

$$Z = \frac{T_S - T_E}{\sqrt{Sv}}$$

where $T_S - T_E$ is for the final event in the network and Sv is the sum of all the variances *in the critical path* of the network. In terms of this formula, can

Yes
Whenever a
"behind-schedule"
condition exists.

the value of Z be negative? [Yes / No] Explain.

_____

_____

79 Find the value of Z for the following network, given the formula

$$Z = \frac{1}{\sqrt{4}} = \frac{1}{2}$$
$$= 0.5$$

$$Z = \frac{T_S - T_E}{\sqrt{Sv}}$$

(Don't forget that variances are summed for the critical path only.)

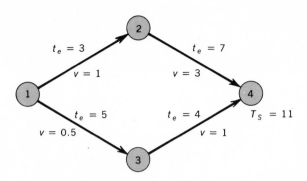

80 The second step in the procedure to determine the value of P_R, which is the probability of completing the project on schedule, is to interpret the meaning of the _____ [symbol] value just computed.

Z

81 The meaning of any value of Z can be determined by reference to the Z table, or the table of areas under the normal distribution curve, which is included in most statistics textbooks. Table 16.1 on page 462 is a condensed version of this table, somewhat modified to facilitate the determination of P_R values. Referring to Table 16.1, we can see that the value of P_R associated with a Z of 0.5 is _____.

0.692

82 Referring to Table 16.1, what is the probability of meeting a scheduled completion date for a project when the Z value is 0? _____. When $Z = 1.0$? _____. When $Z = -0.7$? _____.

0.500
0.841; 0.242

83 Since $T_S - T_E$ is in the numerator of the formula for Z, whenever the scheduled completion date and expected completion date exactly coincide, the numerical probability of completing the project on time is stated as (refer to Table 16.1) _____.

0.500 (since $Z = 0$
in this case)

84 Although a probability of 0.50 indicates a 50 percent chance of completing the project on time, this is usually considered an acceptable level,

Table 16.1 Table of cumulative proportions of area
under the normal curve for various values
of Z

Z	P_R	Z	P_R
0.0	0.500	0.0	0.500
0.1	0.540	−0.1	0.460
0.2	0.579	−0.2	0.421
0.3	0.618	−0.3	0.382
0.4	0.655	−0.4	0.345
0.5	0.692	−0.5	0.308
0.6	0.726	−0.6	0.274
0.7	0.758	−0.7	0.242
0.8	0.788	−0.8	0.212
0.9	0.816	−0.9	0.184
1.0	0.841	−1.0	0.159
1.1	0.864	−1.1	0.136
1.2	0.885	−1.2	0.115
1.3	0.903	−1.3	0.097
1.4	0.919	−1.4	0.081
1.5	0.933	−1.5	0.067
1.6	0.945	−1.6	0.055
1.7	0.955	−1.7	0.045
1.8	0.964	−1.8	0.036
1.9	0.971	−1.9	0.029
2.0	0.977	−2.0	0.023
2.1	0.982	−2.1	0.018
2.2	0.986	−2.2	0.014
2.3	0.989	−2.3	0.011
2.4	0.992	−2.4	0.008
2.5	0.994	−2.5	0.006
2.6	0.995	−2.6	0.005
2.7	0.996	−2.7	0.004
2.8	0.997	−2.8	0.003
2.9	0.998	−2.9	0.002
3.0	0.999	−3.0	0.001

perhaps because any minor "slippage" can be off-set by the addition of resources to the project. On the other hand, a probability less than about 0.25 is usually interpreted as an indication of considerable risk. Ideally, should we try to eliminate risk by getting P_R to be as close to 1.0 as possible? [Yes / No]

No (See next frame.)

85 Although a manager might feel more comfortable with a very high P_R value because of reduced time pressures, in most instances it is also an indication that personnel or other resources are being used extravagantly, so that high P_R values [are / are not] generally considered "good" by management.

are not

86 Whereas it is taken as an indication of considerable risk when the P_R value is less than _____, a P_R greater than 0.60 is taken to indicate that excess resources are possibly being applied to the project.

0.25

87 What is the value of P_R for the network below? $P_R =$ _____

$P_R = 0.500$
(Note that
$T_S - T_E = 0.$)

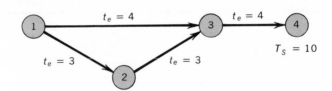

88 When a P_R of 0.500 is obtained, is any corrective action usually called for? [Yes / No]

No (except possibly when termination of the entire project is near at hand)

89 Given the following network, determine the value of P_R, using the formula

$$Z = \frac{T_S - T_E}{\sqrt{S_v}} \qquad P_R = \underline{\hspace{2cm}}$$

$Z = \frac{3}{1} = 3.0$
$P_R = 0.999$

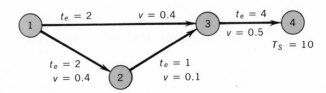

90 What kind of corrective action, if any, is appropriate for the situation just described?

_____

_____

_____

Possibly shifting
personnel and
other resources to
another project
(etc.)

91 Given the following network, determine the probability of completing the project on time:

$$Z = \frac{-3}{2} = -1.5$$

$$P_R = 0.067$$

$$Z = \frac{T_S - T_E}{\sqrt{S_v}}$$

$$P_R = \underline{\hspace{3cm}}$$

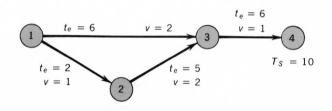

92 In the preceding example, which of the activities in the critical path should be given principal attention in attempting to bring the project back on schedule? Activity [1–2 / 2–3 / 3–4].

2–3 (See next
frame.)

93 It is tempting to assume that the activity that has the largest expected time can be reduced most. However, the relevant value is not t_e itself, but the _____ associated with each expected activity time.

variance

94 For projects extending over a long time period, thousands of activities and events may make up the PERT network. Under these conditions, would the graphic portrayal of the entire network become unwieldy? [Yes / No]

Yes

95 Accordingly, various summary and detail charts are generally prepared when a great many events constitute a project, and critical paths are identified by computer analysis. However, the basic computational and analytical procedure **is** [is / is not] the same as for the simplified examples in this unit.

Review

96 Recently developed control procedures, such as PERT, are mainly directed toward the control of **time** _____. (Frames 1 to 3)

97 An early scheduling method that resembles PERT and CPM, but includes no analysis of interrelationships among all of the events, is the **milestone** Gantt _____ chart. (Frames 4 to 12)

98 A PERT network is made up of a series of **events; activities** _____, connected by _____, which lead to the attainment of an objective. (Frames 13 to 27)

99 The three time estimates for each activity, represented by the symbols *a*, *m*, and *b*, are combined into a weighted average represented by the **t_e** symbol _____. (Frames 28 to 37)

variance **100** *v* is the symbol for the _____ associated with the expected time for each activity. (Frames 38 to 44)

101 The expected completion time for an event **T_E** is represented by the symbol _____, the latest allowable completion time for an event is repre- **T_L** sented by _____, and the scheduled comple- tion time for a project is represented by **T_S** _____. (Frames 45 to 61)

102 The slack associated with an event is the excess time available to reach an event. It is com- **T_E** puted by subtracting the value of _____ from

T_L the value of _____ for that event. (Frames 62 to 68)

103   The path from the first event to the final event in a network that has the least slack is called

critical path   the _____ _____. (Frames 69 to 75).

104 P_R is the notation for the probability of

completing a
project on   _____.
schedule   In order to determine P_R, the value of _____
Z [symbol] must first be computed. (Frames 76 to 80)

105   It is considered an indication of high risk by many when the P_R value is less than about

0.25   _____, whereas it is often taken as an indication that excess resources are being applied to the

0.60   project when the P_R is greater than _____ for an ongoing project. (Frames 81 to 86)

106   Given a project that is behind schedule, it is most fruitful to apply corrective action by trying to reduce the time for those activities with the highest

variance (not
necessarily those   _____. (Frames 92 to 95)
with the highest
expected time t_e)

107   Given the following data for the critical path of a PERT network, complete the table below using the formulas provided. (Frames 36 and 37, 41 to 44)

$$t_e = \frac{a + 4m + b}{6} \qquad v = [(b - a)/6]^2$$

t_e	v	Activity	a	m	b	t_e	v
6	1	1–2	3	6	9	_____	_____
15	4	2–4	9	15	21	_____	_____
10	4	4–7	6	9	18	_____	_____

108   For the data above, compute the value of Z

given that $T_S = 28$. (Frames 76 to 80)

$$= \frac{28 - 31}{3}$$

$$= -1.0$$

$$Z = \frac{T_S - T_E}{\sqrt{Sv}}$$

0.159

109 Referring to Table 16.1, what is the P_R value associated with a Z of -1.0? $P_R = $ _____ . (Frames 87 to 91)

110 For the data in Frame 107, to which activity in the critical path would you give principal attention in attempting to bring the project back on schedule? (Frames 92 to 93) _____

Either 2–4 or 4–7 or both, since the variances are equal

_____

Discussion Questions

1. Why is the use of PERT particularly useful in the aerospace industry?

2. Discuss the importance of the three activity time estimates for PERT analysis. How might these estimates be made more accurate?

3. What is the value of determining the slack associated with each of the paths in a network?

4. At what value is P_R considered to be too low? Too high? What is the remedial action in each case?

5. In what ways can PERT be used as a planning device? In what ways can it be used as a control device?

6. Discuss the similarities and differences between using the Gantt milestone chart and PERT analysis for project planning and controlling.

7. All the examples of applying PERT have implied the development of some type of product or physical component. Consider how PERT analysis might be used by a bank.

8. One criticism directed at PERT as well as certain other methods of analysis is that the quantitative results are misleading because they are in fact based on judgments and subjective approximations. In what respects is this criticism appropriate and in what respects is it inappropriate?

Case Problems: Program Evaluation and Review Technique

1. A professional society holds an annual dinner meeting at which new members are initiated. The number of people attending this meeting has not varied much from year to year. In addition to the initiation itself, a highlight of the evening is an after-dinner report on the current "state of the profession" by a distinguished practitioner. Using the following events, which are *not* listed in order, construct a PERT network representing the pattern of activities leading up to the dinner meeting.

1. The menu is planned.
2. Certificates of membership for new members are received.
3. Replies and payments are received from present members.
4. Program planning is begun.
5. Prospective members are identified.
6. Invitations are mailed to present members.
7. Invitations are mailed to prospective members.
8. A place for the meeting is established.
9. The dinner meeting is held.
10. Certificates of membership are ordered for new members.
11. A price is established.
12. Replies and payments are received from prospective members.
13. An after-dinner speaker is arranged.
14. A seating arrangement is planned.
15. A date for the meeting is established.

2. Identify the errors in the following PERT network.

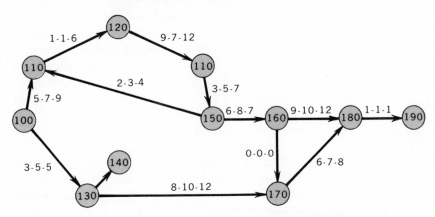

3. Identify the critical path in the network below and compute the amount of slack given that the project is scheduled for completion in thirty months. What can we conclude about the probability that the project will be completed on time? If we are now at event 110, to which activity should we give principal attention in order to accelerate progress toward completion of the project?

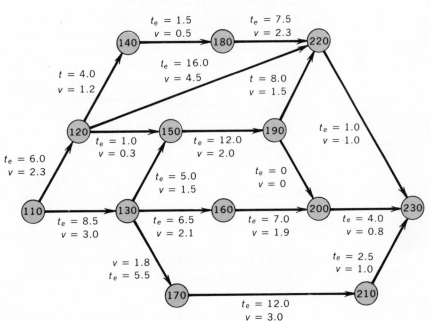

Case Study: An Unsuccessful Application of PERT

For a number of years the Wilson Construction Company has used a modified Gantt chart to help schedule the work activities of the various subcontractors participating in major building projects. After Tom Gadfree, a production superintendent in the company, attended a university-sponsored seminar on PERT analysis, he determined to apply the technique to the next major construction project to which he was assigned.

During the following month an appropriate opportunity presented itself. In conjunction with obtaining the bids from the subcontractors, he also asked each subcontractor to provide an estimate of the optimistic, pessimistic, and most likely amount of time that would be required to do each phase of the work. He then used this information as the quantitative input into the network chart, which he developed based on his knowledge of the interrelationships among and between the various phases of construction.

The following year Tom Gadfree happened to meet Professor Jenkins, who had conducted the seminar on PERT analysis, and the professor asked Tom if he ever got the chance to use the technique. "I sure did," replied Tom, "and I could have lost my job because of it. For one thing, it turned out that all of the time estimates given to me were way low. As a result, the expected time that I came up with for completing the project constituted about 70 percent of the time it actually took. Furthermore, the subcontractors kept slipping back and forth so much in their schedules that I spent a helluva lot of time redrawing that blasted network chart. One tryout of that technique is more than enough for me!"

1. Did Tom Gadfree use an appropriate basis for constructing the network chart in the first place? Why or why not?

2. What errors did he make in obtaining the time estimates for the required activities?

3. What comments might be made in respect to his work in redrawing the network chart during the period of construction?

Suggested Readings*

Avots, I.: "The Management Side of PERT," *California Management Review,* vol. 4, no, 2. Winter 1962.

Berkwitt, G. J.: "Management Rediscovers CPM," *Dun's,* vol. 97, no. 5, May 1971.

Dusenbury, W.: "CPM for New Product Introduction," *Harvard Business Review,* vol. 45, no. 4, July-August 1967.

Evarts, H.F.: *Introduction to PERT,* Allyn and Bacon, Inc., Boston, 1964.

Horowitz, J.: *Critical Path Scheduling,* The Ronald Press Company, New York, 1967.

Levin, R. I., and C. A. Kirkpatrick: *Planning and Control with PERT/CPM,* McGraw-Hill Book Company, New York, 1966.

Miller, R. W.: "How to Plan and Control with PERT," *Harvard Business Review,* vol. 40, no. 2, March-April 1962.

Sherrard, W. R., and F. Mehlick: *"PERT,* A Dynamic Approach," *Decision Sciences,* vol. 3, no. 2, April 1972.

Swanson, L. A., and H. L. Pazer: "Implications of the Underlying Assumptions of PERT," *Decision Sciences,* vol. 2, no. 4, October 1971.

Weist, J. D., and F. K. Levy: *A Management Guide to PERT/CPM,* Prentice-Hall, Inc., Englewood Cliffs, N.J., 1969.

*Also see the cross-reference table in the Preface.

VI
SYSTEMS
CONCEPTS

Throughout this book we have followed the functional approach to management, by which the process of management is described as including the functions of planning, organizing, directing, and controlling. An alternative to the functional approach, and one which has experienced rapid development during the last decade, is based on general systems theory. Although the techniques of the systems approach are particularly associated with the development of new planning and controlling techniques, the approach has broader implications in terms of the way that organizational activities are viewed.

Chapter **seventeen**
THE
SYSTEMS
APPROACH
TO
MANAGEMENT

We begin this chapter by describing the general nature of the systems approach as it has been applied in the physical and biological sciences and then consider its implications for the management functions of planning, organizing, and controlling. A particular development, program management, will then be discussed as an example of the application of a systems-oriented point of view. In the final section of this chapter we describe the development of data processing systems, including electronic data processing, and their use in enhancing effective management. Although data processing methods and applications were not originally developed as an outgrowth of the systems approach, their further development and the utilization of their full potential is closely related to this management orientation.

A SYSTEMS CONCEPTS AND MANAGEMENT

On the most elementary level, systems analysis implies an analysis of wholes rather than parts. In addition to accepting the assertion that "everything depends on everything else," the systems approach is directed toward discovering and explaining the nature of the multiple relationships among the components of a system. As applied in biology, for example, the focus is on the total organism, and functions such as respiration and digestion are viewed as subsystems within the context of the total bodily system, rather than as isolated processes. In management, the systems approach directs our attention to the total firm as an entity, to an identification of the objectives of that firm, and to the identification of the functions necessary for the achievement of those objectives. In this section we begin by offering a definition of a system in general and then we consider the implications of the systems approach to the management functions of planning, organizing, and controlling and to the related organizational processes of communication and decision making.

1 A *system* in general can be defined as an established *arrangement of components* which leads to the attainment of *particular objectives* according to *plan*. By the use of italics, we have stressed three principal ingredients in this definition. In analyzing an established system or devising a new system, we should first identify the _____

particular
objectives _____ of the system.

organizing

2 The objectives of the system should be identified first because these provide the basis for evaluating functions and relationships within the system. In designing a system, establishing the necessary *arrangement of components* is similar to what we have previously designated as the management function of _____.

objectives

3 Of course, the identification of objectives is itself part of the planning process. However, when we say that a system is an established arrangement of components which leads to the attainment of particular objectives *according to plan*, we are referring to the necessity of establishing specific policies, procedures, and methods by which the _____ are to be attained.

components
objectives
plan

4 Thus, in general a system is an established arrangement of _____ which leads to the attainment of particular _____ according to _____.

in addition to

5 Another useful way of considering the meaning of the systems approach in science as well as in administration is to describe how it differs from a nonsystems approach. Sir Arthur Eddington, a noted physicist, has illustrated this difference in his field by the following analogy: "We often think that when we have completed our study of *one* we know all about *two*, because 'two' is 'one and one.' We forget that we still have to make a study of and.' Secondary physics is the study of 'and'—that is to say, of organization."[1] By illustration, Eddington suggests that the study of "and" needs to be done [instead of / in addition to] the study of "one."

[1]Sir Arthur Eddington, *The Nature of the Physical World,* University of Michigan Press, Ann Arbor, 1958, p. 104.

6 Thus, the systems approach cannot take the place of the study of specific or molecular processes. However, beyond some point further attention to specifics is less useful for increasing overall understanding than is the study of their relationships. This suggests that the study of relationships should

follow [precede / follow] the study of specifics.

7 Because the individual scientific disciplines were originally oriented toward research in specific fields, such as physics, chemistry, and astronomy, the later application of the systems orientation has generally resulted in the need for so-called "interdisciplinary approaches," involving

several [only one / several] fields of inquiry.

8 Similarly, in the area of administrative application the systems approach suggests that a firm's plant location decision, for example, [should /

should not should not] be considered solely as a financial problem.

9 Thus, just as the scientist needs to have knowledge in several related fields in order to be able to apply the systems approach, the manager who wishes to apply this approach needs to be a mana-

generalist gerial [specialist / generalist].

10 Being a "managerial generalist" suggests that as he views the organization as a total entity, the

does systems-oriented manager [does / does not] need knowledge in specific functional areas, such as finance and personnel.

11 Turning now to the implications of the systems approach to some of the management functions that we have studied in this book, we can see that once organizational objectives have been defined, the responsibility for the design of the ap-

top propriate system is that of [top / middle / first-level] management.

12 The application of the systems approach to business *planning* results in an emphasis on the several major systems that bear upon the adequacy of planning: the *environmental system*, the *competitive system*, and the *internal system*. These are arranged in a hierarchy, with the broadest system being the

environmental _____ system.

13 As contrasted to the competitive and internal systems, consideration of such factors as population changes, anticipated governmental actions, and international developments are included in

environmental the _____ system.

14 On the other hand, consideration of the past, present, and anticipated actions of other firms in the same product or service field is included in the

competitive _____ system.

15 In addition to the importance of the environmental and competitive systems in the formulation of business plans, particular unique features of the firm itself, including its location, facilities, and personnel, need to be considered as factors in the

internal _____ system.

16 Thus, from the systems viewpoint a hierarchy of three systems impinge on the planning process:

environmental the _____,
competitive _____, and
internal _____ systems.

17 On the level of planning *procedures*, a planning and controlling technique which focuses on the relationships among the events and activities leading to goal attainment is PERT, as discussed in Chapter 16. In its orientation on an entire project,

systems PERT is representative of the [functional / systems] approach to management.

18 Developments in quantitative decision-making techniques have also influenced the application of the systems approach to management. As we indicated in Chapter 5, operations research specifically involves a systemwide approach to management decision making and has thus [accelerated / retarded] the development of the systems approach.

accelerated

19 As is true for the planning function, the function of *organizing* has also been affected by the systems approach. Management historians have described three stages in the development of organization theory: the *classical, neoclassical,* and *modern.* The organization chart can be thought of as one of the first "products" of organization theory, and it is thus associated with _____ organization theory.

classical

20 *Classical organization theory* has stressed description of the formal organization structure, hierarchical relationships, span of control, and line-staff relationships. Therefore, of the following two areas of management concern, the one that particularly reflects the classical orientation is [assignment of authority / determining necessary channels of communication].

assignment of
authority

21 Whereas classical organization theory can be described as being formal and impersonal in its orientation, *neoclassical organization theory* represents a deliberate effort to modify the theory by including human relations considerations and the influence of the informal organization on performance. The development of the neoclassical position was stimulated by the [scientific management movement / Hawthorne studies], as described in Chapter 1.

Hawthorne studies

22 The two approaches to organization theory which we have discussed thus far, both of which begin with the formal organization chart as a point of reference, are the _____ and _____ approaches.

classical
neoclassical

23 On the other hand, *modern organization theory* has extended the modification of the classical theory to the point where the formal structure is not the principal reference point, but rather one of a number of organizational components that need to be considered. Included as organizational components are the individuals, informal groups, and intergroup relationships. Thus modern organiza-

systems

tion theory directly reflects the _____ approach to management that we are discussing in this chapter.

24 Modern organization theory has been a topic of interest and discussion among organization theorists for over a decade. By requiring the manager to have knowledge of the informal and formal parts of the organization *and* their interactions, its application in business organizations has contributed to the concern about developing managerial

generalists

[specialists / generalists].

25 The development of modern organization theory has increased managerial recognition of the "and" in organizational relationships. However, the formal organization chart, developed in the context of classical organization theory, continues to be the principal method by which business firms describe their organization structure. The unavailability of a practical "modern organization chart" to represent all the components within the firm has

limiting

had the effect of [enhancing / limiting] the application of modern organization theory.

26 Turning now to the management function of *controlling,* we can observe that there are two types of control systems from the systems viewpoint: the *open-sequence* and the *closed-sequence* systems. In the open-sequence system, control activity is initiated on the basis of an information source which is unaffected by the system being controlled. Thus, an example of an open-sequence system is [a home ther-

a clock-controlled
sprinkling system

mostat system / a clock-controlled sprinkling system].

27   In engineering parlance the open-sequence system has been referred to as the *open-loop* system. As illustrated in Figure 17.1*a*, for our lawn sprinkler example the "loop" is open because the amount of sprinkler discharge [does / does not] affect the operation of the timing device.

does not

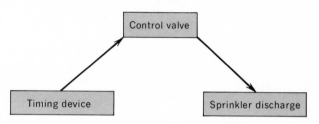

Figure 17.1a   An open-sequence control system.

28   In contrast, in a closed-sequence or *closed-loop* system the information used as the basis for control action *is* affected by the system being controlled. Thus, in Figure 17.1*b* the amount of heat emission [does / does not] affect the thermostat.

does

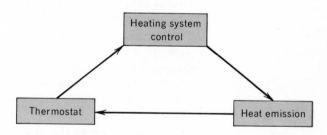

Figure 17.1b   A closed-sequence control system.

29   Whereas the timing mechanism is activated by information outside the system being controlled, the thermostat system is responsive to the effects of the system output. Therefore, the use of the timing mechanism is an example of an open-sequence   _____ system, whereas the use of the thermostat is an example of

closed-sequence   a _____ system.

30 The type of control system that can most realistically be described as being "automatic" is the

closed-   [open- / closed-] sequence system.

31 A key feature of an automatic or closed-sequence system is _feedback_, which we also discussed in Chapter 10 on communication. Figure 17.2 illustrates the operation of feedback in such a system. As indicated, the feedback first affects the

correction process   _____   _____,

process (or   and then through the subsequent corrective action that is initiated, it affects the _____ it-

operation)   self.

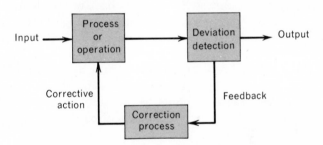

Figure 17.2 Simple feedback in a control system. (Adapted from Harold Koontz and Cyril O'Donnell, _Principles of Management: An Analysis of Managerial Functions_, 5th ed., McGraw-Hill Book Company, New York, 1972, p. 586. Reproduced with permission.)

32 When system output is controlled on the basis of a comparison between established standards and the output of the system itself, the control system can be described as being an automatic, or

closed-sequence   _____, system, and the information used as the basis for system con-

feedback   trol is called _____.

33 Turning now to the organization as a whole, in practice the systems approach to management has typically been associated with the organization being conceived of as an information-decision system whose design ultimately affects organizational success. The "organization structure" of primary interest is therefore the one indicating [division of work / channels of communication].

channels of
communication

34 Thus if the firm were to be designed from the systems point of view, it would be based on the needed communication channels in the system. Since established organization charts are based on the division-of-work concept and the description of only the formal communication channels, redefining the organization from the systems viewpoint would require consideration of the formal and _____ components of the organization.

informal

35 Getting back to the definition of a system offered at the beginning of this section, we suggested that it is an established arrangement of components which leads to particular objectives according to plan. As it has thus far been applied in the systems approach, the arrangement of components is viewed as a [communication / work-group] structure.

communication

36 Figure 17.3 illustrates the design of a basic system. We have not yet discussed the kind of inputs that enter the processor of the system. The basic ingredients of a process have been identified as being *information, energy*, and *materials*. If the system output is a service rather than a product, the ingredient that might not be included as an input in this case is _____.

materials

37 Generally, however, all three ingredients—information, energy, and materials—are required as inputs to produce a product or service. Some of the materials may become part of the product and are thus *product materials*, whereas others are embodied

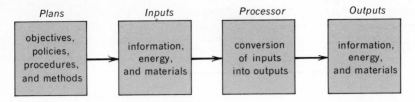

Figure 17.3 The design of a basic system.

product

in the machines and plant and are *operational materials*. In terms of these definitions, the iron ore shipped to a steel mill is _____ material.

operational

38 On the other hand, the furnaces, rolling mills, computers, and other equipment associated with converting product materials into useful outputs are _____ materials.

materials

39 The *output* of a system can also be described as being in the form of information, energy, or materials. The manufacture of automobiles, for example, directly represents a _____ output.

energy

40 The output of an electrical generating station would be described as being in the form of _____.

information

41 Finally, the output of an advisory staff or consulting firm, such as a tax consultant, would be in the form of _____.

output

42 Figure 17.4 on page 488 is a more extensive representation of a system than the examples we have cited up to this point. As is typical of the current systems-oriented approach, the information and decision processes are particularly highlighted in the diagram. There are, for example, five strategic control points represented in the diagram, the final one constituting a measurement of the final _____ itself.

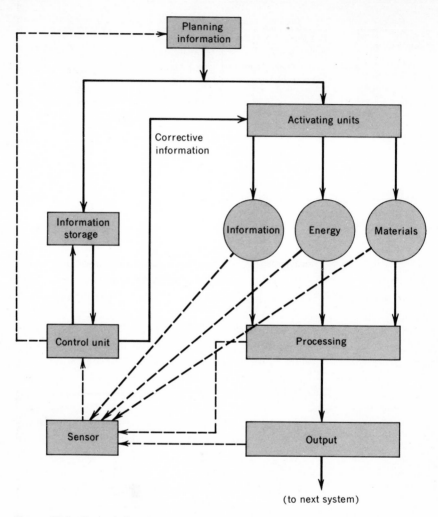

Figure 17.4 Flow of planning and controlling information in a system. (Adapted from Richard A. Johnson, Fremont E. Kast, and James E. Rosenzweig, *The Theory and Management of Systems,* 3d ed., McGraw-Hill Book Company, New York, 1973, p. 125. Reproduced with permission.)

43 As the result of each measurement and comparison at a strategic control point, information is sent to the control and activating units to initiate any needed corrective action. Such information is

feedback   therefore considered to be the _____

in the system, and the overall system would be

closed-sequence

described as being a(n) [open-sequence / closed-sequence] system.

44 In terms of the overall approach to describing the organization and organizational functions, a description of the information and decision processes is represented by the [classical / systems] approach, whereas a description of the division of work and formal authority relationships is represented by the [classical / systems] approach.

systems

classical

B PROGRAM MANAGEMENT

A recently developed set of techniques that is related to the systems approach to management is that of program, or project, management. Although the managerial techniques of program management have been associated with the development of military and space hardware, they are applicable to any situation in which a number of independently operating but mutually dependent organizational groups are working toward the development of a complex product or service. Since the focus is on "development" rather than on "manufacturing," many of the activities require basic research and hence involve uncertainty regarding the time and cost requirements. In this section of the chapter we describe the evolution of program management, identify the product-mission concept that serves as the basis for defining program objectives, and then describe the basic functions required for mission accomplishment.

45 Program management is an outgrowth of the development of systems engineering. Up through World War II systems engineers were primarily concerned with integration of existing subcomponents into a final product, steady improvement in design, and interchangeability of parts and components. These activities were aimed particularly at achieving [new product development / mass production].

mass production

46   After World War II systems engineers became increasingly concerned with the development of new and technologically complex products. In this context, the technical problems encountered and time requirements of the groups participating in the product development are [more / less] certain.

less

47   The coordination of research and development activities in an environment of uncertainty places a particular premium on the development of timely information flow in the system. From this standpoint, program management represents a blending of both systems engineering and information theory. As such, the overall approach to management that is particularly conducive to improving   program   management   is   the _____ approach.

systems

48   The *product-mission concept* has played an important role in the development of program management. In a sense, it is a kind of broader view of the usual product objective. Rather than defining an objective in terms of the desired physical properties of the product, the objective is defined in terms of the mission that the product is intended to perform. One advantage of using the product-mission concept is that preconceptions regarding best product design are [minimized / maximized].

minimized

49   Since designers tend to be influenced by the characteristics of existing products, avoiding design commitments until after the product mission has been defined tends to enhance [continued development of existing products / innovation in product design].

innovation in
product design

50   Thus, the approach by which program objectives are defined in terms of product purposes rather   than   product   specifications   is   the _____ concept.

product-mission

51 We have referred entirely to the design implications of the product-mission approach. In a competitive marketing environment all of the business functions would be oriented toward the product mission as part of a total endeavor. Thus, appropriate methods of advertising and distributing a product [would / would not] depend on the product's defined mission.

would

52 For any development program, five primary functions have to be performed for successful completion of the mission:

1. Perception of need
2. Design
3. Production
4. Delivery
5. Utilization

Using a military problem as an example, not only should perceived needs take into consideration economic and technological feasibility, but the broad initially perceived needs usually have to be made more [general / specific].

specific

53 Since a broad objective may imply several specific objectives, or product missions, these also need to be arranged in order of priority, thus making it feasible to concentrate effort toward the attainment of [arbitrarily chosen / the most important] mission objectives.

the most important

54 Once the *perception of need* is completed, the next step is research and development directed toward *design*. In a new project there is generally a relatively [broad / limited] selection of feasible designs that are evaluated.

broad

55 Following design, the *production* function is performed. As is true for the other functions, the production function typically includes several subfunctions. In this case, these subfunctions include such activities as recruiting manpower, establishing physical facilities, selecting component suppliers, testing and inspection of parts and components, and testing and inspection of the final product. At this stage of the program the problems are concerned with [appropriateness of specifications / coordination of the production subfunctions].

coordination of the
production
subfunctions

56   *Delivery* is the function of transferring ownership physically from producer to user. This typically includes on-site testing by the [producer only / consumer only / both producer and consumer].

both producer and
consumer

57   In military programs the function of *utilization* generally is performed by personnel of the military services. However, need for personnel familiarization and training means that the producing contractors [do / do not] continue to be involved with product functioning after its delivery.

do

58   Returning now to the application of program management within a particular firm, we see that whereas this approach is oriented toward description of the relationship among program subgoals and the overall goal, traditional organization structure is oriented toward describing the functional area of activity within the firm, such as manufacturing and marketing. Program management and functional management are thus [organizational alternatives / two varieties of the same approach to organization].

organizational
alternatives

59   Most companies using program management have in fact combined this approach with the existing functional structure. Figure 17.5 illustrates the organization result, which has been called *matrix organization* by some writers. One difficulty with combining the two approaches is that individuals frequently find themselves working for two or more direct superiors: a manager in the functional program organization and one or more _____ managers.

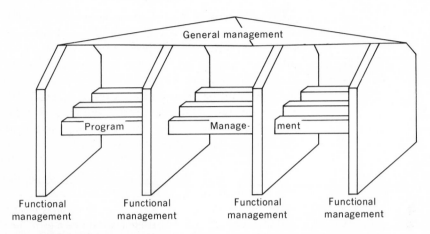

Figure 17-5 Integration of program management within the functionally oriented organization structure. (Adapted from John Stanley Baumgartner, *Project Management,* Richard D. Irwin, Inc., Homewood, Ill., 1963, p. 143. Reproduced with permission.)

more

60 Even though problems like these have been encountered, business firms have generally hesitated to abandon one of these approaches in favor of the other. In addition to the fact that there may be a contractual obligation to use program management in military and space projects, use of this approach and associated techniques such as PERT makes on-schedule program completion [more / less] likely.

is not

61 On the other hand, the unified management of each of the separate activities in the firm [is / is not] attained by use of the program management approach.

62 Therefore the program manager operates as a kind of managerial generalist within the firm and is formally neither superior nor subordinate to the specialized functional managers. This organizational position makes it particularly important that he possess a high degree of [technological / human / relations] skill.

human relations

63 Furthermore, although the functional organization has a limitless life span, the program manager's job is finite. Once a program is completed, he and the other program personnel return to their functional departments on a full-time basis or are assigned to other programs. As individuals, therefore, program personnel need to be attuned to the prospect of continued job and organizational [stability / change].

change

64 From the motivational standpoint, it is particularly important that program personnel look at early program completion as a personal success, rather than as "working their way out of a job." For continued success in program management, a company should [frequently / seldom / never] terminate employment following successful project completion.

never

65 Maintaining the functional organization within a program-oriented firm provides a "home base" for personnel between program assignments. Thus, even though job changes are associated with program completion, providing overall employment security [minimizes / maximizes] the effect of the negative motivational factors in this environment of change.

minimizes

C DATA PROCESSING SYSTEMS

Since the systems approach to business is so closely related to the management of information flow and the making of decisions, developments in data processing have both influenced and been influenced by the systems viewpoint. In our discussion of these developments we are concerned primarily with their management implications, and not with the technical details of these developments as such. We shall first review briefly the early developments in data processing methods that led to mechanized data processing. However, the principal part of our discussion will be concerned with the development of electronic data processing. In discussing current and future developments in information processing systems, we give particular attention to computer programs, computer software versus hardware, and real-time processing versus batch processing of data.

66 In the data processing field there is a basic distinction between *facts* and *information*. One of the principal purposes of a business data processing system is to screen, collate, and relate the various facts available in a firm in order to develop meaningful _____ for management decision making.

information

67 Other than the collection of the facts as such, in a small business firm the "data processing" may simply involve maintaining a *file* of information. For example, use of the employee time cards, inventory ledger cards, and accounts payable statements may all involve simple _____ maintenance.

file

68 Until the development of *mechanized data processing* (MDP), the maintenance of physical card files constituted the principal method of data processing. The needed calculations to update information on the file cards were originally done manually, but they were later supplemented by the use of adding machines and desk calculators to increase the [speed / accuracy / speed and accuracy] of the computations.

speed and accuracy

69 Bookkeeping and accounting machines were also developed to perform calculations, prepare statements, and update records in one combined operation, thus minimizing human errors associated with [original source data / computation and transcription].

computation and transcription

70 A particularly significant occurrence in the history of data processing methods was the development of the punched card as a means of recording information in the 1890 census. Devised by Herman Hollerinth of the Census Bureau, this system permitted mechanical sorting of the cards and

mechanized

thus led to the development of _____ data processing.

71 Although the information "stored" on the cards was originally analyzed by mechanical sorting and subsequent counting of cards in each sorted category, during the first half of this century other mechanical devices were developed which made it possible to do such things as duplicate existing cards, update information on an established set of cards, accumulate numerical values, and print statements and summary reports. Pioneered by the International Business Machines Corporation (IBM), such a data processing system has been

mechanized
data processing

referred   to   as   _____

_____ _____.

72 During World War II the electronic computer was developed for application to scientific and military computational problems. The first business-oriented computer installations were completed during the 1950s, thus signaling the beginning of the *electronic data processing* era, or, as it is

EDP

frequently abbreviated, the _____ era.

73 The *arithmetic unit* of the electronic computer is an extremely fast calculating machine, performing complex calculations in time measured in millionths of a second. But from the standpoint of business applications there are two other attributes of computer systems that are of greater significance. One is that by the use of a set of machine instructions, or a *computer program*, the computer can perform a sequence of computational and decision-making steps yielding intermediate and final values; the second is that the values can be stored and updated in electronic form within the *storage unit* of the computer system. Thus, a computer can perform calculations rapidly by use of its

arithmetic _____ unit, follow a series of instructions as embodied in the computer

program _____, and store and update information in its _____ unit.

storage

74 The earliest applications of EDP in business, and those that are still predominant, were in areas specifically requiring a series of calculations with intermediate and final values. A good example is the application to payroll. Although this may appear to be a simple task at first glance, the need not only to multiply hours worked by wage rates but also to consider overtime premiums, appropriate deductions, and accumulated deductions to date, such as for social security, results in a relatively lengthy set of instructions, or computer

program _____.

75 We have made a point of emphasizing the importance of the computer program because it is in this area that most problems of computer application in business exist, rather than in the technical functioning of the computer as such. Computer errors are generally data input errors or programming errors, rather than equipment errors. For example, if we include the instruction to "deduct $5.60 from gross payroll" as an insurance deduction, but do not first ascertain that the gross figure equals or exceeds $5.60, then the remaining

can payroll amount [can / cannot] be a negative amount.

76 Early computer programs had to be written in *machine language*, which required the mastery of a symbolic notation system and the use of detailed instructions concerned with internal computer processes, such as the storage of intermediate values resulting from each step of a calculation. A shortage of computer programmers with the necessary knowledge and fortitude to develop programs for business applications was itself a barrier to the feasibility of computer use. During the past twenty years the programming task has been simplified by the development of *assembly programs* which translate simpler programming language into the

machine   _____ language.

77   Whereas the physical equipment that makes up the computer system is the *hardware*, the assembly programs and other programs oriented toward simplifying the programming requirement are the *software*. In terms of our discussion, expanded managerial use of EDP as an information source is particularly dependent on the continued develop-

software   ment of computer [hardware / software].

78   The pace of the technological developments in the computational speed and storage capacity of computer systems has been so rapid that many computers now in use are considered to be obso-

hardware   lete in terms of [hardware / software].

79   On the other hand, in addition to the development of assembly programs which simplify programming requirements, libraries of computational subroutines have been developed by manufacturers and users making it possible to construct a program by combining several available subroutines. These, then, represent developments in the

software   area of computer [hardware / software].

80   Although steady progress has been made, developments in computer software have not kept pace with those in hardware. The ultimate development in software will presumably be achieved when an executive can make requests of the EDP system in "everyday language," without the necessity of using an individually prepared computer

program   _____.

81   The programming languages most frequently

used in commercial applications today are FOR-TRAN IV ("Formula Translation, fourth version") and COBOL ("Common Business Oriented Language"). Using either of these programming languages is [easier / more difficult] than using a machine language.

easier

82 To summarize the last few frames, the physical equipment that makes up the EDP system is referred to as the _____, whereas libraries of subroutines, assembly programs, and other items used to simplify the programming task are referred to as the _____.

hardware

software

83 We have already indicated that continued expansion of computer use in business is related to the development of the software. Of the following two general types of business application, the one particularly dependent on the development of software is [*a* / *b*].

b

a. Application to repetitive operations
b. Application involving a series of unique information requests

84 For repetitive applications the difficulties in programming are frequently offset by the fact that the programs are used repeatedly, whereas such is not the case for the series of unique questions associated with managerial decision-making requirements. From this standpoint the integration of EDP with the systems approach to management [has already / has not yet] been achieved.

has not yet

85 As contrasted to the use of EDP in such specialized tasks as payroll and inventory control, integration of the firm's data processing system with the managerial information and decision system would be an application of the _____ approach to management.

systems

86 Finally, there is one other development in

computer use that has affected its application in business firms and will continue to be important as the systems approach is increasingly applied in this area. The computer applications we have discussed so far are examples of *batch processing*; that is, facts are collected over a period of time and then periodically processed. When batch processing is used, the records indicate status [up to the present moment / as of the last time data were compiled].

as of the last time
data were
compiled

87 A development that represents an alternative to batch processing is *real-time processing*. Real-time processing involves updating the master file of information with each and every transaction. In terms of the specialized areas of computer application, real-time processing is most useful for [payroll / inventory control].

inventory control

88 Payroll data are generally needed only periodically, whereas it is a distinct advantage to have inventory records reflect the status to the moment. This kind of perpetual inventory system can be maintained within the context of an EDP system by the use of _____ processing.

real-time

89 Two examples of real-time processing as contrasted to batch processing are the airline reservation systems now generally in use and the SAGE (Semi-Automatic Ground Environment) system used as a continual early warning and air-defense system. In the first case the inputs are reservations and inquiries transmitted from a large number of geographically separated ticket offices, whereas in the latter case the inputs are provided by geographically dispersed radar installations and other data sources. In both cases, processing of data and the compilation of information occur [at designated periodic intervals / with each new input of data].

with each new
input of data

90   The development of real-time data processing makes it feasible to present up-to-the-minute information about a company's operations. This development, combined with further progress in software during the next few years, will increase the applicability of the computer in the total information and decision system in the firm, thus
systems   enhancing use of the _____ approach to management.

Review

91   In general, a system can be defined as an es-
components   tablished   arrangement   of   _____
which   leads   to   the   attainment   of   particular
objectives; plan   _____   according   to   _____.
(Frames 1 to 6)

92   Application of the systems approach to business results in the requirement that executives become "managerial specialists" [instead of / in
in addition to   addition to] having skills in particular functional areas. (Frames 7 to 10)

93   In the area of planning, a hierarchy of three systems are of concern from the systems point of view: the   environmental,   competitive,   and
internal   _____ systems. On the level of procedures, the planning and controlling technique which has been used in conjunction with the systems
PERT   approach is _____. (Frames 11 to 18)

94   In the management function of organizing, the type of organization theory concerned with formal organization structure and hierarchical relationships is classical organization theory, and that which represents a modification of the classical to include human relations and informal organiza-
neoclassical   tion implications is _____
organization theory. The approach that abandons

the formal structure as the principal reference point and considers the relationships among all components that make up the organization is

modern

_____ organization theory. (Frames 19 to 25)

95 In the area of controlling, when a system is controlled by a decision device not affected by system output as such, it is referred to as an

open-sequence

_____ system. On the other hand, a truly self-regulating system includes a comparison of system output with standards and uses this feedback as the basis for control action. Such a system is referred to as a

closed-sequence

_____ system. (Frames 26 to 32)

96 As applied to business firms, the systems approach to management has typically resulted in describing the arrangement of organizational components in terms of [work-group / communication

communication and decision

and decision] structure. (Frames 33 to 35; 42 to 44)

97 Both the inputs and outputs of a system can be in the form of information, energy, or material. Use of electricity in a system, for example, ex-

energy

emplifies the input of _____, whereas the output that is in the form of a consulting ser-

information

vice would exemplify _____ output. (Frames 36 to 41)

98 The set of managerial techniques that represents a blending of systems engineering and infor-

program

mation theory is called _____ management. (Frames 45 to 47)

99 The approach by which program objectives are defined in terms of product purposes rather than product specifications, and which is associated with a number of primary functions beginning with the perception of product need and culminating with product utilization, is called the

product-mission

_____ concept.
(Frames 48 to 57)

100 Program management and traditional organization structure represent [the same / basically different] approach(es) to organization and management. When program management is used, the program managers in the organization are formally [subordinate / superior / neither subordinate nor superior] to the specialized functional managers. (Frames 58 to 65)

basically different

neither
subordinate nor
superior

mechanized data
processing

101 Whereas MDP stands for _____

_____ ,

electronic data
processing

EDP stands for _____
_____. (Frames 66 to 72)

102 In addition to the required input and output equipment, a computer system performs calculations rapidly by the use of the _____ unit, follows a series of instructions as included in the computer _____, and stores and updates information held in the _____ unit. (Frames 73 to 75)

arithmetic

program

storage

103 The physical equipment of the computer system is referred to as _____. The assembly programs and other materials oriented toward simplifying programming requirements are referred to as _____. (Frames 76 to 82)

hardware

software

104 In terms of developments to date, we would conclude that integration of EDP with the systems approach to management [has already / has not yet] been achieved. (Frames 83 to 85)

has not yet

105 When facts are collected over a period of time and processed at periodic intervals, the EDP

batch

procedure is referred to as _____ processing. The procedure by which the master file of information is updated with each transaction

real-time

is referred to as _____ processing. (Frames 86 to 90)

Discussion Questions

1. As compared with the classical approach to organization, which is based on functional specialization, what are the changed executive skill requirements in the systems approach?

2. Is it possible for a particular manager in a particular position to develop as both a specialist and a generalist? In what type of position would development as a specialist take precedence? In what type of position would development as a generalist be particularly important?

3. A chief executive in a pharmaceutical firm, who has a background in marketing, has suggested that the key to his firm's success in planning will depend on knowledge of the potential market. In terms of organizational objectives in general, why is this an appropriate view? In terms of the systems approach to planning, what considerations might be missing?

4. What are the advantages associated with using an organization chart to describe a firm and its activities? What are the advantages associated with describing the firm in terms of the channels of communication that exist and the locations at which decisions are made?

5. Under what circumstances might an open-sequence control system lead to inappropriate control action? Under what circumstances might a closed-sequence control system lead to inappropriate control action? What are the managerial implications of your observations?

6. In this chapter we have suggested that the authority relationship between program managers and functional managers is usually not clearly specified. Do you think this condition is inevitable, or is there a way of integrating the two approaches to organizations?

7. In what respects is the systems approach to management an alternative to the functional approach to management? In what respects is the systems approach compatible with the functional approach?

8. What do you think will be the general role of the computer in management ten years from now?

Case Study: A First Experience with Program Management

Jim Hendrickson has worked with his present employer, a diversified company dedicated to applying the concepts of managerial decentralization, for about fifteen years, ever since he completed his college work in electrical engineering. During this time he has had extensive experience in two of the company's consumer products divisions, and his most recent assignment was as section head of reliability engineering.

Because of the respiratory problems of one of his children, several months ago Hendrickson requested a transfer to the company's aerospace division, located in the Southwest. In requesting the change, he recognized that he had a good deal of work to do in familiarizing himself with the reliability analysis problems associated with aerospace components as contrasted to consumer products, but being just thirty-seven years old, he felt confident that he could make the switch.

In his new position as section head of reliability analysis in the aerospace division he has more direct subordinates than he had in the consumer product division. However, he has found that only about 30 percent of his personnel are in fact working only for him, with the others assigned either full-time or part-time to aerospace programs for which the division is a subcontractor. Consequently, unity of command is the exception rather than the rule, and compared with his previous managerial experience the present situation appears just plain disorganized. In trying to define the appropriate role of the program managers and their relationship with him, he has been particularly frustrated because the program manager positions are not entered on the division organization chart at their actual points of work, but, rather, are simply listed in a box adjoining the chart. In the company policy statement describing the operation of program management, the program manager position is defined as representing the single point of project responsibility to the contracting customer. As to his authority, the release further states that, "The assignment of the program management task is accompanied by delegation of necessary authority to conduct the program with the complete utilization of the technical and supporting facilities of the aerospace division."

Overall, whereas Jim Hendrickson had expected a technical adjustment in his new job, the managerial adjustment has turned out to be the more challenging. As things stand, he is not at all sure that he is really a supervisor in the same sense as was true in the consumer products division, even though he has about the same kind of supervisory title. As if to bring things to a head, the manager of engineering support, who is his direct superior, has just sent Hendrickson a memo informing him that the annual performance appraisal reviews for his personnel are to be completed during the next month. Because of the program assignments of many of his men, he really does not feel qualified to appraise their performance. In order to help clarify authority relationships in the division as a whole as well as in his section, Hendrickson is considering making the following proposal at the next bimonthly supervisor's meeting: that formal responsibility for completing performance appraisals be assigned to a program manager when a man spends more than 50 percent of his time working under that manager's direction during the rating period.

1. What are the organizational advantages, if any, associated with Jim Hendrickson's proposal? How is it likely to be viewed by the other supervisors? By the program managers?
2. What are the organizational disadvantages, if any, associated with the proposal?
3. In what way has Hendrickson possibly misconstrued the relationship between himself and program managers and between himself and those of his subordinates who are assigned to program work?

Case Study: A Systems-Oriented Manager of Data Processing

Merrill Frazier was hired by the office machines division of a multiproduct corporation about a year ago to replace the previous manager of the data processing department, who accepted a similar position in a larger data processing facility. The data processing department had been established for over fifteen years and was principally oriented toward such functions as payroll, billing, and inventory control.

Mr. Frazier presented two requests as a condition of his accepting the position: first, that the department be redesignated as the information systems department, and second, that as manager of this department he also be appointed a member of the executive committee of the division, which meets every two weeks with the division general manager to review operations and to serve as an advisory committee. The division general manager accepted both of Merrill's conditions.

Frazier has been a long-standing proponent of the philosophy of managerial decentralization and, accordingly, after assuming the department manager position he proceeded to assign specific managerial responsibilities for all the continuing data processing tasks to subordinate personnel in his department. In turn, this gave him the time to devote to his main objective: developing a data base such that all information relevant to the division's products would be integrated within one overall system. It was his contention that such a data base would be instrumental in leading to better decisions in product design, pricing, and marketing, and would thereby lead to improved division profitability. Frazier was quite aggressive, but not in an abrasive way, and was able to schedule discussions on data base design in several meetings of the executive committee. These discussions culminated in his receiving the approval of the division general manager for the project, with the concurrence of the committee.

Within several weeks after approval of the data-base project was given, the division general manager began receiving informal complaints from the other managers about the amount of involvement of their people in the project. As one manager put it, "Merrill is as sharp as a tack, and the objectives he described to us and the logic of his proposals are unassailable. But he's got people involved in this thing from all over the division, and I'm afraid he's off on cloud nine. You know, he's kept so distant from the regular data processing tasks that his department has pretty well run itself. Along these lines, I've wondered whether he was really interested in being a data processing manager when he took this job or whether he came in to reorganize and take over the division. In any event, I suggest we reconsider the entire data-base project."

The division general manager took comments such as these under advisement, but as things turned out he never got to act on them. During his attendance at a two-week program in the company's management institute, Merrill Frazier so impressed several corporate-level managers with his analytical ability and persuasive skills that he was offered a managerial position in corporate headquarters with a substantial increase in salary. After some deliberation because of the geographic move involved, he accepted the position with the understanding that he would have a month to help make arrangements for his replacement and to wind up his personal affairs.

1. How would you evaluate Merrill Frazier's overall strategy in attempting to develop an integrated management information system?
2. Should Frazier have more explicitly made known his interest in developing a division data base at the time of his employment interview?
3. In what respects might Merrill Frazier have done a more effective job in his position?
4. What kind of replacement should the division general manager now seek to fill the managerial opening?

Suggested Readings*

Ackoff, R. L.: "Towards a System of Systems Concepts," *Management Science*, vol. 17, no. 11, July 1971.

Baumgartner, J. S.: *Project Management,* Richard D. Irwin, Inc., Homewood, Ill., 1963.

Butler, A. G., Jr.: "Project Management: A Study in Organizational Conflict," *Academy of Management Journal*, vol. 16, no. 1, March 1973.

Drucker, P. F.: *Technology, Management, and Society,* Harper & Row, Publishers, Incorporated, New York, 1970.

*Also see the cross-reference table in the Preface.

Grimes, A. J., S. M. Klein, and F. A. Shull: "Matrix Model: A Selective Empirical Test," *Academy of Management Journal,* vol. 15, no. 1, March 1972.

Johnson, R. A., F. E. Kast, and J. E. Rosenzweig: *The Theory and Management of Systems,* 3d ed., McGraw-Hill Book Company, New York, 1973.

Kast, F. E., and J. E. Rosenzweig: "General Systems Theory: Applications for Organization and Management," *Academy of Management Journal,* vol. 15, no. 4, December 1972.

Kelly, J. F.: *Computerized Management Information Systems,* The Macmillan Company, New York, 1970.

Lawrence, P. R., and J. W. Lorsch: *Studies in Organization Design,* Richard D. Irwin, Inc., and the Dorsey Press, Homewood, Ill., 1970.

Maurer, J. G.: *Readings in Organization Theory: Open-Systems Approaches,* Random House, Inc., New York, 1971.

Moan, F. E.: "Does Management Practice Lag Behind Theory in the Computer Environment?" *Academy of Management Journal,* vol. 16, no. 1, March 1973.

Philippakis, A. S., and L. J. Kazmier: *Information Systems through COBOL,* McGraw-Hill Book Company, New York, 1974.

Reeser, C.: "Some Potential Human Problems of the Project Form of Organization," *Academy of Management Journal,* vol. 12, no. 4, December 1969.

Sayles, L. R., and M. K. Chandler: *Managing Large Systems.* Harper & Row, Publishers, Incorporated, New York, 1971.

Schoderbek, P. P.: *Management Systems,* 2d ed., John Wiley & Sons, Inc., New York, 1971.

Thayer, F.: "General System(s) Theory: The Promise that Could Not Be Kept," *Academy of Management Journal,* vol. 15, no. 4, December 1972.

Von Bertalanffy, L.: "The History and Status of General Systems Theory," *Academy of Management Journal,* vol. 15, no. 4, December 1972.

Whisler, T. L.: *Information Technology and Organizational Change,* Wadsworth Publishing Company, Inc., Belmont, Calif., 1970.

Zani, W. M.: "The Computer Utility," *California Management Review,* vol. 12, no. 1, Fall 1970.

INDEX